Y0-ABA-075

CHEVY & GMC PICKUPS

1967-1978 · INCLUDES SUBURBANS
SHOP MANUAL

By
MIKE BISHOP

ERIC JORGENSEN
Editor

JEFF ROBINSON
Publisher

CLYMER PUBLICATIONS

*World's largest publisher of books
devoted exclusively to automobiles and motorcycles*

12860 MUSCATINE STREET · P.O. BOX 20 · ARLETA, CALIFORNIA 91331

Copyright © 1979 Clymer Publications

*All rights reserved. No part of this publication may
be reproduced, stored in a retrieval system, or transmitted,
in any form or by any means, electronic, mechanical,
photocopying, recording or otherwise,
without the prior written permission of Clymer Publications.*

FIRST EDITION
First Printing May, 1979
Second Printing April, 1980

Printed in U.S.A.

ISBN: 0-89287-301-9

Sharon Buck, production coordinator.

•

*Troubleshooting equipment in Chapter One courtesy of
Hank Rose, Executive Vice-president, Rite Autotronics Corp., Los Angeles, California.*

*We wish to thank RVI, Inc., Torrance, California, for
their assistance in the preparation of the Customizing chapter.*

•

COVER:

*Photographed by Mike Brown/Visual Imagery, Los Angeles, California;
assisted by Dennis Gilmore.*

*1967 Stepside pickup courtesy of Sam Head. 1974 Fleetside pickup
courtesy of Orbit Garritano.*

CONTENTS

CHEVY &
GMC PICKUPS
1967-1978 · INCLUDES SUBURBANS
SHOP MANUAL

QUICK REFERENCE DATA

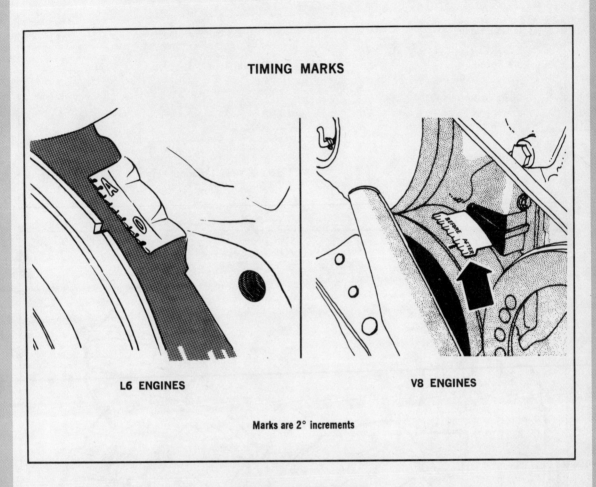

TIMING MARKS

L6 ENGINES   V8 ENGINES

Marks are 2° increments

TUNE-UP SPECIFICATIONS

Cylinder Head Bolt Torque
L6 — 95 ft.-lb.
Small block V8 — 65 ft.-lb.
Mark IV V8 — 80 ft.-lb.

Valve Clearance — Hydraulic lifters — adjustment is automatic.

Spark Plugs
Type — See Chapter Four — Tune-Up
Gap
1967-1974 (all) — 0.035 in.
1975 (all) — 0.060 in.
1976-1978 (all) — 0.045 in.

Point Gap
1967-1974 (all) — 0.016 in. (used); 0.019 in. (new)

(continued)

Dwell Angle (continued)
L6 — 1967-1974 (all)	31-34 degrees
V8 — 1967-1971 (all)	28-32 degrees
V8 — 1972-1974 (all)	29-31 degrees

Ignition Timing   See Chapter Four — Tune-Up

Idle Speed   See Chapter Four — Tune-Up

Compression
L6	130 psi
V8	150-160 psi

Firing order
L6	1-5-3-6-2-4 (No. 1 cylinder — front)
V8	1-8-4-3-6-5-7-2 (No. 1 cylinder — left front)

DISTRIBUTOR

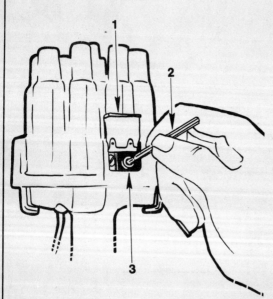

1967-1974 V8 ENGINES

1. Window
2. Hexagon wrench
3. Adjusting screw

1967-1974 L6 ENGINES

1. Breaker plate attaching screws
2. Point gap
3. Contact set attaching screws
4. Quick disconnect terminal
5. Cam lubricator

Table 1   MINIMUM TIRE INFLATION PRESSURE AT GROSS VEHICLE WEIGHT RATING

Tire	Load Range	C10, 15 Pickups & Cab — Chassis								C10, 15 Suburbans					
GVWR (lb.)		4900		5300		5400		6000 & 6200		5400		6400		6800 & 7000	
		FR	R	FR	R	FR	R	FR	R	FR	R	FR	R	FR	R
G78-15	B	32	32	32	32	—	—	—	—	32	32	—	—	—	—
H78-15	B	32	32	—	—	32	32	—	—	32	32	32	32	—	—
6.50-16LT	C	45	45	—	—	45	45	—	—	45	45	45	45	—	—
7.00-15LT	C	40	45	—	—	40	45	—	—	40	45	40	45	—	—
L78-15	B	28	32	—	—	28	32	28	32	28	32	28	32	—	—
7.00-16LT	C	40	45	—	—	40	45	40	45	40	45	40	45	—	—
LR78-15	C	28	36	—	—	28	36	28	36	28	36	28	36	28	36
L78-15	D	—	—	—	—	—	—	—	—	28	36	28	36	28	36

Tire	Load Range	C20, 25 Pickup & Cab — Chassis								C20, 25 Suburban					
GVWR (lb.)		6400		7100		7500		8200		7100		7500		8200	
		FR	R	FR	R	FR	R	FR	R	FR	R	FR	R	FR	R
8.75-16.5	C	45	45	45	—	—	—	—	—	45	45	—	—	—	—
8.75-16.5	D	45	60	45	60	—	—	—	—	45	60	—	—	—	—
7.50-16LT	C	40	45	40	60	—	—	—	—	40	45	—	—	—	—
10-16.5	C	35	45	35	45	—	—	—	—	—	—	—	—	—	—
7.50-16LT	D	40	60	40	60	—	—	—	—	40	60	—	—	—	—
7.50-16LT	E	40	75	40	75	40	75	40	75	40	75	40	75	40	75
9.50-16.5	D	35	60	35	50	35	60	35	60	35	60	35	60	35	60

Note: The tire pressures shown are for original equipment tires. Because of the wide variety of tire types and makes available, it is impractical to set down all of the tire pressures in this table. When buying tires other than original equipment sizes, check with manufacturer for recommended pressures. In all cases, never exceed the maximum pressure embossed on the side of the tire.

(continued)

APPROXIMATE REFILL CAPACITIES

Engine crankcase	5 quarts with filter
Transmission	
Manual	Fill to level hole with GL-5
Automatic	
Turbo Hydramatic 400	7½ U.S. pints
Turbo Hydramatic 375	7½ U.S. pints
Turbo Hydramatic 350	5 U.S. pints
Turbo Hydramatic 250	5 U.S. pints
Powerglide	3 U.S. pints
Torque Drive	4 U.S. pints (approximately)
Differential	
8.5 in. ring gear	3.5 pints GL-5
10.5 in. ring gear	
Chevrolet	5.4 pints GL-5
Dana	7.2 pints GL-5
9.75 in. Dana	6.0 pints GL-5
12.25 in. ring gear	14.0 pints GL-5

RECOMMENDED LUBRICANTS

	Grade	Temperature Range
Engine	5W-20*, 5W-30	20°F and below
	10W, 5W-30, 10W-30, 10W-40	0° to 60°F
	20W-20, 10W-30, 10W-40, 20W-40, 20W-50	20°F and above
Transmission		
3-speed/4-speed synchromesh	SAE 80W**, SAE 80W-90, GL-5	—
Powerglide/Powerflo	Dexron automatic transmission fluid or equivalent	—
Turbo-Hydramatic		
350	Dexron automatic transmission fluid or equivalent	—
400	Dexron automatic transmission fluid or equivalent	—
Axle	SAE 80	Below 10°F
	SAE 90	Up to 100°F
	SAE 140	Consistently above 100°F

*If vehicle is being operated at sustained highway speeds. The next heavier grade of oil should be used.

**SAE 80 should be used if sustained ambient temperature is below 32°F.

INTRODUCTION

This detailed, comprehensive manual covers 1967-1978 Chevy and GMC pickups and Suburbans. The expert text gives complete information on maintenance, tune-up, repair, and overhaul. Hundreds of photos and drawings guide you through every step. The book includes all you need to know to keep your vehicle running right.

Where repairs are practical for the owner/mechanic, complete procedures are given. Equally important, difficult jobs are pointed out. Such operations are usually more economically performed by a dealer or independent garage.

A shop manual is a reference. You want to be able to find information fast. As in all Clymer books, this one is designed with this in mind. All chapters are thumb tabbed. Important items are extensively indexed at the rear of the book. Finally, all the most frequently used specifications and capacities are summarized on the blue *Quick Reference* pages at the front of the book.

Keep the book handy. Carry it in your glove box. It will help you to better understand your van, lower repair and maintenance costs, and generally improve your satisfaction with your vehicle.

CHAPTER ONE

GENERAL INFORMATION

The troubleshooting, tune-up, maintenance, and step-by-step repair procedures in this book are written for the owner and home mechanic. The text is accompanied by useful photos and diagrams to make the job as clear and correct as possible.

Troubleshooting, tune-up, maintenance, and repair are not difficult if you know what tools and equipment to use and what to do. Anyone not afraid to get their hands dirty, of average intelligence, and with some mechanical ability can perform most of the procedures in this book.

In some cases, a repair job may require tools or skills not reasonably expected of the home mechanic. These procedures are noted in each chapter and it is recommended that you take the job to your dealer, a competent mechanic, or machine shop.

MANUAL ORGANIZATION

This chapter provides general information and safety and service hints. Also included are lists of recommended shop and emergency tools as well as a brief description of troubleshooting and tune-up equipment.

Chapter Two provides methods and suggestions for quick and accurate diagnosis and repair of problems. Troubleshooting procedures discuss typical symptoms and logical methods to pinpoint the trouble.

Chapter Three explains all periodic lubrication and routine maintenance necessary to keep your vehicle running well. Chapter Three also includes recommended tune-up procedures, eliminating the need to constantly consult chapters on the various subassemblies.

Subsequent chapters cover specific systems such as the engine, transmission, and electrical systems. Each of these chapters provides disassembly, repair, and assembly procedures in a simple step-by-step format. If a repair requires special skills or tools, or is otherwise impractical for the home mechanic, it is so indicated. In these cases it is usually faster and less expensive to have the repairs made by a dealer or competent repair shop. Necessary specifications concerning a particular system are included at the end of the appropriate chapter.

When special tools are required to perform a procedure included in this manual, the tool is illustrated either in actual use or alone. It may be possible to rent or borrow these tools. The inventive mechanic may also be able to find a suitable substitute in his tool box, or to fabricate one.

The terms NOTE, CAUTION, and WARNING have specific meanings in this manual. A NOTE provides additional or explanatory information. A CAUTION is used to emphasize areas where equipment damage could result if proper precautions are not taken. A WARNING is used to stress those areas where personal injury or death could result from negligence, in addition to possible mechanical damage.

SERVICE HINTS

Observing the following practices will save time, effort, and frustration, as well as prevent possible injury.

Throughout this manual keep in mind two conventions. "Front" refers to the front of the vehicle. The front of any component, such as the transmission, is that end which faces toward the front of the vehicle. The "left" and "right" sides of the vehicle refer to the orientation of a person sitting in the vehicle facing forward. For example, the steering wheel is on the left side. These rules are simple, but even experienced mechanics occasionally become disoriented.

Most of the service procedures covered are straightforward and can be performed by anyone reasonably handy with tools. It is suggested, however, that you consider your own capabilities carefully before attempting any operation involving major disassembly of the engine.

Some operations, for example, require the use of a press. It would be wiser to have these performed by a shop equipped for such work, rather than to try to do the job yourself with makeshift equipment. Other procedures require precision measurements. Unless you have the skills and equipment required, it would be better to have a qualified repair shop make the measurements for you.

Repairs go much faster and easier if the parts that will be worked on are clean before you begin. There are special cleaners for washing the engine and related parts. Brush or spray on the cleaning solution, let it stand, then rinse it away with a garden hose. Clean all oily or greasy parts with cleaning solvent as you remove them.

WARNING
Never use gasoline as a cleaning agent. It presents an extreme fire hazard. Be sure to work in a well-ventilated area when using cleaning solvent. Keep a fire extinguisher, rated for gasoline fires, handy in any case.

Much of the labor charge for repairs made by dealers is for the removal and disassembly of other parts to reach the defective unit. It is frequently possible to perform the preliminary operations yourself and then take the defective unit in to the dealer for repair, at considerable savings.

Once you have decided to tackle the job yourself, make sure you locate the appropriate section in this manual, and read it entirely. Study the illustrations and text until you have a good idea of what is involved in completing the job satisfactorily. If special tools are required, make arrangements to get them before you start. Also, purchase any known defective parts prior to starting on the procedure. It is frustrating and time-consuming to get partially into a job and then be unable to complete it.

Simple wiring checks can be easily made at home, but knowledge of electronics is almost a necessity for performing tests with complicated electronic testing gear.

During disassembly of parts keep a few general cautions in mind. Force is rarely needed to get things apart. If parts are a tight fit, like a bearing in a case, there is usually a tool designed to separate them. Never use a screwdriver to pry apart parts with machined surfaces such as cylinder head and valve cover. You will mar the surfaces and end up with leaks.

Make diagrams wherever similar-appearing parts are found. You may think you can remember where everything came from — but mistakes are costly. There is also the possibility you may get sidetracked and not return to work for days or even weeks — in which interval, carefully laid out parts may have become disturbed.

Tag all similar internal parts for location, and mark all mating parts for position. Record number and thickness of any shims as they are removed. Small parts such as bolts can be iden-

tified by placing them in plastic sandwich bags that are sealed and labeled with masking tape.

Wiring should be tagged with masking tape and marked as each wire is removed. Again, do not rely on memory alone.

When working under the vehicle, do not trust a hydraulic or mechanical jack to hold the vehicle up by itself. Always use jackstands. See **Figure 1**.

Disconnect battery ground cable before working near electrical connections and before disconnecting wires. Never run the engine with the battery disconnected; the alternator could be seriously damaged.

Protect finished surfaces from physical damage or corrosion. Keep gasoline and brake fluid off painted surfaces.

Frozen or very tight bolts and screws can often be loosened by soaking with penetrating oil like Liquid Wrench or WD-40, then sharply striking the bolt head a few times with a hammer and punch (or screwdriver for screws). Avoid heat unless absolutely necessary, since it may melt, warp, or remove the temper from many parts.

Avoid flames or sparks when working near a charging battery or flammable liquids, such as brake fluid or gasoline.

No parts, except those assembled with a press fit, require unusual force during assembly. If a part is hard to remove or install, find out why before proceeding.

Cover all openings after removing parts to keep dirt, small tools, etc., from falling in.

When assembling two parts, start all fasteners, then tighten evenly.

The clutch plate, wiring connections, brake shoes, drums, pads, and discs should be kept clean and free of grease and oil.

When assembling parts, be sure all shims and washers are replaced exactly as they came out.

Whenever a rotating part butts against a stationary part, look for a shim or washer. Use new gaskets if there is any doubt about the condition of old ones. Generally, you should apply gasket cement to one mating surface only, so the parts may be easily disassembled in the future. A thin coat of oil on gaskets helps them seal effectively.

Heavy grease can be used to hold small parts in place if they tend to fall out during assembly. However, keep grease and oil away from electrical, clutch, and brake components.

High spots may be sanded off a piston with sandpaper, but emery cloth and oil do a much more professional job.

Carburetors are best cleaned by disassembling them and soaking the parts in a commercial carburetor cleaner. Never soak gaskets and rubber parts in these cleaners. Never use wire to clean out jets and air passages; they are easily damaged. Use compressed air to blow out the carburetor, but only if the float has been removed first.

Take your time and do the job right. Do not forget that a newly rebuilt engine must be broken in the same as a new one. Refer to your owner's manual for the proper break-in procedures.

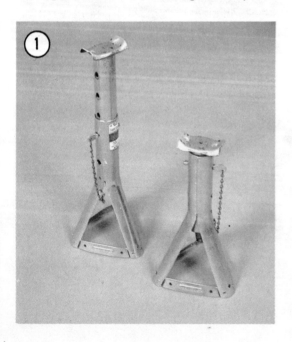

SAFETY FIRST

Professional mechanics can work for years and never sustain a serious injury. If you observe a few rules of common sense and safety, you can enjoy many safe hours servicing your vehicle. You could hurt yourself or damage the vehicle if you ignore these rules.

1. Never use gasoline as a cleaning solvent.

2. Never smoke or use a torch in the vicinity of flammable liquids such as cleaning solvent in open containers.

3. Never smoke or use a torch in an area where batteries are being charged. Highly explosive hydrogen gas is formed during the charging process.

4. Use the proper sized wrenches to avoid damage to nuts and injury to yourself.

5. When loosening a tight or stuck nut, be guided by what would happen if the wrench should slip. Protect yourself accordingly.

6. Keep your work area clean and uncluttered.

7. Wear safety goggles during all operations involving drilling, grinding, or use of a cold chisel.

8. Never use worn tools.

9. Keep a fire extinguisher handy and be sure it is rated for gasoline (Class B) and electrical (Class C) fires.

EXPENDABLE SUPPLIES

Certain expendable supplies are necessary. These include grease, oil, gasket cement, wiping rags, cleaning solvent, and distilled water.

Also, special locking compounds, silicone lubricants, and engine cleaners may be useful. Cleaning solvent is available at most service stations and distilled water for the battery is available at most supermarkets.

SHOP TOOLS

For proper servicing, you will need an assortment of ordinary hand tools (**Figure 2**).

As a minimum, these include:

a. Combination wrenches
b. Sockets
c. Plastic mallet
d. Small hammer
e. Snap ring pliers
f. Gas pliers
g. Phillips screwdrivers
h. Slot (common) screwdrivers
i. Feeler gauges
j. Spark plug gauge
k. Spark plug wrench

Special tools necessary are shown in the chapters covering the particular repair in which they are used.

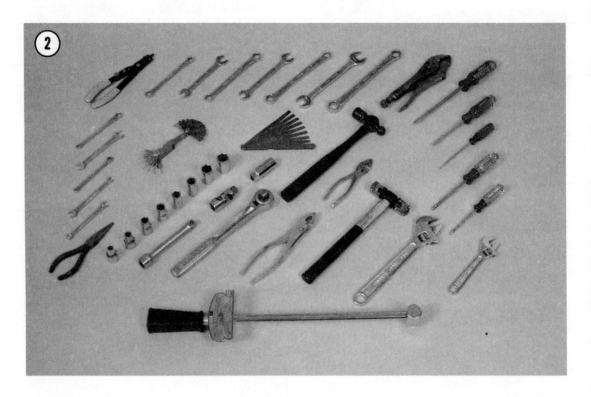

Engine tune-up and troubleshooting procedures require other special tools and equipment. These are described in detail in the following sections.

EMERGENCY TOOL KIT

A small emergency tool kit kept in the trunk is handy for road emergencies which otherwise could leave you stranded. The tools listed below and shown in **Figure 3** will let you handle most roadside repairs.

a. Combination wrenches

b. Crescent (adjustable) wrench

c. Screwdrivers — common and Phillips

d. Pliers — conventional (gas) and needle nose

e. Vise Grips

f. Hammer — plastic and metal

g. Small container of waterless hand cleaner

h. Rags for clean up

i. Silver waterproof sealing tape (duct tape)

j. Flashlight

k. Emergency road flares — at least four

l. Spare drive belts (water pump, alternator, etc.)

TROUBLESHOOTING AND TUNE-UP EQUIPMENT

Voltmeter, Ohmmeter, and Ammeter

For testing the ignition or electrical system, a good voltmeter is required. For automotive use, an instrument covering 0-20 volts is satisfac-

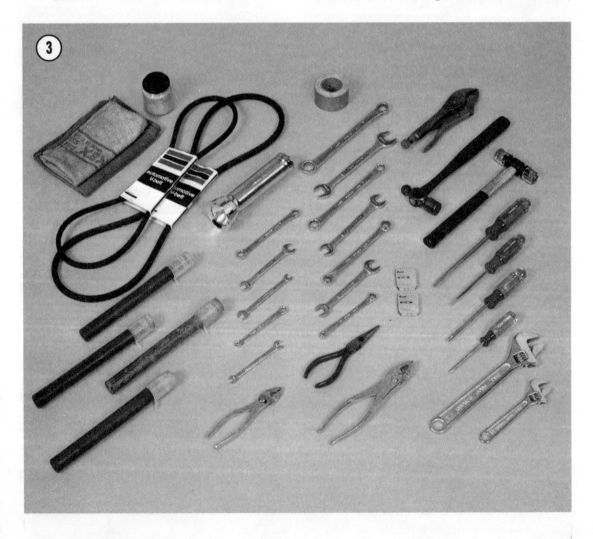

tory. One which also has a 0-2 volt scale is necessary for testing relays, points, or individual contacts where voltage drops are much smaller. Accuracy should be ± ½ volt.

An ohmmeter measures electrical resistance. This instrument is useful for checking continuity (open and short circuits), and testing fuses and lights.

The ammeter measures electrical current. Ammeters for automotive use should cover 0-50 amperes and 0-250 amperes. These are useful for checking battery charging and starting current.

Several inexpensive VOM's (volt-ohm-milli-ammeter) combine all three instruments into one which fits easily in any tool box. See **Figure 4**. However, the ammeter ranges are usually too small for automotive work.

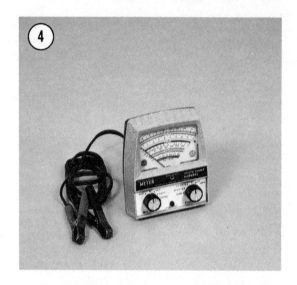

Hydrometer

The hydrometer gives a useful indication of battery condition and charge by measuring the specific gravity of the electrolyte in each cell. See **Figure 5**. Complete details on use and interpretation of readings are provided in the electrical chapter.

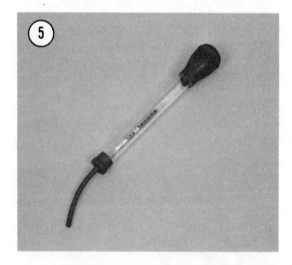

Compression Tester

The compression tester measures the compression pressure built up in each cylinder. The results, when properly interpreted, can indicate general cylinder and valve condition. See **Figure 6**.

Vacuum Gauge

The vacuum gauge (**Figure 7**) is one of the easiest instruments to use, but one of the most difficult for the inexperienced mechanic to interpret. The results, when interpreted with other findings, can provide valuable clues to possible trouble.

To use the vacuum gauge, connect it to a vacuum hose that goes to the intake manifold. Attach it either directly to the hose or to a T-fitting installed into the hose.

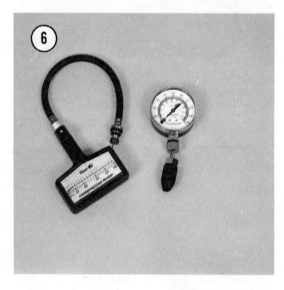

NOTE: *Subtract one inch from the reading for every 1,000 ft. elevation.*

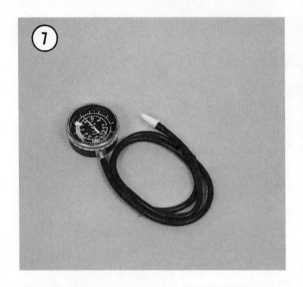

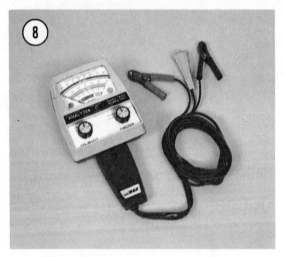

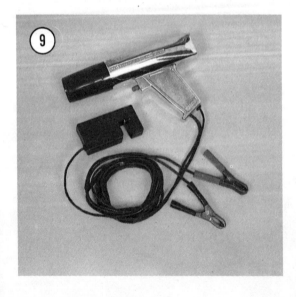

Fuel Pressure Gauge

This instrument is invaluable for evaluating fuel pump performance. Fuel system trouble-shooting procedures in this manual use a fuel pressure gauge. Usually a vacuum gauge and fuel pressure gauge are combined.

Dwell Meter (Contact Breaker Point Ignition Only)

A dwell meter measures the distance in degrees of cam rotation that the breaker points remain closed while the engine is running. Since this angle is determined by breaker point gap, dwell angle is an accurate indication of breaker point gap.

Many tachometers intended for tuning and testing incorporate a dwell meter as well. See **Figure 8**. Follow the manufacturer's instructions to measure dwell.

Tachometer

A tachometer is necessary for tuning. See **Figure 8**. Ignition timing and carburetor adjustments must be performed at the specified idle speed. The best instrument for this purpose is one with a low range of 0-1,000 or 0-2,000 rpm for setting idle, and a high range of 0-4,000 or more for setting ignition timing at 3,000 rpm. Extended range (0-6,000 or 0-8,000 rpm) instruments lack accuracy at lower speeds. The instrument should be capable of detecting changes of 25 rpm on the low range.

Strobe Timing Light

This instrument is necessary for tuning, as it permits very accurate ignition timing. The light flashes at precisely the same instant that No. 1 cylinder fires, at which time the timing marks on the engine should align. Refer to Chapter Three for exact location of the timing marks for your engine.

Suitable lights range from inexpensive neon bulb types ($2-3) to powerful xenon strobe lights ($20-40). See **Figure 9**. Neon timing lights are difficult to see and must be used in dimly lit areas. Xenon strobe timing lights can be used outside in bright sunlight. Both types work on this vehicle; use according to the manufacturer's instructions.

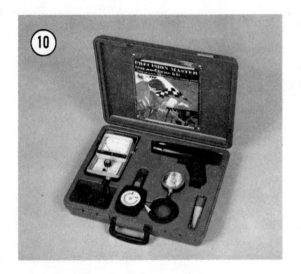

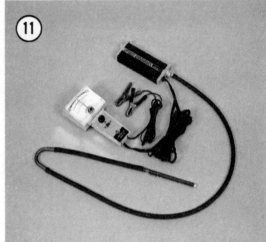

Tune-up Kits

Many manufacturers offer kits that combine several useful instruments. Some come in a convenient carry case and are usually less expensive than purchasing one instrument at a time. **Figure 10** shows one of the kits that is available. The prices vary with the number of instruments included in the kit.

Exhaust Gas Analyzer

Of all instruments described here, this is the least likely to be owned by a home mechanic. This instrument samples the exhaust gases from the tailpipe and measures the thermal conductivity of the exhaust gas. Since different gases conduct heat at varying rates, thermal conductivity of the exhaust is a good indication of gases present.

An exhaust gas analyzer is vital for accurately checking the effectiveness of exhaust emission control adjustments. They are relatively expensive to buy ($70 and up), but must be considered essential for the owner/mechanic to comply with today's emission laws. See **Figure 11**.

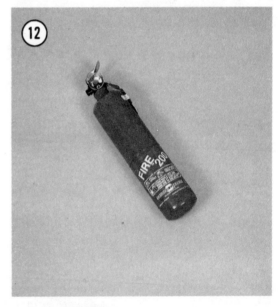

Fire Extinguisher

A fire extinguisher is a necessity when working on a vehicle. It should be rated for both *Class B* (flammable liquids — gasoline, oil, paint, etc.) and *Class C* (electrical — wiring, etc.) type fires. It should always be kept within reach. See **Figure 12**.

CHAPTER TWO

TROUBLESHOOTING

Troubleshooting can be a relatively simple matter if it is done logically. The first step in any troubleshooting procedure must be defining the symptoms as closely as possible. Subsequent steps involve testing and analyzing areas which could cause the symptoms. A haphazard approach may eventually find the trouble, but in terms of wasted time and unnecessary parts replacement, it can be very costly.

The troubleshooting procedures in this chapter analyze typical symptoms and show logical methods of isolation. These are not the only methods. There may be several approaches to a problem, but all methods must have one thing in common — a logical, systematic approach.

STARTING SYSTEM

The starting system consists of the starter motor and the starter solenoid. The ignition key controls the starter solenoid, which mechanically engages the starter with the engine flywheel, and supplies electrical current to turn the starter motor.

Starting system troubles are relatively easy to find. In most cases, the trouble is a loose or dirty electrical connection. **Figures 1 and 2** provide routines for finding the trouble.

CHARGING SYSTEM

The charging system consists of the alternator (or generator on older vehicles), voltage regulator, and battery. A drive belt driven by the engine crankshaft turns the alternator which produces electrical energy to charge the battery. As engine speed varies, the voltage from the alternator varies. A voltage regulator controls the charging current to the battery and maintains the voltage to the vehicle's electrical system at safe levels. A warning light or gauge on the instrument panel signals the driver when charging is not taking place. Refer to **Figure 3** for a typical charging system.

Complete troubleshooting of the charging system requires test equipment and skills which the average home mechanic does not possess. However, there are a few tests which can be done to pinpoint most troubles.

Charging system trouble may stem from a defective alternator (or generator), voltage regulator, battery, or drive belt. It may also be caused by something as simple as incorrect drive belt tension. The following are symptoms of typical problems you may encounter.

1. *Battery dies frequently, even though the warning lamp indicates no discharge* — This can be caused by a drive belt that is slightly too

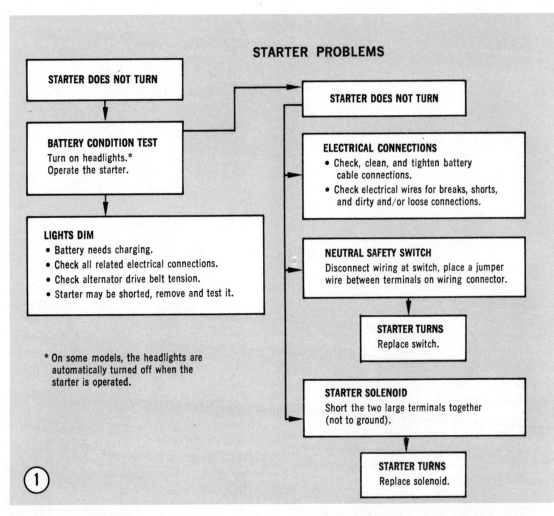

STARTER PROBLEMS

STARTER DOES NOT TURN

BATTERY CONDITION TEST
Turn on headlights.*
Operate the starter.

LIGHTS DIM
• Battery needs charging.
• Check all related electrical connections.
• Check alternator drive belt tension.
• Starter may be shorted, remove and test it.

* On some models, the headlights are
automatically turned off when the
starter is operated.

STARTER DOES NOT TURN

ELECTRICAL CONNECTIONS
• Check, clean, and tighten battery
  cable connections.
• Check electrical wires for breaks, shorts,
  and dirty and/or loose connections.

NEUTRAL SAFETY SWITCH
Disconnect wiring at switch, place a jumper
wire between terminals on wiring connector.

STARTER TURNS
Replace switch.

STARTER SOLENOID
Short the two large terminals together
(not to ground).

STARTER TURNS
Replace solenoid.

①

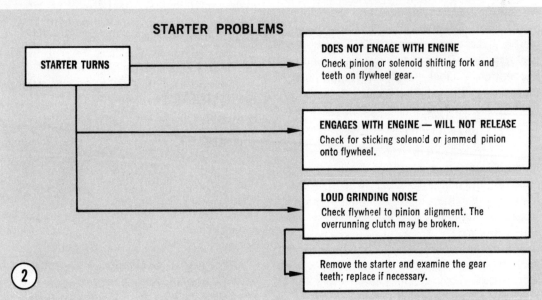

STARTER PROBLEMS

STARTER TURNS

DOES NOT ENGAGE WITH ENGINE
Check pinion or solenoid shifting fork and
teeth on flywheel gear.

ENGAGES WITH ENGINE — WILL NOT RELEASE
Check for sticking solenoid or jammed pinion
onto flywheel.

LOUD GRINDING NOISE
Check flywheel to pinion alignment. The
overrunning clutch may be broken.

Remove the starter and examine the gear
teeth; replace if necessary.

②

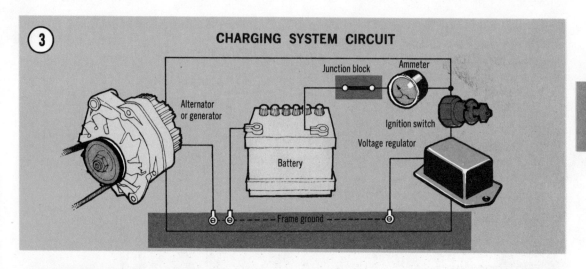

③ CHARGING SYSTEM CIRCUIT

2

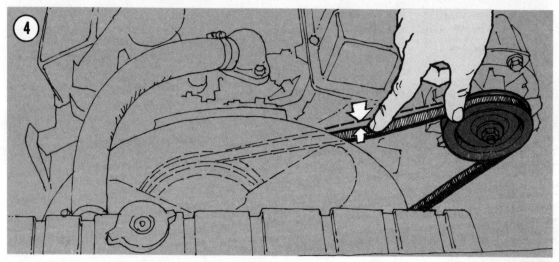

④

loose. Grasp the alternator (or generator) pulley and try to turn it. If the pulley can be turned without moving the belt, the drive belt is too loose. As a rule, keep the belt tight enough that it can be deflected about ½ in. under moderate thumb pressure between the pulleys (**Figure 4**). The battery may also be at fault; test the battery condition.

2. *Charging system warning lamp does not come on when ignition switch is turned on* — This may indicate a defective ignition switch, battery, voltage regulator, or lamp. First try to start the vehicle. If it doesn't start, check the ignition switch and battery. If the car starts, remove the warning lamp; test it for continuity with an ohmmeter or substitute a new lamp. If the lamp is good, locate the voltage regulator

and make sure it is properly grounded (try tightening the mounting screws). Also the alternator (or generator) brushes may not be making contact. Test the alternator (or generator) and voltage regulator.

3. *Alternator (or generator) warning lamp comes on and stays on* — This usually indicates that no charging is taking place. First check drive belt tension (**Figure 4**). Then check battery condition, and check all wiring connections in the charging system. If this does not locate the trouble, check the alternator (or generator) and voltage regulator.

4. *Charging system warning lamp flashes on and off intermittently* — This usually indicates the charging system is working intermittently.

Check the drive belt tension (**Figure 4**), and check all electrical connections in the charging system. Check the alternator (or generator). *On generators only*, check the condition of the commutator.

5. *Battery requires frequent additions of water, or lamps require frequent replacement* — The alternator (or generator) is probably overcharging the battery. The voltage regulator is probably at fault.

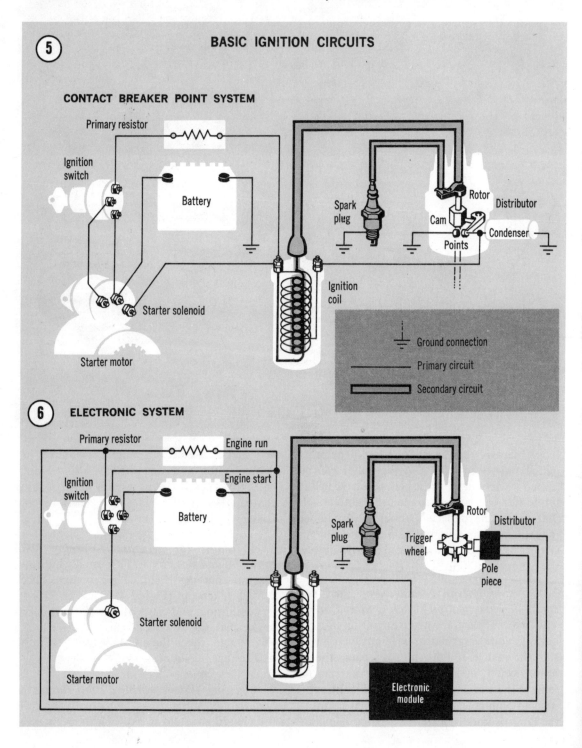

6. *Excessive noise from the alternator (or generator)* — Check for loose mounting brackets and bolts. The problem may also be worn bearings or the need of lubrication in some cases. If an alternator whines, a shorted diode may be indicated.

IGNITION SYSTEM

The ignition system may be either a conventional contact breaker type or an electronic ignition. See electrical chapter to determine which type you have. **Figures 5 and 6** show simplified diagrams of each type.

Most problems involving failure to start, poor performance, or rough running stem from trouble in the ignition system, particularly in contact breaker systems. Many novice troubleshooters get into trouble when they assume that these symptoms point to the fuel system instead of the ignition system.

Ignition system troubles may be roughly divided between those affecting only one cylinder and those affecting all cylinders. If the trouble affects only one cylinder, it can only be in the spark plug, spark plug wire, or portion of the distributor associated with that cylinder. If the trouble affects all cylinders (weak spark or no spark), then the trouble is in the ignition coil, rotor, distributor, or associated wiring.

The troubleshooting procedures outlined in **Figure 7** (breaker point ignition) or **Figure 8**

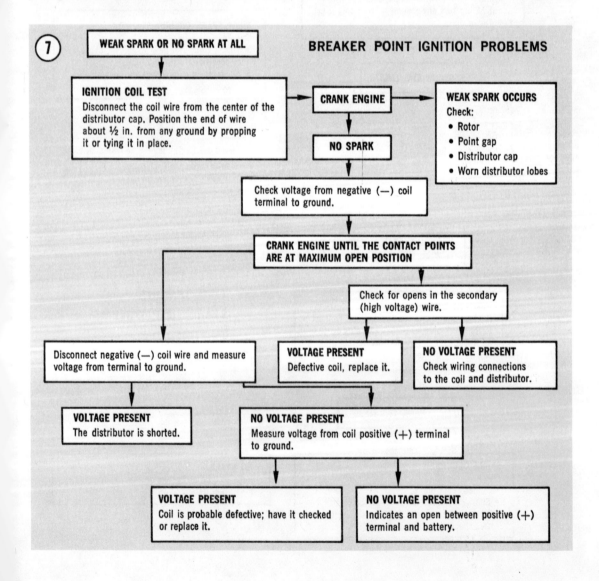

BREAKER POINT IGNITION PROBLEMS

(electronic ignition) will help you isolate ignition problems fast. Of course, they assume that the battery is in good enough condition to crank the engine over at its normal rate.

ENGINE PERFORMANCE

A number of factors can make the engine difficult or impossible to start, or cause rough running, poor performance and so on. The majority of novice troubleshooters immediately suspect the carburetor or fuel injection system. In the majority of cases, though, the trouble exists in the ignition system.

The troubleshooting procedures outlined in **Figures 9 through 14** will help you solve the majority of engine starting troubles in a systematic manner.

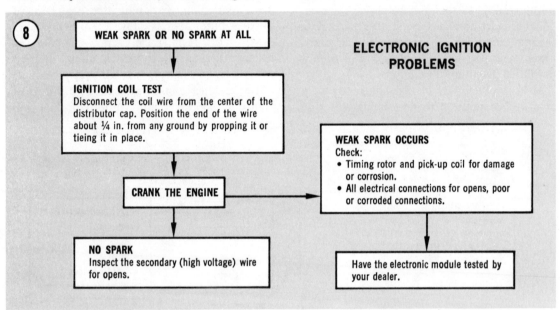

(8) WEAK SPARK OR NO SPARK AT ALL

ELECTRONIC IGNITION PROBLEMS

IGNITION COIL TEST
Disconnect the coil wire from the center of the distributor cap. Position the end of the wire about ¼ in. from any ground by propping it or tieing it in place.

CRANK THE ENGINE

WEAK SPARK OCCURS
Check:
• Timing rotor and pick-up coil for damage or corrosion.
• All electrical connections for opens, poor or corroded connections.

NO SPARK
Inspect the secondary (high voltage) wire for opens.

Have the electronic module tested by your dealer.

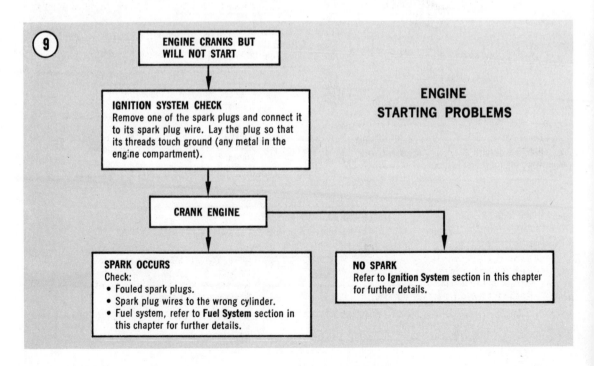

(9) ENGINE CRANKS BUT WILL NOT START

ENGINE STARTING PROBLEMS

IGNITION SYSTEM CHECK
Remove one of the spark plugs and connect it to its spark plug wire. Lay the plug so that its threads touch ground (any metal in the engine compartment).

CRANK ENGINE

SPARK OCCURS
Check:
• Fouled spark plugs.
• Spark plug wires to the wrong cylinder.
• Fuel system, refer to **Fuel System** section in this chapter for further details.

NO SPARK
Refer to **Ignition System** section in this chapter for further details.

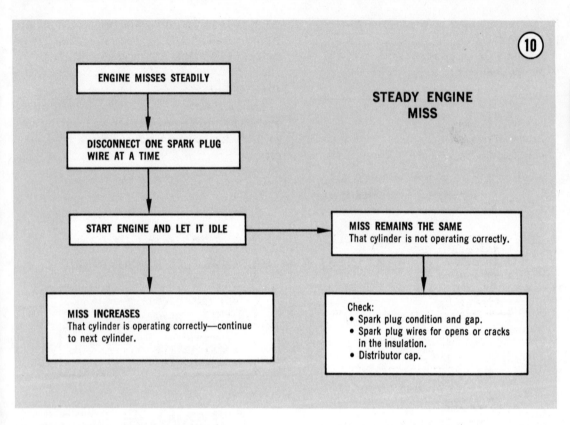

⑩

STEADY ENGINE
MISS

ENGINE MISSES STEADILY

↓

DISCONNECT ONE SPARK PLUG
WIRE AT A TIME

↓

START ENGINE AND LET IT IDLE → MISS REMAINS THE SAME
That cylinder is not operating correctly.

↓ ↓

MISS INCREASES
That cylinder is operating correctly—continue
to next cylinder.

Check:
• Spark plug condition and gap.
• Spark plug wires for opens or cracks
  in the insulation.
• Distributor cap.

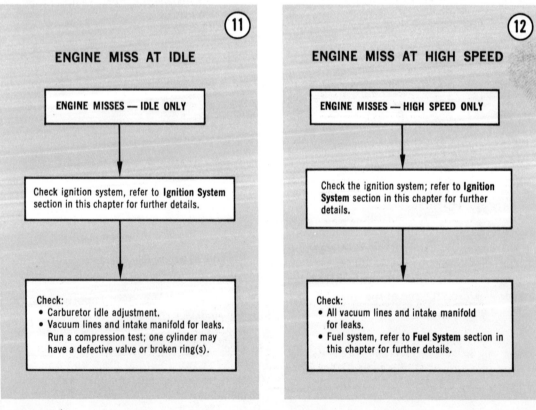

⑪

ENGINE MISS AT IDLE

ENGINE MISSES — IDLE ONLY

↓

Check ignition system, refer to **Ignition System**
section in this chapter for further details.

↓

Check:
• Carburetor idle adjustment.
• Vacuum lines and intake manifold for leaks.
  Run a compression test; one cylinder may
  have a defective valve or broken ring(s).

⑫

ENGINE MISS AT HIGH SPEED

ENGINE MISSES — HIGH SPEED ONLY

↓

Check the ignition system; refer to **Ignition
System** section in this chapter for further
details.

↓

Check:
• All vacuum lines and intake manifold
  for leaks.
• Fuel system, refer to **Fuel System** section in
  this chapter for further details.

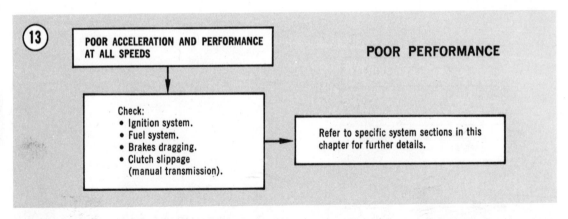

POOR PERFORMANCE

⑬ POOR ACCELERATION AND PERFORMANCE AT ALL SPEEDS

Check:
- Ignition system.
- Fuel system.
- Brakes dragging.
- Clutch slippage (manual transmission).

Refer to specific system sections in this chapter for further details.

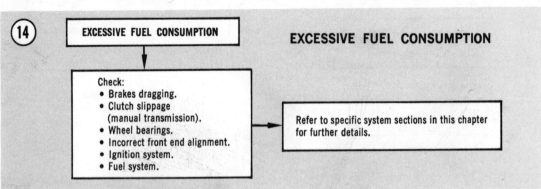

EXCESSIVE FUEL CONSUMPTION

⑭ EXCESSIVE FUEL CONSUMPTION

Check:
- Brakes dragging.
- Clutch slippage (manual transmission).
- Wheel bearings.
- Incorrect front end alignment.
- Ignition system.
- Fuel system.

Refer to specific system sections in this chapter for further details.

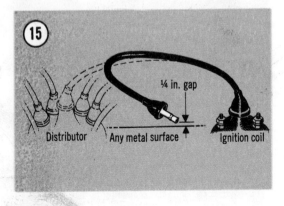

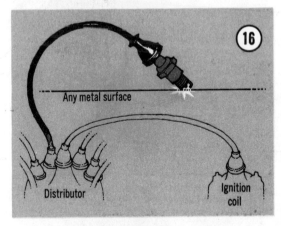

Some tests of the ignition system require running the engine with a spark plug or ignition coil wire disconnected. The safest way to do this is to disconnect the wire with the engine stopped, then prop the end of the wire next to a metal surface as shown in **Figures 15 and 16.**

WARNING
Never disconnect a spark plug or ignition coil wire while the engine is running. The high voltage in an ignition system, particularly the newer high-energy electronic ignition systems could cause serious injury or even death.

Spark plug condition is an important indication of engine performance. Spark plugs in a properly operating engine will have slightly pitted electrodes, and a light tan insulator tip. **Figure 17** shows a normal plug, and a number of others which indicate trouble in their respective cylinders.

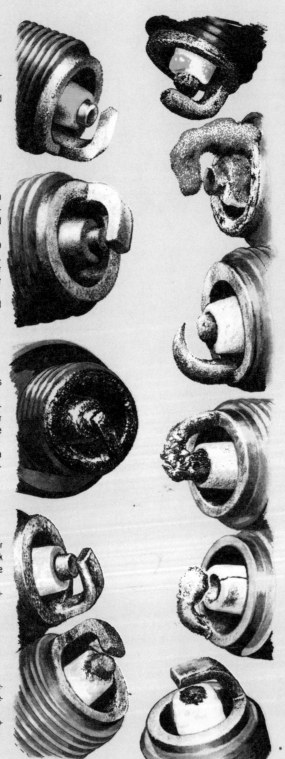

NORMAL
- Appearance—Firing tip has deposits of light gray to light tan.
- Can be cleaned, regapped and reused.

CARBON FOULED
- Appearance—Dull, dry black with fluffy carbon deposits on the insulator tip, electrode and exposed shell.
- Caused by—Fuel/air mixture too rich, plug heat range too cold, weak ignition system, dirty air cleaner, faulty automatic choke or excessive idling.
- Can be cleaned, regapped and reused.

OIL FOULED
- Appearance—Wet black deposits on insulator and exposed shell.
- Caused by—Excessive oil entering the combustion chamber through worn rings, pistons, valve guides or bearings.
- Replace with new plugs (use a hotter plug if engine is not repaired).

LEAD FOULED
- Appearance — Yellow insulator deposits (may sometimes be dark gray, black or tan in color) on the insulator tip.
- Caused by—Highly leaded gasoline.
- Replace with new plugs.

LEAD FOULED
- Appearance—Yellow glazed deposits indicating melted lead deposits due to hard acceleration.
- Caused by—Highly leaded gasoline.
- Replace with new plugs.

OIL AND LEAD FOULED
- Appearance—Glazed yellow deposits with a slight brownish tint on the insulator tip and ground electrode.
- Replace with new plugs.

FUEL ADDITIVE RESIDUE
- Appearance — Brown colored hardened ash deposits on the insulator tip and ground electrode.
- Caused by—Fuel and/or oil additives.
- Replace with new plugs.

WORN
- Appearance — Severely worn or eroded electrodes.
- Caused by—Normal wear or unusual oil and/or fuel additives.
- Replace with new plugs.

PREIGNITION
- Appearance — Melted ground electrode.
- Caused by—Overadvanced ignition timing, inoperative ignition advance mechanism, too low of a fuel octane rating, lean fuel/air mixture or carbon deposits in combustion chamber.

PREIGNITION
- Appearance—Melted center electrode.
- Caused by—Abnormal combustion due to overadvanced ignition timing or incorrect advance, too low of a fuel octane rating, lean fuel/air mixture, or carbon deposits in combustion chamber.
- Correct engine problem and replace with new plugs.

INCORRECT HEAT RANGE
- Appearance—Melted center electrode and white blistered insulator tip.
- Caused by—Incorrect plug heat range selection.
- Replace with new plugs.

2

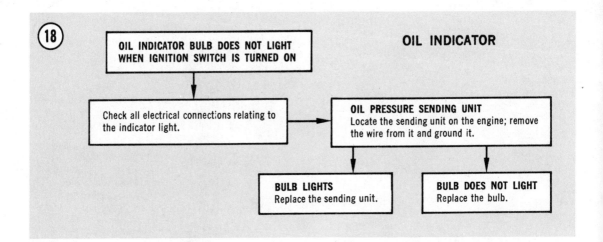

18 OIL INDICATOR BULB DOES NOT LIGHT WHEN IGNITION SWITCH IS TURNED ON — **OIL INDICATOR**

Check all electrical connections relating to the indicator light.

OIL PRESSURE SENDING UNIT
Locate the sending unit on the engine; remove the wire from it and ground it.

BULB LIGHTS
Replace the sending unit.

BULB DOES NOT LIGHT
Replace the bulb.

ENGINE OIL PRESSURE LIGHT

Proper oil pressure to the engine is vital. If oil pressure is insufficient, the engine can destroy itself in a comparatively short time.

The oil pressure warning circuit monitors oil pressure constantly. If pressure drops below a predetermined level, the light comes on.

Obviously, it is vital for the warning circuit to be working to signal low oil pressure. Each time you turn on the ignition, but before you start the car, the warning light should come on. If it doesn't, there is trouble in the warning circuit, not the oil pressure system. See **Figure 18** to troubleshoot the warning circuit.

Once the engine is running, the warning light should stay off. If the warning light comes on or acts erratically while the engine is running there is trouble with the engine oil pressure system. *Stop the engine immediately*. Refer to **Figure 19** for possible causes of the problem.

FUEL SYSTEM (CARBURETTED)

Fuel system problems must be isolated to the fuel pump (mechanical or electric), fuel lines, fuel filter, or carburetor. These procedures assume the ignition system is working properly and is correctly adjusted.

1. *Engine will not start* — First make sure that fuel is being delivered to the carburetor. Remove the air cleaner, look into the carburetor throat, and operate the accelerator

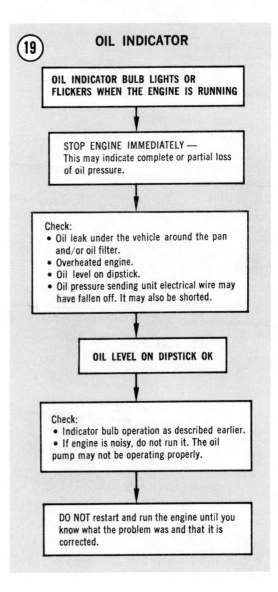

19 OIL INDICATOR

OIL INDICATOR BULB LIGHTS OR FLICKERS WHEN THE ENGINE IS RUNNING

STOP ENGINE IMMEDIATELY —
This may indicate complete or partial loss of oil pressure.

Check:
• Oil leak under the vehicle around the pan and/or oil filter.
• Overheated engine.
• Oil level on dipstick.
• Oil pressure sending unit electrical wire may have fallen off. It may also be shorted.

OIL LEVEL ON DIPSTICK OK

Check:
• Indicator bulb operation as described earlier.
• If engine is noisy, do not run it. The oil pump may not be operating properly.

DO NOT restart and run the engine until you know what the problem was and that it is corrected.

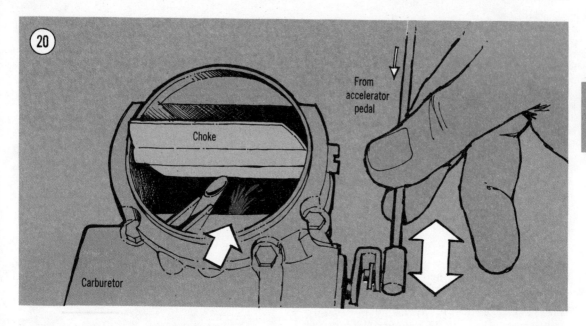

linkage several times. There should be a stream of fuel from the accelerator pump discharge tube each time the accelerator linkage is depressed (**Figure 20**). If not, check fuel pump delivery (described later), float valve, and float adjustment. If the engine will not start, check the automatic choke parts for sticking or damage. If necessary, rebuild or replace the carburetor.

2. *Engine runs at fast idle* — Check the choke setting. Check the idle speed, idle mixture, and decel valve (if equipped) adjustment.

3. *Rough idle or engine miss with frequent stalling* — Check idle mixture and idle speed adjustments.

4. *Engine "diesels" (continues to run) when ignition is switched off* — Check idle mixture (probably too rich), ignition timing, and idle speed (probably too fast). Check the throttle solenoid (if equipped) for proper operation. Check for overheated engine.

5. *Stumbling when accelerating from idle* — Check the idle speed and mixture adjustments. Check the accelerator pump.

6. *Engine misses at high speed or lacks power* — This indicates possible fuel starvation. Check fuel pump pressure and capacity as described in this chapter. Check float needle valves. Check for a clogged fuel filter or air cleaner.

7. *Black exhaust smoke* — This indicates a badly overrich mixture. Check idle mixture and idle speed adjustment. Check choke setting. Check for excessive fuel pump pressure, leaky floats, or worn needle valves.

8. *Excessive fuel consumption* — Check for overrich mixture. Make sure choke mechanism works properly. Check idle mixture and idle speed. Check for excessive fuel pump pressure, leaky floats, or worn float needle valves.

FUEL SYSTEM (FUEL INJECTED)

Troubleshooting a fuel injection system requires more thought, experience, and know-how than any other part of the vehicle. A logical approach and proper test equipment are essential in order to successfully find and fix these troubles.

It is best to leave fuel injection troubles to your dealer. In order to isolate a problem to the injection system make sure that the fuel pump is operating properly. Check its performance as described later in this section. Also make sure that fuel filter and air cleaner are not clogged.

FUEL PUMP TEST (MECHANICAL AND ELECTRIC)

1. Disconnect the fuel inlet line where it enters the carburetor or fuel injection system.

2. Fit a rubber hose over the fuel line so fuel can be directed into a graduated container with about one quart capacity. See **Figure 21**.

3. To avoid accidental starting of the engine, disconnect the secondary coil wire from the coil.

4. Crank the engine for about 30 seconds.

5. If the fuel pump supplies the specified amount (refer to the fuel chapter later in this book), the trouble may be in the carburetor or fuel injection system. The fuel injection system should be tested by your dealer.

6. If there is no fuel present or the pump cannot supply the specified amount, either the fuel pump is defective or there is an obstruction in the fuel line. Replace the fuel pump and/or inspect the fuel lines for air leaks or obstructions.

7. Also pressure test the fuel pump by installing a T-fitting in the fuel line between the fuel pump and the carburetor. Connect a fuel pressure gauge to the fitting with a short tube (**Figure 22**).

8. Reconnect the primary coil wire, start the engine, and record the pressure. Refer to the fuel chapter later in this book for the correct pressure. If the pressure varies from that specified, the pump should be replaced.

9. Stop the engine. The pressure should drop off very slowly. If it drops off rapidly, the outlet valve in the pump is leaking and the pump should be replaced.

EMISSION CONTROL SYSTEMS

Major emission control systems used on nearly all U.S. models include the following:

    a. Positive crankcase ventilation (PCV)

    b. Thermostatic air cleaner

    c. Air injection reaction (AIR)

    d. Fuel evaporation control

    e. Exhaust gas recirculation (EGR)

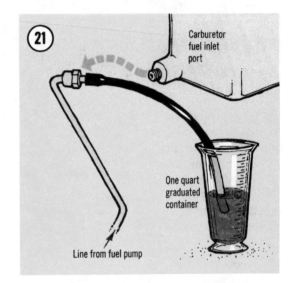

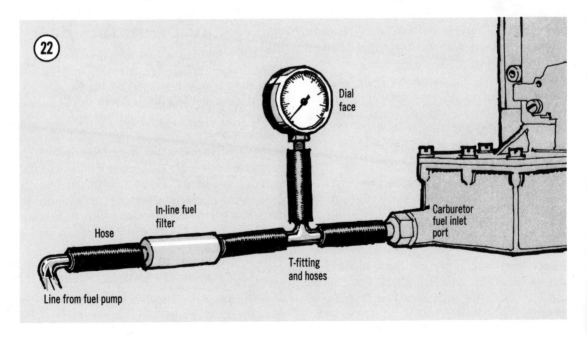

Emission control systems vary considerably from model to model. Individual models contain variations of the four systems described here. In addition, they may include other special systems. Use the index to find specific emission control components in other chapters.

Many of the systems and components are factory set and sealed. Without special expensive test equipment, it is impossible to adjust the systems to meet state and federal requirements.

Troubleshooting can also be difficult without special equipment. The procedures described below will help you find emission control parts which have failed, but repairs may have to be entrusted to a dealer or other properly equipped repair shop.

With the proper equipment, you can test the carbon monoxide and hydrocarbon levels.

Figure 23 provides some sources of trouble if the readings are not correct.

Positive Crankcase Ventilation

Fresh air drawn from the air cleaner housing scavenges emissions (e.g., piston blow-by) from the crankcase, then the intake manifold vacuum draws emissions into the intake manifold. They can then be reburned in the normal combustion process. **Figure 24** shows a typical system. **Figure 25** provides a testing procedure.

Thermostatic Air Cleaner

The thermostatically controlled air cleaner maintains incoming air to the engine at a predetermined level, usually about 100°F or higher. It mixes cold air with heated air from the exhaust manifold region. The air cleaner in-

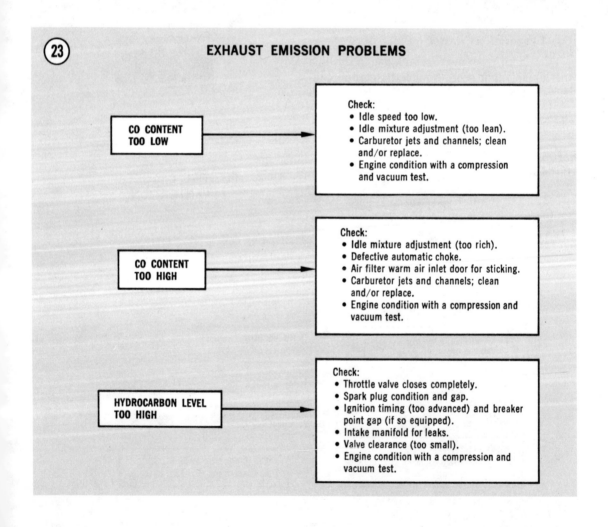

(23) **EXHAUST EMISSION PROBLEMS**

CO CONTENT TOO LOW

Check:
- Idle speed too low.
- Idle mixture adjustment (too lean).
- Carburetor jets and channels; clean and/or replace.
- Engine condition with a compression and vacuum test.

CO CONTENT TOO HIGH

Check:
- Idle mixture adjustment (too rich).
- Defective automatic choke.
- Air filter warm air inlet door for sticking.
- Carburetor jets and channels; clean and/or replace.
- Engine condition with a compression and vacuum test.

HYDROCARBON LEVEL TOO HIGH

Check:
- Throttle valve closes completely.
- Spark plug condition and gap.
- Ignition timing (too advanced) and breaker point gap (if so equipped).
- Intake manifold for leaks.
- Valve clearance (too small).
- Engine condition with a compression and vacuum test.

cludes a temperature sensor, vacuum motor, and a hinged door. See **Figure 26**.

The system is comparatively easy to test. See **Figure 27** for the procedure.

Air Injection Reaction System

The air injection reaction system reduces air pollution by oxidizing hydrocarbons and carbon monoxide as they leave the combustion chamber. See **Figure 28**.

The air injection pump, driven by the engine, compresses filtered air and injects it at the exhaust port of each cylinder. The fresh air mixes with the unburned gases in the exhaust and promotes further burning. A check valve prevents exhaust gases from entering and damaging the air pump if the pump becomes inoperative, e.g., from a fan belt failure.

Figure 29 explains the testing procedure for this system.

Fuel Evaporation Control

Fuel vapor from the fuel tank passes through the liquid/vapor separator to the carbon canister. See **Figure 30**. The carbon absorbs and

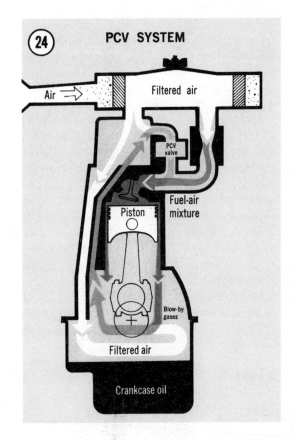

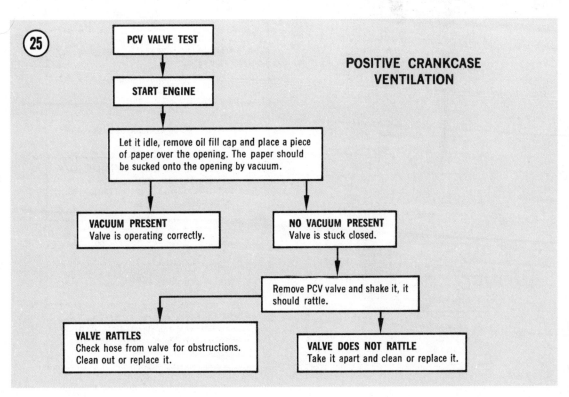

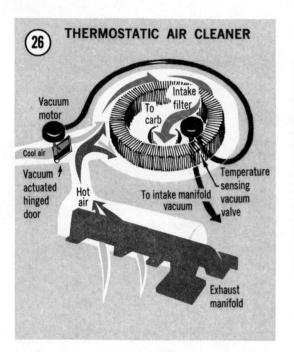

THERMOSTATIC AIR CLEANER

26

Vacuum motor

Cool air

Vacuum actuated hinged door

Hot air

Intake filter

To carb

Temperature sensing vacuum valve

To intake manifold vacuum

Exhaust manifold

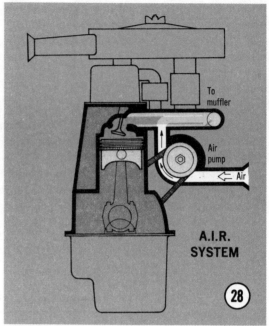

To muffler

Air pump

Air

A.I.R. SYSTEM

28

2

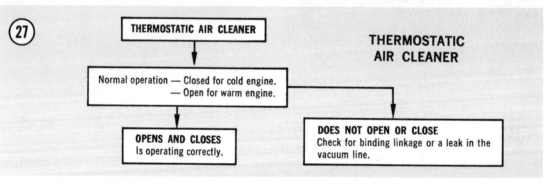

27

THERMOSTATIC AIR CLEANER

THERMOSTATIC AIR CLEANER

Normal operation — Closed for cold engine.
— Open for warm engine.

OPENS AND CLOSES
Is operating correctly.

DOES NOT OPEN OR CLOSE
Check for binding linkage or a leak in the vacuum line.

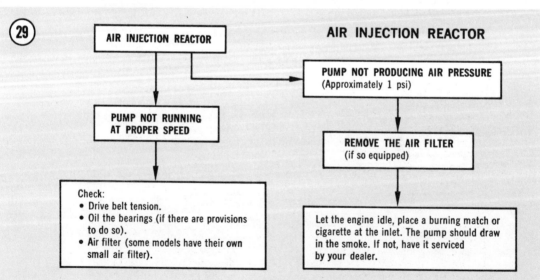

29

AIR INJECTION REACTOR

AIR INJECTION REACTOR

PUMP NOT PRODUCING AIR PRESSURE
(Approximately 1 psi)

PUMP NOT RUNNING AT PROPER SPEED

REMOVE THE AIR FILTER
(if so equipped)

Check:
• Drive belt tension.
• Oil the bearings (if there are provisions to do so).
• Air filter (some models have their own small air filter).

Let the engine idle, place a burning match or cigarette at the inlet. The pump should draw in the smoke. If not, have it serviced by your dealer.

stores the vapor when the engine is stopped. When the engine runs, manifold vacuum draws the vapor from the canister. Instead of being released into the atmosphere, the fuel vapor takes part in the normal combustion process.

Exhaust Gas Recirculation

The exhaust gas recirculation (EGR) system is used to reduce the emission of nitrogen oxides (NOx). Relatively inert exhaust gases are introduced into the combustion process to slightly reduce peak temperatures. This reduction in temperature reduces the formation of NOx.

Figure 31 provides a simple test of this system.

ENGINE NOISES

Often the first evidence of an internal engine trouble is a strange noise. That knocking, clicking, or tapping which you never heard before may be warning you of impending trouble.

While engine noises can indicate problems, they are sometimes difficult to interpret correctly; inexperienced mechanics can be seriously misled by them.

Professional mechanics often use a special stethoscope which looks similar to a doctor's stethoscope for isolating engine noises. You can do nearly as well with a "sounding stick" which can be an ordinary piece of doweling or a section of small hose. By placing one end in contact with the area to which you want to listen and the other end near your ear, you can hear

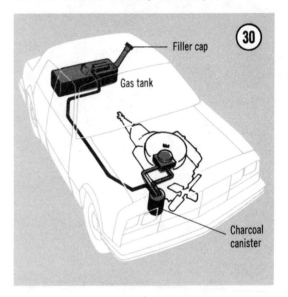

(30)

Filler cap

Gas tank

Charcoal canister

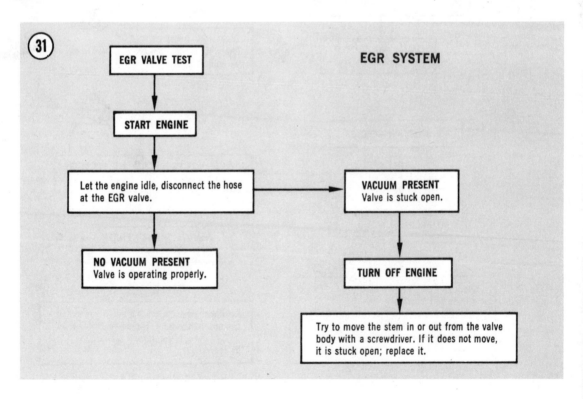

(31)

EGR VALVE TEST

EGR SYSTEM

START ENGINE

Let the engine idle, disconnect the hose at the EGR valve.

VACUUM PRESENT
Valve is stuck open.

NO VACUUM PRESENT
Valve is operating properly.

TURN OFF ENGINE

Try to move the stem in or out from the valve body with a screwdriver. If it does not move, it is stuck open; replace it.

sounds emanating from that area. The first time you do this, you may be horrified at the strange noises coming from even a normal engine. If you can, have an experienced friend or mechanic help you sort the noises out.

Clicking or Tapping Noises

Clicking or tapping noises usually come from the valve train, and indicate excessive valve clearance.

If your vehicle has adjustable valves, the procedure for adjusting the valve clearance is explained in Chapter Three. If your vehicle has hydraulic lifters, the clearance may not be adjustable. The noise may be coming from a collapsed lifter. These may be cleaned or replaced as described in the engine chapter.

A sticking valve may also sound like a valve with excessive clearance. In addition, excessive wear in valve train components can cause similar engine noises.

Knocking Noises

A heavy, dull knocking is usually caused by a worn main bearing. The noise is loudest when the engine is working hard, i.e., accelerating hard at low speed. You may be able to isolate the trouble to a single bearing by disconnecting

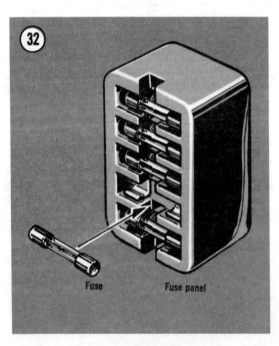

Fuse   Fuse panel

the spark plugs one at a time. When you reach the spark plug nearest the bearing, the knock will be reduced or disappear.

Worn connecting rod bearings may also produce a knock, but the sound is usually more "metallic." As with a main bearing, the noise is worse when accelerating. It may even increase further just as you go from accelerating to coasting. Disconnecting spark plugs will help isolate this knock as well.

A double knock or clicking usually indicates a worn piston pin. Disconnecting spark plugs will isolate this to a particular piston, however, the noise will *increase* when you reach the affected piston.

A loose flywheel and excessive crankshaft end play also produce knocking noises. While similar to main bearing noises, these are usually intermittent, not constant, and they do not change when spark plugs are disconnected.

Some mechanics confuse piston pin noise with piston slap. The double knock will distinguish the piston pin noise. Piston slap is identified by the fact that it is always louder when the engine is cold.

ELECTRICAL ACCESSORIES

Lights and Switches (Interior and Exterior)

1. *Bulb does not light* — Remove the bulb and check for a broken element. Also check the inside of the socket; make sure the contacts are clean and free of corrosion. If the bulb and socket are OK, check to see if a fuse has blown or a circuit breaker has tripped. The fuse panel (**Figure 32**) is usually located under the instrument panel. Replace the blown fuse or reset the circuit breaker. If the fuse blows or the breaker trips again, there is a short in that circuit. Check that circuit all the way to the battery. Look for worn wire insulation or burned wires.

If all the above are all right, check the switch controlling the bulb for continuity with an ohmmeter at the switch terminals. Check the switch contact terminals for loose or dirty electrical connections.

2. *Headlights work but will not switch from either high or low beam* — Check the beam selector switch for continuity with an ohmmeter

at the switch terminals. Check the switch contact terminals for loose or dirty electrical connections.

3. *Brake light switch inoperative* — On mechanically operated switches, usually mounted near the brake pedal arm, adjust the switch to achieve correct mechanical operation. Check the switch for continuity with an ohmmeter at the switch terminals. Check the switch contact terminals for loose or dirty electrical connections.

4. *Back-up lights do not operate* — Check light bulb as described earlier. Locate the switch, normally located near the shift lever. Adjust switch to achieve correct mechanical operation. Check the switch for continuity with an ohmmeter at the switch terminals. Bypass the switch with a jumper wire; if the lights work, replace the switch.

Directional Signals

1. *Directional signals do not operate* — If the indicator light on the instrument panel burns steadily instead of flashing, this usually indicates that one of the exterior lights is burned out. Check all lamps that normally flash. If all are all right, the flasher unit may be defective. Replace it with a good one.

2. *Directional signal indicator light on instrument panel does not light up* — Check the light bulbs as described earlier. Check all electrical connections and check the flasher unit.

3. *Directional signals will not self-cancel* — Check the self-cancelling mechanism located inside the steering column.

4. *Directional signals flash slowly* — Check the condition of the battery and the alternator (or generator) drive belt tension (**Figure 4**). Check the flasher unit and all related electrical connections.

Windshield Wipers

1. *Wipers do not operate* — Check for a blown fuse or circuit breaker that has tripped; replace or reset. Check all related terminals for loose or dirty electrical connections. Check continuity of the control switch with an ohmmeter at the switch terminals. Check the linkage and arms

for loose, broken, or binding parts. Straighten out or replace where necessary.

2. *Wiper motor hums but will not operate* — The motor may be shorted out internally; check and/or replace the motor. Also check for broken or binding linkage and arms.

3. *Wiper arms will not return to the stowed position when turned off* — The motor has a special internal switch for this purpose. Have it inspected by your dealer. Do not attempt this yourself.

Interior Heater

1. *Heater fan does not operate* — Check for a blown fuse or circuit breaker that has tripped. Check the switch for continuity with an ohmmeter at the switch terminals. Check the switch contact terminals for loose or dirty electrical connections.

2. *Heat output is insufficient* — Check the heater hose/engine coolant control valve usually located in the engine compartment; make sure it is in the open position. Ensure that the heater door(s) and cable(s) are operating correctly and are in the open position. Inspect the heat ducts; make sure that they are not crimped or blocked.

COOLING SYSTEM

The temperature gauge or warning light usually signals cooling system troubles before there is any damage. As long as you stop the vehicle at the first indication of trouble, serious damage is unlikely.

In most cases, the trouble will be obvious as soon as you open the hood. If there is coolant or steam leaking, look for a defective radiator, radiator hose, or heater hose. If there is no evidence of leakage, make sure that the fan belt is in good condition. If the trouble is not obvious, refer to **Figures 33 and 34** to help isolate the trouble.

Automotive cooling systems operate under pressure to permit higher operating temperatures without boil-over. The system should be checked periodically to make sure it can withstand normal pressure. **Figure 35** shows the equipment which nearly any service station has for testing the system pressure.

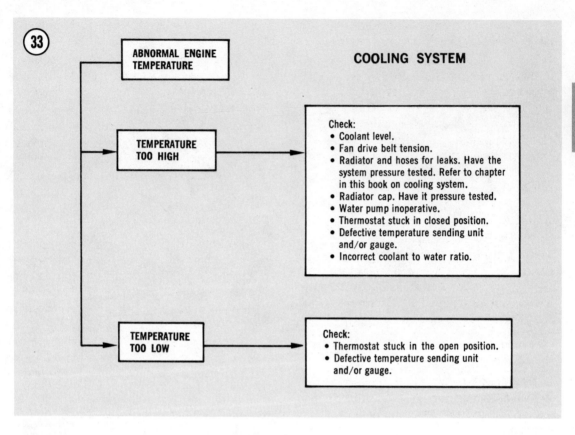

2

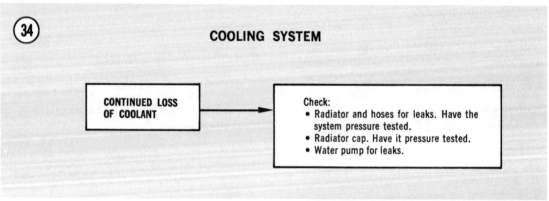

CLUTCH

All clutch troubles except adjustments require transmission removal to identify and cure the problem.

1. *Slippage* — This is most noticeable when accelerating in a high gear at relatively low speed. To check slippage, park the vehicle on a level surface with the handbrake set. Shift to 2nd gear and release the clutch as if driving off. If the clutch is good, the engine will slow and stall. If the clutch slips, continued engine speed will give it away.

Slippage results from insufficient clutch pedal free play, oil or grease on the clutch disc, worn pressure plate, or weak springs.

2. *Drag or failure to release* — This trouble usually causes difficult shifting and gear clash, especially when downshifting. The cause may be excessive clutch pedal free play, warped or bent pressure plate or clutch disc, broken or

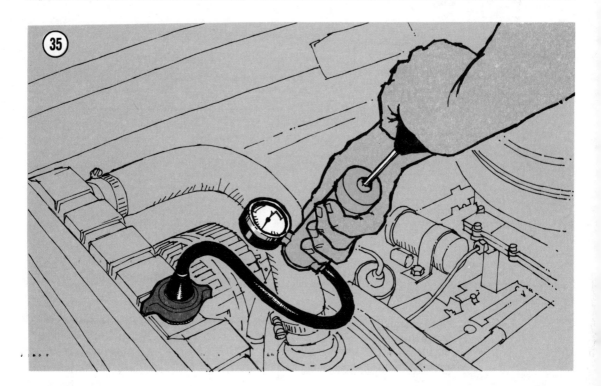

loose linings, or lack of lubrication in pilot bearing. Also check condition of transmission main shaft splines.

3. *Chatter or grabbing* — A number of things can cause this trouble. Check tightness of engine mounts and engine-to-transmission mounting bolts. Check for worn or misaligned pressure plate and misaligned release plate.

4. *Other noises* — Noise usually indicates a dry or defective release or pilot bearing. Check the bearings and replace if necessary. Also check all parts for misalignment and uneven wear.

MANUAL
TRANSMISSION/TRANSAXLE

Transmission and transaxle troubles are evident when one or more of the following symptoms appear:

   a. Difficulty changing gears

   b. Gears clash when downshifting

   c. Slipping out of gear

   d. Excessive noise in NEUTRAL

   e. Excessive noise in gear

   f. Oil leaks

Transmission and transaxle repairs are not recommended unless the many special tools required are available.

Transmission and transaxle troubles are sometimes difficult to distinguish from clutch troubles. Eliminate the clutch as a source of trouble before installing a new or rebuilt transmission or transaxle.

AUTOMATIC TRANSMISSION

Most automatic transmission repairs require considerable specialized knowledge and tools. It is impractical for the home mechanic to invest in the tools, since they cost more than a properly rebuilt transmission.

Check fluid level and condition frequently to help prevent future problems. If the fluid is orange or black in color or smells like varnish, it is an indication of some type of damage or failure within the transmission. Have the transmission serviced by your dealer or competent automatic transmission service facility.

BRAKES

Good brakes are vital to the safe operation of the vehicle. Performing the maintenance speci-

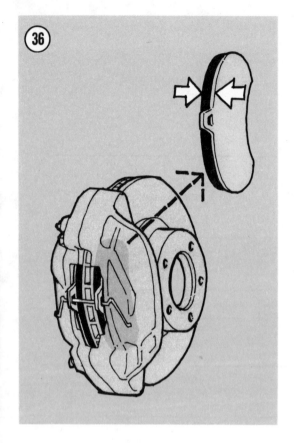

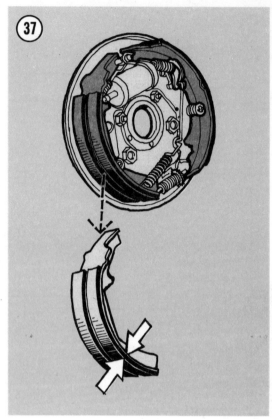

fied in Chapter Three will minimize problems with the brakes. Most importantly, check and maintain the level of fluid in the master cylinder, and check the thickness of the linings on the disc brake pads (**Figure 36**) or drum brake shoes (**Figure 37**).

If trouble develops, **Figures 38 through 40** will help you locate the problem. Refer to the brake chapter for actual repair procedures.

STEERING AND SUSPENSION

Trouble in the suspension or steering is evident when the following occur:

a. Steering is hard

b. Car pulls to one side

c. Car wanders or front wheels wobble

d. Steering has excessive play

e. Tire wear is abnormal

Unusual steering, pulling, or wandering is usually caused by bent or otherwise misaligned suspension parts. This is difficult to check without proper alignment equipment. Refer to the suspension chapter in this book for repairs that you can perform and those that must be left to a dealer or suspension specialist.

If your trouble seems to be excessive play, check wheel bearing adjustment first. This is the most frequent cause. Then check ball-joints as described below. Finally, check tie rod end ball-joints by shaking each tie rod. Also check steering gear, or rack-and-pinion assembly to see that it is securely bolted down.

TIRE WEAR ANALYSIS

Abnormal tire wear should be analyzed to determine its causes. The most common causes are the following:

a. Incorrect tire pressure

b. Improper driving

c. Overloading

d. Bad road surfaces

e. Incorrect wheel alignment

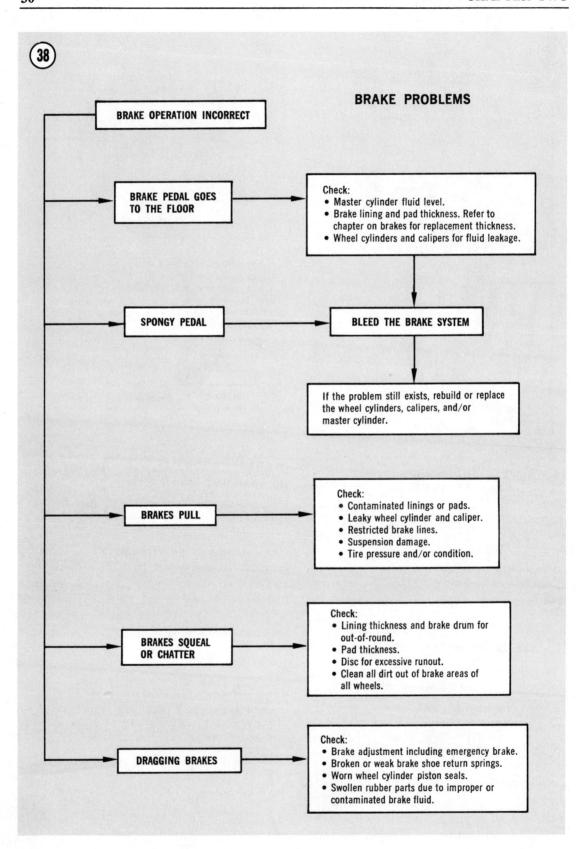

38

BRAKE PROBLEMS

BRAKE OPERATION INCORRECT

BRAKE PEDAL GOES TO THE FLOOR

Check:
- Master cylinder fluid level.
- Brake lining and pad thickness. Refer to chapter on brakes for replacement thickness.
- Wheel cylinders and calipers for fluid leakage.

SPONGY PEDAL

BLEED THE BRAKE SYSTEM

If the problem still exists, rebuild or replace the wheel cylinders, calipers, and/or master cylinder.

BRAKES PULL

Check:
- Contaminated linings or pads.
- Leaky wheel cylinder and caliper.
- Restricted brake lines.
- Suspension damage.
- Tire pressure and/or condition.

BRAKES SQUEAL OR CHATTER

Check:
- Lining thickness and brake drum for out-of-round.
- Pad thickness.
- Disc for excessive runout.
- Clean all dirt out of brake areas of all wheels.

DRAGGING BRAKES

Check:
- Brake adjustment including emergency brake.
- Broken or weak brake shoe return springs.
- Worn wheel cylinder piston seals.
- Swollen rubber parts due to improper or contaminated brake fluid.

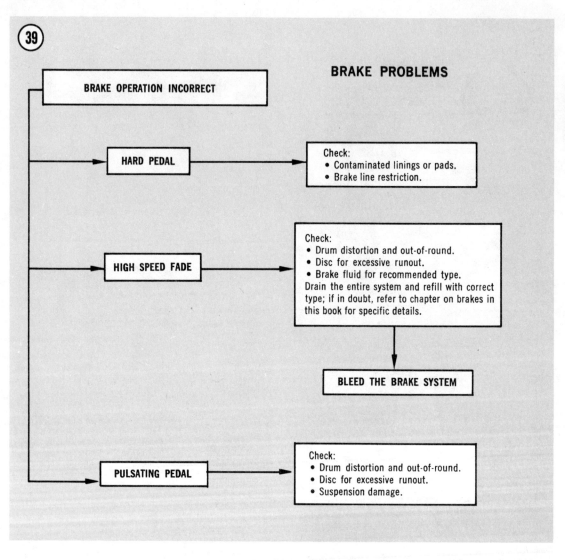

39

BRAKE PROBLEMS

BRAKE OPERATION INCORRECT

2

HARD PEDAL

Check:
• Contaminated linings or pads.
• Brake line restriction.

HIGH SPEED FADE

Check:
• Drum distortion and out-of-round.
• Disc for excessive runout.
• Brake fluid for recommended type.
Drain the entire system and refill with correct type; if in doubt, refer to chapter on brakes in this book for specific details.

BLEED THE BRAKE SYSTEM

PULSATING PEDAL

Check:
• Drum distortion and out-of-round.
• Disc for excessive runout.
• Suspension damage.

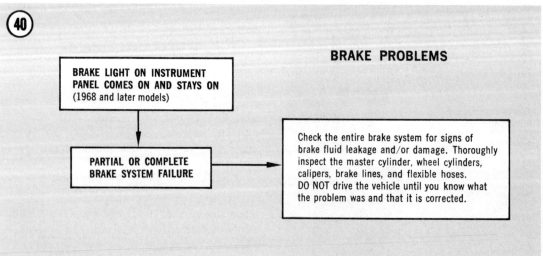

40

BRAKE PROBLEMS

BRAKE LIGHT ON INSTRUMENT PANEL COMES ON AND STAYS ON
(1968 and later models)

PARTIAL OR COMPLETE BRAKE SYSTEM FAILURE

Check the entire brake system for signs of brake fluid leakage and/or damage. Thoroughly inspect the master cylinder, wheel cylinders, calipers, brake lines, and flexible hoses.
DO NOT drive the vehicle until you know what the problem was and that it is corrected.

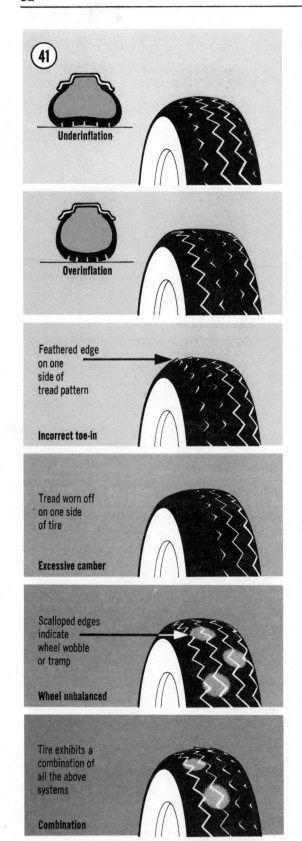

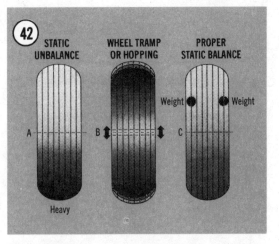

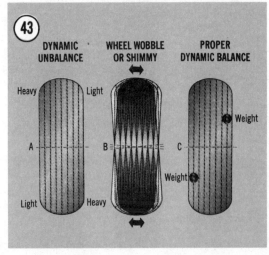

Figure 41 identifies wear patterns and indicates the most probable causes.

WHEEL BALANCING

All four wheels and tires must be in balance along two axes. To be in static balance (**Figure 42**), weight must be evenly distributed around the axis of rotation. (A) shows a statically unbalanced wheel; (B) shows the result — wheel tramp or hopping; (C) shows proper static balance.

To be in dynamic balance (**Figure 43**), the centerline of the weight must coincide with the centerline of the wheel. (A) shows a dynamically unbalanced wheel; (B) shows the result — wheel wobble or shimmy; (C) shows proper dynamic balance.

CHAPTER THREE

MAINTENANCE AND LUBRICATION

To ensure good performance, dependability, and safety, regular preventive maintenance and timely lubrication are essential. This chapter outlines periodic maintenance and lubrication for a vehicle subjected to average use (a combination of urban and highway driving and light-duty off-road use). A vehicle that is driven extensively off-road or used primarily in stop-and-go traffic may require more frequent attention than that recommended. But even without use, rust, dirt, and corrosion will cause unnecessary damage if the vehicle is neglected. Whether maintenance and lubrication are carried out by the owner or a dealer, regular routine attention helps avoid expensive repairs.

Carefully read the maintenance and lubrication schedule (**Table 1 or 2**, depending on model year). They represent a complete maintenance and lubrication plan that, if followed faithfully, will ensure good performance and long service life for your vehicle.

ROUTINE CHECKS

The following simple checks should be performed at each fuel stop.

1. Check the engine oil level. The oil should be checked with the engine warm and the vehicle sitting on level ground. Opinions differ on when the oil should be checked during a fuel stop. Some feel that it should be checked last so oil has had a chance to drain back into the sump from the cam valley and the cylinder heads. Others feel that it has little effect on the oil level. Remove the dipstick and wipe it with a clean rag or paper towel. Reinsert it all the way and withdraw it once again. The level should be between the 2 marks — never above and never below (**Figure 1**). The difference between the 2 marks represents about 1 quart, so if it is close to the ADD mark but still above it, don't add oil (unless you have a chronic oil consumption problem) — just be sure to pay particular attention to the oil level at the next fuel stop.

When adding oil, make sure it is the same viscosity grade as the oil that is in the engine.

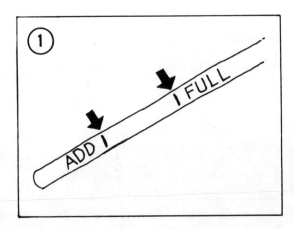

Table 1   VEHICLE MAINTENANCE SCHEDULE — 1974 AND EARLIER

Interval	Service
Every 4 months or 6,000 miles	Chassis lubrication Fluid levels ① ② Engine oil ① Air conditioning system
Every 6,000 miles	Tire rotation
At 1st oil change—then every 2nd	Engine oil filter ①
Every 12,000 miles	Rear axle
Every 12 months or 12,000 miles	Cooling system ①
Every 24,000 miles	Wheel bearings Automatic transmission ①
Every 36,000 miles	Manual steering gear
Every 4 months or 6,000 miles	Owner safety checks Tires and wheels Exhaust system Drive belts ① Suspension and steering Brakes and power steering
Every 6,000 miles	Disc brakes
Every 12 months or 12,000 miles	Drum brakes and parking brake Throttle linkage Headlights Underbody

At 1st 4 months or 6,000 miles—
   then at 12-month/12,000-mile
   intervals
	Thermostatically controlled air cleaner
	Carburetor choke
	Timing, dwell, carburetor idle, distributor and coil
	Manifold heat valve

At 1st 4 months or 6,000 miles	Carburetor mounting
Every 6,000 miles	Spark plugs (vehicles using leaded fuels)
Every 12 months or 12,000 miles	EGR system (vehicles using leaded fuels) Carburetor fuel inlet filter Thermal vacuum switch and hoses Vacuum advance solenoid and hoses Transmission control switch Idle stop solenoid PCV system
Every 24 months or 24,000 miles	Engine compression ECS system Fuel cap, tank, and lines AIR system
Every 24,000 miles	Air cleaner element
At 1st 24/24—then every 12/12	Spark plug and ignition coil wires

① Also an emission control service   ② Also a safety service

Table 2   VEHICLE MAINTENANCE SCHEDULE — 1975 AND LATER

Interval	Service
Every 6 months or 7,500 miles	Chassis lubrication ② Fluid levels check ① ② Engine oil change ②
At 1st oil change—then every 2nd	Oil filter change ②
See explantion ③	Tire rotation (steel belted radial) Rear axle lube change
Every 12 months	Air conditioning check
Every 12 months or 15,000 miles	Cooling system check ② Coolant change and hose replacement
Every 30,000 miles	Wheel bearing repack Automatic transmission fluid and filter change ② Manual steering gear check Clutch cross shaft lubrication
Every 6 months or 7,500 miles	Owner safety checks Tire and wheel inspection Exhaust system check ② Drive belt check ② Belt replacement ② Suspension and steering check Brake and power steering check
Every 12 months or 15,000 miles	Drum brake and parking brake check Throttle linkage check Underbody flush and check Bumper check
At first 6 months or 7,500 miles—then at 18-month/ 22,500-mile intervals	Thermostatically controlled air cleaner check Carburetor choke check Engine idle speed adjustment EFE valve check Carburetor mounting torque
Every 12 months or 15,000 miles	Fuel filter replacement Vacuum advance system and hoses check PCV system check PCV valve and filter replacement
Every 18 months or 22,500 miles	Idle stop solenoid check Spark plug wires check
Every 22,500 miles	Spark plug replacement Engine timing adjustment and distributor check
Every 24 months or 30,000 miles	ECS system check and filter replacement Fuel cap, tank, and lines check
Every 30,000 miles	Air cleaner element replacement

① Also a safety service
② Also an emission control service

③ Steel-belted radials should be rotated (front/ rear on same side only) at 7,500 and then 15,000-mile intervals. Bias-belted tires should be rotated every 7,500 miles.

2. Check the battery electrolyte level. For batteries equipped with level indicator caps, read the level as shown in **Figure 2**. For late model Delco Freedom batteries, the electrolyte level is correct if it can be seen at the bottom of the inspection window (**Figure 3**). For other batteries, the electrolyte level should be at the bottom of the vent plug bores. Top up any cells that are low with distilled water. Never add electrolyte to a battery that is in service.

Normal electrolyte usage is about 2 ounces per month — for the entire battery, not each cell. If more water must be added, the battery may be overcharged, commonly caused by high battery operating temperatures (frequent or prolonged starts), incorrect voltage regulator adjustment, or a poor ground connection from the regulator.

While you're checking the electrolyte level, check the terminals for powdery, white corrosion; at your first opportunity, clean the terminals and the battery as described in Chapter Eight if corrosion is present.

3. Check the radiator coolant level. If the vehicle is equipped with a coolant recovery tank, the level should be between the 2 level marks (**Figure 4**). If the vehicle does not have a recovery tank, carefully loosen the radiator cap to the first notch, using a shop rag folded in several thicknesses to protect your hand. Wait a couple of minutes until you are sure the pressure in the system has been relieved, then unscrew the cap and visually check the level. The coolant should be above the tubes in the top radiator tank. If the level is low, add water (or coolant if the vehicle is operated in freezing weather). For recovery tank systems, add the water or coolant to the recovery tank. For other systems, add it to the radiator.

4. Check the windshield washer fluid level and top it up if necessary (**Figure 5**). If the vehicle is operated in freezing temperatures, use a washer fluid that is compounded to resist freezing. Don't add cooling system antifreeze; it will damage painted surfaces.

5. Check tire pressure. Refer to **Table 3**.

> NOTE: *Ideally, tire pressure should be checked when the tires are cold (before the vehicle has been run). For this reason, and because the integral gauges*

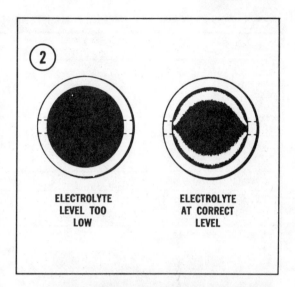

ELECTROLYTE LEVEL TOO LOW   ELECTROLYTE AT CORRECT LEVEL

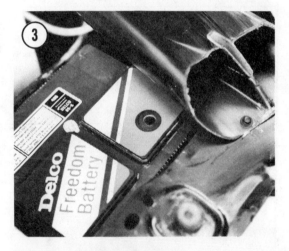

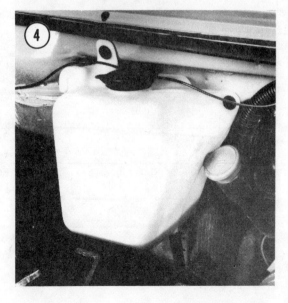

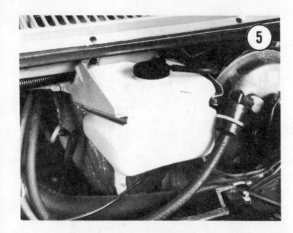

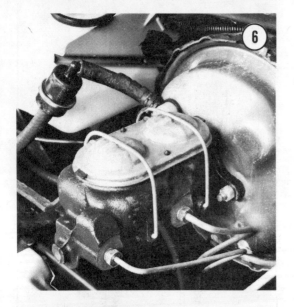

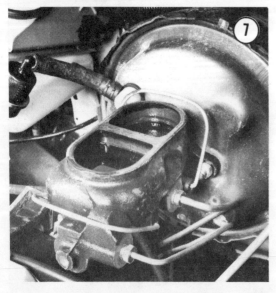

on service station air lines are notoriously inaccurate, it is a good idea to keep a tire gauge in the glove compartment. If the tire pressure is checked when the tires are warm, it will be about 3 psi higher than recommended following a low-speed drive and about 7 psi higher following a high-speed drive.

In addition to pressure, check the condition of the tread and sidewalls for wear, damage, or cracking. Wear patterns are a good indicator for diagnosing chassis and suspension problems and alignment (see Chapter Two). If incorrect alignment is detected early, it can be corrected before the tires have worn severely. Checking tire condition for damage is particularly important following hard off-road use. Pay special attention to signs of rock damage, usually evidenced by cuts or bubbles in the tread and sidewalls. This type of damage represents an extreme driving hazard when the vehicle is operated at highway speeds. Replace a damaged tire as soon as it is detected.

PERIODIC CHECKS AND INSPECTIONS

The following checks and inspections should be made at least monthly or at the intervals indicated in **Table 1 or 2**. In addition, it is a good idea to perform these checks after the vehicle has been used off-road for an extended period of time.

Brake Fluid Level

The brake fluid level should be checked monthly as well as any time the pedal can be pushed to within a couple of inches from the floor. Release the clamp that secures the master cylinder reservoir cap (**Figure 6**), remove the cap taking care not to allow dirt to fall into the reservoir, and visually check the level. The level should be ¼ in. below the upper edge of the reservoir (**Figure 7**). If level is low, add brake fluid that is clearly marked SAE 70R3, SAE J1703 (which supercedes 70R3), or DOT 3.

If the level is extremely low, it may be necessary to bleed the system to remove air that was drawn into it. See *Bleeding the Brake System* in Chapter Eleven. However, before the

Table 1   MINIMUM TIRE INFLATION PRESSURE AT GROSS VEHICLE WEIGHT RATING

C10, 15 Pickups & Cab — Chassis / C10, 15 Suburbans

		4900		5300		5400		6000 & 6200		5400		6400		6800 & 7000	
Tire	**Load Range**	FR	R	FR	R	FR	R	FR	R	FR	R	FR	R	FR	R
G78-15	B	32	32	32	32	—	32	—	—	32	32	—	32	—	—
H78-15	B	32	32	—	—	32	32	—	—	32	32	32	32	—	—
6.50-16LT	C	45	45	—	60	45	45	—	—	45	45	45	45	—	—
7.00-15LT	C	40	45	—	60	40	45	—	—	40	45	40	45	—	—
L78-15	B	28	32	35	45	28	32	28	32	28	32	28	32	—	—
7.00-16LT	C	40	45	40	60	40	45	40	45	40	45	40	45	—	—
LR78-15	C	28	36	—	75	28	36	28	36	28	36	28	36	28	36
L78-15	D	—	—	—	60	—	—	—	—	28	36	28	36	28	36

C20, 25 Pickup & Cab — Chassis / C20, 25 Suburban

		6400		7100		7500		8200		7100		7500		8200	
Tire	**Load Range**	FR	R	FR	R	FR	R	FR	R	FR	R	FR	R	FR	R
8.75-16.5	C	45	45	45	—	—	—	—	—	45	45	—	—	—	—
8.75-16.5	D	45	60	45	60	—	—	—	—	45	60	—	—	—	—
7.50-16LT	C	40	45	40	60	—	—	—	—	40	45	—	—	—	—
10-16.5	C	35	45	35	45	—	—	—	—	—	—	—	—	—	—
7.50-16LT	D	40	60	40	60	—	—	—	—	40	60	40	60	—	—
7.50-16LT	E	40	75	40	75	40	75	40	75	40	75	40	75	40	75
9.50-16.5	D	35	60	35	60	35	60	35	60	35	60	35	60	35	60

Note: The tire pressures shown are for original equipment tires. Because of the wide variety of tire types and makes available, it is impractical to set down all of the tire pressures in this table. When buying tires other than original equipment sizes, check with manufacturer for recommended pressures. In all cases, never exceed the maximum pressure embossed on the side of the tire.

(continued)

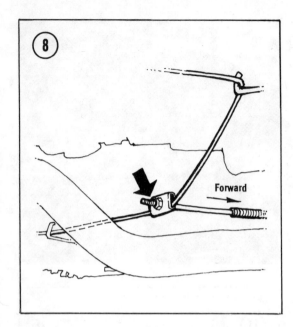

Forward

system is filled and bled, refer to *Brake Lines and Hoses* in this chapter and check for and correct any leaks that are found.

When the system has been filled (and bled if necessary), install the reservoir cap and pump the brake pedal several times to restore system pressure. Drive the vehicle, slowly at first, and check to make sure the brakes are operating correctly.

Brake Adjustment

Service brakes are self-adjusting. As disc brake pads wear, fluid is drawn into the wheel circuits from the master cylinder reservoir to compensate for increased piston travel. For this reason it's important to maintain the fluid level in the reservoir.

Drum brakes are adjusted when the vehicle is driven in reverse and the brakes are applied. If the brake pedal can be pushed to within a couple of inches from the floor, back the vehicle up several times and sharply apply the brakes. Test the adjustment by driving the vehicle at about 20 mph forward and then braking to a smooth stop. If the pedal travel is still excessive, adjust them once again as just described. If pedal travel cannot be corrected by this method, refer to Chapter Eleven — *Brake Inspection and Cleaning, Drum Brakes,* and check for wear and damage.

Parking Brake Adjustment

The parking brake should be adjusted whenever the pedal can be depressed six or more clicks. Before adjusting the parking brake, adjust service brakes as just described.

1. Depress the parking brake pedal one click.

2. Tighten the adjuster nut (**Figure 8**) until there is a slight drag on the rear wheels when they are rotated forward.

3. Release the parking brake and rotate the wheels. There should be no drag; if there is, back off the adjuster just until there is no drag with the brake released.

Brake Pad and Lining Condition

Disc brake pads and drum brake shoe linings should be checked for oil or grease on the friction material and measured for serviceability every 6,000-10,000 miles or when long pedal travel indicates the likelihood of extreme wear. Refer to *Brake Inspection and Cleaning* in Chapter Eleven.

Brake Lines and Hoses

Brake lines and hoses should be routinely checked for signs of deterioration, chafing, and kinks each time the brake pad and lining condition is checked, and following hard, off-road use where the possibility of rock and brush damage is great. Any line or hose that is less than perfect should be replaced immediately.

Check all the connections for tightness and look for signs of leakage which may indicate a cracked or otherwise unserviceable fitting. As with lines and hoses, any connections or fittings that are less than perfect should be replaced immediately.

When a line has been replaced, or in any situation where a brake line or hose has been disconnected, refer to Chapter Eleven, *Bleeding the Brake System,* and fill and bleed the system before operating the vehicle.

Manual Transmission Oil Level

The vehicle must be sitting level when the transmission oil level is checked. If you do not have access to a hoist, a mechanic's "creeper" will be helpful.

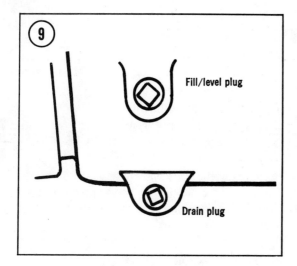

Fill/level plug

Drain plug

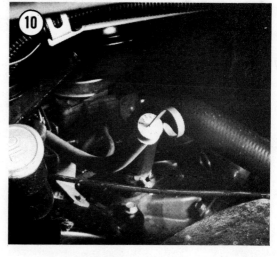

Before checking the level, drive the vehicle for several miles to warm up the oil. Then, unscrew the level plug on the transmission (**Figure 9**). If the level is correct, a small amount of oil will seep out the level hole. If necessary, carefully add fresh oil up to the bottom of the hole and install the plug and tighten it snugly.

> NOTE: *If the vehicle has been operated in deep water, pay particular attention to the condition of the oil. If water droplets are present, indicating that water has entered the transmission, change the oil immediately. See* **Manual Transmission Oil Change** *later in this chapter.*

Automatic Transmission Oil Level

The vehicle must be sitting level and the engine and transmission warmed up to operating temperature when the transmission oil level is checked. If the level is checked with the transmission cold, the level will appear to be low.

1. Set the handbrake. Set the selector at PARK, and start the engine and allow it to run for a couple of minutes to ensure that the torque converter is full of fluid. Shift the selector through all positions and return it to PARK.

2. Wipe the transmission dipstick handle and filler tube clean with a dry rag (**Figure 10**). Withdraw the dipstick and wipe it with a clean, lint-free cloth. *Do not use the rag that was used to clean the tube and handle.* Any contamina-

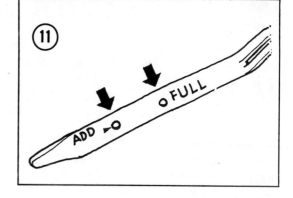

tion that might find its way into the transmission — even lint from a rag — could cause serious damage.

3. Insert the dipstick all the way into the filler tube, wait for a few seconds, and then withdraw it and check the level. It should be above the ADD mark (**Figure 11**). If the level is low, add fresh Dexron (type A) transmission fluid. The distance between the 2 marks represents about 1 pint.

Use a clean funnel with a fine-mesh filter. Slowly add the fluid, a little at a time, with the engine running. Recheck level as fluid is added.

CAUTION
Do not overfill the transmission. Too much fluid creates high internal pressures and will cause the transmission to overheat.

If the level is extremely low, the fluid pump will draw air into the transmission, causing the

Table **4**   INTAKE AND EXHAUST MANIFOLD FASTENER TORQUE

Engine	Fastener	Torque
In-line 6 1967-1972	Exhaust manifold to intake manifold	25 ft.-lb.
1973-on	Exhaust manifold to intake manifold	30 ft.-lb.
V8 (all) 1967-on	Intake manifold to cylinder head	30 ft.-lb.
	Exhaust manifold to cylinder head	20 ft.-lb.

fluid to foam and making it difficult to obtain an accurate reading. If this occurs, shut off the engine and wait several minutes for the fluid to settle. Then, restart the engine and add about ½ pint of fluid. Recheck the level and continue to add fluid until the level is correct.

4. Set the parking brake, hold the footbrake down, and select each of the gear positions for several seconds to allow the servo pistons to fill. Recheck the level and correct it once again if necessary.

> NOTE: *If the vehicle has been operated in deep water, pay particular attention to the condition of the fluid. If water droplets are present, indicating that water may have entered the transmission, change the oil immediately (see* **Automatic Transmission Fluid Change** *later in this chapter).*

Intake/Exhaust Manifold Nuts and Bolts

The nuts and bolts on the intake and exhaust manifolds should be checked for tightness and for broken or missing lockwashers. Nuts that are snug need be tightened no further, but loose nuts should be tightened to appropriate torque shown in **Table 4**. Overtightening can cause studs to break or castings to crack, requiring expensive repairs.

Drive Belts

The water pump/fan drive belt, as well as the belts which drive the alternator, air conditioning, power steering pump, etc., should be inspected monthly for condition and adjustment.

Worn, frayed, cracked, or glazed belts should be replaced at once. The components to which they direct power are essential to the safe and reliable operation of the vehicle. If correct adjustment is maintained on the belts they will usually all enjoy the same service life. For this reason, and because of the labor involved in replacing an inboard belt (requiring the removal of the outer belts), it's a good idea to replace all of the belts as a set. The low added expense is well worth the time involved in doing the job twice, to say nothing of the consequences of a failed belt.

Drive Belt Tension Adjustment

In addition to being in good condition, it's important that the drive belts be correctly adjusted. A belt that is too loose does not permit the driven components to operate at maximum efficiency. In addition, the belt wears rapidly because of increased friction caused by slipping. A belt that is adjusted too tight wears prematurely and overstresses bearings in driven components.

Drive belt tension (adjustment) is measured by deflection of the belt midway between two pulleys at the belt's longest run (**Figure 12**).

Alternator/Fan-Water Pump Belt (Without Air Conditioning)

For maximum belt life and component efficiency, the belt tension should be checked with a tester like that shown in **Figure 13**. The tension for a new belt should be 125 ± 5 lb. and for a used belt (one that has been in operation for more than 10 minutes) the tension should be

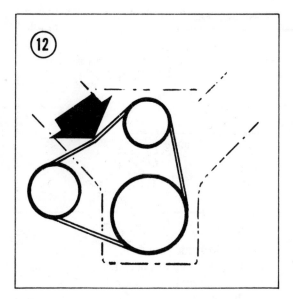

75 ± 5 lb. As a temporary setting, until the actual tension can be adjusted, a deflection of about ½ in. with moderate force applied to the belt is a reasonable compromise.

To adjust the tension, loosen the pivot bolt located beneath the alternator and then loosen the lock bolt (**Figure 14**). Move the alternator toward or away from the engine as required until the tension is correct, then tighten the lock bolt and then the pivot bolt without further moving the alternator. When the adjustment has been made, double check to ensure that it is correct.

To replace the belt, loosen the alternator bolts as just described and swing the alternator toward the engine as far as it will go so the belt can be removed from the pulleys.

Alternator Belt
(With Air Conditioning)

Adjust the alternator drive belt as described above, using a belt tension tester (**Figure 13**). The tension for a new belt should be 125 ± 5 lb. and for a used belt (one that has been in operation for more than 10 minutes), the tension should be 75 ± 5 lb.

Fan-Water Pump/Air Conditioning Belt

Measure the belt tension with a tester, midway between the fan-water pump pulley and the air conditioning compressor pulley (**Figure 15**).

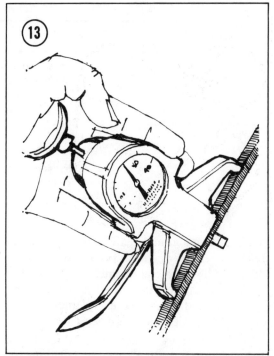

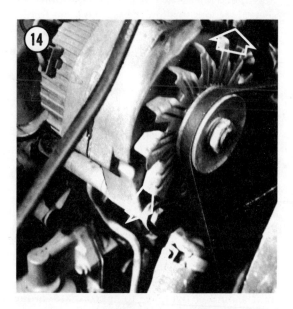

The tension for a new belt should be 140 ± 5 lb. and for a used belt (one that has been in service for more than 10 minutes), the tension should be 95 ± 5 lb.

To adjust the belt tension, loosen the pivot and lock bolts that attach the compressor to its mount and move the compressor until the tension is correct. Then, without further movement, tighten the bolts and recheck the tension.

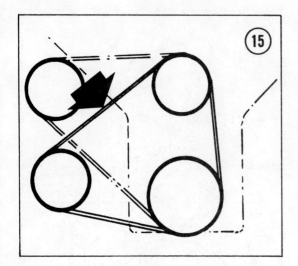

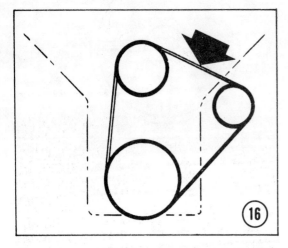

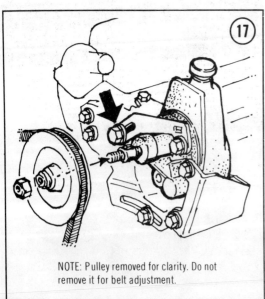

NOTE: Pulley removed for clarity. Do not remove it for belt adjustment.

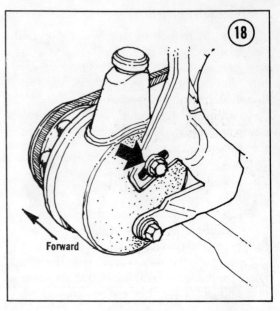

Forward

To replace the belt, loosen the compressor pivot and lock bolts and swing the compressor toward the engine until the belt can be removed. Install a new belt and adjust it as described above.

Power Steering Pump Belt

Measure the tension of the power steering pump belt with a tester, midway between the fan-water pump pulley and the power steering pump pulley (**Figure 16**). The tension for a new belt should be 125 ± 5 lb. For a used belt (one that has been in service for more than 10 minutes), the tension should be 75 ± 5 lb.

To adjust the tension of the belt, loosen the bolts which attach the pump or pump mounting bracket to the adjusting bracket (**Figures 17 and 18**) and move the pump by applying pressure at the web behind the pulley.

CAUTION
Do not apply pressure to the reservoir; it will bend and leak.

When the tension is correct, tighten the bolts without further moving the pump. Then recheck the tension to make sure it has not changed.

To replace the belt, loosen the adjusting and pivot bolts and swing the pump toward the engine as far as it will go so the belt can be removed.

Air Injection Pump Belt

Check the tension of the air injection pump belt as shown in **Figure 19**. The tension for a new belt should be 75 ± 5 lb. For a used belt (one that has been in service for more than 10 minutes), the tension should be 55 ± 5 lb.

To adjust the tension of the belt, loosen the pump mounting bolt and the adjusting bolt and move the pump as necessary.

CAUTION
Do not pry on the pump body.

When the tension is correct, tighten both bolts without further moving the pump and then recheck the tension.

To replace the belt, loosen both bolts and move the pump toward the crankshaft pulley as far as possible so the belt can be removed.

Vacuum Fittings and Hoses

Check the vacuum fittings and connections to make sure they are tight, and inspect the hoses for cracking, kinking, or deterioration. Any unsatisfactory hoses should be replaced.

Coolant Condition

Start the engine and allow it to run for a couple of minutes to circulate coolant through the system; don't run it long enough to bring the engine to operating temperature. Remove the radiator cap and check the condition of the coolant. If it is dirty or oily, drain the cooling system, flush it, and refill it as described in Chapter Nine — *Periodic Maintenance*.

It's recommended that coolant be changed every 24 months, regardless of condition or mileage.

Coolant Hoses

Inspect the radiator and heater hoses visually and by feel. Replace any that are cracked or deteriorated, or are spongy or extremely hard.

Make sure the hoses are correctly routed so they do not chafe on metal. Make sure all hose clamps are tight.

Have the cooling system and the radiator cap pressure checked by a service station at least once each year or after a hose has been replaced. Often there is no charge for this service which requires just a few minutes.

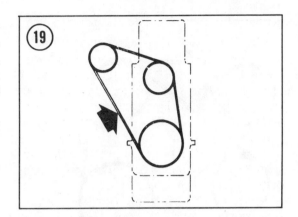

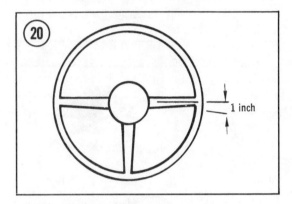

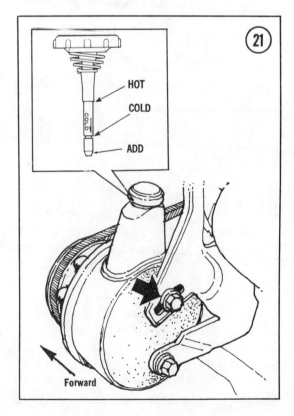

Radiator

Check the radiator for leaks and damage at least once a year or when coolant loss indicates possible trouble. Blow bugs and debris out of the radiator fins from the rear with compressed air. Carefully straighten bent fins with a small screwdriver, taking care not to dent or puncture the tubes.

Have the radiator cap pressure tested as suggested above. It should maintain a pressure of 13 psi before the relief valve opens.

Pressure test the radiator and cooling system when it is cold. Make sure the coolant level is correct. Install the tester and pressurize the system to 18-21 psi. Inspect the radiator and all hoses and connections for leaks. Check also for swollen hoses which should be replaced.

If a leak is found in the radiator core or the tanks, have it repaired by a dealer or radiator specialist, and when the radiator has been reinstalled, have the system pressure tested to make sure all connections are tight.

Wheel Alignment

Wheel alignment should be checked following hard off-road use, when steering and handling problems are experienced, when new tires or wheels are installed, or when abnormal tire wear patterns indicate that there may be trouble (see Chapter Two). Refer this work to a dealer or alignment specialist; specialized equipment and experience are required.

Steering

1. With the vehicle on level ground, and with the front wheels lined up straight ahead, grasp the steering wheel and turn it from right to left and check for rotational free play. The free play should not be greater than about one inch (**Figure 20**). If it is, the front wheel bearings should be checked for condition and adjustment (see Chapter Twelve), and the kingpins, steering linkage, and steering arm should be checked as possible causes of excessive play. These checks should be referred to a dealer.

2. Try to move the steering wheel in and out and check for axial play. If any play is felt, check the tightness of the steering wheel center nut.

3. Attempt to move the steering wheel from side to side without turning it. Movement is an indication of loose steering column mounting bolts or worn column bushings. Check and tighten the mounting bolts if necessary, and if the movement is still present, the vehicle should be referred to a dealer for corrective service.

Power Steering
Fluid Level

The power steering fluid level can be checked cold or with the engine and fluid warmed up to operating temperature.

1. Turn the steering wheel to right and left lock several times and then turn the wheels straight ahead. Shut off the engine.

2. Remove the dipstick from the pump reservoir (**Figure 21**), wipe it clean with a lint-free cloth, reinsert it all the way into the tube, and withdraw it. If the fluid is at operating temperature (hot to the touch) the level should be between the HOT and COLD marks (**Figure 21**). If the fluid is "cold" (about 70°F) the level should be between the ADD and COLD marks. If the level is not correct, carefully add GM Power Steering Fluid or Dexron automatic transmission fluid, or an equivalent, and recheck the level. Do not overfill the reservoir. If the level, after filling, is above the FULL mark, fluid must be siphoned off until the level is correct.

LUBRICATION

Strict adherence to a detailed lubrication schedule is at least as important as timely preventive maintenance. The recommended lubrication schedules (**Figures 22 and 23**) are based on average vehicle use — a combination of highway and urban driving with some light-duty off-road use, in moderate weather and climate. Abnormal use, such as mostly off-road use, in dusty and dirty conditions, or in extremely hot or cold climates, requires that the lubrication schedule be modified so that the lubricants are checked and changed more frequently.

Acids that form in the engine, transmission, and differential oil during short-haul driving, or during operation in extremely cold climates will wear out parts as quickly as dirty lubricants.

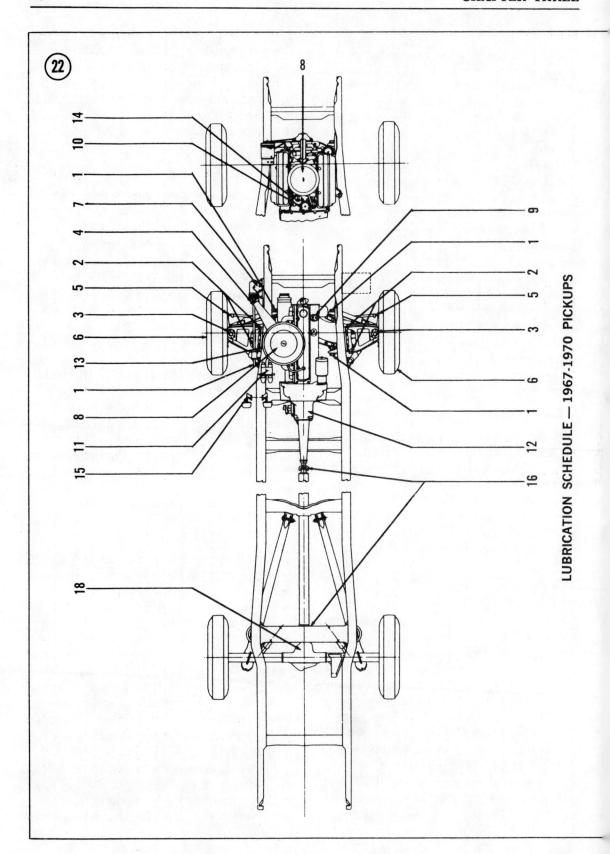

LUBRICATION SCHEDULE — 1967-1970 PICKUPS

No.	Lubrication Points	Lubrication Period	Type of Lubrication	Quantity	Remarks
1	Lower control arms	6,000 miles	Chassis lubricant	4 places as required	
2	Upper control arms	6,000 miles	Chassis lubricant	4 places as required	
3	Upper and lower control arm ball-joints	6,000 miles	Chassis lubricant	4 places as required	
4	Intermediate steering shaft (PA10)	6,000 miles	Chassis lubricant	2 places as required	
5	Tie rod ends	6,000 miles	Chassis lubricant	4 places as required	
6	Wheel bearings	30,000 miles	Wheel bearing lubricant	2 places as required	
7	Steering gear	36,000 miles	Chassis lubricant	As required	Check only—do not drain
8	Air cleaner—oil bath	12,000 miles	Engine oil SAE 50 above freezing Engine oil SAE 20 below freezing	As required	Check—clean and refill if necessary
	Air cleaner—paper element	12,000 miles			Check—if satisfactory reuse but recheck every 6,000 miles
9	Distributor—L6	12,000 miles			½ turn of cam lubricator*
10	Distributor—V8	12,000 miles			Rotate cam lubricator*
11	Master cylinder	6,000 miles	Delco Supreme No. 11	As required	Check—add fluid when necessary
12	Transmission—synchromesh —automatic	6,000 miles 6,000 miles	Multipurpose AQ-ATF-A (Dexron®)	As required As required	Keep even with filler plug. Check—see lubrication section
13	Throttle bell crank—L6	6,000 miles	Engine oil	As required	
14	Carburetor linkage—V8	6,000 miles	Engine oil	As required	
15	Brake and clutch pedal springs	6,000 miles	Engine oil	As required	
16	Universal joints	6,000 miles	Chassis lubricant	As required	
17	Propeller shaft slip joint	6,000 miles	Chassis lubricant	As required	Not shown
18	Rear axle	6,000 miles	Multipurpose	As required	Check See lubrication section

*Replace lubricator at 24,000 mile intervals.

3

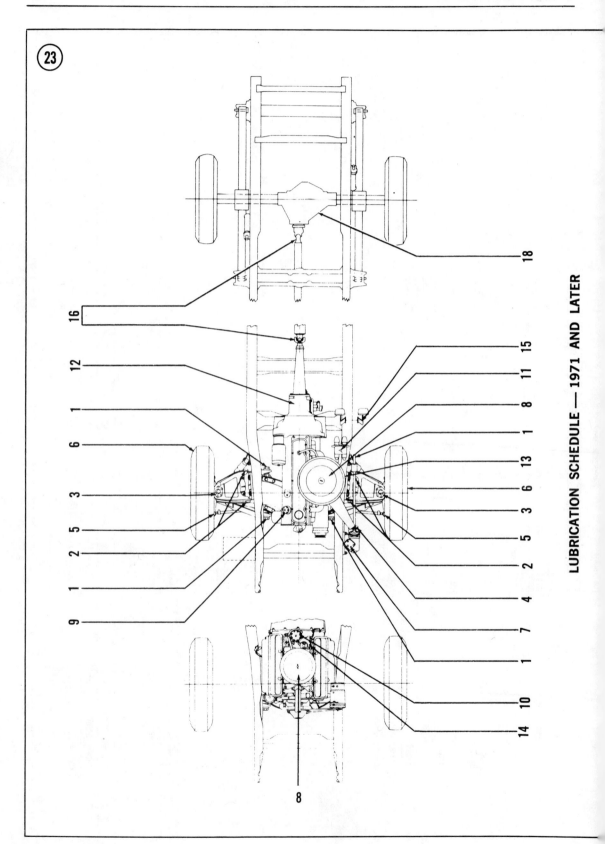

LUBRICATION SCHEDULE — 1971 AND LATER

No.	Lubrication Points	Lubrication Period	Type of Lubrication	Quantity	Remarks
1	Lower control arms	6,000 miles ①	Chassis lubricant	4 places as required	
2	Upper control arms	6,000 miles ①	Chassis lubricant	4 places as required	
3	Upper and lower control arm ball-joints	6,000 miles ①	Chassis lubricant	4 places as required	
4	Intermediate steering shaft (PA10)	6,000 miles ①	Chassis lubricant	2 places as required	
5	Tie rod ends	6,000 miles ①	Chassis lubricant	4 places as required	
6	Wheel bearings	24,000 miles ②	Wheel bearing lubricant	2 places as required	Check for grease leak—do not lubricate
7	Steering gear	36,000 miles ③			See vehicle maintenance schedule
8	Air cleaner element	12,000 miles ④			
9	Distributor—L6	24,000 miles ②			Replace cam lubricator*
10	Distributor—V8	24,000 miles ②			Replace cam lubricator*
11	Master cylinder	6,000 miles ①	Delco Supreme No. 11 or DOT-3 fluids	As required	Check—add fluid when necessary
12	Transmission—manual	6,000 miles ①	GL-5	As required	Keep even with filler plug
	—automatic	6,000 miles ①	Dexron® or equivalent	As required	See lubrication section
13	Throttle bell crank—L6	12,000 miles ④	Engine oil	As required	
14	Carburetor linkage—V8	12,000 miles ④	Engine oil	As required	
15	Brake and clutch pedal springs	6,000 miles ①	Engine oil	As required	
16	Universal joints	6,000 miles ①	Chassis lubricant	As required	
17	Propeller shaft slip joint	6,000 miles ①	Chassis lubricant	As required	Not shown
18	Rear axle	6,000 miles ①	GL-5	As required	Check See lubrication section

*Replace points at 12,000 mile intervals.

① = 7,500 miles—1975 ② = 30,000 miles—1975 ② = 30,000 miles—1975 ③ = 30,000 miles—1975 ④ = 15,000 miles—1975

3

ENGINE OIL
AND FILTER CHANGE

For average use (see above) the engine oil and filter should be changed at the following intervals:

a. 1974 and earlier models — 6,000 miles or 4 months

b. 1975 and later models — 7,500 miles or 6 months

NOTE: *Many experienced mechanics feel that these factory-recommended intervals are too long and that oil and filter changes at 3,000-mile intervals will significantly increase engine life.*

Shorter oil change intervals (3,000 miles) are essential to long engine life if the vehicle is subjected to any of the following use conditions:

a. Consistently short trips

b. Constant stop-and-go driving

c. Primary use off-road in dusty conditions

d. Extensive use at temperatures below 10°F

In addition, if the vehicle is driven only a few hundred miles each month, the oil change interval should be based on time — 6 to 8 weeks; acids form rapidly in the oil of an engine that is used very little and will damage sliding and rotating contact surfaces as quickly as dirt in the oil.

Recommended oil grades (by operating temperature range) are shown in **Table 5**. Use only a detergent oil with an API rating of SE or SD. These quality ratings are stamped on the top of the can.

Try always to use the same brand of oil. If the oil you select to use is not from one of the major oil companies, it may not always be available when you are travelling or when you are operating the vehicle for extended periods off-road. For these reasons, it's a good idea to carry a couple of quarts of oil in your vehicle.

If you carry out your own oil changes it's a good idea to buy oil by the case. Good quality name brand oil can be purchased from any one of a number of national chain stores at savings in excess of 30 percent. Case lots of filters can also be purchased at similar savings.

The use of oil additives is not necessary nor is it recommended for an engine that is in good

Table 5   RECOMMENDED GRADES OF OIL

Oil Grade	Temperature Range
5W-20*, 5W-30	20°F and below
10W, 5W-30, 10W-30, 10W-40	0° to 60°F
20W-20, 10W-30, 10W-40, 20W-40, 20W-50	20°F and above

*If the vehicle is being operated at sustained highway speeds, the next heavier grade of oil should be used.

operating condition. Specialized "cures," such as additives that free sticky valve lifters or piston rings, may seem to correct a problem for the time, but abnormal conditions such as excessive oil consumption, blow-by, low oil pressure, and sticking valve lifters should be corrected with engine reconditioning.

1. Thoroughly warm up the engine so the old oil will drain freely. Place a drip pan beneath the engine and unscrew the drain plug (**Figure 24**). Allow 10-15 minutes for the oil to drain. Then install the drain plug.

2. Unscrew the oil filter (**Figure 24**) and allow an additional 5 minutes for draining. Discard the filter. When oil has ceased to drain, clean the filter mounting flange. Lightly coat the sealing ring of the new filter with fresh oil and screw the filter onto the block. When it makes contact with the sealing flange, tighten it ¼ turn by hand.

3. Fill the engine with the correct grade of oil (see **Table 5**). Six-cylinder engines require 6 quarts with a filter change; 8-cylinder engines require 5 quarts. See **Figure 25**.

4. Start the engine and allow it to idle for several minutes to ensure that oil has had a chance to circulate throughout the system. On some vehicles, the oil pressure warning light may remain on for several seconds after the engine is first started; this is normal.

While the engine is running, check the filter and drain plug for leaks and tighten them if necessary. Then, shut off the engine and check the oil level with the dipstick. If necessary, add oil to correct the level. See **Figure 1**.

NOTE: *Discard the drained oil by pouring it into a plastic bleach bottle or a similar container, capping it, and putting it in the trash.*

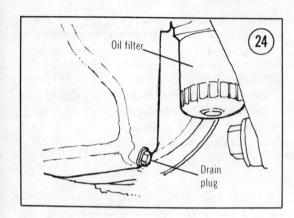

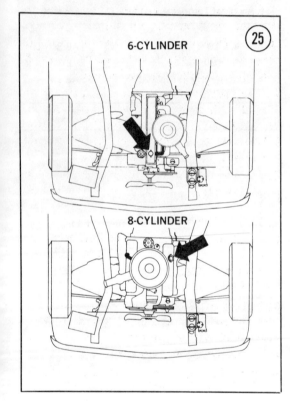

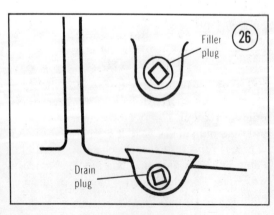

CHASSIS AND DRIVE TRAIN LUBRICATION

Figures 22 and 23 detail lubrication points, service intervals, type of lubrication and quantity required. The procedures that follow explain some of the less obvious points.

TRANSMISSION

Procedures for checking the oil or fluid level in both manual and automatic transmissions are presented earlier in this chapter (see *Manual Transmission Oil Level* or *Automatic Transmission Oil Level*).

The oil in a manual transmission need not be changed unless it has been contaminated with water. Oil change in automatic transmissions is recommended at 24,000-mile intervals with normal use. The change interval should be cut in half — 12,000 miles — if the vehicle is subjected to any of the following use conditions:

a. Consistently short trips

b. Constant stop-and-go driving

c. Trailer towing

d. Extensive use at temperatures below 10°F

e. Consistently low mileage (a couple of hundred miles a month)

In addition, the oil should be changed immediately if water is discovered in the oil.

Manual Transmission Oil Change

Prior to draining the transmission, drive the vehicle for several miles to warm the oil so that it will flow freely. Remove the fill/level plug (**Figure 26**). Place a drip pan beneath the transmission and unscrew the drain plug (**Figure 26**). Allow the oil to drain for 10-15 minutes. Clean the drain plug and install it. Tighten the plug firmly but be careful not to overtighten it and risk stripping the threads on the transmission housing.

Refer to **Table 6** and fill the transmission with the correct amount and grade of oil. The transmission oil level is correct when oil just begins to seep out of the fill/level hole. Screw in and tighten the fill/level plug taking care not to overtighten, and wipe excess oil from the outside of the transmission. Check to make sure the drain plug does not leak.

Table 6   TRANSMISSION OIL

Transmission	Oil Grade	Capacity
3-speed/4-speed synchromesh	SAE 80W*, SAE 80W-90, GL-5	**
Powerglide/Powerflo	Dexron automatic transmission fluid or equivalent	2 quarts
Turbo Hydramatic 350	Dexron automatic transmission fluid or equivalent	2.5 quarts
400	Dexron automatic transmission fluid or equivalent	7.5 pints

*SAE 80W should be used if sustained ambient temperature is below 32°F.
**Fill to bottom of fill/level hole in the side of the transmission.

Automatic Transmission Fluid Change

Prior to draining the transmission, drive the vehicle for several miles to warm up the fluid so it will drain freely. The vehicle must sit level during draining and filling. If a hoist or a pit is not available, a mechanic's "creeper" will be helpful for working beneath the vehicle.

1. Place a drip pan beneath the transmission and unscrew the drain plug from the pan (**Figure 27**). Allow about 5 minutes for the fluid to drain.

2. When draining is complete, screw in the plug.

3. Using a clean funnel with a fine-mesh filter, pour the correct amount (see **Table 6**) of fresh Dexron automatic transmission fluid through the filler pipe. Start the engine and allow it to idle for 2 minutes with the gear selector in the PARK position. Increase the engine speed to a fast idle (no more than about 1,200 rpm) and allow the engine and transmission to reach normal operating temperature.

4. With the handbrake set and the service brake depressed, slowly move the selector through all of the gear positions. Return the selector to PARK and recheck the fluid level. If necessary, add fluid and bring the level midway between the ADD and FULL marks on the dipstick. Remember: Do not overfill the transmission; too much fluid is harmful. If the level is above the maximum mark on the dipstick, sufficient fluid must be drained to correct the level.

5. When the fluid level is correct, check for and correct any leaks at the filler tube connection and around the edge of the pan. Then road test the vehicle to ensure the transmission operates correctly. After the vehicle has been driven

Table 7   AXLE LUBRICANTS

Ambient Temperature	Viscosity
Below 10°F	SAE 80
Up to 100°F	SAE 90
Consistently above 100°F	SAE 140

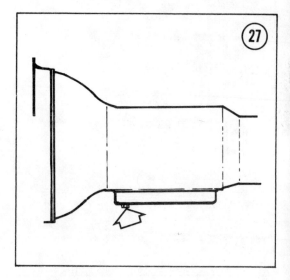

about 125 miles check the level once again and correct it if necessary.

DIFFERENTIAL

The oil level in the axle differential should be checked and corrected if necessary every 6,000 miles of road use, every 1,000 miles of off-road use, and daily if the vehicle is operated in deep water. (In this instance, the check is essential to determine if water has entered the axle, in which case contaminated oil must be drained and the axle filled with fresh oil.)

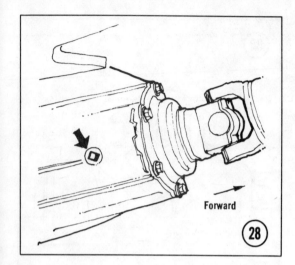

Forward

(28)

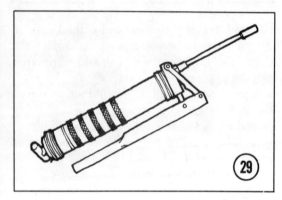

(29)

Oil Level

The vehicle must be sitting level when the axle oil level is checked. Wipe the area around the fill/level plug clean. Unscrew the fill/level plug from the differential case (**Figure 28**). If the level is correct, a small amount of oil will begin to seep out of the hole. If it does not, slowly add oil to correct the level. For standard differentials, add hypoid gear lubricant (see **Table 7**). For Positraction and Power-Lok (limited-slip) differentials, add hypoid gear lubricant compounded for these units, and clearly identified as such on the container.

When the level is correct, screw in and tighten the fill/level plug and wipe any excess oil from the outside of the differential case.

Oil Changing

Prior to draining the oil from the differential, drive the vehicle for several miles to warm up the oil so it will flow freely. With the vehicle

sitting level, wipe the area around the fill/level plug clean and unscrew the plug. Place a drip pan beneath the differential and unscrew the drain plug (if fitted). Allow 10-15 minutes for the oil to drain and then screw in and tighten the drain plug.

> NOTE: *If the differential is not equipped with a drain plug, the oil can be removed with a suction pump available at most service stations. If you do not have access to a suction pump, the differential cover bolts can be loosened several turns and the cover carefully pried away from the differential to permit the oil to drain. Be careful not to damage the gasket. When the oil has ceased to drain, tighten the bolts securely in a criss-cross pattern.*

Refer to *Oil Level* above and fill the differential with the appropriate type of hypoid gear lubricant until the oil level reaches the bottom of the fill/level hole and just begins to seep out. Then install the fill/level plug and tighten it securely. Wipe any spilled oil from the differential housing.

After the vehicle has been driven for about 100 miles, check for and correct any leaks around the edge of the cover, particularly in the area of the bottom bolt. If leakage is found, recheck and correct the oil level after the leak has been corrected.

CHASSIS LUBRICATION

Complete chassis lubrication should be performed at the intervals shown in **Figures 22 and 23**. For extensive off-road use, the interval should be every 1,000 miles, and if the vehicle is operated in deep water, chassis lubrication should be attended to daily.

Lubrication points and fittings, along with recommended lubricants, are shown in **Figures 22 and 23**. Equivalent lubricants available through most major oil companies can be used. However, make sure the dealer knows the specific application so that he can recommend a suitable substitute.

A simple hand-operated grease gun like the one shown in **Figure 29** is a worthwhile investment, particularly if the vehicle was used extensively off-road and in mud, snow, and water.

3

Do not overlook items such as gear selector linkage, clutch linkage, parking brake linkage, speedometer cable, clutch release equalizer, and the steering gearbox. Lack of lubrication on these items will make control operation difficult in addition to causing premature wear. However, lubricants should be used sparingly and excess oil should be wiped away to prevent it from attracting dirt which will also accelerate wear.

BODY LUBRICATION

Door, hood, and tailgate hinges and latches, and front seat tracks should be lubricated at the 6,000-mile intervals to ensure smooth operation and reduce wear.

Apply all lubricant sparingly, operating the mechanism several times to aid penetration. Then, wipe off the excess lubricant with a clean, dry cloth to prevent it from attracting dirt and from soiling clothing, carpeting, or upholstery.

STEERING GEAR

The steering gearbox on late model vehicles (1971-1975) is permanently lubricated and should require no service other than checking

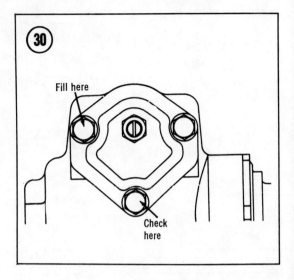

for seal leakage, indicated by thick grease deposits on the steering gearbox around the cover. In such case, the unit should be referred to a dealer for repair.

Early models, fitted with a fill plug on top of the steering gearbox, should be checked every 36,000 miles and steering gear lubricant added if necessary, until it is level with the bottom of the filler hole.

Figure 22 shows the location. **Figure 30** indentifies the fill/check plug.

CHAPTER FOUR

TUNE-UP

To ensure maximum operating economy and service life, and to comply with regulated exhaust emission standards, a complete tune-up should be performed at 12,000-mile intervals for 1974 and earlier models, and at 22,500 miles for 1975 and later.

These recommended intervals are based on normal use — a combination of highway, city, and off-road driving. If the vehicle is used extensively for stop-and-go city driving, more frequent tune-ups may be required. Extensive off-road use should have little effect on tune and the recommended intervals can generally be followed with little degradation of performance or economy.

The firing order for 6-cylinder engines is 1-5-3-6-2-4; for V8 engines, it is 1-8-4-3-6-5-7-2. Cylinder numbering is shown in **Figure 1**. Distributor rotation is clockwise, viewed from the top.

Tune-up specifications are shown in **Table 1** at the end of this chapter.

EXPENDABLE PARTS

The expendable ignition parts (spark plugs, points, and condenser) should be routinely replaced during the tune-up. In addition, some expendable emission control devices on some models must also be replaced if the vehicle is to remain within legal emission standards. These devices are shown in Chapter Seven. You should have all of the necessary parts on hand before you begin a tune-up.

TUNE-UP SEQUENCE

Because different systems in an engine interact, the procedures should be done in the following order.

1. Check cylinder head bolt torque.
2. Check compression.
3. Work on ignition system.
4. Adjust carburetor.

CYLINDER HEAD BOLTS

It is generally not necessary to tighten the cylinder head bolts of an engine that has been in service for some time, unless leakage is suspected. However, the torque can be periodically checked and corrected if necessary.

1. Note the location of breather hoses and disconnect them and the oil fill cap from the valve cover. Unscrew the bolts which hold the valve cover to the cylinder head and remove the valve cover. It may be necessary to tap the valve cover rearward, using the heel of your hand or a soft mallet, to break the gasket loose.

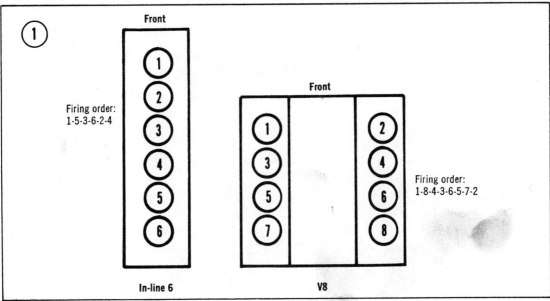

① Firing order:
1-5-3-6-2-4

Front

In-line 6

Front

Firing order:
1-8-4-3-6-5-7-2

V8

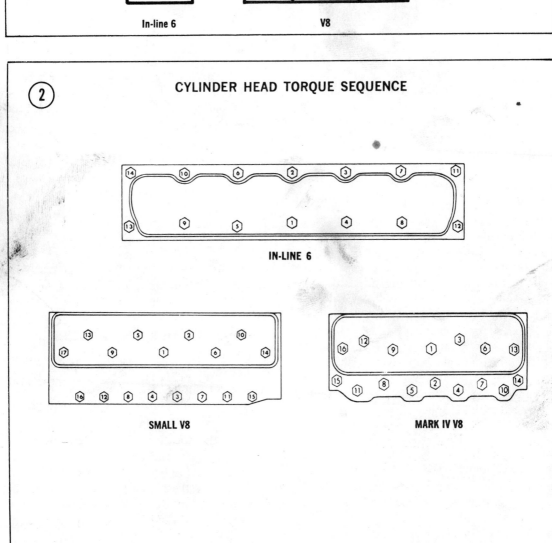

② CYLINDER HEAD TORQUE SEQUENCE

IN-LINE 6

SMALL V8

MARK IV V8

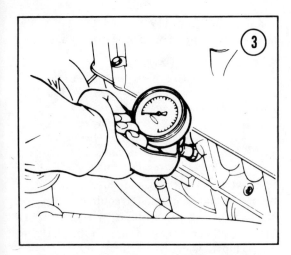

Table 2   CYLINDER HEAD BOLT TORQUE

Engine	Torque
In-line 6 (all)	95 ft.-lb.
Small block V8 (all)	65 ft.-lb.
Mark IV V8 (all)	80 ft.-lb.

2. Tighten the cylinder head bolts in the appropriate pattern shown in **Figure 2** to torque specified in **Table 2**.

Valve Clearance Adjustment

Correct valve clearance in engines equipped with hydraulic lifters is maintained automatically in many cases throughout the life of the engine. However, if incorrect valve clearance is suspected as a possible cause of poor performance or the engine has logged many thousands of miles, the valve clearance should be checked and corrected if necessary by a dealer or automotive specialist.

COMPRESSION TEST

An engine with low or uneven compression cannot be properly tuned. In view of this, the engine should be given a compression test before proceeding with the tune-up.

1. Remove the spark plugs as described below. Remove the air cleaner from the carburetor and block the throttle and choke wide open.

2. Remove the distributor primary lead from the negative terminal on the coil.

3. Connect a remote starter switch in accordance with the manufacturer's instructions, or have an assistant operate the starter with the ignition key. See **Figure 3**.

4. Firmly insert a compression gauge in each spark plug hole in order, and crank the engine through at least 4 compression strokes to obtain the highest possible reading. Record the reading for each cylinder.

> NOTE: *If there is more than 20 pounds difference between the high and low reading cylinders, the engine cannot be properly tuned until repairs have been made. The remainder of this procedure may be performed to help determine the kind of repairs that are needed.*

5. If low or uneven compression readings were recorded for one or more cylinders, inject about a tablespoon of motor oil through the spark plug hole of each low-reading cylinder. Crank the engine through several compression strokes and recheck compression. If compression improves, the problem is probably worn rings. If no improvement is noted, in all probability the valves are burned, sticking, or not seating properly. If 2 adjacent cylinders read low and the oil injection does not increase compression, the problem may be a defective head gasket.

IGNITION SYSTEM

Two basic types of ignition systems are used on Chevrolet/GMC vehicles covered in this manual: conventional mechanical contact breaker ignition (1967-1974) and breakerless electronic ignition (1975 and later).

Service to breakerless ignition systems is limited to replacement of spark plugs, checking and correcting ignition timing, and inspection and repair of wiring. Total ignition service is presented for mechanical contact breaker systems. The service procedures are presented separately.

SPARK PLUGS

Removal

1. Remove all foreign matter from around spark plugs, using compressed air if available.

A tire pump, vacuum cleaner, or a small paint-brush can also be used.

2. Disconnect spark plug wires by grasping the *boot* portion of the wire and applying only enough twisting force to remove the wire from the plug.

CAUTION
Spark plug wires should never be removed by yanking on the wire, as damage could result.

NOTE: *Tag each spark plug wire (a strip of masking tape will do) and mark the proper cylinder number. The cylinder closest to the front of the car is No. 1. (On V8 engines the left front cylinder is No. 1. The left bank contains cylinders 1, 3, 5, and 7 and the right bank cylinders 2, 4, 6, and 8 from front to back).*

3. Using a spark plug wrench, remove the spark plugs in order.

4. Inspect each spark plug as it is removed and compare its appearance to the color chart in Chapter Two. Electrode appearance is a good indicator of performance in each cylinder and permits early recognition of trouble.

Replacement

Spark plugs should be replaced at each tune-up. If misfiring occurs earlier than the tune-up intervals, spark plugs in good condition can often be cleaned, regapped, and reinstalled with acceptable results. If all new plugs are being in-stalled, skip to Step 3 in the following pro-cedure.

1. Inspect plugs and discard and replace them if they have badly worn electrodes and/or glazed, blistered, or broken porcelain in-sulators.

2. Clean serviceable plugs with an abrasive cleaner, such as sandblast. File center electrode flat.

3. Verify that all plugs to be installed are of the same make and of the proper heat range number (**Table 1**).

4. Adjust spark gap to 0.035 in. (all models, 1967-1974, and all 1976 and later 6-cylinder engines), 0.060 in. (1975), or 0.045 (1976 and later V8's), using a round wire-type gauge.

CAUTION
Always adjust gap by bending negative or side (never center) electrode. Most spark plug feeler gauges have a slot which can be used for bending the electrode. Never adjust plugs by tapping the electrode on a hard surface. This can cause damage to the plug insulator.

5. Inspect spark plug hole threads and clean before installing plugs. If required, corrosion can be removed with a 14mm x 1.25 SAE spark plug thread chaser (use grease on the chaser to catch chips).

CAUTION
Use extreme care when using thread chaser to avoid cross-threading. Also crank engine several times to blow out any dislodged material from the engine.

6. Apply a thin film of oil — a drop from engine dipstick will do — to spark plug threads. Install plug in hole and torque to 15 ft.-lb. (1971 and later and 1970 14mm x $^{13}/_{16}$) or 25 ft.-lb. (1967-1969 and 1970 14mm x $^{5}/_{8}$).

NOTE: *If a torque wrench is not available, tighten spark plugs as tight as possible by hand, then, using wrench, tighten another ½ turn. Do not over-tighten. Excessive torque may change gap setting or squash the gasket so badly it cannot seal.*

7. Reconnect the spark plug wires.

NOTE: *If spark plug wires have been in service for a year or longer, or appear cracked, oil soaked, or brittle, check them with an ohmmeter. Any wire with a resistance over 20,000 ohms or "infinity" should be replaced. Use only brand name (Delco, Belden, etc.) replacement resistance cable.*

BREAKER POINT IGNITION SYSTEMS

Ignition System Inspection

1. Remove and clean distributor cap. Inspect for cracks, carbon tracks, and burned, worn, or corroded terminals, etc. (**Figure 4**). Replace cap if necessary.

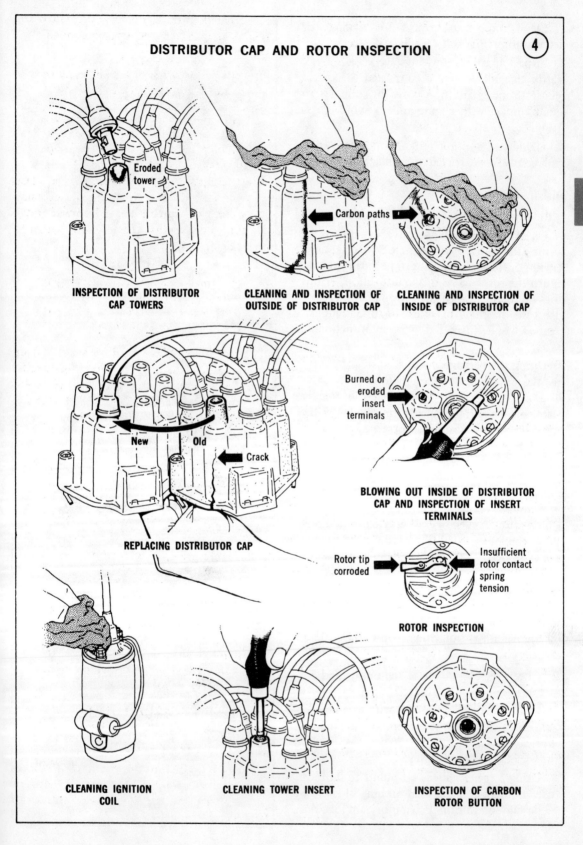

DISTRIBUTOR CAP AND ROTOR INSPECTION ④

Eroded tower

INSPECTION OF DISTRIBUTOR CAP TOWERS

Carbon paths

CLEANING AND INSPECTION OF OUTSIDE OF DISTRIBUTOR CAP

CLEANING AND INSPECTION OF INSIDE OF DISTRIBUTOR CAP

New Old Crack

REPLACING DISTRIBUTOR CAP

Burned or eroded insert terminals

BLOWING OUT INSIDE OF DISTRIBUTOR CAP AND INSPECTION OF INSERT TERMINALS

Rotor tip corroded Insufficient rotor contact spring tension

ROTOR INSPECTION

CLEANING IGNITION COIL

CLEANING TOWER INSERT

INSPECTION OF CARBON ROTOR BUTTON

2. Clean rotor and inspect for damage or deterioration (**Figure 4**). Replace if necessary.

3. Inspect spark plug wiring (see NOTE above). Verify that all wires are connected to correct plugs. Properly position wires in supports to avoid contact with engine and to avoid cross-firing.

4. Tighten all ignition system connections and replace any loose, frayed, or damaged wires.

Distributor Inspection

Refer to **Figure 5 or 6** for this procedure.

1. Check the centrifugal advance system by turning the distributor rotor clockwise as far as it will go. Release the rotor. The spring should return the rotor to its original position. If this does not happen, or if the return action is sluggish, the mechanism must be disassembled, cleaned, and inspected for malfunctioning parts.

2. Check the vacuum advance system by turning the moveable breaker plate counterclockwise as far as it will go. Release the breaker plate and see if the spring returns it to the original retarded position. Correct any interference or binding condition.

Breaker Point Inspection

Examine breaker point contact surfaces. Points with an even overall gray color and only slight roughness or pitting need not be replace, but may be dressed with a clean point file as follows:

1. File the points, using only a few strokes and a clean fine-cut, contact point file. Never use sandpaper or emery cloth, and do not attempt to remove all irregularities — just the scale or dirt.

2. Check the alignment of the points and correct as necessary. See **Figure 7**.

3. Clean the distributor cam with cleaning solvent and a clean, lint-free cloth. Rotate the cam lubricator wick ½ turn or 180 degrees. Replace the wick every 24,000 miles.

4. Using a feeler gauge, set points to 0.016 in. (used points). Breaker arm rubbing block must be on high point of a distributor cam lobe during adjustment.

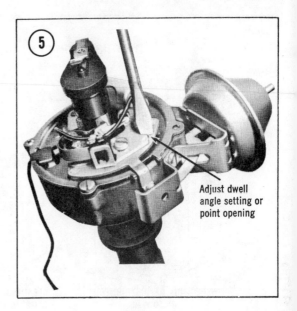

Adjust dwell angle setting or point opening

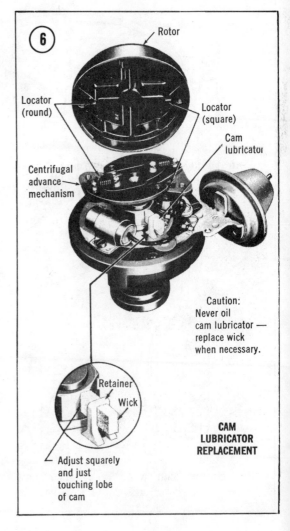

Rotor

Locator (round)

Locator (square)

Cam lubricator

Centrifugal advance mechanism

Caution: Never oil cam lubricator — replace wick when necessary.

Retainer

Wick

Adjust squarely and just touching lobe of cam

CAM LUBRICATOR REPLACEMENT

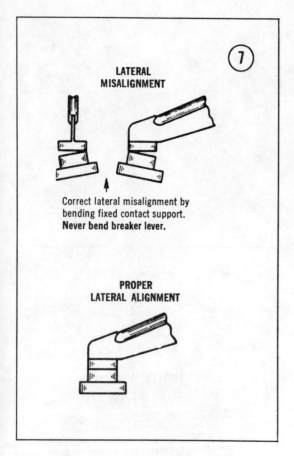

LATERAL
MISALIGNMENT

Correct lateral misalignment by
bending fixed contact support.
Never bend breaker lever.

PROPER
LATERAL ALIGNMENT

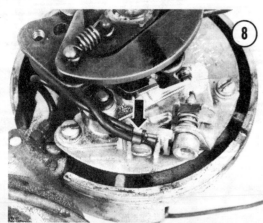

If points are badly pitted or burned, they must be replaced. However, these conditions are usually caused by improper conditions in other parts of the ignition system or by dirt or other contamination in the distributor. The cause must be corrected when installing new points, or the same condition will rapidly develop again.

Breaker Point Replacement (6-cylinder)

1. Remove the distributor cap by releasing hold-down screws. Move the cap out of the way.

2. Remove the rotor.

3. Remove condenser and primary lead wires from quick disconnect terminal (**Figure 8**).

4. Remove the contact set attaching screw and remove the point set.

5. If the condenser is to be replaced, remove attaching screw and remove the condenser from the breaker plate.

6. Using a clean, lint-free cloth, wipe the breaker plate free of oil and smudge.

7. Install a new point set on breaker plate and attach with the screw.

> NOTE: *The pilot on the point set must engage the matching hole in the breaker plate.*

8. If the condenser was removed, install a new condenser on the breaker plate.

9. Connect the primary and condenser lead wires to quick disconnect terminal on point set.

10. Using a feeler gauge, set the new points to 0.019 inch. Rubbing block of points must be resting on the highest point of a cam lobe when this adjustment is made (see *Dwell Angle Procedure* below).

11. Rotate cam lubricator 180 degrees at 12,000 mile intervals and replace lubricator every 24,000 miles.

12. Install the rotor and distributor cap. Lock cap to distributor housing with hold-down screws.

13. Start engine and check dwell angle (see below).

Breaker Point Replacement (8-cylinder)

> NOTE: *The contact point set (and condenser on 1974 models) is replaced as a single unit. Breaker lever tension and point gap are pre-set at the factory, and only dwell angle requires adjustment after replacement.*

1. Remove the distributor cap by placing a screwdriver blade in the slotted head of each latch screw, pressing down, and rotating a

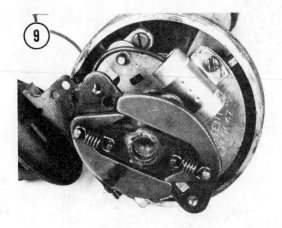

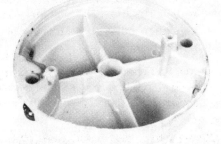

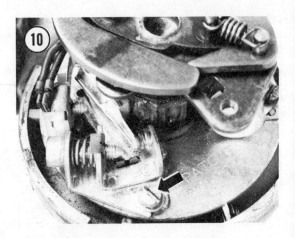

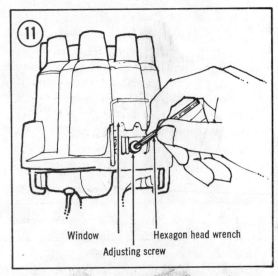

Window   Hexagon head wrench

Adjusting screw

quarter turn in either direction. Move the cap out of the way.

2. Remove the rotor attaching screws, then remove rotor (see **Figure 9**).

3. Remove the 2-piece RFI shield, if so equipped, by removing attaching screws.

4. Loosen the 2 point set assembly attaching screws and remove the set from the breaker plate. Disconnect the primary.

5. Remove the primary and condenser lead wires from the nylon insulated connector in the point set.

6. If the condenser is to be replaced (1973 and earlier), remove attaching screw and then remove condenser.

7. Install a new condenser (if old condenser was removed).

8. Install a new point set.

9. Connect primary and condenser lead wires to nylon insulated connector on point set. Make certain lead wires are routed so they will not interfere with point set operation.

10. Install the rotor and install and tighten the attaching screws.

11. Rotate the cam lubricator 180 degrees at 12,000 mile intervals. Replace every 24,000 miles.

12. Install the distributor cap and lock into place with latches.

13. Start the engine and check the dwell angle (see below).

DWELL ANGLE

The preferred method for setting dwell angle is to first set the breaker point gap with a feeler gauge (6-cylinder engines only — points for 8-cylinder engines are factory pre-set) and then check the setting with a dwell meter. It is very important that breaker points be set to the proper gap. Points set too closely tend to burn and pit rapidly. Points with an excessive gap result in a weak spark at high speeds. New points

must be set to a wider gap than used points to compensate for wear of the rubbing block while seating to the distributor cam.

Adjusting Dwell Angle (6-Cylinder Engines)

1. Remove the distributor cap and motor.

2. Verify alignment of points. See **Figure 7**. If necessary, align by bending fixed contact arm. Do not bend the breaker lever (moveable arm). Do not attempt to align used points. Instead, replace them if serious misalignment is present.

3. Crank or turn the engine until the rubbing block on breaker lever is resting on the high point of a distributor cam lobe (this provides maximum point gap).

4. Loosen the point set attaching screw (see **Figure 10**) and insert a screwdriver in the opposing slots in the point set and the breaker plate. Move the point set to obtain a setting of 0.019 in. (new points) or 0.016 in. (used points), measured with blade-type feeler gauge.

5. Tighten the attaching screw and remeasure the gap. Readjust if setting was moved during the tightening of the screw.

6. Reassemble the rotor and distributor cap.

7. Connect a dwell meter and tachometer to the engine, using manufacturer's instructions.

8. Disconnect vacuum line from distributor and plug line with sharp end of a pencil, a golf tee, or other similar pointed object.

9. Operate engine at normal idle speed and check dwell angle. For 6-cylinder engines, angle should be between 31 and 34 degrees.

> NOTE: *If dwell angle is not within these limits, points should be reset. Check for misalignment of points or worn distributor cam lobes.*

10. Accelerate engine to 1,750 rpm. Variation in dwell angle should not exceed 3 degrees. Higher variation indicates excessive distributor wear or loose breaker plate.

11. Reconnect vacuum line to distributor.

Adjusting Dwell Angle (8-Cylinder Engines)

1. After installing point set and reassembling distributor, start engine and allow to warm up to normal operating temperature. Disconnect and plug vacuum line to distributor.

2. Attach a dwell meter and tachometer to the engine, using the manufacturer's instructions.

3. Raise window in distributor cap and insert a hex wrench in the adjusting screwhead (see **Figure 11**).

4. Turn adjusting screw until a dwell angle of 29-31 degrees (30 degrees preferred) is reached.

> NOTE: *If a dwell meter is not available, turn the adjusting screw clockwise until the engine begins to misfire. Then turn screw ½ turn in opposite direction. This method will give an approximate dwell angle setting, but should be used only when a dwell meter is not available.*

5. Accelerate the engine to 1,750 rpm and check for variation in dwell angle. The angle should not vary more than 3 degrees. Variation in excess of this indicates excessive distributor wear or loose breaker plate.

6. Remove hex wrench and close access window in distributor cap. Unplug and replace vacuum line to distributor.

IGNITION TIMING ADJUSTMENT

Ignition timing should be checked and adjusted (if required) after point replacement and dwell angle adjustment have been completed.

1. Connect timing light in accordance with the manufacturer's instructions.

2. Determine the timing specifications from **Table 1**.

> NOTE: *Use chalk or white paint, etc., to emphasize the proper markings on the timing tab and the harmonic balancer.*

3. Disconnect the vacuum line to the distributor and plug line with sharp end of pencil or a golf tee.

4. Operate the engine at normal idle speed.

5. Aim the timing light at the timing tab (see **Figure 12**).

6. Adjust timing by loosening distributor clamp bolt and rotating distributor body as required while watching timing marks on engine tab and harmonic balancer and operation of

timing light. When the marks appear to stand still directly opposite each other, retighten the distributor clamp bolt. Recheck timing and readjust if required.

7. Stop engine, disconnect timing light, and reconnect vacuum hose.

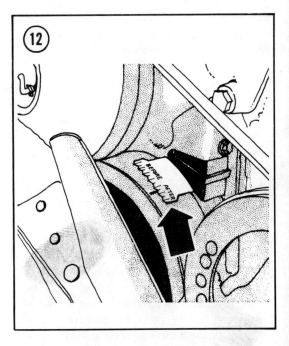

HIGH ENERGY
IGNITION SYSTEM

Routine maintenance is not required for the HEI system itself. If parts or components fail, they are not repairable and must be replaced. However, engine timing should be checked and the disributor components visually checked for cracks, wear, dust, moisture, burns, etc., every 18 months or 22,500 miles, whichever comes first. At the same time, the secondary wiring (spark plug wires) should be inspected, checked out with an ohmmeter, and replaced if necessary. Spark plugs also should be replaced after every 22,500 miles.

> NOTE: *The* HEI *system has larger (8mm) diameter, silicone-insulated, spark plug wires. While these gray-colored wires are more heat resistant and less vulnerable to deterioration than conventional wires, they should not be mistreated. When removing wires from spark plugs, grasp only on the boots. Twist boot ½ turn in either direction to break seal, then pull to remove.*

The procedure for ignition timing is identical to that given above for conventional ignition systems, except that timing light connections should be made in parallel using an adapter at the No. 1 spark plug wire terminal on the distributor. The distributor cap also has a special terminal marked TACH. Connect one lead of the tachometer to this terminal and the other to ground.

> NOTE: *Some tachometers must connect from the* TACH *terminal to the battery positive terminal. Check the manufacturer's instructions before making connections.*

CARBURETOR ADJUSTMENT

> NOTE: *Carburetors on 1971 and later models are equipped with limiter caps on idle mixture screws. These caps,*

which should not be altered or removed, are a part of the emission control system and restrict the richness of the fuel/air mixture. This mixture ratio is pre-set at the factory and a satisfactory idle can be obtained within the range (usually ½-¾ turn) allowed by the cap. If the cap has been damaged or removed on your vehicle, a procedure is included which will permit setting the idle mixture to an acceptable ratio.

> NOTE: *Before attempting to adjust idle settings on carburetor, the ignition system should be tuned and timed, using the procedures given earlier in this chapter.*

Engine idle speed is controlled by a combination of adjustments to the fuel/air mixture screw(s) and the throttle linkage. Throttle linkage adjustment is made by adjusting either an idle stop screw, an idle stop solenoid, or both.

During the period covered, vehicles used 1-barrel (1-BBL) carburetors on 6-cylinder engines, and 2- and 4-barrel carburetors on V8 engines.

> NOTE: *In making idle adjustments, always refer to the Vehicle Emission Control Information* (VECI) *decal*

located in the engine compartment for correct idle speeds for your vehicle. The speeds listed in **Table 1** *should be used only if the decal is missing or cannot be read.*

ROCHESTER CARBURETORS (1975 AND LATER VEHICLES)

Idle Mixture Adjustment (1-BBL Carburetors)

1. Start engine and allow to reach operating temperature. Air cleaner should be on, choke should be fully open, and air conditioner off.

2. Connect a tachometer to the distributor, following manufacturer's instructions.

3. Set parking brake and block rear wheels.

4. Disconnect fuel tank hose from vapor canister and disconnect vacuum hose from distributor and plug hose. Check VECI decal and disconnect and plug other hoses as directed.

5. Check engine timing and correct if required. Reconnect vacuum hose to distributor.

6. If vehicle is equipped with automatic transmission, place selector in DRIVE. If equipped with manual transmission, place selector in NEUTRAL and disconnect electrical lead wire to idle stop solenoid.

7. Adjust idle stop solenoid (**Figure 13**) to set idle speed to higher specified rpm.

8. Turn idle mixture screw (**Figure 13**) counterclockwise until maximum idle speed is obtained. Repeat Step 7, if required, to reset idle speed to higher specified rpm on VECI decal.

9. Observe tachometer and adjust idle speed with the idle stop solenoid to lower specified rpm on VECI decal.

10. Stop engine and remove tachometer.

11. Connect fuel tank hose to vapor canister. Reconnect electrical lead wire to idle stop solenoid on vehicles equipped with manual transmission.

Low and Curb Idle Adjustment (1-BBL Carburetor)

Refer to **Figure 13**.

1. Start engine and allow it to reach normal operating temperature. Air cleaner should be installed, choke fully open, and air conditioner

off. Connect a tachometer to engine, using manufacturer's instructions.

2. Set parking brake and block rear wheels.

3. Disconnect the fuel tank line from the vapor canister and disconnect the vacuum hose from the distributor.

4. Verify that timing is correctly set, then reconnect vacuum hose to distributor.

5. Adjust idle stop solenoid to obtain specified curb idle speed.

6. Disconnect electrical lead wire from idle stop solenoid (**Figure 13**).

7. Place transmission selector in DRIVE (automatic) or NEUTRAL (manual). Turn ⅛ inch hex screw in end of solenoid to obtain the specified low idle speed.

8. Reconnect solenoid lead and crank throttle slightly. Verify that curb idle specified rpm is obtained when throttle is released.

9. Stop engine and remove tachometer.

10. Reconnect fuel tank hose to vapor canister.

Fast Idle Adjustment (1-BBL Carburetor)

Refer to **Figure 14**.

1. Verify that low and curb idle speeds are correctly set.

2. Start engine and allow it to reach normal operating speed. Air cleaner should be installed, choke should be fully open, EGR valve signal line should be removed and plugged, and air conditioner should be off. Connect tachometer to engine, using manufacturer's instructions.

3. Disconnect vacuum hose from distributor and plug hose.

4. With transmission in NEUTRAL, set fast idle cam follower so that tank is on high step of cam.

5. Bend cam follower tang to arrive at fast idle speed listed on emissions control decal.

Idle Mixture Adjustment (2-BBL Carburetor)

1. Start engine and allow it to reach normal operating temperature. Air cleaner should be on, air conditioner should be off, and choke should be fully open. Connect tachometer to engine, using manufacturer's instructions.

⑬
ROCHESTER CARBURETORS
(1975 AND LATER VEHICLES)

SINGLE-BARREL

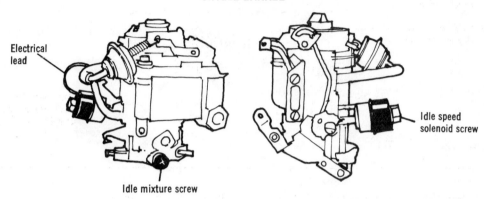

Electrical lead

Idle speed solenoid screw

Idle mixture screw

TWO-BARREL

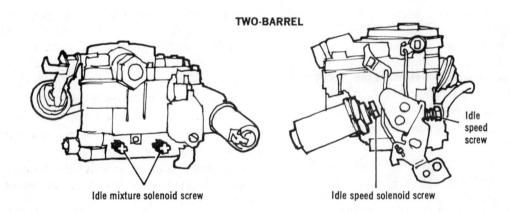

Idle speed screw

Idle mixture solenoid screw

Idle speed solenoid screw

FOUR-BARREL

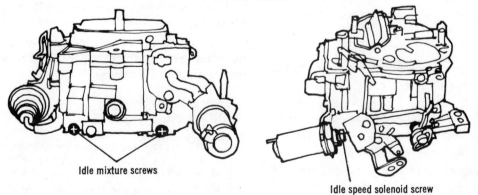

Idle mixture screws

Idle speed solenoid screw

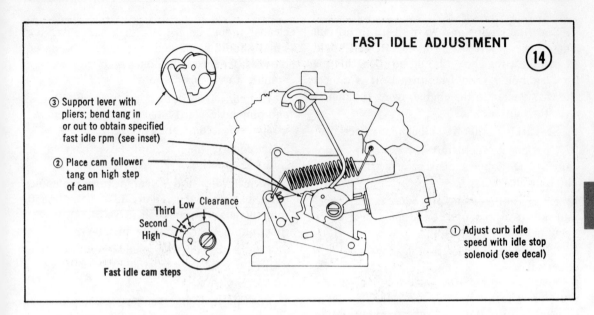

FAST IDLE ADJUSTMENT ⑭

③ Support lever with pliers; bend tang in or out to obtain specified fast idle rpm (see inset)

② Place cam follower tang on high step of cam

Third Low Clearance
Second
High

Fast idle cam steps

① Adjust curb idle speed with idle stop solenoid (see decal)

2. Set parking brake and block rear wheels.

3. Disconnect fuel tank hose from vapor canister. Disconnect vaccum hose from distributor and plug hose. Disconnect and plug other hoses as directed by VECI decal.

4. Check engine timing and adjust if required, using the procedures given above. Reconnect vacuum hose to distributor.

5. Position the transmission selector in DRIVE (automatic transmission) or NEUTRAL (manual transmission).

> NOTE: *Obtain idle speeds from Vehicle Emission Control Information decal located in engine compartment. If decal is missing or cannot be read, specifications given in* **Table 1** *can be used.*

> NOTE: *Idle mixture screws are equipped with factory-installed caps. These caps allow acceptable adjustment and must not be removed or altered.*

6. Adjust idle speed screw to obtain the higher of 2 idle speeds given (**Figure 13**).

7. Turn idle mixture screws (**Figure 13**) out equally to obtain highest possible idle speed. Reset idle speed screw to higher specified rpm if required.

8. Turn idle mixture screws in equally until the lower specified idle speed is achieved.

9. Reconnect fuel tank hose to vapor canister.

**Idle Speed Adjustment
(2-BBL Carburetor)**

1. Start engine and allow it to warm up to normal operating temperature. Air cleaner should be installed, choke should be fully open, and air conditioner should be off. Connect tachometer to engine, using manufacturer's instructions.

2. Set parking brake and block rear wheels.

3. Disconnect fuel tank hose at vapor canister.

4. Disconnect vacuum hose from distributor and plug hose.

5. Verify that timing is properly set or adjust if required, using the procedure given above. Reconnect vacuum hose.

6. Place the transmission selector in DRIVE (automatic transmission) or NEUTRAL (manual transmission).

7. Adjust idle speed screw to specified rpm (**Figure 13**).

8. Stop engine and remove tachometer. Connect fuel tank hose to vapor canister and remove blocks from wheels.

**Low and Curb Idle Adjustment
(4-BBL Carburetor)**

> NOTE: *Obtain low and curb idle speeds from Vehicle Emission Control Information decal in engine compartment. If decal is missing or cannot be read, speeds given in* **Table 1** *can be used.*

4

1. Start the engine and warm it up to normal operating temperature. The air cleaner should be installed, the choke should be open, and the air conditioner should be turned off. Connect the tachometer to the engine, using the manufacturer's instructions.

2. Set parking brake and block rear wheels.

3. Disconnect fuel tank hose from vapor canister. Disconnect distributor vacuum hose and plug hose.

4. Check timing, using procedure given above, and adjust as required. Reconnect distributor vacuum hose.

5. Disconnect the electrical lead at idle stop solenoid.

6. Place transmission selector in DRIVE (automatic transmission) or NEUTRAL (manual transmission). Adjust low idle screw to obtain specified low idle speed.

7. Reconnect idle stop solenoid electrical lead and open throttle slightly to extend solenoid plunger.

8. Adjust solenoid plunger screw to set specified curb idle speed.

9. Stop engine and remove tachometer. Reconnect hose to vapor canister.

**Fast Idle Adjustment
(4-BBL Carburetor)**

Refer to **Figure 15**.

1. Place cam follower on highest step of fast idle cam.

2. Adjust fast idle screw out until primary throttle valves are closed.

3. Turn fast idle screw into contact lever, then give screw 3 additional turns.

4. Connect tachometer to engine, start engine and check fast idle against specifications listed on Vechicle Emission Control Information decal. Readjust as required.

ROCHESTER CARBURETORS
(1972-1974 VEHICLES)

**Idle Mixture Adjustment
(All Carburetors)**

1. Start engine and allow it to reach normal operating temperature. Air conditioner should be off, choke should be fully open, and air cleaner should be installed on engine. Parking brake should be on and rear wheels should be blocked. Connect a tachometer to engine using manufacturer's instructions.

2. Disconnect vacuum hose from distributor and plug hose. Verify that timing has been set, using the procedure given above.

3. Disconnect the fuel tank hose from vapor canister.

4. Adjust idle stop solenoid (turn solenoid body, using hex nut, **Figure 13**) to obtain 850 rpm (manual transmission in NEUTRAL) or 600 rpm (automatic transmission in DRIVE).

5. De-energize idle stop solenoid and use Allen wrench to adjust solenoid for 450 rpm. Energize solenoid.

6. Position fast idle lever on high step of fast idle cam. Place transmission in NEUTRAL or PARK. Set fast idle to 1,800 rpm by bending fast idle tang on throttle lever if required (**Figure 16**).

7. Reconnect vacuum hose to distributor and fuel tank line to vapor canister. Remove the tachometer.

**Idle Speed Adjustment
(2-BBL Carburetor)**

NOTE: *Fast idle is preset in factory at approximately 1,600 rpm.*

1. Start engine and allow it to reach normal operating temperature. Air conditioner should be off, choke should be fully open, and air cleaner should be installed. Parking brake should be on and rear wheels should be blocked. Connect a tachometer to engine, using manufacturer's instructions.

2. Disconnect vacuum hose from distributor and plug hose. Verify that timing has been properly set, using the procedure given above.

3. Disconnect the fuel tank hose from vapor canister.

4. Adjust idle stop solenoid screw (**Figure 13**) to obtain 900 rpm (manual transmission in NEUTRAL) or 600 rpm (automatic transmission in DRIVE).

5. De-energize idle stop solenoid by disconnecting electrical lead. Place automatic transmission in DRIVE or manual transmission in

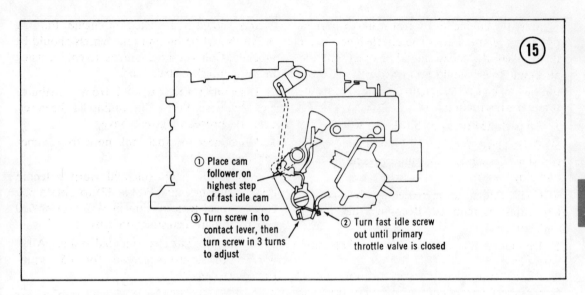

⑮

① Place cam
follower on
highest step
of fast idle cam

③ Turn screw in to
contact lever, then
turn screw in 3 turns
to adjust

② Turn fast idle screw
out until primary
throttle valve is closed

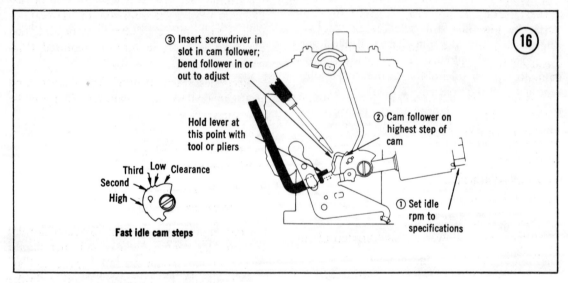

⑯

③ Insert screwdriver in
slot in cam follower;
bend follower in or
out to adjust

Hold lever at
this point with
tool or pliers

② Cam follower on
highest step of
cam

Third Low Clearance
Second
High

Fast idle cam steps

① Set idle
rpm to
specifications

NEUTRAL. Adjust idle cam screw (with screw on low step of cam) to obtain 400 rpm on engines with automatic transmissions and 500 rpm on 350 cu. in. engines (manual transmissions).

6. Reconnect idle stop solenoid electrical lead, distributor vacuum line, and fuel tank hose to vapor canister. Disconnect and remove the tachometer.

**Idle Speed Adjustment
(4-BBL Carburetors)**

1. Start engine and allow it to warm up to normal operating temperature. Air conditioner should be off, choke should be wide open, and air cleaner should be installed. Set parking brake and block rear wheels. Connect tachometer to engine, using manufacturer's instructions.

2. Disconnect distributor vacuum hose and plug hose. Verify that timing has been properly set, using procedure given above.

3. Disconnect the fuel tank line from vapor canister.

4. Adjust idle stop solenoid screws as follows:

   a. Automatic transmissions (in DRIVE) 350 cu. in. engines — 600 rpm

   b. Manual transmissions (in NEUTRAL) 350 cu. in. engines — 900 rpm

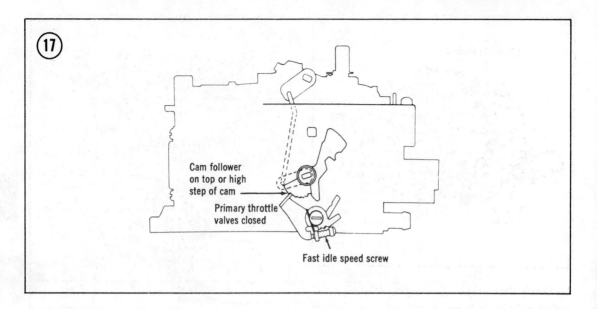

Cam follower
on top or high
step of cam

Primary throttle
valves closed

Fast idle speed screw

5. De-energize idle stop solenoid and adjust idle speed to low idle rpm given in **Table 1** for your engine, using low idle screw on low step of cam. Reconnect solenoid and check curb idle, readjusting if required.

6. Connect vacuum hose to distributor and place fast idle cam follower on top step of fast idle cam. Adjust fast idle speed as follows (see **Figure 17**).

   a. Automatic transmissions (in PARK) 350 cu. in engines — 1,600 rpm

   b. Manual transmissions (in NEUTRAL) 350 cu. in. engines — 1,300 rpm

7. Reconnect fuel tank line to vapor canister. Disconnect and remove tachometer.

HOLLEY CARBURETOR 4150-4160 (1967-1972 VEHICLES)

Idle Mixture Screw

If idle mixture screw (**Figure 18**) is equipped with a limiter cap, no attempt should be made to adjust fuel/air mixture setting — do not remove or alter limiter cap. If limiter cap is not present, or if carburetor overhaul or idle mixture screw replacement has been performed, the following procedure must be followed.

1. Follow instructions on tune-up decal in engine compartment. Remove the distributor vacuum hose and plug hose. Disconnect fuel tank hose from vapor canister.

2. Turn idle mixture screw in until it seats, then back out 4 full turns.

3. Adjust idle stop solenoid screw to specified idle rpm, using procedure given below.

4. Turn idle mixture ¼ turn rich and install limiter cap on idle mixture cap.

5. Connect vacuum hose to distributor and fuel tank hose to vapor canister.

Idle Speed Adjustment

Refer to **Figure 18**.

1. Start engine and warm up to normal operating temperature. Choke should be fully open, air conditioner off, parking brake on, and rear wheels blocked. Remove fuel tank hose from vapor canister. Connect tachometer to engine, using manufacturer's instructions.

2. Remove and plug distributor vacuum hose.

3. Adjust idle stop solenoid screw to obtain 900 rpm (manual transmission in NEUTRAL) or 700 rpm (automatic transmission in DRIVE).

4. Unplug and reconnect distributor vacuum hose. Reconnect the fuel tank hose to vapor canister.

Fast Idle Adjustment

Refer to **Figure 19**.

1. Start engine and warm up to normal operating temperature.

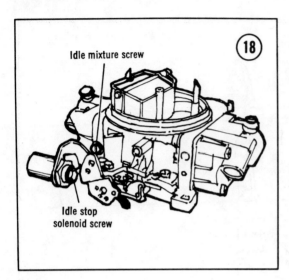

Idle mixture screw

Idle stop solenoid screw

2. Verify that choke valve is properly adjusted and in wide open position.

3. Place transmission in NEUTRAL and position fast idle lever on high step of fast idle cam.

4. Bend fast idle lever, if required, to obtain 2,350 rpm.

CARTER YF AND ROCHESTER CARBURETORS (1967-1971 VEHICLES)

Idle Mixture Adjustment (All Models)

> NOTE: *The 1971 model carburetors are equipped with limiter caps on idle mixture screws. These caps, which should not be removed, do not permit adjustment of the idle mixture.*

1. Start engine and warm up to normal operating temperature (air cleaner installed, preheater valve, if so equipped, and choke valve wide open). Connect tachometer to engine, using manufacturer's instructions.

> NOTE: *Air conditioner, if so equipped, should be turned on or off, per instructions on the Tune-up decal located in engine compartment.*

3. Adjust idle mixture screw to obtain highest steady idle speed.

4. Adjust idle speed screw to rpm recommended on Tune-up decal (adjust idle stop solenoid, if so equipped).

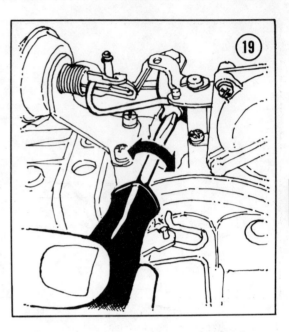

CAUTION
On 1971 vehicles only, do not adjust combination emissions control solenoid to set idle speed. Instead, use carburetor idle speed screw to make adjustments. See Figure 20.

5. If carburetor is equipped with idle stop solenoid, disconnect solenoid electrical lead and set idle speed to low rpm recommended on Tune-up decal. Reconnect solenoid electrical lead, crack throttle slightly, and recheck idle speed per Step 4, if required.

6. Adjust mixture screw in (lean) to obtain a 20 rpm drop (lean roll). Then turn mixture screw out ¼ turn.

7. Repeat Steps 2 through 6 for second mixture screw, if so equipped.

8. Readjust idle speed screw (or solenoid) as required to achieve specified rpm.

Fast Idle Adjustment (All Models)

> NOTE: *No fast idle adjustment is required for 2-barrel carburetors.*

1. Start and warm up engine to normal operating temperature. Choke should be in wide open position.

2. Verify that ignition has been tuned and timed and that curb idle has been set, using the procedure above.

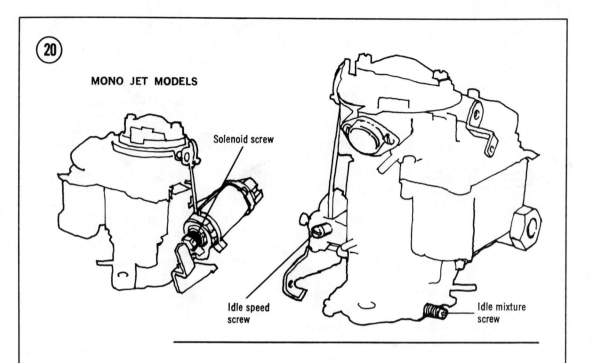

20

MONO JET MODELS

Solenoid screw

Idle speed screw

Idle mixture screw

1971
ROCHESTER
CARBURETORS

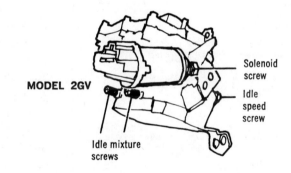

MODEL 2GV

Solenoid screw

Idle speed screw

Idle mixture screws

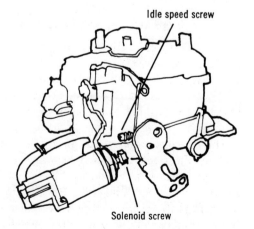

Idle speed screw

4MV QUADRAJET MODEL

Solenoid screw

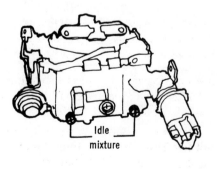

Idle mixture

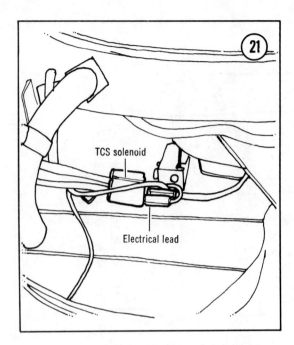

TCS solenoid

Electrical lead

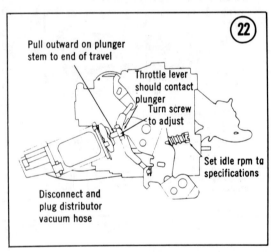

Pull outward on plunger stem to end of travel

Throttle lever should contact plunger

Turn screw to adjust

Set idle rpm to specifications

Disconnect and plug distributor vacuum hose

NOTE: *Disconnect electrical lead to Transmission Controlled Spark* (TCS) *solenoid on 1970 models so equipped. See Figure 21.*

3. Place transmission in NEUTRAL and position fast idle lever on high step (second step for 1970-1971 4-bbl carburetors) of fast idle cam.

4. Adjust fast idle to specifications (see Tune-up decal or **Table 1**) with fast idle screw (4- barrel) or by bending fast idle lever (1-barrel).

5. Reconnect electrical leads to TCS solenoid (1970 models).

6. Disconnect and remove tachometer.

CEC Solenoid Adjustment (All 1971 Models)

Refer to **Figure 22**.

CAUTION
If the CEC *solenoid is used to set idle speed or is adjusted out of limits (see* **Table 1**), *decrease in engine braking may result.*

NOTE: *The* CEC *solenoid is adjusted only after replacement of solenoid, major overhaul of carburetor, or after throttle body is removed and replaced. Also, instructions on Tune-up sticker in engine compartment must be completed before making adjustment.*

1. Start engine and warm up to normal operating temperature. Transmission should be in NEUTRAL (manual) or DRIVE (automatic) with parking brake set and rear wheels blocked. Air conditioner should be off, distributor vacuum hose removed and plugged, and fuel tank hose removed from vapor canister. Tachometer should be connected to engine, using the manufacturer's instructions.

2. Manually extend CEC solenoid plunger to control throttle lever.

3. Adjust plunger length to obtain idle speed of 850 rpm.

4. Disconnect tachometer and reconnect distributor vacuum hose and fuel tank to vapor canister.

AIR INJECTION REACTOR SYSTEM

The Air Injection Reactor (AIR) system is an exhaust emission aid that promotes a more complete burning of the exhaust gases to reduce hydrocarbon and carbon monoxide content by injecting air in the gases as they leave the cylinders.

Three things are essential to combustion — fuel, oxidizer (oxygen), and heat. As the exhaust gases leave the cylinders, 2 of these things are present — fuel and heat. By injecting air (oxygen) at this point, before the exhaust gases reach the exhaust system and cool down, the exhaust gases continue to burn and expend much of the hydrocarbon and carbon monoxide that

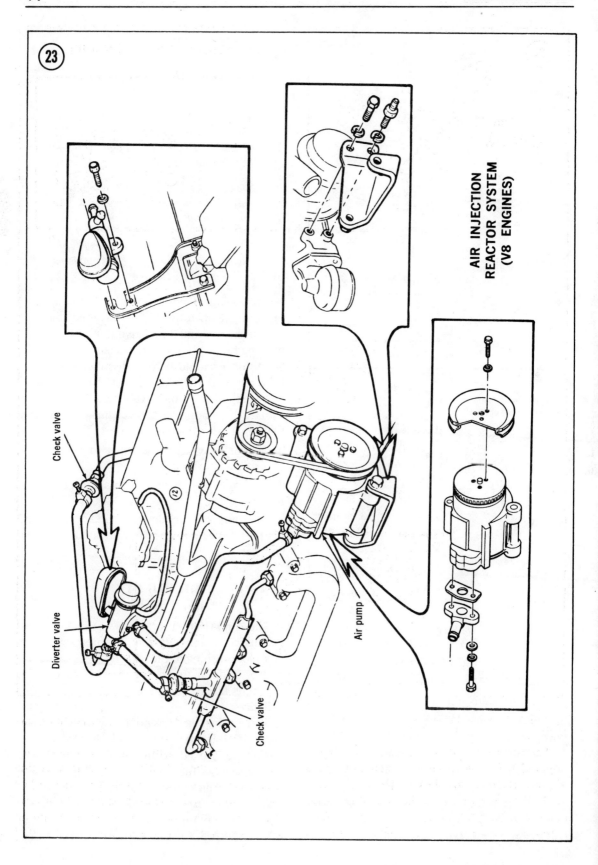

AIR INJECTION
REACTOR SYSTEM
(V8 ENGINES)

Check valve

Diverter valve

Check valve

Air pump

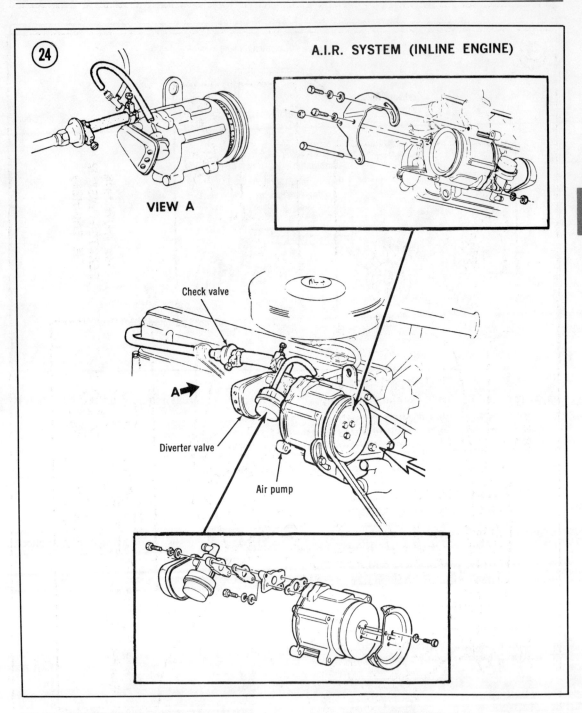

VIEW A

A.I.R. SYSTEM (INLINE ENGINE)

Check valve

Diverter valve

Air pump

would otherwise be exhausted into the atmosphere.

The AIR used with V8 engines is shown in **Figure 23**. The AIR system used on inline engines (**Figure 24**) injects the air into the cylinder head at the exhaust ports rather than into the exhaust manifolds. The check valves prevent exhaust gases from entering the air pump if the air

pump were to become inoperative (such as during a drive belt failure).

The diverter valve prevents air from being injected into the exhaust gases during engine overrun (such as occurs during gear changes) or deceleration when the exhaust gases are overly rich with fuel vapor. If the air from the pump was not diverted at these times a substantial

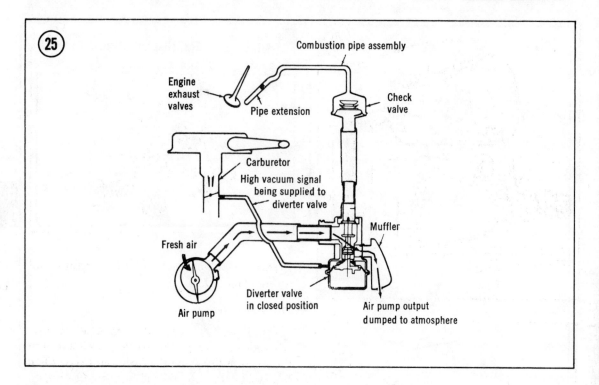

(25)

Combustion pipe assembly

Engine exhaust valves

Pipe extension

Check valve

Carburetor

High vacuum signal being supplied to diverter valve

Muffler

Fresh air

Air pump

Diverter valve in closed position

Air pump output dumped to atmosphere

backfire would occur. A sharp increase in manifold vacuum (such as during deceleration) signals the diverter valve to close and vent the air from the pump to atmosphere, through the muffler on the diverter valve (**Figure 25**).

AIR System Inspection

The inspection of the AIR system can be performed without the aid of special test equipment. Replacement of faulty hoses, check valves, diverter valve, or drive belt are routine. However, when replacing hoses, make sure they are designed for use with the AIR system and will withstand high operating temperatures. Also, use an anti-seize compound on the threads of all connectors that attach to the exhaust manifold or cylinder head.

Drive Belt

Check the condition of the drive belt. If it is cracked, worn, excessively glazed, or if the rubber is deteriorated, replace it. Also check the tension of the belt. If the belt is in good condition, it should be adjusted to a tension of 50 lb. using a belt tension gauge.

If adjustment is required, loosen the pump pivot bolt and the bracket adjustment bolt.

Move the pump as required until the tension is correct.

CAUTION
Do not pry on the pump housing to move it. This can severely damage the pump.

Air Manifold, Hoses, and Tubes

Inspect the hoses for deterioration and check the hoses and tubes for cracks. Replace any that are not satisfactory. Check the connections to make sure they are tight and leak free. Test the pressure side of the system with a soapy water solution applied to each of the connections with the engine idling (**Figure 26**). Bubbling and foaming are indications that a connection is not tight and leak free. Correct any leaks that are found.

NOTE: *The connectors at the cylinder head (L6 engine) or exhaust manifold (V8 engines) are ¼ in. straight pipe threads; do not use a ¼ in. tapered tap to clean them.*

If a hose or tube is to be replaced, pay careful attention to the routing of the piece being removed and route the new piece in the same

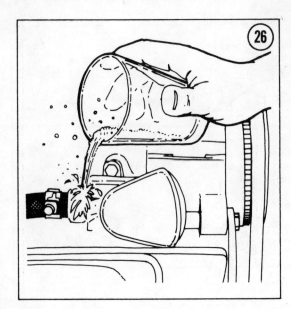

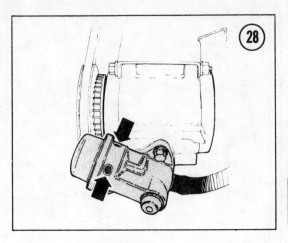

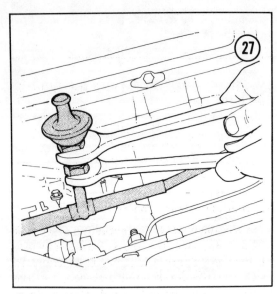

wrenches of comparable shaft length for equal torque (**Figure 27**).

Diverter Valve

Check the condition and tightness of the lines to the diverter valve. Pay particular attention to the vacuum line from the carburetor base plate or manifold to the valve; it must not be kinked, damaged, or deteriorated. With the engine idling, disconnect the vacuum line from the diverter valve and see if vacuum is present. If it is not, the line or the ports in the carburetor base plate may be clogged.

Check the outlets in the diverter valve muffler. At idle, no air should escape through the muffler. Quickly open and close the throttle; a blast of air at least one second in duration should be discharged through the muffler (**Figure 28**). If valve fails to operate correctly in either mode, it should be replaced.

> NOTE: *Make certain a new valve is the same as, or equivalent to, the one being replaced to ensure that it was designed for your engine and its operating specifications.*

Air Injection Pump

All of the inspections, checks, and corrections just described should be carried out first. Then, with the air pressure hoses disconnected from the check valves, accelerate the engine to about 1,500 rpm and check the air flow from the hoses. It should increase as engine speed increases. If it does not, or if there is no air pressure at all, the air pump can be assumed to

manner. Tighten all the connections securely and check for leaks as described above.

Check Valve

If a check valve is suspected of being faulty, disconnect its hose from the diverter valve and blow through it. There should be no resistance. Then, attempt to suck air through the hose. If the valve is in good condition this will not be possible. If the valve fails to perform satisfactorily in either direction, replace it. When removing and installing a check valve, be careful not to bend the air manifold. Use two

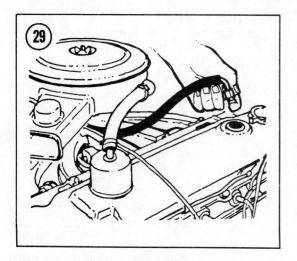

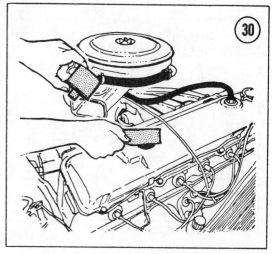

be faulty. Service to or replacement of the pump should be entrusted to a dealer.

> NOTE: *If, after inspection and correction of any defects found in the* AIR *system have been carried out, the vehicle performs poorly or does not idle smoothly, the earlier tune-up procedures and inspections should be rechecked. The pump and the pressure-side lines and fittings have no effect on engine performance. Rough idling or poor performance could be caused by a leaking diverter valve vacuum line, or backfiring could be caused by a defective diverter valve or connections. The* AIR *system has no effect on performance other than these points.*

POSITIVE CRANKCASE VENTILATION (PCV) VALVE

The PCV valve should be checked and replaced if necessary at each tune-up. Remove the valve from the rocker cover but leave it connected to the vent hose.

If the valve is clear, a hissing sound will be heard when the engine is idling, and a strong vacuum will be felt when a finger is placed over the valve (**Figure 29**).

Reinstall the valve in the rocker cover and disconnect the crankcase inlet air cleaner from the rocker cover. Hold a stiff piece of paper over the opening (**Figure 30**). After about a minute, when the crankcase pressure has subsided, the paper should be sucked down against the hole. Shut off the engine and once again disconnect the PCV valve from the rocker cover. Shake it and listen for a clicking sound that indicates the valve is free. If it is not, it should be replaced.

When a new valve is installed, check it as before, with a piece of paper held over the inlet. If the force is not considerable, it is necessary to clean the vent hose and the passages in the carburetor. Clean the hose with solvent and blow it dry with compressed air. The carburetor must be removed to clean the passages; this should be entrusted to a dealer.

Table 1   TUNE-UP SPECIFICATIONS — 1967

Spark plug gap — all engines		0.035 in.	
Point gap — all engines		0.016 in. used	
		0.019 in. new	
Dwell angle — L6 Engines		31-34 degrees	
V8 Engines		28-32 degrees	

Engine	Spark Plug Type (AC)	Timing (°BTDC)	Idle Speed, rpm
230-6	46N	4	700 (M); 500 (A)
250-6	46N	4	700 (M); 500 (A)
292-6	44N	2 (M); 4 (A)	700 (M); 500 (A)
283-8	44N	6 ATDC (M); 4 BTDC (A)	700 (M); 600 (A)
327-8/185 HP	C43	8	500
327-8/220 HP	42-1	2 with AIR; O others	700 (M); 600 (A)

(M) = manual transmission
(A) = automatic transmission
AIR = air injection reactor system

Table 1   TUNE-UP SPECIFICATIONS — 1968

Spark plug gap — all engines		0.035 in.	
Point gap — all engines		0.016 in. used;	
		0.019 in. new	
Dwell angle — L6 Engines		31-34 degrees	
V8 Engines		28-32 degrees	

Engine	Spark Plug Type (AC)	Timing (°BTDC)	Idle Speed, rpm
230-6	46N	w/o AIR—4 w/AIR—0	w/o AIR—500 (M & A) w/AIR—700 (M); 500 (A)
250-6	46N	w/o AIR—4 w/AIR—0 (M); 4 (A)	w/o AIR—500 (M & A) w/AIR—700 (M); 500 (A)
292-6	44N	w/o AIR—4 w/AIR—0 (M); 4 (A)	w/o AIR—500 (M & A) w/AIR—700 (M); 600 (A)
307-8	44S	2 (all)	w/o AIR—500 (M & A) w/AIR—700 (M); 600 (A)
327-8/185 HP		8 (all)	700 (M); 500 (A)
327-8/220 HP	44	w/o AIR—4 w/AIR—0 (M); 4 (A)	700 (M); 600 (A)

(M) = manual transmission
(A) = automatic transmission
AIR = air injection reactor system

Table 1   TUNE-UP SPECIFICATIONS — 1969-1970

Spark plug gap — all engines	0.035 in.
Point gap — all engines	0.016 in. used; 0.019 in. new
Dwell angle — L6 Engines	31-34 degrees
V8 Engines	28-32 degrees

Engine	Spark Plug Type (AC)	Timing (°BTDC)	Idle Speed, rpm
230-6	R46N	0 (M); 4 (A)	700 (M); 550 (A)
250-6	R46N	0 (M); 4 (A)	700 (M); 550 (A)
292-6	CR44N	0 (M); 4 (A)	700 (M); 550 (A)
307-8	R44	2 (all)	700 (M); 600 (A)
350-8/215 HP	CR43	4 (all)	500 (all)
350-8/255 HP	R44	0 (M); 4 (A)	700 (M); 600 (A)

(M) = manual transmission
(A) = automatic transmission

Table 1   TUNE-UP SPECIFICATIONS—1971

Spark plug gap — all engines	0.035 in.
Point gap — all engines	0.016 in. used; 0.019 in. new
Dwell angle — L6 Engines	31-34 degrees
V8 Engines	28-32 degrees

Engine	Spark Plug Type (AC)	Timing (°BTDC)	Idle Speed, rpm
250-6	R46TS	4 (all)	550 (M); 500 (A)
292-6	R44T	4 (all)	700 (all)
307-8/200 HP	R45TS	4 (M); 8 (A)	600 (M); 500 (A)
307-8/215 HP	R45TS	4 (all)	550 (M); 500 (A)
350-8	R44TS	4 (M); 8 (A)	600 (M); 550 (A)

(M) = manual transmission
(A) = automatic transmission

Table 1   TUNE-UP SPECIFICATIONS—1972

Spark plug gap — all engines	0.035 in.
Point gap — all engines	0.016 in. used; 0.019 in. new
Dwell angle — L6 Engines	31-34 degrees
V8 Engines	29-31 degrees

Engine	Spark Plug Type (AC)	Timing (°BTDC)	Idle Speed, rpm
250-6	R46T	4 (all)	700 (M); 600 (A)
292-6	R44T	4 (all)	700 (all)
307-8	R44T	4 (all except "10" auto) 8 ("10" auto)	900 (M) Fed.; 950 (M) Cal. 600 (A) all
350-8	R44T	4 (M); 8 (A)	800 (M); 600 (A)

(M) = manual transmission
(A) = automatic transmission
Fed. = for vehicles subject to Federal emission regulations
Cal. = for vehicles subject to California emission regulations
"10" = Series 10 vehicles

Table 1   TUNE-UP SPECIFICATIONS—1973

Spark plug gap — all engines	0.035 in.
Point gap — all engines	0.016 in. used; 0.019 in. new
Dwell angle — L6 Engines	31-34 degrees
V8 Engines	29-31 degrees

Engine	Spark Plug Type (AC)	Timing (°BTDC)	Idle Speed, rpm
250-6	R46T	6 (all)—LD 4 (all)—HD	700 (M); 600 (A)
292-6	R44T	4 (all)—Fed. 8 (all)—Cal.	700 (all)—Fed. 600 (all)—Cal.
307-8	R44T	4 (M); 8 (A)—LD 0 (M & A)—HD	900 (M)—Fed.; 600 (M)—Cal. 600 (A)—Fed. & Cal.
350-8	R44T	8 (M); 12 (A)—LD 4 (all)—HD	900 (M); 600 (A)—LD 600 (all)—HD

(M) = manual transmission
(A) = automatic transmission
LD = light duty
HD = heavy duty
Fed. = for vehicles subject to Federal emission regulations
Cal. = for vehicles subject to California emission regulations

Table 1   TUNE-UP SPECIFICATIONS—1974

Spark plug gap — all engines	0.035 in.
Point gap — all engines	0.016 in. used; 0.019 in. new
Dwell angle — L6 engines	31-34 degrees
V8 engines	29-31 degrees

Engine	Spark Plug Type (AC)	Timing (°BTDC)	Idle Speed, rpm
250-6	R46T	8 (all)	850 (M); 600 (A)—LD 600 (M & A)—HD
292-6	R44T	8 (all)	600 (all)
350-8/2BBL	R44T	0 (M); 8 (A)—Fed.	900 (M); 600 (A)—LD 600 (M & A)—HD
350-8/4BBL	R44T	8 (M & A) Fed.—LD except Suburban 6 (M); 12 (A) Fed. Suburban 4 (M); 8 (A) Cal.—LD except Suburban 6 (A) Cal. Suburban 4 (M & A)—HD	900 (M); 600 (A)—LD 600 (M & A)—HD

(M) = manual transmission
(A) = automatic transmission
LD = light duty
HD = heavy duty
Fed. = for vehicles subject to Federal emission regulations
Cal. = for vehicles subject to California emission regulations

Table 1   TUNE-UP SPECIFICATIONS—1975

| Spark plug gap — all engines | 0.060 in. |

Engine	Spark Plug Type (AC)	Timing (°BTDC)	Idle Speed, rpm
250-6	R46TX	6 (M); 10 (A)	900 (M); 550 (A)—Fed. 1000 (M); 600 (A)—Cal.
292-6	R44TX	8 (all)	600 (all)
350-8	R44TX	8 (all)—Fed. 6 (all)—Cal.	800 (M); 600 (A)
454-8	R44TX	8 (all)—Fed. 12 (all)—Cal.	600 (all)

(M) = manual transmission
(A) = automatic transmission
Fed. = for vehicles subject to Federal emission regulations
Cal. = for vehicles subject to California emission regulations

Table 1   TUNE-UP SPECIFICATIONS—1976

Spark plug gap — all engines		0.045 in.	
Engine	**Spark Plug Type (AC)**	**Timing (°BTDC)**	**Idle Speed, rpm***
250-6	R46TS	6 (M); 10 (A)	900 (M); 550 (A)—Fed. 1000 (M); 600 (A)—Cal.
292-6	R44T	8 (all)	600 (all)
350-8	R45TS	8 (all)—Fed. 6 (all)—Cal.	800 (M); 600 (A)
454-8	R45TS	8 (all)—Fed. 12 (all)—Cal.	600 (all)

(M) = manual transmission
(A) = automatic transmission
Fed. = for vehicles subject to Federal emission regulations
Cal. = for vehicles subject to California emission regulations
*For automatic transmissions, idle speed is set with selector in DRIVE.

4

Table 1   TUNE-UP SPECIFICATIONS—1977-1978

Spark plug gap—all engines		0.045 in.	
Engine	**Spark Plug Type (AC)**	**Timing (°BTDC)**	**Idle Speed, rpm***
250-6	R46TS	6 (M); 10 (A)—Fed. 8 (M); 12 (A)—Cal.	750 (M); 600 (A)—Fed. 850 (M); 600 (A)—Cal.
305-8	R45TS	8 (all)	600 (M); 500 (A)
350-8	R45TS	8 (M & A)—Fed. 6 (M & A)—Cal.	700 (M); 500 (A) 600 (high altitude)
454-8	R45TS	4 (all)	600 (all)

(M) = manual transmission
(A) = automatic transmission
Fed. = for vehicles subject to Federal emission regulations
Cal. = for vehicles subject to California emission regulations
*For automatic transmission, idle speed is set with selector in DRIVE.

CHAPTER FIVE

ENGINE

Three basic engines are used in the vehicles covered in this handbook — the inline 6-cylinder (L6) engine; small block V8; and Mark IV V8. Service procedures on all engines are very similar and where differences occur they are noted in the procedure involved.

All engines operate on the 4-cycle principle. The crankshaft turns two complete revolutions during each cycle. A single camshaft, operating at ½ crankshaft speed, operates the valves through hydraulic lifters, pushrods, and rocker arms. The camshaft also operates the distributor, fuel pump, and oil pump. The L6 engine has 7 main bearings and 4 camshaft bearings. The V8 engines have 5 main bearings and 5 camshaft bearings.

This chapter covers removal and installation of the engine, removal and replacement of subassemblies, and inspection, adjustment, and repair of some subassemblies and components. Although the illustrations usually show workbench operations, many single procedures, when not a part of a general overhaul, can be performed successfully with the engine in the vehicle.

ENGINE REMOVAL

NOTE: *The engine and transmission should be removed as a unit.*

1. Remove the hood.

2. Disconnect the battery cables (negative first), drain the cooling system, and remove the air cleaner.

3. Remove the radiator and fan shroud.

4. Disconnect the wires from the starter solenoid, alternator temperature sensing switch, oil pressure switch, coil, and CEC solenoid.

> NOTE: *For vehicles equipped with air conditioning, carefully read the air conditioning section in Chapter Nine to acquaint yourself with the system. Then, remove clamps that attach the hoses to the fender wells and the engine. Remove the compressor and position it out of the way. There is usually no need to disconnect the lines from the components. Make certain that there is no strain on any of the hoses or lines.*

5. Disconnect the following items:
   a. Accelerator linkage (at the manifold bell crank)
   b. Fuel feed line (from the fuel tank) at the fuel pump
   c. Heater hoses from the engine connections
   d. Oil pressure gauge line (if equipped)
   e. Vacuum lines from the engine

f. Power steering pump with hoses attached (set out of the way)

g. Electrical ground straps from the engine

h. TCS switch from the transmission

i. Exhaust pipe from the manifold (support the pipe with a length of wire)

6. Remove the fan and drive clutch (if equipped).

7. Drain the crankcase.

8. Remove the drive shaft. If a plug is not available for the tailshaft opening in the rear of the transmission, drain the transmission.

9. Disconnect the following items:

a. Transmission cooler lines (if equipped)

b. Transmission control switch (if equipped)

c. Shift linkage from the transmission

d. Speedometer cable from the transmission

10. If the vehicle is equipped with a manual transmission, disconnect the clutch linkage from the cross shaft and remove the cross shaft engine mount.

11. Connect a lifting device to the engine lifting eyes and lift the engine just enough to unweight the engine mounts. Then remove the through bolts from the engine mounts. See **Figure 1**.

12. Remove the bolts that attach the rear mount to the frame crossmember.

CAUTION
Double check to make sure all electrical leads, vacuum lines, and control links between the engine/transmission assembly and the vehicle have been disconnected or removed. Check also to ensure that air conditioning lines, oil lines, and wiring harness will not snag on the engine when it is removed.

13. Raise the engine/transmission assembly with the lifting device and remove it from the vehicle.

14A. If vehicle is equipped with a manual transmission, remove it and the clutch as follows:

a. Remove the screws from the clutch housing cover.

b. Unscrew the bolts that connect the transmission bell housing to the engine. Support the transmission and remove it from the engine.

CAUTION
Do not allow the transmission to hang by the input shaft. Pull it straight back from the engine to disengage the shaft from the clutch disc, taking care not to damage the splines.

c. Remove the starter and the clutch housing rear cover.

d. Loosen the clutch mounting bolts in a crisscross pattern, progressively, one turn at a time until the clutch spring has been relaxed. This is necessary to prevent warping the clutch body. Then, remove the bolts, the clutch assembly, and the clutch disc.

14B. If the vehicle is equipped with an automatic transmission, remove it as follows:

a. Support the engine and transmission on blocks.

b. Remove the starter and the bottom pan from the torque converter.

c. Remove the bolts that connect the flywheel to the torque converter. It will be necessary to rotate the crankshaft to gain access to all of the bolts.

d. Remove the bolts that attach the transmission bell housing to the engine.

e. Slowly raise the engine with the lifting device and remove it from the transmission.

15. If an engine stand is available, raise the engine with the lifting device and mount it on the stand. If a stand is not available, support the engine on wooden blocks.

ENGINE INSTALLATION

1. Attach the lifting device to the engine and remove it from the stand or blocks.

2A. If the vehicle is equipped with a manual transmission, proceed as follows:

a. Install the clutch as described in Chapter Ten.

b. Install the starter and clutch housing front cover.

c. Install the transmission as described in Chapter Ten.

d. Install the clutch housing cover.

5

(1)

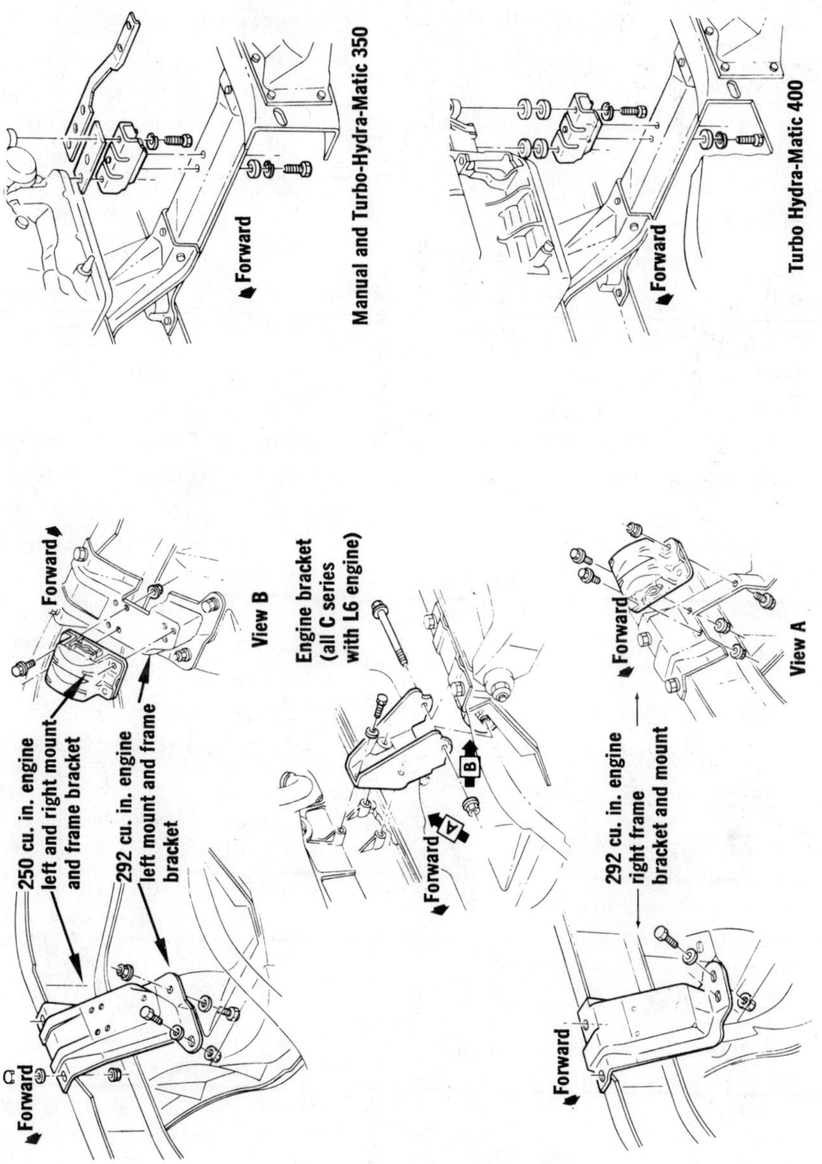
Forward
Manual and Turbo-Hydra-Matic 350
Forward
Turbo Hydra-Matic 400
Forward
250 cu. in. engine left and right mount and frame bracket
292 cu. in. engine left mount and frame bracket
Forward
View B
Forward
A
B
Engine bracket (all C series with L6 engine)
Forward
292 cu. in. engine right frame bracket and mount
Forward
View A

6-CYLINDER

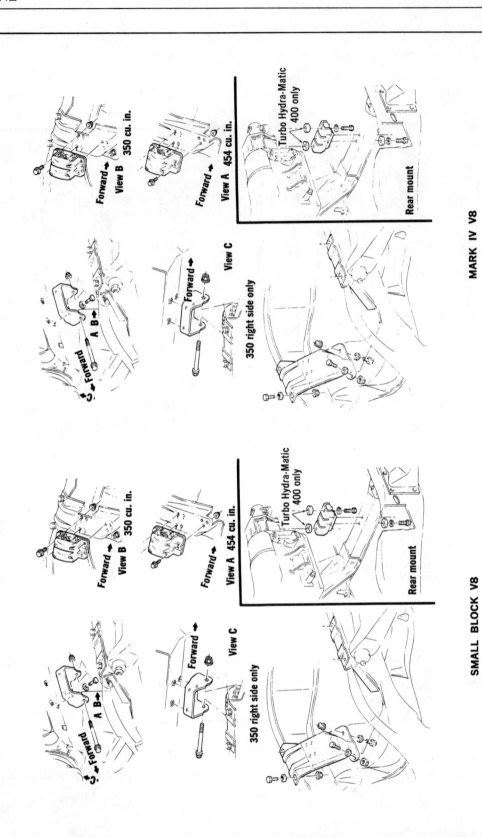

Forward

View B   350 cu. in.

Forward

View A   454 cu. in.

Turbo Hydra-Matic
400 only

Rear mount

Forward

A B

Forward

View C

350 right side only

MARK IV V8

Forward

View B   350 cu. in.

Forward

View A   454 cu. in.

Turbo Hydra-Matic
400 only

Rear mount

Forward

A B

Forward

View C

350 right side only

SMALL BLOCK V8

5

2B. If the vehicle is equipped with an automatic transmission, proceed as follows:

  a. Align the engine with the transmission, using the lifting device.

  b. Bolt the transmission bell housing to the engine.

  c. Raise the engine/transmission assembly and install bolts that connect the torque converter to the flywheel.

  d. Install the starter and the torque converter bottom pan.

3. Raise the engine/transmission assembly with the lifting device until it clears the front of the vehicle. Tilt the tailshaft of the transmission down and guide the assembly into the vehicle. Lower it slowly, checking for lines, hoses, and wires that may become snagged. Align the front motor mounts and install the through bolts but do not tighten them.

4. Raise the rear of the engine with a floor jack and install the rear mount. Then lower the engine and connect it to the mount. Remove the lifting device.

5. Tighten the front mount through bolts to 55 ft.-lb. and the rear mount bolts to 30 ft.-lb.

6. If the vehicle is equipped with a manual transmission, install the clutch cross shaft engine mount. Connect and adjust the clutch linkage as described in Chapter Ten. Connect and adjust the shifting linkage as described in Chapter Ten.

7. Connect the transmission control switch (if equipped) and the speedometer cable.

8. Install the drive shaft.

9. Connect the following items:

  a. Power steering pump (if equipped)

  b. Power brake booster vacuum line

  c. Fuel line to the fuel pump

  d. Vapor canister hoses (if equipped)

  e. Exhaust pipe

  f. Accelerator linkage

10. Connect the following wires:

  a. Vacuum advance solenoid (at the carburetor)

  b. Coil

  c. Oil pressure sensor

  d. Temperature sensor

  e. Delcotron

  f. Starter solenoid

11. Install the fan clutch (if equipped), fan, and fan belt.

12. Install the radiator and the fan shroud, taking care not to damage the radiator fins and tubes.

13. Connect the cooling system and heater hoses and tighten them securely. Fill the system with coolant as described in Chapter Nine.

14. Fill the engine and transmission with oil as described in Chapter Three.

15. Connect the battery leads.

16. Start the engine and check for oil and coolant leaks. Repair any that are found.

CAUTION
Do not rev the engine when it is first started. Allow several minutes for the oil to circulate thoroughly.

17. Install the air cleaner and adjust timing and idle speed as described in Chapter Four, Tune-Up.

GENERAL OVERHAUL SEQUENCE

NOTE: *For partial disassembly of the engine, see the applicable procedure later in this chapter. For complete disassembly, follow sequence outlined below. This sequence presumes that the engine has been removed from the vehicle and mounted on an engine stand or suitable workbench.*

1. Remove the following accessories or components from the engine (if present):

  a. Air injection reactor system (and brackets)

  b. Alternator (and brackets)

  c. Accessory drive pulleys

  d. Fuel pump (and pushrod, V8 engine)

  e. Water pump and hoses

  f. Spark plug wires and distributor cap

  g. Carburetor and fuel lines

  h. Oil filter

  i. Starter

j. Clutch pressure plate and disc

k. Ground strap

l. Oil dipstick and tube

2. Remove intake and exhaust manifolds.

3. Remove pushrod covers (inline engines).

4. Loosen valve rocker arm nuts and remove pushrods and valve lifters. Store removed items in racks so they can be reinstalled in the same locations from which they were removed.

5. Remove cylinder head(s).

6. Remove torsional damper.

7. Remove oil pan.

8. Remove front cover from crankcase.

9. Remove oil baffle, if so equipped.

10. Remove oil pump and screen. Remove extension shaft (V8 engines).

11. If connecting rods and caps are not marked with cylinder number identification, mark them. Also check cylinder bores for ridges. If necessary, remove ridges.

12. Remove connecting rod caps, then remove connecting rod-piston assemblies from engine.

NOTE: *Turn crankshaft as required to remove rods and bearings.*

CAUTION
Use care when removing camshaft to avoid damaging bearings.

13A. Remove the camshaft from V8 as follows:

a. Remove attaching bolts from camshaft sprocket, tap lower edge of sprocket lightly with plastic hammer to dislodge, and remove sprocket and timing chain.

b. Install two 5/16-18 bolts in camshaft sprocket bolt holes and carefully pull out camshaft.

13B. Remove the camshaft from inline engines as follows:

a. Remove the camshaft thrust plate screws, using holes in the camshaft gear for access.

b. Remove the camshaft and gear as an assembly.

14. Remove the flywheel.

15. Remove the caps from main bearings and remove the crankshaft from the cylinder block.

16. Remove the rear main bearing oil seal from the cylinder block and bearing cap.

17. Discard all gaskets and seals removed during the above steps.

NOTE: *See procedures later in this chapter for further disassembly, cleaning, and inspection of the parts or subassemblies removed during this procedure.*

GENERAL REASSEMBLY SEQUENCE

NOTE: *Use only new gaskets and seals on engine during assembly.*

1. Install the crankshaft as follows:

a. Place the rear main bearing oil seal in grooves in the cylinder block and bearing cap. Make certain the seal lip faces toward the front of the engine. If the seal has two lips, the one with a helix should face front of engine.

b. Lubricate the seal lips with engine oil. Keep oil off the parting line surface.

c. Install the main bearings in the block and bearing caps and lubricate the bearing surfaces with engine oil.

d. Carefully install the crankshaft in the cylinder block.

e. Brush a thin coat of Gasgacinch or equivalent sealer on the block mating surface (**Figure 2**) and on the corresponding surface on the bearing cap.

CAUTION
Do not allow sealer on crankshaft or seal.

f. Install the main bearing caps, with arrows pointing to the front of the engine. Tighten all bolts (except rear cap) to specifications (see **Table 1** at end of chapter). Tighten the rear bearing cap bolts to 10-12 ft.-lb., then tap the end of the crankshaft, first to the rear and to the front, with a lead hammer to line up rear main bearing and crankshaft thrust surfaces. Retighten all bolts to specifications.

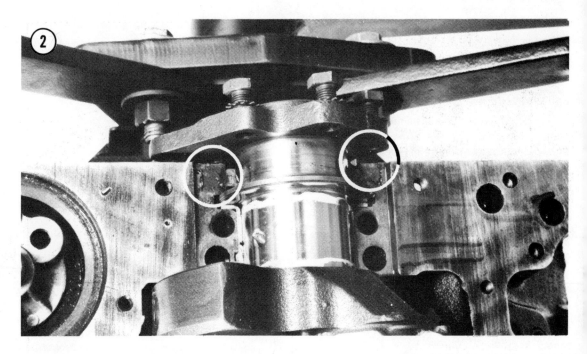

g. Measure crankshaft end play with a feeler gauge (**Figure 3**). Force the crankshaft forward as far as it will go and measure between the front of the rear main bearing and the crankshaft thrust surface. See **Table 2**, at end of chapter, for allowable end play.

2. Install a wood block between the crankshaft and cylinder block to prevent rotation and install the flywheel. Tighten to specifications (see **Table 1**).

> NOTE: *Align dowel holes in the flywheel and crankshaft. If the vehicle has an automatic transmission, make certain converter attaching pads on flywheel are facing toward transmission.*

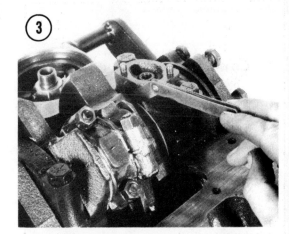

> NOTE: *If the camshaft or lifters are new, lubricate cam lobes and lifter feet with Molykote or equivalent.*

3A. Install the camshaft on V8 as follows:

a. Thread 5/16-18 bolts into the camshaft sprocket bolt holes, lubricate camshaft journals with engine oil, and install the camshaft. **Figure 4** is typical. Take care not to damage the bearings. Remove the bolts.

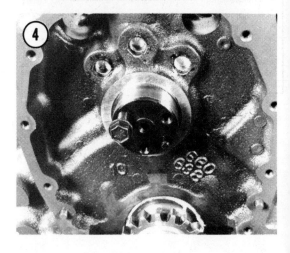

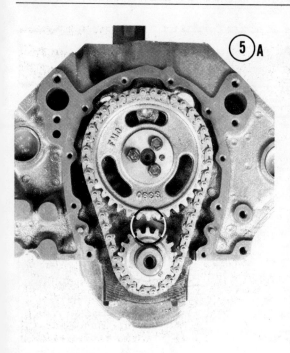

5 A

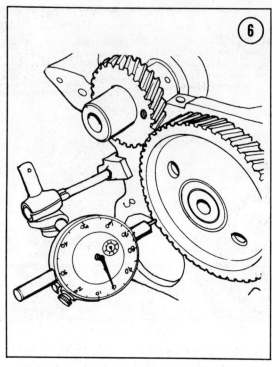

6

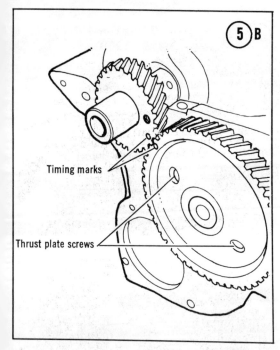

5 B

Timing marks

Thrust plate screws

b. Install the timing chain on the camshaft sprocket. Align the marks on the camshaft and crankshaft sprockets (see **Figure 5A**) and install the chain on the crankshaft sprocket. Align the dowel on the camshaft with the hole in the camshaft sprocket and install the sprocket on the camshaft.

CAUTION
Do not hammer on the camshaft sprocket during installation; the camshaft rear expansion plug could be loosened.

c. Use mounting bolts to draw the sprocket onto the camshaft. Tighten to specifications (see **Table 1**), and lubricate the chain with engine oil.

3B. Install the camshaft in inline engines as follows:

a. Lubricate the journals on the camshaft with engine oil.

b. Position the crankshaft and camshaft so that timing marks are aligned (see **Figure 5B**) and install camshaft and gear assembly. Take care not to damage the camshaft bearings.

c. Using a dial indicator, check gear runout (see **Figure 6**). Camshaft gear runout should not exceed 0.004 in. and crankshaft gear should not exceed 0.003 in.

d. Use a dial indicator to check backlash between timing gear teeth. Backlash should be not less than 0.004 in. and not more than 0.006 in.

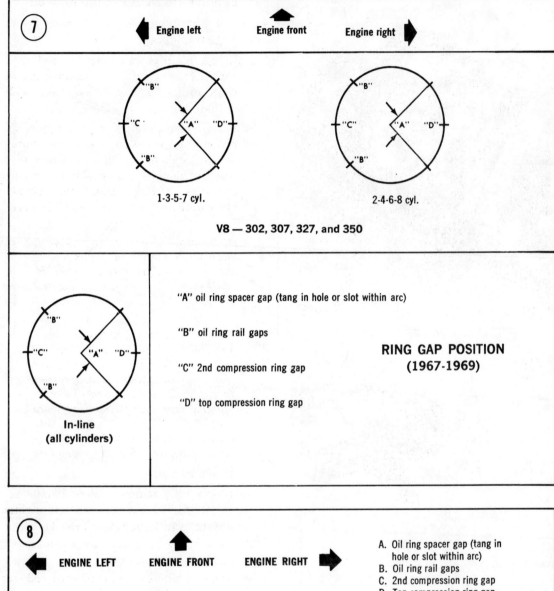

⑦ Engine left   Engine front   Engine right

1-3-5-7 cyl.   2-4-6-8 cyl.

V8 — 302, 307, 327, and 350

In-line (all cylinders)

"A" oil ring spacer gap (tang in hole or slot within arc)

"B" oil ring rail gaps

"C" 2nd compression ring gap

"D" top compression ring gap

RING GAP POSITION (1967-1969)

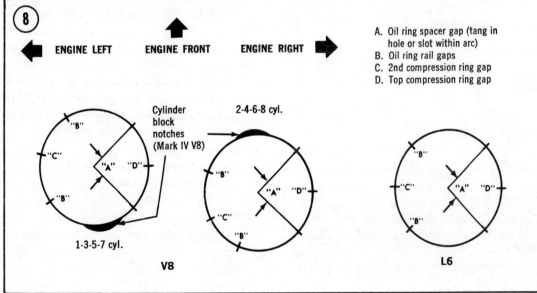

⑧ ENGINE LEFT   ENGINE FRONT   ENGINE RIGHT

A. Oil ring spacer gap (tang in hole or slot within arc)
B. Oil ring rail gaps
C. 2nd compression ring gap
D. Top compression ring gap

Cylinder block notches (Mark IV V8)

2-4-6-8 cyl.

1-3-5-7 cyl.

V8   L6

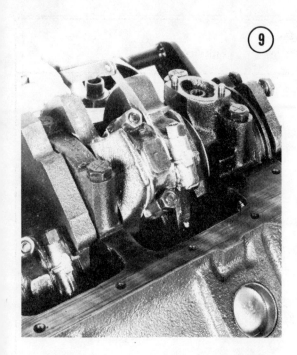

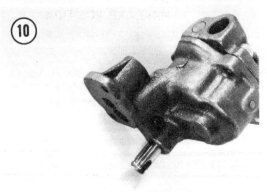

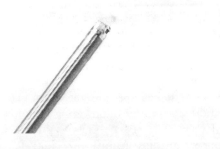

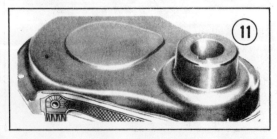

e. Lubricate timing gears with engine oil.

4. Install the connecting rod and piston assemblies as follows:

a. Install bearings in connecting rods and caps. Lubricate bearings, pistons, piston rings, bolts, and cylinder walls with engine oil.

b. Using a ring compressor to compress the piston rings, insert No. 1 piston assembly in No. 1 cylinder, using light taps with a wooden hammer handle. Hold the ring compressor firmly against the cylinder block until all rings have entered the bore.

CAUTION
Make certain ring gaps are properly positioned on piston and piston is properly positioned in cylinder. See Figure 7 (1967-1969 models) and Figure 8 (1970 and later models).

NOTE: *A connecting rod guide tool set will greatly help in installing piston and rod assemblies. If not available, use care to avoid damage to bearing surfaces, threads and crankshaft journals. Masking tape over threads and sharp projections will help. However, make certain all adhesive from the tape is removed before assembling rods to the crankshaft.*

c. If installed, remove the rod guide set. Install connecting rod cap and tighten nuts to specifications (see **Table 1**).

d. Repeat Steps b and c for remaining rod and piston assemblies.

e. Measure side clearance of each rod (see **Table 2**). Make measurement between connecting rod cap and side of crankpin (inline engines) or between connecting rod caps (V8 engines). Refer to **Figure 9**.

5. Install the oil pump and screen assembly, extension shaft (V8 engines), and oil baffle, if so equipped. (See **Figure 10**.)

6A. Install the crankcase front cover on inline engines as follows:

a. Lubricate the lip seal with engine oil and install the crankcase front cover aligning tool (GM tool No. J-23042 or equivalent) in seal (see **Figure 11**).

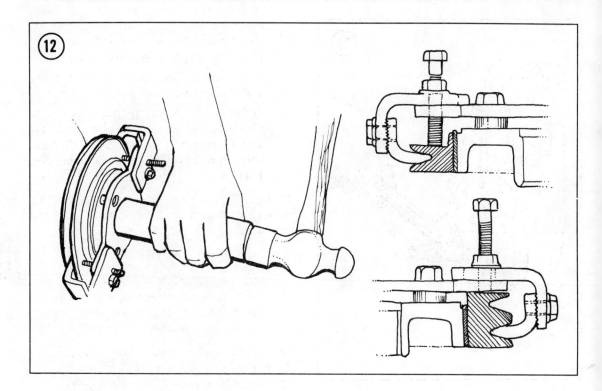

b. Position the gasket on the cover and install the cover on the cylinder block. Tighten to specifications (see **Table 1**) and remove the tool.

6B. Install the crankcase front cover on V8 engines as follows:

a. Place the gasket in position on dowels on cylinder block.

b. Lubricate the lip seal with engine oil. Place the cover in position on dowel pins. Install bolts and tighten to specifications (see **Table 1**).

7. Install the oil pan as follows:

a. Place side gaskets on cylinder block sealing surfaces and apply sealer at the intersection of the end seals and side gaskets.

b. Place the oil pan rear seal in groove in rear main bearing cap. Ends of seal should butt against side gaskets.

c. Place the oil pan front seal in the crankcase front cover. Ends of seal should butt against side gaskets.

d. Install the oil pan and tighten to specifications (see **Table 1**).

CAUTION
The installation procedures in Step 8 must be followed, using the proper tool, or movement of the inertial weight section (assembled to hub with rubber-like material) or the hub may destroy the tuning of the torsional damper.

8A. Install the drive-on torsional damper as follows:

a. Coat the seal contact area on damper with engine oil.

b. Attach the installer tool (GM Part J-22197) to damper (see **Figure 12**). Tighten fingers of tool to keep weight from moving.

c. Position the damper on the crankshaft and drive it into position, using a hollow drift bar (GM Part J-5590), until the damper bottoms against the crankshaft gear or sprocket. Remove the tool.

8B. Install the pull-on type torsional damper as follows:

a. Coat seal contact area on damper with engine oil.

b. Position the damper over the key on the crankshaft.

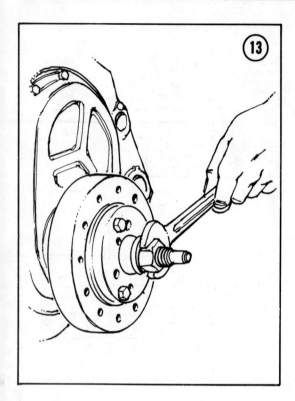

(13)

c. Using GM tool Part J-23523, pull the damper onto crankshaft (see **Figure 13**).

> **CAUTION**
> *Bolt should be installed in crankshaft with a minimum of ½ in. thread engagement.*

d. Remove the tool and install retaining bolts. Tighten to specifications (see **Table 1**).

9. Install the cylinder head(s) as follows:

> **CAUTION**
> *Make certain that gasket surfaces on head(s) and cylinder block are clean and free of nicks and deep scratches. Threads in the block and on cylinder head bolts must be clean, as dirty threads will affect bolt torques.*

a. Apply a thin coat of sealer on both sides of steel gaskets.

> **CAUTION**
> *Too much sealer will affect the sealing quality of the gasket.*

> **CAUTION**
> *Do not use sealer on either side of a composite steel-asbestos gasket.*

b. Place the gasket over the dowel pins on the cylinder block with bead side up.

c. Carefully lower cylinder head into place.

d. Apply sealing compound to bolt threads and install them finger-tight.

e. Following the torque sequence shown in **Figure 14**, tighten each cylinder head bolt a small amount at a time until all bolts have been tightened to specifications (see **Table 1**).

10. Install valve lifters and pushrods, making certain they are replaced in the same locations from which they were removed.

> NOTE: *If new lifters and/or rocker arms and balls are installed, coat feet of valve lifters and surfaces of rocker arm and balls with Molykote or equivalent.*

5

11. Install rocker arms, balls, and nuts. Tighten nuts to take up all pushrod end play.

12. Install pushrod covers (inline engines).

13. Install exhaust and intake manifolds, and torque bolts in sequence shown in **Figure 14** to specifications (see **Table 1**).

14. Install the following applicable subassemblies or components, using the appropriate procedures given later in this chapter.

a. Engine oil dipstick tube and dipstick

b. Clutch pressure plate and disc

c. Ground strap

d. Starter

e. New oil filter

f. Fuel lines and carburetor

g. Distributor (See Chapter Eight)

h. Distributor cap and spark plug wires

i. Fuel pump (and pushrod on V8 engines)

j. Water pump and bypass hose

k. Accessory drive pulleys and belts

l. Alternator and bracket

m. Air injector reactor system with brackets

15. Adjust all belts to proper tension.

16. Adjust valves (see *Valve Mechanism*).

17. Connect lifting device to engine lifting brackets and install in car (see *Engine Installation*).

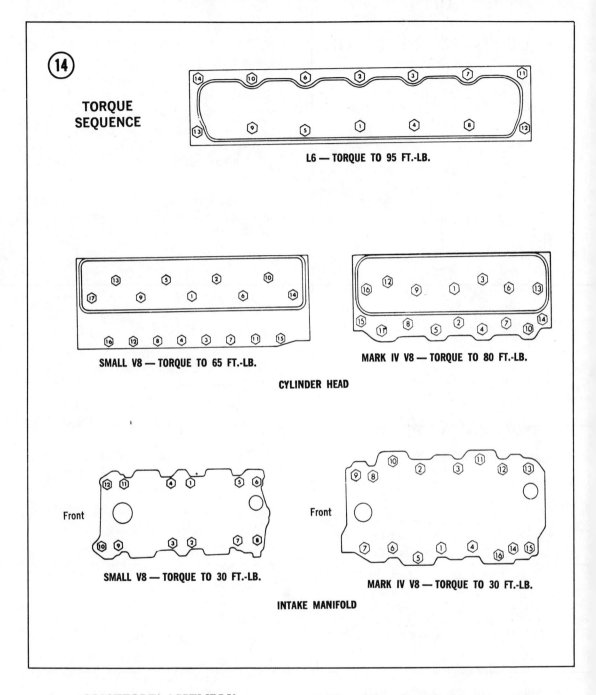

TORQUE SEQUENCE

L6 — TORQUE TO 95 FT.-LB.

SMALL V8 — TORQUE TO 65 FT.-LB.

MARK IV V8 — TORQUE TO 80 FT.-LB.

CYLINDER HEAD

SMALL V8 — TORQUE TO 30 FT.-LB.

MARK IV V8 — TORQUE TO 30 FT.-LB.

INTAKE MANIFOLD

MANIFOLD ASSEMBLY (INLINE ENGINES)

Removal

1. Remove the air cleaner and disconnect both throttle rods at bellcrank and remove throttle spring.

2. Disconnect the vacuum and fuel lines from carburetor.

3. Disconnect the ventilation hose from rocker arm cover and hose at vapor canister.

4. Disconnect the exhaust pipe from manifold flange and discard packing.

5. Remove the attaching bolts and clamps and then remove manifold assembly. Discard all gaskets.

6. Check for cracks in the manifold assembly.

7. Separate the manifolds by removing the bolt and nuts at center.

Installation

1. Clean all gasket surfaces on the manifold and cylinder head.

2. Check the manifold exhaust ports for gaps by placing a straightedge along the full length of the port faces. If at any point a gap of 0.030 in. exists, the manifold will not, in all probability, seal and the manifold should be replaced.

3. Rejoin the exhaust and intake manifolds by installing the center bolt and nuts (finger-tight).

4. Place a new gasket on the cylinder head manifold end studs. Place the manifold assembly on the cylinder head and install bolts and clamps. Tighten to 25-30 ft.-lb. (inner bolts) and 20 ft.-lb. (outer bolts).

5. Tighten the exhaust-to-intake manifold bolt and nuts to 30 ft.-lb.

6. Using a new packing, connect the exhaust pipe to the manifold flange.

7. Connect the ventilation hose to the rocker arm cover and connect the hoses to the vapor canister.

8. Connect vacuum and fuel lines to carburetor.

9. Reconnect the throttle linkage and install the throttle spring.

10. Install the air cleaner, start the engine, and check for manifold leaks and adjust the idle speed.

INTAKE MANIFOLD (V8 ENGINES)

Removal

NOTE: *If engine has been removed from vehicle, skip to Step 5.*

1. Remove the air cleaner and drain the radiator.

2. Disconnect the following:

    a. Battery cables (at battery)

    b. Radiator hoses (at manifold)

    c. Accelerator linkage (at pedal lever)

    d. Fuel line (at carburetor)

    e. All coil and temperature sender wires

    f. Power brake vacuum hose

    g. Crankcase ventilation hoses (if so equipped)

    h. Vacuum hose (at distributor)

3. Remove the cap from distributor and mark position of rotor. First remove the distributor clamp, then remove the distributor from the engine. Position the distributor cap rearward so it is clear of manifold.

4. Remove the alternator upper bracket.

5. Remove the coil bracket and coil.

6. Remove the attaching bolts and then remove intake manifold and carburetor from the engine. Discard all gaskets and seals.

7. If the manifold is to be replaced, transfer the following to the new manifold, using new gaskets:

    a. Carburetor (and attaching bolts)

    b. Water outlet and thermostat

    c. Heater hose adapter

    d. Choke coil

    e. EGR valve, if so equipped

Installation

1. Clean all sealing and gasket surfaces on the cylinder block, cylinder heads, and intake manifold.

2. Install new end seals and side gaskets as shown in **Figure 15**. Use sealing compound around water passages.

3. Install the manifold **(Figure 16)** and attaching bolts and tighten to specifications (see **Table 1**), using the tightening pattern shown in **Figure 14**.

4. Install the coil bracket and coil.

5. Install the distributor and distributor clamp. Make certain the rotor points toward the mark made during removal. Install the distributor cap.

NOTE: *If the crankshaft was rotated while the distributor was removed, see* **Distributor Removal/Installation** *in Chapter Eight for installation instructions.*

6. Install the alternator upper bracket and adjust the belt tension and tighten bolts.

5

7. Connect the following components:

    a. Battery cables

    b. Radiator hoses

    c. Accelerator linkage

    d. Fuel line

    e. Wires to coil

    f. Power brake vacuum hose

    g. Distributor vacuum hose

    h. Crankcase ventilation hoses

8. Fill the cooling system with coolant, start the engine, and check the manifold and cooling system for leaks. Adjust the timing and idle speed, using the procedures given in Chapter Four.

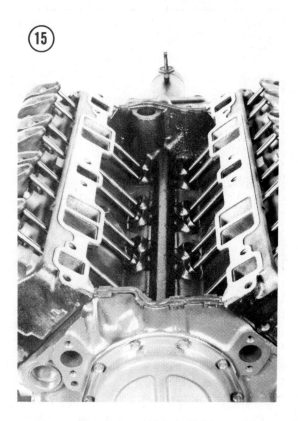

EXHAUST MANIFOLD
(V8 ENGINES)

Removal

> NOTE: *If the engine is equipped with Air Injection Reactor system, remove the* AIR *manifold and tubes, using the procedure given in Chapter Seven.*

1. Disconnect the battery ground cable and remove the pre-heater air stove from air cleaner. Remove the alternator.

2. Remove the flange nuts and lower and support the exhaust pipe assembly.

3. Remove the bolts (end bolts first) and remove the exhaust manifold from the engine. Discard the gaskets.

Installation

1. Clean mating surfaces on manifolds and cylinder heads. Install the manifolds and secure with center bolts.

2. Install the end bolts and snug up all bolts. Tighten the center bolts to specifications (see **Table 1**), then tighten end bolts.

3. Using a new gasket, connect the exhaust pipe to the manifold flange.

4. Install the alternator (if removed), and connect the battery ground cable.

5. Install the air cleaner pre-heater, and AIR manifold and tubes, if so equipped.

6. Start the engine and check for leaks.

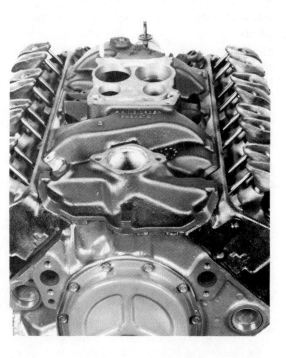

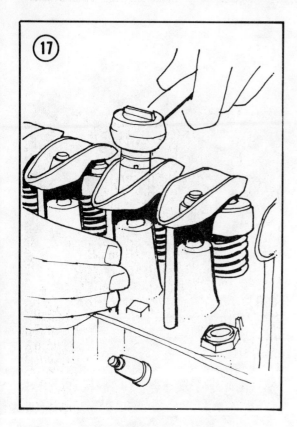

ROCKER ARM COVER
(ALL MODELS)

Removal/Installation

1. Remove the air cleaner and disconnect the crankcase ventilation hose(s) at rocker arm cover(s).

2. Remove all wires from the clips on the rocker arm cover. Remove the air injection hose from the check valve of AIR pipe, if so equipped.

3. Remove the attaching bolts and remove the rocker arm cover. If so equipped, rotate the cover out from under the AIR pipe.

4. To install, clean all gasket surfaces on cylinder head and rocker cover, install a new gasket, and reverse Steps 1 through 3.

VALVE MECHANISM

Removal

1. Remove the rocker arm cover(s), using procedure above.

2. Remove the rocker arm nuts, balls, arms, and pushrods.

NOTE: *Store nuts, balls, arms, and pushrods in a rack, properly identified, so they can be reinstalled in the same locations from which they were removed. A rack can be built by drilling a series of 12 or 16 holes in a piece of wood and marking them with the cylinder numbers.*

Installation and Adjustment
(Inline Engines)

CAUTION
Whenever new rocker arms and/or rocker arm balls are installed, coat bearing surfaces with Molykote or equivalent.

1. Install the pushrods, making certain rods seat in lifter sockets.

2. Install the rocker arms, balls, and nuts. Tighten the nuts until all lash is eliminated.

3. Adjust valves when lifter is on base circle of camshaft lobe as follows:

a. Mark distributor housing with chalk at No. 1 and No. 6 cylinder positions, then disconnect wires from spark plugs and coil. Remove the distributor cap and wires.

b. Crank the engine until the distributor rotor points to No. 1 cylinder position and breaker points are open, and adjust the following valves:

   No. 1 cylinder exhaust and intake

   No. 2 cylinder intake

   No. 3 cylinder exhaust

   No. 4 cylinder intake

   No. 5 cylinder exhaust

c. Back out the adjusting nut until lash is felt at the pushrod, then turn the nut to eliminate all lash. Verify by checking pushrod end play while turning nut (see **Figure 17**). When all play has been removed, tighten the nut one additional full turn (to center lifter plunger).

d. Crank the engine until rotor points to No. 6 cylinder position and breaker points are open. Adjust the following valves:

   No. 2 cylinder exhaust

   No. 3 cylinder intake

No. 4 cylinder exhaust

No. 5 cylinder intake

No. 6 cylinder intake and exhaust

4. Reinstall the distributor cap and spark plug wires.

5. Install the rocker arm cover, using the procedure given above.

6. Adjust the idle speed.

**Installation and Adjustment
(V8 Engines)**

> NOTE: *If new rocker arms and/or rocker arm balls are being installed, coat bearing surfaces with Molykote or equivalent.*

1. Install the pushrods in same locations from which they were removed. Make sure the rods are seated in lifter sockets (**Figure 18**).

2. Install the rocker arms, balls, and nuts.

3. Adjust the valves (hydraulic lifters only) as follows:

a. Crank the engine until the mark on the torsional damper is aligned with the zero mark on the timing tab. Engine is then in No. 1 firing position.

> NOTE: *When the marks are aligned as described above, the engine may be in either No. 1 or No. 6 firing position. To determine No. 1 firing position, hold fingers on No. 1 cylinder valves while cranking engine. If valves are not moving as mark on damper comes near the zero mark, engine is in No. 1 firing position. If valves move, engine is in No. 6 firing position.*

b. With the engine in No. 1 position, adjust the following valves (see Step d):

Exhaust: 1, 3, 4, 8

Intake: 1, 2, 5, 7

c. Crank the engine one revolution to No. 6 firing position and adjust the following valves (see Step d):

Exhaust: 2, 5, 6, 7

Intake: 3, 4, 6, 8

d. Adjust the valves by backing off the adjusting nut (rocker arm stud nut) until

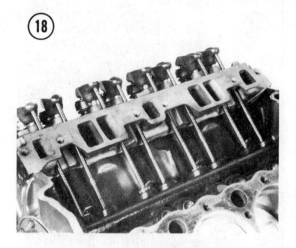

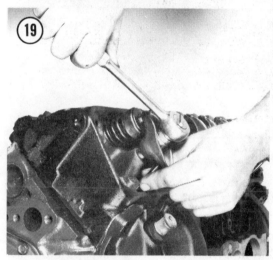

play can be felt in the pushrod. Tighten the nut to the point that all pushrod-to-rocker arm clearance is removed. This can be determined by rotating the pushrod while tightening the nut (see **Figure 19**). When the pushrod does not turn easily, clearance has been eliminated. Now tighten the nut one additional turn to center the hydraulic lifter plunger. No other adjustment is required.

4. Install the rocker arm cover(s) with new gaskets and procedure given elsewhere in this chapter.

HYDRAULIC VALVE LIFTERS

All engines covered are equipped with hydraulic valve lifters, which seldom require at-

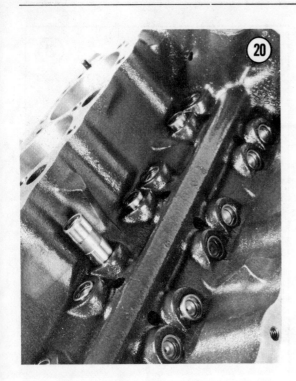

tention and do not require readjustment. Exercise care and cleanliness when handling parts, however.

Valve Lifter Removal
(Inline Engines)

1. Remove the valve mechanism, using procedure given above.

2. Mark No. 1 and No. 6 cylinder positions on the distributor housing, then disconnect the coil and spark plug wires and remove wires and distributor cap.

3. Turn the engine over until the distributor rotor points to No. 1 cylinder position. Disconnect the primary lead at the coil and remove the distributor.

4. Remove the pushrod covers and discard gaskets.

5. Remove the valve lifters.

> NOTE: *Store valve lifters in order in a rack so they may be reinstalled in the same locations from which they were removed.*

Valve Lifter Installation
(Inline Engines)

1. Install the valve lifters in the engine.

> NOTE: *If new valve lifters are being installed, coat the foot of each lifter with Molykote or equivalent.*

2. Install the pushrod covers, using new gaskets. Tighten to 80 in.-lb. (1967-1970 models) or 50 in.-lb. (1971 and later models).

3. Install the distributor and secure with clamp and bolts. Make certain the rotor is pointing to No. 1 cylinder position. Connect primary lead to coil.

4. Reinstall and adjust the valve mechanism and distributor cap and wires, using the procedure given above.

5. Set ignition timing and idle speed, using the procedures given in Chapter Four.

Valve Lifter Removal
(V8 Engines)

1. Remove the intake manifold, using the procedure given above.

2. Remove the valve mechanism, using the procedure given above.

3. Remove the valve lifters (**Figure 20**). Store lifters in a rack so they can be reinstalled in the locations from which they were removed.

Valve Lifter Installation
(V8 Engines)

1. Install the valve lifters.

> NOTE: *If new lifters are being installed, coat feet of lifters with Molykote or equivalent.*

2. Install the intake manifold, using the procedure given above.

3. Install and adjust the valve mechanism, using the procedure given above.

VALVE STEM OIL SEAL
AND/OR VALVE SPRING
(ALL ENGINES)

Removal/Installation

1. Remove the rocker arm cover, using procedure given above.

2. Remove the spark plug, rocker arm, and pushrod on valve to be serviced.

3. Install an air line adapter tool in the spark plug hole and apply compressed air to hold the valves.

> NOTE: *The recommended tool is GM Part No. J-23590. A suitable substitute can be made by removing the porcelain and side electrode from an old spark plug (see* **Figure 21**). *Drive out porcelain, after cutting as shown, by tapping on center electrode. Using a ⅛ in. pipe tap, cut thread in remaining body of plug and assemble air connection as shown. A suitable tool also may be available at an auto parts dealer.*

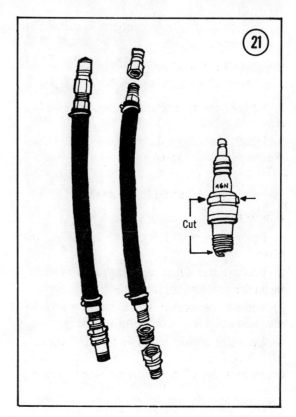

4. Using a valve spring compressor tool (GM Part No. J-5892 or equivalent), applied as shown in **Figure 22**, remove the valve locks, valve cap, and valve spring and damper.

5. Remove the valve stem oil seal (if replacement is required).

6. On inline and small V8 engines, replace as follows:

   a. Set the valve spring and damper, valve shield, and valve cup in place.

   b. Compress the spring and install oil seal in lower groove of stem, taking care that seal is flat and not twisted.

> NOTE: *A light coat of oil on seal will help avoid twisting.*

   c. Install valve locks and release the spring compression. Make sure locks seat properly in upper groove of valve stem.

> NOTE: *A small amount of grease can be used to hold locks in place.*

7. On large (Mark IV) V8 engines, replace as follows:

   a. Coat the new valve stem oil seal with oil and position over valve guide.

> NOTE: *Follow seal installation procedures supplied with service kit.*

   b. Set the valve spring and damper and cap in place.

   c. Compress the spring, install the valve locks, then release compression. Make

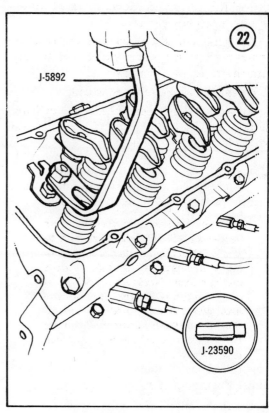

sure that lock seats properly in valve stem groove.

NOTE: *A small amount of grease can be used to hold locks in place.*

8. Remove the air line adapter tool and replace the spark plug.

9. Install and adjust the valve mechanism, using the procedures given above.

CYLINDER HEAD

Removal

1. Drain the cooling system, including the block.

2. Remove the intake and exhaust manifolds, using the procedures given above.

3. Remove the rocker arm cover(s) and valve mechanisms, using procedure given above.

4. On inline engines, remove fuel and vacuum lines from retaining clip at water outlet and disconnect wires from temperature sending units.

5. On vehicles so equipped, disconnect Air Injection Reactor system hoses at check valve, vapor canister hose, and EGR valve.

6. On inline engines, disconnect the radiator upper hose at the water outlet and battery ground strap at the cylinder head.

7. On inline engines, remove the coil.

8. Remove the cylinder head bolts, cylinder head(s), and gasket(s). Support the heads on wood blocks to prevent damage.

Installation

CAUTION
Clean gasket sealing surfaces on both head and block. These surfaces must be free of all foreign matter and nicks or heavy scratches. All threads on bolts and in cylinder blocks must be clean, as dirt will affect bolt torque. If an all-steel head gasket is used, give both sides a thin coat of sealing compound. Do not use sealer on combination metal and asbestos gaskets.

1. Place gasket in position over dowel pins with bead side up.

2. Using care, lower and guide the cylinder head into position.

3. Lightly coat the cylinder head bolt threads with sealing compound and install finger-tight.

4. Tighten the bolts, applying a small amount of torque at a time and following the sequence shown in **Figure 14**, until the specified torque is reached (see **Table 1**).

5. On inline engines, perform the following:

   a. Install the coil.

   b. Connect the engine ground strap and upper radiator hose.

   c. Connect the fuel and vacuum lines in clip at water outlet.

   d. Connect the temperature sender wires.

6. Connect vapor canister hose, if so equipped.

7. Fill the cooling system and check for leaks.

8. Install the intake and exhaust manifolds, using the procedures given above.

9. Install and adjust the valve mechanism, using the procedures given elsewhere in this chapter.

10. Install the rocker arm cover.

11. Connect the AIR pipe, if so equipped.

12. Connect the EGR valve, if so equipped.

13. Start the engine and allow it to warm up to operating temperature. Stop the engine and retighten the cylinder head bolts to specification.

14. Adjust the timing and idle speed, using the procedures given in Chapter Four.

Disassembly

NOTE: *This procedure is performed after rocker arm nuts, balls, and rocker arms have been removed and the cylinder head has been removed from the engine.*

1. Using a spring compressor, compress the valve springs and remove valve keys. Release the compressor and remove the rotators or spring caps, shields (if so equipped), and spring damper. Then remove the oil seals and valve spring shims.

2. Remove the valves from cylinder head and store them in sequence in a rack so they can be replaced in their original positions.

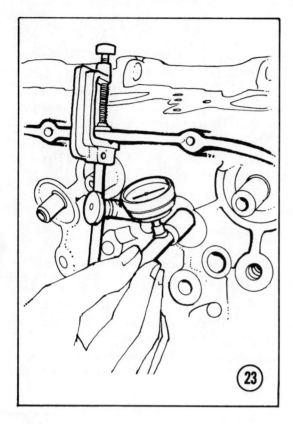

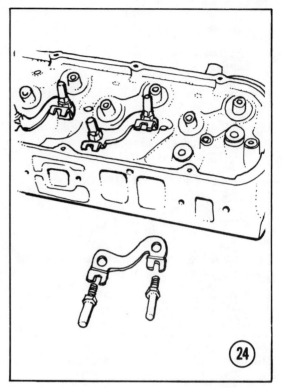

Cleaning

1. Clean all carbon from the combustion chambers and valve ports, using a wire brush.

2. Clean the valve guides, using a suitable tool (GM Part No. J-8101 or equivalent).

3. Clean all carbon and sludge from pushrods, rocker arms, and rocker arm guides.

4. Clean the valve stems and heads, using a buffing wheel.

5. Clean all foreign material from head gasket mating surface.

Inspection

1. Inspect for cracks in exhaust ports, combustion chambers, and water chambers.

2. Check valves for damaged stems, cracked faces, or burned heads.

> NOTE: *Excessive valve stem clearance will result in excessive oil usage and could cause stems to break. Insufficient clearance can result in noisy operation and sticking of valves.*

3. Measure valve stem clearance as follows:

> NOTE: *Valve stem clearance measurement and valve guide reaming, if required, are tasks which should be performed by competent automotive machinists.*

a. Install a dial indicator as shown in **Figure 23,** so that side-to-side (crosswise to head) movement of valve stem will cause direct movement of the indicator stem. The indicator stem must contact the valve stem just above the valve guide.

b. Drop the valve head about $\frac{1}{16}$ inch off valve seat. Move valve stem from side to side, using light pressure, and take indicator reading. If reading exceeds specified tolerance (see **Table 2**), valve guide must be reamed and oversized valves installed.

4. Have valve spring tension checked by an automotive machine shop. Springs should be replaced if not within 10 lb. of specified load (without dampers). See **Table 2.**

5. Inspect the rocker arm studs for wear or damage. On Mark IV engines, inspect the pushrod guides for wear or damage.

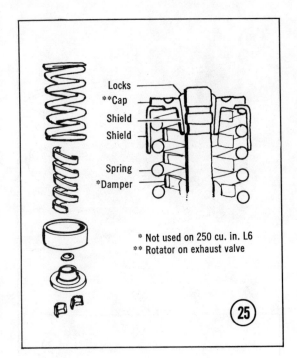

* Not used on 250 cu. in. L6
** Rotator on exhaust valve

(25)

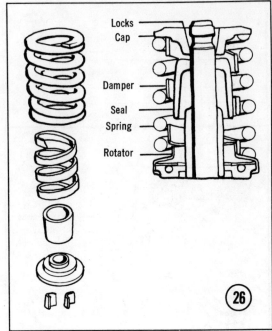

(26)

Repairs

Rocker arm studs and pushrod guides:

1. On Mark IV engines, pushrod guides are related to the cylinder head by rocker arm studs (see **Figure 24**). If necessary, replace and tighten to specifications (see **Table 1**).

> NOTE: *Before assembling rocker arm studs to cylinder head, coat threads with sealer.*

2. On inline and small V8 engines, damaged or loose rocker arm studs should be replaced with oversized studs (available in 0.003 in. and 0.03 in. oversize). This task should be performed by an experienced automotive machinist; holes must be reamed before the oversized studs can be installed and special tools and skills are required.

Valve guide bores, valve seats, and valves (all models):

The reconditioning of valve guide bores, valve seats, and valves requires the use of precision special equipment and should not be attempted by the home mechanic. These tasks can be performed competently and economically by a well-equipped automotive machine shop. Specifications are given in **Table 2**.

Assembly

1. Insert a valve in the port from which it was removed.

2. Assemble related parts, including spring as follows:

  a. For inline and small V8 engines:

> NOTE: *If the engine uses exhaust valve rotators, make certain that the shorter springs are used on exhaust valves.*

    (1) Position valve spring shim, spring, damper (if used), shield and cap or rotator on valve stem (**Figure 25**).

    (2) Compress the spring with a spring compressor.

    (3) Install the oil seal in stem lower groove. Make sure the seal is not twisted.

    (4) Install the valve locks and remove the compressor. Make sure that lock seats in upper valve stem groove.

  b. On Mark IV V8 engines:

    (1) Install the shim on valve spring seat and install a new oil seal over the valve and valve guide.

    (2) Install the valve spring (with damper) and valve cap (see **Figure 26**).

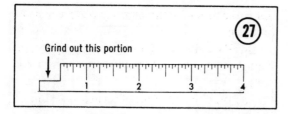

Grind out this portion

See specifications

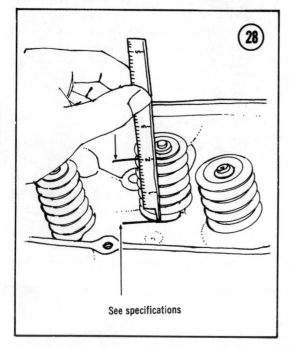

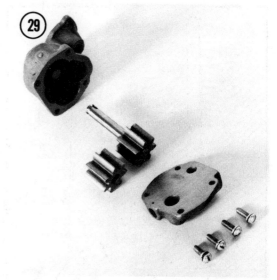

(3) Compress the spring with a spring compressor.

(4) Install the valve locks and release the compressor. Make sure locks seat in the valve stem groove.

3. Install the remaining valves.

4. Check height of installed springs against specification (see **Table 2**). A cutaway scale (see **Figure 27**) will help. Measure from shim or spring seat top to valve spring or valve spring shield top (see **Figure 28**). If height exceeds specification, install a valve seat shim (approximately ¼₆ in. thick). Do not shim spring to give an installed height under the specified minimum.

OIL PUMP

Removal/Installation

1. Remove the oil pan.

2. On inline engines, remove 2 flange mounting

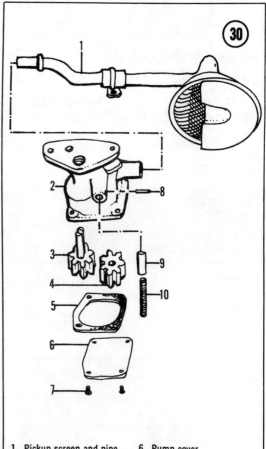

1. Pickup screen and pipe	6. Pump cover
2. Pump body	7. Screws
3. Drive gear and shaft	8. Retaining pin
4. Idler gear	9. Pressure regulator valve
5. Cover gasket	10. Pressure regulator spring

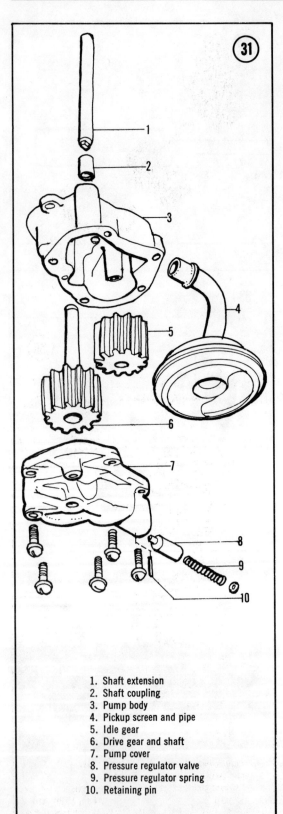

1. Shaft extension
2. Shaft coupling
3. Pump body
4. Pickup screen and pipe
5. Idle gear
6. Drive gear and shaft
7. Pump cover
8. Pressure regulator valve
9. Pressure regulator spring
10. Retaining pin

bolts, then remove the pump and screeen as an assembly.

3. On V8 engines, remove the pump-to-rear main bearing cap bolt and remove pump and seal.

4. To install the oil pump, proceed as follows:

   a. On inline engines, align the oil pump drive shaft to match with distributor tang and install oil pump. Position flange over lower distributor bushing. No gasket is required.

      NOTE: *If the oil pump does not slide easily into place, remove and realign slot with distributor tang.*

   b. On V8 engines, assemble the pump and extension shaft to rear main bearing cap, aligning slot in shaft top end with tang on lower end of distributor shaft. Install the bolt and tighten to specification (see **Table 1**).

      NOTE: *The bottom edge of oil pump screen should be parallel to oil pan rails.*

Disassembly

Refer to **Figures 29, 30, and 31** for this procedure.

1. Remove the pump cover attaching screws and the pump cover. On inline engines, remove the gasket.

   NOTE: *Mark gear teeth so same indexing of teeth can be duplicated when reassembling pump.*

2. Remove the idler and drive gears and drive shaft from the pump body.

3. Remove the retaining pin, then remove the pressure regulator valve and related parts.

4. If replacement is indicated, mount the pump in a soft-jawed vise and extract the pickup screen and pipe from pump body.

Cleaning and Inspection

1. Wash all parts in solvent and dry them with compressed air.

2. Inspect the pump body for cracks and signs of wear.

3. Inspect the gears for excessive wear or damage.

4. Check the shaft of the drive gear for looseness in the pump body.

5. Inspect the inside of the cover for wear which would allow oil to leak past the ends of the gears.

6. Inspect the pickup screen and pipe for damage.

7. Check the pressure regulator valve for fit.

> NOTE: *Pump body and gears cannot be replaced separately. If damage or excessive wear is present, entire pump must be replaced.*

Assembly

Refer to **Figures 29, 30, and 31** for this procedure.

> CAUTION
> *If pickup screen and pipe assembly was removed, install new assembly. Do not attempt to install old assembly; loss of press fit could result in loss of oil pressure.*

1. To install a new pickup screen and pipe assembly, mount the pump in a soft-jawed vise. Apply sealer to the end of the pipe and tap it into place with a plastic hammer.

> CAUTION
> *Avoid twisting, shearing, or collapsing pipe while installing. Screen on inline engines must be parallel to bottom of oil pan when pump is installed.*

2. Install the pressure regulator valve and related parts with the retaining pin.

3. Install the drive gear and shaft in the body, then install the idler gear so that the teeth mesh in original position and the smooth side of the gear is facing the pump cover opening.

4. Install the pump cover (using new gasket on inline engine) and tighten screws to 70 in.-lb. (inline engine) or 80 in.-lb. (V8 engine).

5. Check for smooth operation by turning the pump drive shaft by hand.

REAR MAIN OIL
SEAL REPLACEMENT

> NOTE: *Upper and lower seal must be replaced as a unit. Install seal with lip facing front of engine.*

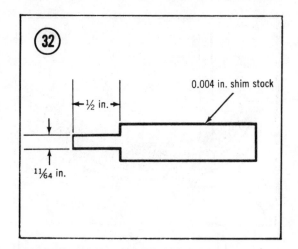

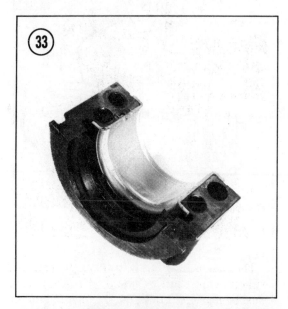

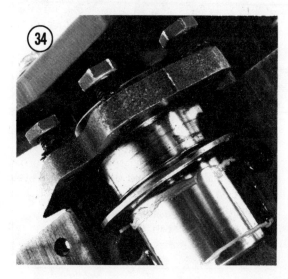

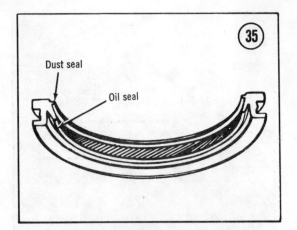

Dust seal

Oil seal

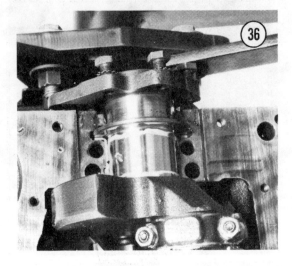

The rear main bearing seal can be replaced without crankshaft removed. However, care must be taken to protect the sealing bead on the outside diameter of the seal. An installation tool (see **Figure 32**) can be used to protect the bead.

1. Remove the oil pan.

2. Remove the oil pump, using the procedure given above.

3. Remove the rear main bearing cap. Use a small screwdriver to remove the seal half from bearing cap (**Figure 33**).

4. Tap one end of the upper half of the seal with a small hammer and brass pin punch (see **Figure 34**) until other end protrudes enough to grasp and remove with pliers.

5. Use a non-abrasive cleaner to remove all traces of sealant and other foreign matter from cylinder block, crankshaft, and bearing cap.

6. Inspect all components for defects on sealing surfaces, case assembly, and crankshaft. Coat seal lips and bead with engine oil, keeping oil off seal mating ends.

7. Position the tool tip between crankshaft and cylinder block seal seat.

8. Position the seal between crankshaft and tip of tool so that sealing bead contacts tip of tool, making certain that seal lip points toward front of engine (see **Figure 35**).

9. Roll seal around crankshaft using tool as a "shoehorn" to protect seal bead.

CAUTION
Tool must remain in position until seal is positioned with both ends flush with block to protect seal bead from sharp edge of seal seat surface in cylinder block.

10. Remove the tool. Use care not to remove or displace seal.

11. Again using the tool as a "shoehorn", install the seal half in the bearing cap. Feed the seal into the cap, using light pressure with thumb and finger.

12. Apply sealant as shown in **Figure 36** and install the bearing cap. Take care to avoid getting sealant on the seal split line. Tighten to specifications (see **Table 1**).

MAIN BEARINGS

Precision insert type bearing are used in all engines covered, and shims are not required for fitting. At any time bearing clearance is found to be excessive, a new bearing (both upper and lower halves) is required. Bearings are available in standard and 0.001, 0.002, 0.009, 0.010, 0.020, and 0.030 in. undersize. Close tolerances are obtained in production by selective fitting of rod and main bearing inserts. Thus one half of a bearing may be standard and the other half 0.001 in. undersize (this decreases clearance by 0.0005 in.). If a production crankshaft cannot be properly fitted in this manner it is ground 0.009 in. undersize on the main journals only and again is selectively fitted. If your engine has a 0.009 in. undersize crankshaft, the counterweight forward of the center main journal will

be stamped with ".009", and the number 9 will be stamped on the block at the left front oil pan rail.

> NOTE: *In repair work, shimming may be required if bearing caps are replaced for any reason. Laminated shims are available.*

Inspection

As a rule, the lower bearing half shows greater wear and distress from fatigue. If inspection shows lower half is suitable for use, it can usually be assumed that the upper half also is satisfactory without removing it. If the lower half is unsatisfactory, replace both halves (never replace only one half of a main bearing).

Checking Bearing Clearance

> NOTE: *Use Plastigage or equivalent for checking bearing clearances. All bearing cap bolts should be tightened to specification, and surfaces to be measured should be wiped free of oil. If engine is still installed in vehicle, support crankshaft at flywheel and torsional damper to remove clearance from upper bearing half.*

1. With the oil pan and pump removed, and starting with rear main bearing, remove cap and wipe oil from journal and bearing half in cap.

2. Place a piece of Plastigage the full width of the bearing on the journal, parallel to crankshaft (see **Figure 37**).

> CAUTION
> *Do not rotate crankshaft while Plastigage is between journal and bearing, as false reading will be obtained.*

3. Install the bearing cap and evenly tighten bolts to specification (see **Table 1**).

4. Remove the bearing cap. Flattened Plastigage will be found either on journal or bearing.

5. Using the scale printed on the Plastigage package, measure the width of compressed plastic at its widest point. Do not remove plastic before measurement is made (see **Figure 38**).

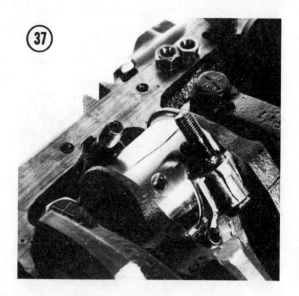

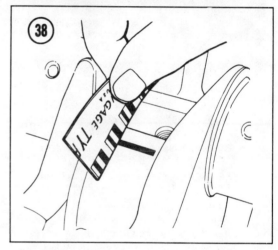

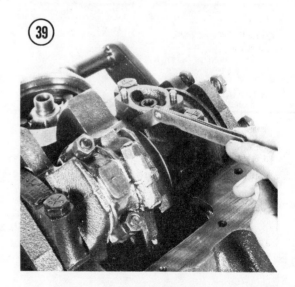

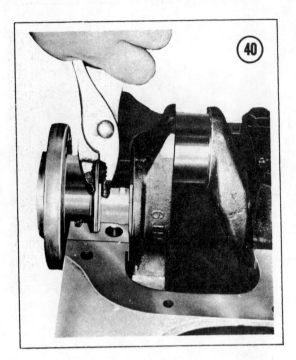

NOTE: *As a rule, main bearings wear evenly and are not out-of-round. If a bearing is fitted to an out-of-round journal (0.001 in. max.), the bearing must be fitted to the maximum diameter of the journal. Otherwise rapid wear of the bearing can be expected. If the flattened plastic tapers toward the center or ends, and a difference of more than 0.001 in. is indicated, the crankshaft journal should be checked for taper, and corrected if required, before proceeding.*

6. If clearance is within specifications, the insert is satisfactory. If not, replace both halves of the insert.

NOTE: *If a new bearing cap is being installed and clearance is less than 0.001 in., inspect for nicks and burrs. If none are found, use shims to obtain specified clearance.*

7. If a standard or 0.001 in. or 0.002 in. undersize bearing fails to produce proper clearance, the journal must be ground for the next undersize bearing.

8. Repeat the above steps for the remaining bearings, then rotate the crankshaft to verify that excessive drag is not present.

9. Measure crankshaft end play (see specifications, **Table 2**) by forcing the crankshaft to extreme front. Measure at front end of rear main bearing. See **Figure 39**.

10. Install new rear main bearing oil seal, using the procedure given above.

**Main Bearing Replacement
(With Crankshaft Removal)**

1. Remove and inspect the crankshaft.

2. Remove the old bearings from cylinder block and caps.

3. Select new bearings of correct size (see *Checking Bearing Clearance* procedure above) and coat them with engine oil. Install in the cylinder block and bearing caps.

4. Install the crankshaft in cylinder block and install bearing caps with arrows pointing to front of engine.

5. Install the bolts and tighten to specification (see **Table 1**).

**Main Bearing Replacement
(Without Crankshaft Removal)**

1. Remove oil pan, oil pump, and spark plugs from engine. Remove the cap from the main bearing to be replaced and remove the bearing from the cap.

2. On inline engine crankshafts, the rear main bearing journal has no oil hole. Rear main bearing upper half is removed as follows:

   a. Use hammer and small drift punch to start bearing half out of block.

   b. Grasp the bearing thrust surface and oil slinger with a pair of pliers (with taped jaws) and rotate the crankshaft to remove the bearing half (see **Figure 40**).

   c. Select a new bearing of correct size and coat it with oil. Insert unnotched end between crankshaft and notched side of block.

   d. Using pliers as in Step b, rotate the bearing half into place. During the last fourth of movement, pliers may be used on slinger only, or, if care is taken, bearing may be tapped into place with a soft drift.

3. All remaining main bearing journals on in-line crankshafts and all V8 crankshaft journals have oil holes. Upper bearing halves may be installed as follows:

   a. Install a long cotter pin in the oil hole in the crankshaft journal and rotate the crankshaft clockwise (viewed from front of engine) to roll out insert.

   b. Select and oil a correct size upper bearing (see *Checking Bearing Clearance* above) and insert unnotched end between crankshaft and notched side of block. Rotate into place and remove the cotter pin from the journal oil hole.

4. Oil a new lower bearing insert and install it in bearing cap. Install the cap with arrows pointing to engine front. Tighten cap bolts to specifications (see **Table 1**).

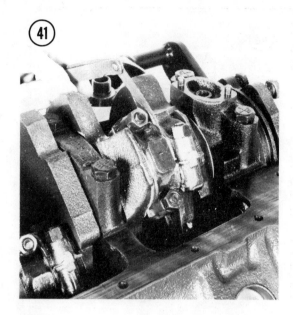

CONNECTING ROD BEARING REPLACEMENT

CAUTION
Do not file rods or rod caps to obtain specified clearance. If clearance is excessive, new bearings are required. Bearings are available in standard and 0.001 in. and 0.002 in. undersize for use with new and used standard size crankshafts, and in 0.010 in. and 0.020 in. undersize for use with reconditioned crankshafts.

1. Remove the oil pan and oil pump.

2. Remove the connecting rod cap and bearing, and inspect the bearing for wear or damage. Do not reuse it if either is in evidence.

3. Clean bearings and crankpin to remove all oil.

4. Using a micrometer, measure crankpin for out-of-round or taper. If not within specifications (see **Table 2**), replace or recondition the crankshaft. If it is within tolerances and a new bearing is to be installed, measure maximum diameter of the crankpin to determine required bearing size.

CAUTION
If a new bearing is fitted to the minimum diameter of an out-of-round crankpin, rapid bearing failure will result.

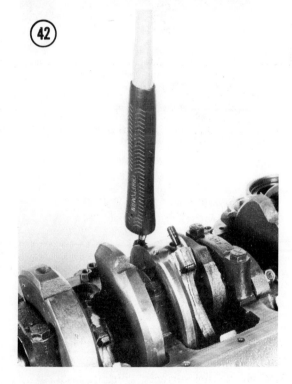

5. Install the new or used bearing and check clearance with Plastigage or equivalent as follows:

   a. Place a piece of Plastigage on crankpin (parallel to crankshaft). Plastigage should cover the full width contacted by the bearing (see **Figure 37**).

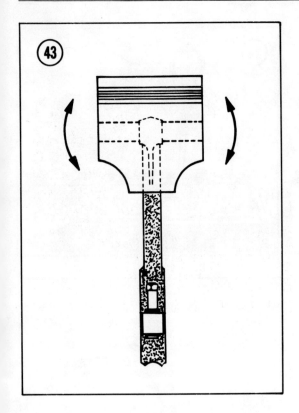

b. Install the bearing halves in the connecting rod and bearing cap.

c. Install the connecting rod and cap on crankpin and tighten nuts evenly to specification (see **Table 1**).

CAUTION
Do not turn the crankshaft while Plastigage is installed. To do so will distort Plastigage which will result in incorrect measurement.

d. Remove the cap and measure Plastigage at widest point, using the scale on the Plastigage package (see **Figure 38**).

6. If clearance is not within specified tolerances, select and install a different, correct size bearing and remeasure clearance.

7. Coat bearing surfaces with oil, install the rod and cap on crankpin, and tighten nuts to specification.

8. When all bearings have been installed, tap each connecting rod lightly to assure clearance, and measure side clearances (see **Table 2**) as shown in **Figure 41**.

9. Replace the oil pump and oil pan.

CONNECTING ROD AND PISTON ASSEMBLIES

Removal

1. Remove the oil pan, oil pump, and cylinder head, using the procedures given earlier in this chapter.

2. If ridges or deposits are found in the upper end of the cylinder bore, remove them as follows:

a. Turn the crankshaft until piston is at bottom of the stroke and place a cloth on top of piston to catch cuttings.

b. Use a ridge reamer to remove the ridge or deposit.

c. Turn crankshaft until piston is at top of its stroke and remove the cloth and all cuttings.

3. Inspect rods and bearing caps for cylinder identification markings. If none are present, mark rods and caps so they can be replaced in proper cylinders.

4. Remove bearing caps and push out assembly as shown in **Figure 42**. Tape ends of rod and threads of bolts to prevent cylinder wall damage and push out the rod and piston assembly with a piece of hardwood or a hammer handle.

NOTE: *It will be necessary to rotate crankshaft slightly to remove some assemblies.*

Disassembly

1. Remove the piston rings with a ring expander tool.

2. Support the rod tightly and rock piston as shown in **Figure 43**. Any rocking motion (do not confuse with sliding) indicates wear in the piston pin, rod bushing, pin bore, or more likely, a combination of all three. Mark the assembly for further inspection.

NOTE: *Disassembly and assembly of the piston, piston pin, and rod requires an arbor press and special tools. These jobs are best performed by an automotive machine shop, as the use of makeshift tools could result in damage.*

Inspection

1. Clean the pistons thoroughly in solvent. Scrape carbon deposits from top and grooves. Take care to avoid damage to piston.

CAUTION

Do not use wire brush on piston skirts.

2. Examine grooves for burrs, dented edges, and side wear. Pay particular attention to top compression ring groove, as it usually wears more than the others.

3. Measure piston-to-cylinder clearance, using the procedure given below.

4. If damage or wear indicates piston replacement, select a new piston as described in *Piston Clearance and Selection* procedure.

5. Measure all parts marked in Step 2 of the *Disassembly* procedure above with micrometer and dial bore gauge to determine which parts are worn (this can be done by an automotive machine shop if measuring equipment is not available). Replace piston and pin set as a unit if either or both are worn.

Piston Clearance and Selection

1. Make sure the cylinder walls are clean and dry.

2. Measure the cylinder bore with a telescope bore gauge. Make measurement 2½ in. from top of bore (see **Figure 44**).

3. Measure the outside diameter of piston at the bottom of the skirt (see **Figure 45**).

4. The difference between the 2 readings is the piston clearance. Compare difference with the specification in **Table 3**. If greater than specified, select another piston size from **Table 2**.

Piston Ring Installation

> NOTE: *All compression rings have marks on their upper sides. Install these rings with marks toward top of piston. Oil control rings are made of 3 pieces, including 2 rails and a spacer.*

1. Select new rings of correct size for the piston being used.

2. Insert the compression ring into bore of cylinder, about ¼ in. above ring travel. Square

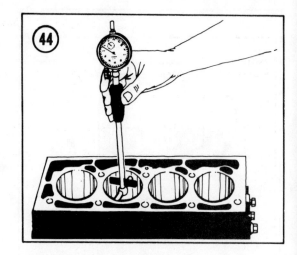

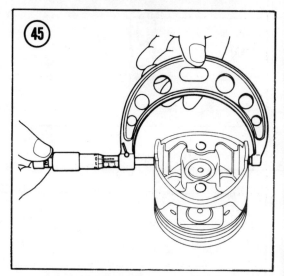

the ring with the cylinder wall by tapping it in with a piston. Use a feeler gauge to measure the gap (see **Figure 46**) and compare to specifications (see **Table 2**). If the gap is too large, fit another ring. If it is smaller than specified, hold a small file in a vise, grip the ends of ring with fingers, and carefully enlarge the gap as shown in **Figure 47**.

3. Fit each cylinder with 2 compression rings, using the instructions in Step 2.

4. Roll each ring around its piston groove as shown in **Figure 48** to check for binding. Minor binding may be cleaned up with a fine cut file, if care is used.

5. Using a ring expander tool, install oil ring spacer in groove and, except on 1970 or later in-line engines, install the anti-rotational tang in

Table 3 PISTON SIZE CHART

Engine Displacement	Years	Standard (in.)	0.010 in.	0.020 in.	0.030 in.	0.040 in.
230	1967-69	3.8750-3.8760	3.8760-3.8770	3.8937-3.8957	3.9037-3.9057	3.9137-3.9157
250-307	1967-70	3.8750-3.8760	3.8760-3.8770	3.8937-3.8957	3.9037-3.9057	—
250-307	1971	3.8750-3.8760	3.8760-3.8770	3.8935-3.8955	3.9035-3.9055	
250-307	1972-on	3.8750-3.8760	3.8760-3.8770	—	3.9035-3.9055	—
302	1968-1969	3.9953-3.9963	3.9963-3.9973	4.0138-4.0158	4.0252-4.0272	—
305	1976-on	3.7360-3.7370	3.7370-3.7380	—	3.7390-3.7400	—
327 350	1967-69 1967-70	4.0000-4.0010	4.0010-4.0020	4.0187-4.0207	4.0287-4.0370	—
350	1971	3.9998-4.0008	4.0008-4.0010	4.0183-4.0203	4.0283-4.0303	—
350	1972-on	3.9998-4.0008	4.0008-4.0018	—	4.0283-4.0303	—
402	1971-72	4.1237-4.1247	4.1245-4.1257	4.1450-4.1470[1]	4.1550-4.1570	—
454[2]	1970	4.2455-4.2465	4.2465-4.2475	—	4.2760-4.2780	—

1. 1971 only.   2. 0.060 in. oversize = 4.3060-4.3080.

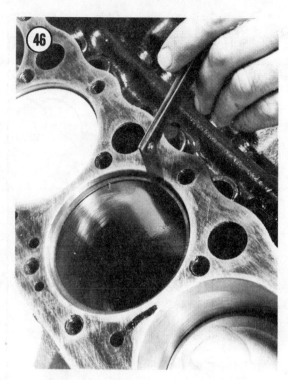

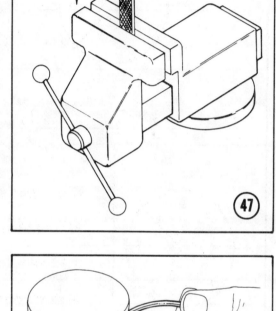

the oil hole. Hold spacer ends butted and install lower steel rail with gap correctly located. Then install the upper steel rail with the gap correctly located (see **Figure 49** for gap locations).

6. Flex the oil ring assembly in its groove to make sure it is free and binding does not occur at any point. Minor binding can be cleaned up with a fine cut file.

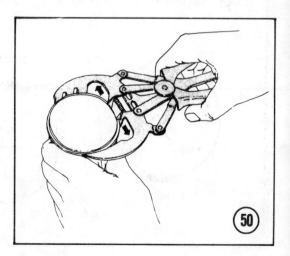

7. Install 2 compression rings, marked side up, using ring expander tool (see **Figure 50**). Make certain the rings fitted to each cylinder are installed on the correct pistons.

8. Check the side clearance of each ring as shown in **Figure 51**. Compare with specifications for your engine (see **Table 2**).

9. Verify that ring gaps are correctly positioned as shown in **Figure 49**.

Piston Installation

> NOTE: *Used pistons must be installed in the cylinders from which they were removed, and new pistons must be installed in the cylinders to which they were fitted.*

1. Coat cylinder walls, piston, and rings with light engine oil.

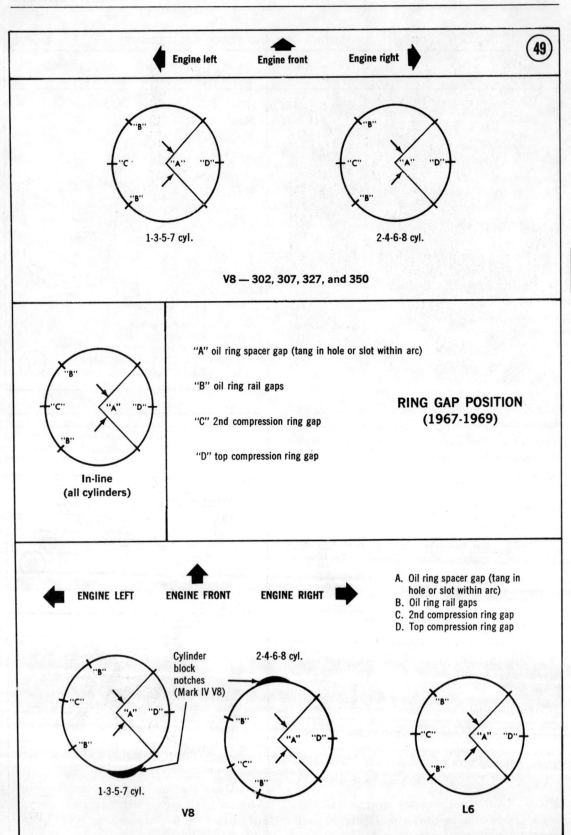

Engine left   Engine front   Engine right

49

1-3-5-7 cyl.   2-4-6-8 cyl.

V8 — 302, 307, 327, and 350

5

"A" oil ring spacer gap (tang in hole or slot within arc)

"B" oil ring rail gaps

"C" 2nd compression ring gap

"D" top compression ring gap

**RING GAP POSITION
(1967-1969)**

In-line
(all cylinders)

ENGINE LEFT   ENGINE FRONT   ENGINE RIGHT

A. Oil ring spacer gap (tang in hole or slot within arc)
B. Oil ring rail gaps
C. 2nd compression ring gap
D. Top compression ring gap

Cylinder block notches (Mark IV V8)

2-4-6-8 cyl.

1-3-5-7 cyl.

V8   **L6**

Table 4   CONNECTING ROD AND PISTON RELATIONSHIP

Engine (cu.in.)	Piston Type (Figure 52)	Side of Piston Aligned with Connecting Rod Bearing Tangs
230	A	Notch to front
250	C	Notch to front
302 (1968)	B	All cylinders; left side
302 (1969)	D	All cylinders; left side
305, 307	A	Cylinders 1-3-5-7; left side Cylinders 2-4-6-8; right side
327, 350 (1967)	A	Cylinders 1-3-5-7; right side Cylinders 2-4-6-8; left side
327, 350 (1968-1969)	A	Cylinders 1-3-5-7; left side Cylinders 2-4-6-8; right side
350 (1970, 250 hp)	A	Cylinders 1-3-5-7; left side Cylinders 2-4-6-8; right side
350 (1971-1978)	F or G	Cylinders 1-3-5-7; left side Cylinders 2-4-6-8; right side
402	E	Cylinders 1-3-5-7; left side Cylinders 2-4-6-8; right side
454	E	All cylinders; left side

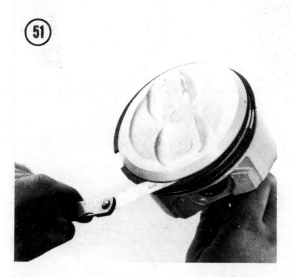

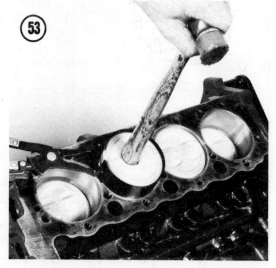

2. With bearing caps removed, tape bearing end of rod, including bolt threads, and have an assistant help you to slowly guide rods into place.

3. Install each piston in its correct cylinder bore. Orient rod as shown in **Figure 52** and **Table 4**.

4. Compress the rings with a ring compressor tool and press pistons into bores with a wooden hammer handle (**Figure 53**).

5. Guide the bearing carefully onto the journal. Install bearing caps and check clearances as described above. Tighten nuts to specifications (**Table 1**).

PISTON — VIEWED FROM TOP

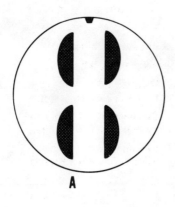

A

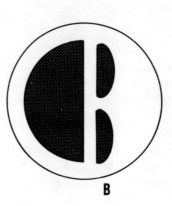

B

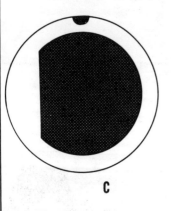

C

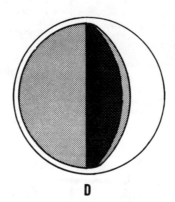

D

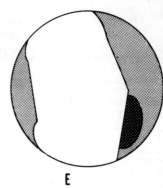

E

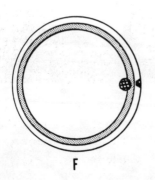

F

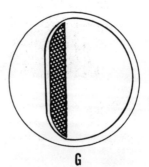

G

52

CAMSHAFT

Camshaft removal and installation procedures are given in Steps 13 and 3 of the *General Overhaul* and *Reassembly* sequences, respectively.

Inspection

> NOTE: *If measuring equipment is not available, take the camshaft to an automotive machinist for the measurements described in this procedure.*

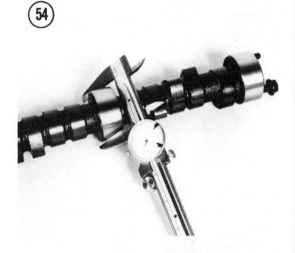

1. Measure the camshaft bearing journals for out-of-round condition, using a micrometer or vernier caliper (**Figure 54**). Replace the camshaft if out-of-round exceeds 0.001 in.
2. Mount the camshaft in V-blocks, and, using a dial indicator, check bearing journals for alignment. Replace camshaft if out of alignment more than 0.0015 in.
3. On inline engines, check the gear and thrust plate for wear and damage. Check end play (**Figure 55**). End play should be between 0.001 and 0.005 in.

Oil Nozzle Replacement
(Inline Engines)

1. Pull out the nozzle with pliers (**Figure 56**).
2. Drive a new nozzle in with a plastic hammer. Make sure the oil hole is vertical.

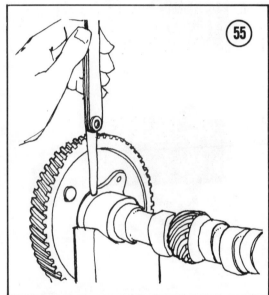

Camshaft Gear Replacement
(Inline Engines)

Replacement of camshaft gear requires an arbor press and special tools. This job should be referred to an automotive machine shop.

Camshaft Bearing Replacement

Bearing replacement requires special tools and adequate substitutes are not easily improvised. An automotive machine shop will replace the bearings for a small fee.

CRANKSHAFT

The engine must be removed from the vehicle in order to remove the crankshaft. The procedures for crankshaft removal; bearing

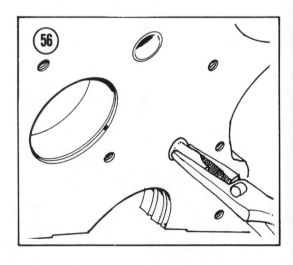

removal, inspection, and replacement; and installation are given in Step 15 of the *General Overhaul* sequence and Step 1 of the *Reassembly* sequence.

Crankshaft Inspection

> NOTE: *If measuring equipment is not available, take the crankshaft to an automotive machine shop to have the checks described in this procedure performed.*

1. Using a micrometer, check crankshaft journals and crankpins for out-of-round, taper, or undersize. See **Table 2** for specifications.

2. Mount the front and rear main journals in V-blocks and check at intermediate main journals with a dial indicator for runout. See **Table 2** for specifications.

3. Replace the crankshaft or have it reconditioned if it is out of specifications.

CYLINDER BLOCK

Cleaning and Inspection

1. Clean the block with solvent and remove all foreign material from gasket surfaces.

2. Remove the plugs from oil galleries and clean all oil passages.

3. Clean and inspect all water passages.

4. Check for cracks in cylinder walls, water jacket, valve lifter bores, and main bearing webs.

5. Check cylinder walls for out-of-round, taper, or excessive ridges, using a dial indicator (this job should be referred to an automotive machinist). If cylinders exceed specifications, honing or reboring will be required.

5

Table 1   TIGHTENING TORQUES

Bolt Size	Usage	Inline	Small V8	Mark IV V8
¼ - 20	Camshaft thrust plate	80 in. lb.	——	——
	Crankcase front cover	80 in. lb.	80 in.-lb.	80 in.-lb.
	Flywheel housing cover	80 in. lb.	80 in.-lb.	80 in.-lb.
	Oil filter bypass valve	——	80 in.-lb.	80 in.-lb.
	Oil pan (to crankcase)	80 in.-lb.	80 in.-lb.	80 in.-lb.
	Oil pan (to front cover) 1967-1973	55 in.-lb.	——	80 in.-lb.
	Oil pan (to front cover) 1974-on	50 in.-lb.	——	55 in.-lb.
	Oil pump cover	70 in.-lb.	80 in.-lb.	80 in.-lb.
	Rocker arm cover 1967-1970	55 in.-lb.	55 in.-lb.	50 in.-lb.
	Rocker arm cover 1971-on	45 in.-lb.	45 in.-lb.	50 in.-lb.
¹¹⁄₃₂ - 24	Connecting rod cap 1967-1968	35 ft.-lb.	35 ft.-lb.	——
	Connecting rod cap 1969-on	35 ft.-lb.	——	——
⁵⁄₁₆ - 18	Camshaft sprocket	20 ft.-lb.	20 ft.-lb.	20 ft.-lb.
	Clutch pressure plate	20 ft.-lb.	——	——
	Oil pan (to crankcase) 1967-1970	125 in.-lb.	65 in.-lb.	135 in.-lb.
	Oil pan (to crankcase) 1971-1973	75 in.-lb.	65 in.-lb.	135 in.-lb.
	Oil pan (to crankcase) 1974-on	75 in.-lb.	265 in.-lb.	135 in.-lb.
	Oil pump	115 in.-lb.	——	——
	Pushrod cover 1967-1970	80 in.-lb.	——	——
	Pushrod cover 1971-on	50 in.-lb.	——	——
	Water pump	15 ft.-lb.	——	——
⅜ - 16	Clutch pressure plate	——	——	35 ft.-lb.
	Distributor clamp 1967-1968	10 ft.-lb.	10 ft.-lb.	10 ft.-lb.
	Distributor clamp 1969-on	20 ft.-lb.	20 ft.-lb.	20 ft.-lb.
	Flywheel housing	30 ft.-lb.	30 ft.-lb.	30 ft.-lb.
	Manifold, exhaust	——	——	20 ft.-lb. ①
	Manifold (exhaust to inlet) 1967-1972	25 ft.-lb.	——	——
	Manifold (exhaust to inlet) 1973-on	30 ft.-lb.	——	——
	Manifold (inlet)	——	30 ft.-lb.	30 ft.-lb.
	Manifold-to-head (outer) 1967-1971	20 ft.-lb.	——	——
	Manifold-to-head (all others) 1967-1971	30 ft.-lb.	——	——
	Manifold-to-head 1972-on	35 ft.-lb.	——	——
	Thermostat housing	30 ft.-lb.	——	——
	Water outlet 1967-1970	20 ft.-lb.	20 ft.-lb.	20 ft.-lb.
	Water outlet 1971-on	30 ft.-lb.	30 ft.-lb.	30 ft.-lb.
	Water pump	——	30 ft.-lb.	30 ft.-lb.

(continued)

Table 1   TIGHTENING TORQUES (continued)

Bolt Size	Usage	Inline	Small V8	Mark IV V8
3/8 - 24	Connecting rod cap 1967-1968	——	——	50 ft.-lb.
	Connecting rod cap 1969-on	——	45 ft.-lb.	50 ft.-lb.
7/16 - 14	Cylinder head	——	65 ft.-lb.	80 ft.-lb.
	Main bearing cap 1967	65 ft.-lb.	80 ft.-lb.	——
	Main bearing cap 1968-1970	65 ft.-lb.	75 ft.-lb. ②	——
	Main bearing cap 1971-1975	65 ft.-lb.	70 ft.-lb. ②	——
	Main bearing cap 1976-on	65 ft.-lb.	80 ft.-lb. ③	——
	Oil pump 1967-1969	——	65 ft.-lb.	65 ft.-lb.
	Oil pump 1970-on	65 ft.-lb.	65 ft.-lb.	65 ft.-lb.
	Rocker arm stud	——	——	50 ft.-lb.
7/16 - 20	Flywheel 1967-1968	60 ft.-lb.	60 ft.-lb.	60 ft.-lb.
	Flywheel 1969-on	60 ft.-lb.	60 ft.-lb.	65 ft.-lb.
	Torsional damper 1967-1968 (327)	——	60 ft.-lb.	——
	Torsional damper 1969 (302 and 350)	——	60 ft.-lb.	——
	Torsional damper 1970-on	60 ft.-lb.	60 ft.-lb.	——
1/2 - 13	Cylinder head	95 ft.-lb.	——	——
	Main bearing cap (2 bolt) 1967-1968	——	——	95 ft.-lb.
	Main bearing cap (4 bolt) 1967	——	——	115 ft.-lb.
	Main bearing cap (4 bolt) 1968-1970	——	——	105 ft.-lb.
	Main bearing cap 1971-on	——	——	110 ft.-lb.
1/2 - 14	Temperature sending unit	20 ft.-lb.	20 ft.-lb.	20 ft.-lb.
1/2 - 20	Torsional damper	——	——	85 ft.-lb.
	Oil filter	Hand tight	25 ft.-lb.	25 ft.-lb.
	Oil pan drain plug	20 ft.-lb.	20 ft.-lb.	20 ft.-lb.
14mm (5/8 in.)	Spark plug 1967-1970	25 ft.-lb.	25 ft.-lb.	25 ft.-lb.
	Spark plug 1971-on	15 ft.-lb.	15 ft.-lb.	15 ft.-lb.

① Inside bolts on 302, 307, and 350 engines = 30 ft.-lb.

② Outer bolts on engines with 4 bolt caps = 65 ft.-lb.

③ Outer bolts only (2, 3, and 4) = 70 ft.-lb.

5

Table 2   ENGINE SPECIFICATIONS

	230 CID L6	250 CID L6
General		
Bore	3⅞ in.	3⅞ in.
Stroke	3.25 in.	3.53 in.
Firing order	1-5-3-6-2-4	1-5-3-6-2-4
Cylinder bore		
Diameter	3.8745 in.	3.8775 in.
Out-of-round, new (wear limit)	0.0005 in.	(0.005 in. maximum)
Piston		
Clearance in bore	0.0005 in.	0.0015 in.
Piston rings		
Number per cylinder	3	3
Ring end gap		
Top	0.010 in.	0.010-0.020 in.
2nd	0.010 in.	0.010-0.020 in.
Oil control	0.015 in.	0.015-0.055 in.
Ring side clearance		
Top	0.0012 in.	0.0012-0.0027 in.
2nd	0.0012 in.	0.0012-0.0032 in.
Oil control	0.000 in.	0.002-0.005 in.
Piston pin		
Diameter	0.9270 in.	0.9270-0.9273 in.
Clearance		
In piston	0.00015 in.	0.0015-0.00025 in.
In rod	0.0008 in.	0.0008-0.0016 in.
Crankshaft		
End play	0.002 in.	0.002-0.006 in.
Main bearing journal		
Diameter (all)	2.2983 in.	2.2983-2.993 in.
Taper	0.0002 in. maximum	0.0002 in. maximum
Out-of-round	0.0002 in. maximum	0.0002 in. maximum

(continued)

Table 2   ENGINE SPECIFICATIONS   (continued)

	230 CID L6	250 CID L6
Crankshaft (continued)		
Main bearing clearance (all)	0.0003-0.0029 in.	0.0003-0.0029 in.
Crankpin		
Diameter	1.999-2.000 in.	1.928-2.000 in.
Taper, new (wear limit)	0.0003 in. maximum (0.001 in.)	0.0003 in. maximum (0.001 in.)
Out-of-round, new (wear limit)	0.002 in. maximum (0.001 in.)	0.002 in. maximum (0.001 in.)
Connecting rods		
Side clearance	0.0085-0.0135 in.	0.007-0.016 in.
Bearing clearance	0.0007-0.0027 in.	0.0007-0.0027 in.
Camshaft		
Journal diameter	1.8682-1.8692 in.	1.8677-1.8697 in.
Runout	0.0015 in. maximum	0.0015 in. maximum
Valve system		
Lifter type	Hydraulic	Hydraulic
Rocker arm ratio	1.75:1	1.75:1
Valve lash (intake & exhaust)	One turn down from zero lash	One turn down from zero lash
Intake valve		
Face angle	45°	45°
Seat angle	46°	46°
Seat width	$\frac{1}{32}$-$\frac{1}{16}$ in.	$\frac{1}{32}$-$\frac{1}{16}$ in.
Stem-to-guide clearance	0.0010-0.0027 in.	0.0010-0.0027 in.
Seat runout	0.002 in. maximum	0.002 in. maximum
Exhaust valve		
Face angle	45°	45°
Seat angle	46°	46°
Seat width	$\frac{1}{16}$-$\frac{3}{32}$ in.	$\frac{1}{16}$-$\frac{3}{32}$ in.
Stem-to-guide clearance	0.0015-0.0032 in.	0.0015-0.0032 in.
Seat runout	0.002 in. maximum	0.002 in. maximum
Valve springs (outer)		
Free length	1.92 in.	1.92 in. (to 1975) 1.94 in. (1976-on)
Load @ length (lbs. @ in.)		
Closed	54-64 @ 1.66 in.	55-64 @ 1.66 in. (to 1975) 78-86 @ 1.66 in. (1976-on)
Open	170-184 @ 1.33 in.	180-192 @ 1.27 in. (to 1975) 170-180 @1.26 in. (1976-on)
Installed height ($\pm\frac{1}{32}$ in.)	$1\frac{21}{32}$ in.	$1\frac{21}{32}$ in.

5

Table 2   ENGINE SPECIFICATIONS

305 CID V8	
General	
Bore	3.736 in.
Stroke	3.48 in.
Firing order	1-8-4-3-6-5-7-2
Cylinder bore	
Diameter	3.7350-3.7385 in.
Out-of-round, new (wear limit)	0.001 (0.002) in.
Piston	
Clearance in bore	0.0007-0.0017 in.
Piston rings	
Number per cylinder	3
Ring end gap	
Top	0.010-0.020 in.
2nd	0.010-0.025 in.
Oil control	0.015-0.055 in.
Ring side clearance	
Top	0.0012-0.0032 in.
2nd	0.0012-0.0027 in.
Oil control	0.002-0.007 in.
Piston pins	
Diameter	0.9270-0.9273 in.
Clearance	
In piston	0.00015-0.00025 in.
In rod	0.0008-0.0016 in.
Crankshaft	
End play	0.002-0.006 in.
Main bearing journal	
Diameter	No. 1 — 2.4484-2.4493 in.
	No. 2-3-4 — 2.4481-2.4490 in.
	No. 5 — 2.4479-2.4484 in.
Taper	0.0002 in. (0.001 in. maximum)
Out-of-round	0.0002 in. (0.001 in. maximum)

(continued)

Table 2   ENGINE SPECIFICATIONS (continued)

305 CID V8

Crankshaft (continued)

Main bearing clearance	No. 1 — 0.0008-0.0020 in.
	No. 2-3-4 — 0.0011-0.0023 in.
	No. 5 — 0.0017-0.0032 in.
Crankpin	
Diameter	2.099-2.100 in.
Taper, new (wear limit)	0.0002 in. (0.001 in. maximum)
Out-of-round, new (wear limit)	0.0002 in. (0.001 in. maximum)

Connecting rods

Side clearance	0.008-0.014 in.
Bearing clearance	0.0013-0.0035 in.

Camshaft

Journal diameter	1.8682-1.8692 in.
Runout	0.0015 in. maximum

Valve system

Lifter type	Hydraulic
Rocker arm ratio	1.50:1
Valve lash — intake and exhaust	¾ turn down from zero lash
Intake valve	
Face angle	45°
Seat angle	46°
Seat width	$\frac{1}{32}$-$\frac{1}{16}$ in.
Stem-to-guide clearance	0.0010-0.0027 in.
Seat runout	0.001 in.
Exhaust valve	
Face angle	45°
Seat angle	46°
Seat width	$\frac{1}{16}$-$\frac{3}{32}$ in.
Stem-to-guide clearance	0.0010-0.0027 in.
Seat runout	0.002 in.
Valve springs (outer)	
Free length	2.03 in.
Load @ length (lbs. @ in.)	
Closed	76-84 @ 1.61 in.
Open	194-206 @ 1.16 in.
Installed height	$1\frac{19}{32}$ in. exhaust, $1\frac{23}{32}$ intake
Damper free length	1.86 in.

5

Table 2   ENGINE SPECIFICATIONS

307 CID V8		
General		
Bore	3⅞ in.	
Stroke	3.25 in.	
Firing order	1-8-4-3-6-5-7-2	
Cylinder bore		
Diameter	3.8745-3.8775 in.	
Out-of-round, new (wear limit)	0.001 in. (0.002 in.)	
Piston		
Clearance in bore	0.0005-0.0011 in.	
Piston rings		
Number per cylinder	3	
Ring end gap		
Top	0.010-0.020 in.	
2nd	0.010-0.020 in.	
Oil control	0.015-0.055 in.	
Ring side clearance		
Top	0.0012-0.0027 in.	
2nd	0.0012-0.0032 in.	
Oil control	0.055 in. maximum	
Piston pins		
Diameter	0.9270-0.9273 in.	
Clearance		
In piston (wear limit)	0.00015-0.00025 in. (0.001 in.)	
In rod	0.0008-0.0016 in.	
Crankshaft		
End play	0.002-0.006 in.	
Main bearing journal diameter	1970-71:	1972-73:
No. 1	2.4484-2.4493 in.	2.4484-2.4493 in.
Nos. 2-3-4	2.4484-2.4493 in.	2.4481-2.4490 in.
No. 5	2.4479-2.4488 in.	2.4479-2.4488 in.
Taper	0.0002 in.	0.0002 in.
Out-of-round	0.0002 in.	0.0002 in.

(continued)

Table 2   ENGINE SPECIFICATIONS   (continued)

307 CID V8		
Crankshaft (continued)		
Main bearing clearance	1970:	1971-73:
No. 1	0.0003-0.0015 in.	0.0008-0.0020 in.
Nos. 2-3-4	0.0006-0.0016 in.	0.0011-0.0023 in.
No. 5	0.0008-0.0023 in.	0.0017-0.0033 in.
Crankpin		
Diameter	2.099-2.100 in.	2.099-2.100 in.
Taper, new (wear limit)	0.0003 in. (0.001 in.)	0.0003 in. (0.001 in.)
Out-of-round, new (wear limit)	0.002 in. (0.001 in.)	0.002 in. (0.001 in.)
Connecting rods	1970:	1971-73:
Side clearance	0.008-0.014 in.	0.008-0.014 in.
Bearing clearance	0.0007-0.0028 in.	0.0013-0.0035 in.
Camshaft		
Journal diameter	1.8682-1.8692 in.	1.8682-1.8692 in.
Runout	0.015 in. maximum	0.015 in. maximum
Valve system		
Lifter type	Hydraulic	Hydraulic
Rocker arm ratio	1.50:1	1.50:1
Valve lash	One turn down from zero lash	One turn down from zero lash
Intake valve		
Face angle	45°	45°
Seat angle	46°	46°
Seat width	$\frac{1}{32}$-$\frac{1}{16}$ in.	$\frac{1}{32}$-$\frac{1}{16}$ in.
Stem-to-guide clearance	0.0010-0.0027 in.	0.0010-0.0027 in.
Seat runout	0.002 in. maximum	0.002 in. maximum
Exhaust valve		
Face angle	45°	45°
Seat angle	46°	46°
Seat width	$\frac{1}{16}$-$\frac{3}{32}$ in.	$\frac{1}{16}$-$\frac{3}{32}$ in.
Stem-to-guide clearance	0.0012-0.0029 in.	0.0012-0.0029 in.
Seat runout	0.002 in. maximum	0.002 in. maximum
Valve springs (outer)	1970-72 & 1973 intake:	1973 exhaust:
Free length	2.03 in.	1.91 in.
Load @ length (lb. @ in.)		
Closed	76-84 @ 1.70 in.	76-84 @ 1.61 in.
Open	194-206 @ 1.25 in.	183-195 @ 1.20 in.
Installed height	1$\frac{23}{32}$ in.	1.518 in.
Damper free length	1.94 in.	1.94 in.

5

Table 2   ENGINE SPECIFICATIONS

327 CID V8			
General			
Bore	4.0 in.		
Stroke	3.25 in.		
Firing order	1-8-4-3-6-5-7-2		
Cylinder bore			
Diameter	3.9995-4.0025 in.		
Out-of-round, new (wear limit)	0.001 in. (0.002 in.)		
Piston			
Clearance in bore	0.0005-0.0011 in.		
Piston rings			
Number per cylinder	3		
Ring end gap			
Top	0.013-0.023 in.		
2nd	0.013-0.025 in.		
Oil control	0.015-0.055 in.		
Ring side clearance			
Top	0.0012-0.0027 in.		
2nd	0.0012-0.0032 in.		
Oil control	0.000-0.005 in.		
Piston pins			
Diameter	0.9270-0.9273 in.		
Clearance			
In piston	0.00015-0.00025 in.		
In rod	0.0008-0.0016 in.		
Crankshaft			
End play	0.003-0.011 in.		
Main bearing journals			
Diameter	1967:	1968:	1969:
No. 1	2.2984-2.2993 in.	2.4484-2.4493 in.	2.4479-2.4488 in.
Nos. 2-3-4	2.2983-2.2993 in.	2.4484-2.4493 in.	2.4479-2.4488 in.
No. 5	2.2978-2.2988 in.	2.4470-2.4488 in.	2.4479-2.4488 in.
Taper	0.001 in. maximum	0.0003 in. maximum	0.0002 in. maximum
Out-of-round	0.0002 in. maximum	0.0002 in. maximum	0.0002 in. maximum

(continued)

Table 2   **ENGINE SPECIFICATIONS**   (continued)

327 CID V8			
Crankshaft (continued)			
Main bearing clearance	1967:	1968:	1969:
No. 1	0.0008-0.0020 in.	0.0008-0.0020 in.	0.0008-0.0020 in.
Nos. 2-3-4	0.0018-0.0020 in.	0.0008-0.0020 in.	0.0008-0.0020 in.
No. 5	0.0010-0.0036 in.	0.0018-0.0034 in.	0.0018-0.0034 in.
Crankpin			
Diameter	1.999-2.000 in.	2.099-2.001 in.	2.099-2.001 in.
Taper, new (wear limit)	0.0003 in. maximum (0.001 in.)		
Out-of-round, new (wear limit)	0.002 in. maximum (0.001 in.)		

Connecting rods	
Side clearance	0.009-0.013 in.
Bearing clearance	0.0007-0.0028 in.

Camshaft	
Journal diameter	1.8682-1.8692 in.
Runout	0.0015 in. maximum

Valve system	
Lifter type	Hydraulic
Rocker arm ratio	1.50:1
Valve lash (intake & exhaust)	One turn down from **zero lash**
Intake valve	
Face angle	45°
Seat angle	46°
Seat width	$\frac{1}{32}$-$\frac{1}{16}$ in.
Stem-to-guide clearance	0.0010-0.0027 in.
Seat runout	0.002 in. maximum
Exhaust valve	
Face angle	45°
Seat angle	46°
Seat width	$\frac{1}{16}$-$\frac{3}{32}$ in.
Stem-to guide clearance	0.0010-0.0027 in.
Seat runout	0.002 in. maximum
Valve springs (outer)	
Free length	2.03 in.
Load @ length (lb. @ in.)	
Closed	76-84 @ 1.70 in.
Open	194-206 @ 1.25 in.
Installed height	$1\frac{5}{32}$ in.

5

Table 2   ENGINE SPECIFICATIONS

350 CID V8		
General		
Bore	4.0 in. ①	3⅞ in. ②
Stroke	3.48 in. ①	3.25 in. ②
Firing order	1-8-4-3-6-5-7-2	
Cylinder bore		
Diameter	3.9995-4.0025 in. ①	3.8745-3.8775 in. ②
Out-of-round, new (wear limit)	0.001 in. (0.002 in.)	
Piston		
Clearance in bore	See Table 3, Chapter 5	
Piston rings		
Number per cylinder	3	
Ring end gap		
Top	0.010-0.020 in.	
2nd	0.013-0.023 in.	
Oil control	0.015-0.055 in.	
Ring side clearance		
Top	0.0012-0.0032 in.	
2nd	0.0012-0.0027 in.	
Oil control	0.0000-0.005 in. maximum	
Piston pins		
Diameter	0.9270-0.9273 in.	
Clearance		
In piston	0.00015-0.00025 in.	
In rod	0.0008-0.0016 in.	
Crankshaft		
End play	0.003-0.011 in. (1967-69) 0.002-0.006 in. (1970-75)	
Main bearing journals		
Diameter		
Nos. 1-2-3-4	2.4483-2.4493 in. (1967-68-70-71) 2.4479-2.4488 in. (1969)	
No. 5	2.4478-2.4488 in. (1967-71)	
No. 1	2.4484-2.4493 in. (1972-75)	
Nos. 2-3-4	2.4481-2.4490 in. (1972-75)	
No. 5	2.4479-2.4488 in. (1972-75)	
Taper	0.0002 in. maximum	
Out-of-round	0.0002 in. maximum	
Main bearing clearance		
No. 1	0.0008-0.0020 in. (1967-68-69) 0.003-0.0015 in. (1970)	
Nos. 2-3-4	0.0008-0.0020 in. (1967-68-69) 0.0006-0.0018 in. (1970)	
No. 5	0.0018-0.0034 in. (1967-68-69) 0.0008-0.0023 in. (1970)	
No. 1	0.0008-0.0020 in. (1971-on)	
Nos. 2-3-4	0.0011-0.0023 in. (1971-on)	
No. 5	0.0017-0.0033 in. (1971-on)	

(continued)

Table 2   ENGINE SPECIFICATIONS   (continued)

350 CID V8

Crankshaft (continued)
Crankpin

Diameter	2.099-2.100 in.
Taper, new (wear limit)	0.0003 in. (0.001 in. maximum)
Out-of-round, new (wear limit)	0.0002 in. (0.001 in. maximum)

Connecting rods

Side clearance	0.008-0.014 in.
Bearing clearance	0.0013-0.0035 in.

Camshaft

Journal diameter	1.8682-1.8692 in.
Runout	0.0015 in. maximum

Valve system

Lifter type	Hydraulic
Rocker arm ratio	1.50:1
Valve lash	See Table 2, Chapter 4 for mechanical lifters; $3/4$ turn down from zero lash for hydraulic.

Intake valve

Face angle	45°
Seat angle	46°
Seat width	$1/32$-$1/16$ in.
Stem-to-guide clearance	0.0010-0.0027 in.
Seat runout	0.002 maximum

Exhaust valve

Face angle	45°
Seat angle	46°
Seat width	$1/16$-$3/32$ in.
Stem-to-guide clearance	0.0012-0.0029 in.
Seat runout	0.002 in. maximum

Valve springs (outer)

Free length	2.03 (1967-72 and 1976-on intake/exhaust; 1973-75 intake valves)
	1.90 (1973-75 exhaust valves)
Load @ length (lb. @ in.)	
Closed	76-84 @ .1.70 in. (1967-72 and 1976-on intake/exhaust; 1973-75 intake valves)
Open	194-206 @ 1.25 in. (1967-72 intake/exhaust; 1973-75 intake valves)
Closed	76-84 @ 1.61 in. (1973-75 exhaust valves)
Open	183-195 @ 1.20 in. (1973-75 exhaust valves)
Installed height	$1 5/32$ in. (1967-69)
	$1 23/32$ in. (1970-72 and 1976-on intake)
	$1 5/8$ in. (1973-75)
	$1 19/32$ in. (1976-on exhaust)
Damper free length	1.94 in. (to 1975); 1.86 in. (1976-on)

① All except 1974-on 145 hp.   ② 1974-on 145 hp. only.

Table 2   ENGINE SPECIFICATIONS

402 CID V8		
General		
Bore	4⅛ in.	
Stroke	3.76 in.	
Firing order	1-8-4-3-6-5-7-2	
Cylinder bore		
Diameter	4.1246-4.1274 in.	
Out-of-round, new (wear limit)	0.001 in. (0.002 in. maximum)	
Piston		
Clearance in bore	See Table 3, Chapter 5	
Piston rings	1970:	1971-72:
Number per cylinder	3	3
Ring end gap		
Top	0.010-0.020 in.	0.010-0.020 in.
2nd	0.010-0.020 in.	0.010-0.020 in.
Oil control	0.010-0.030 in.	0.015-0.055 in.
Ring side clearance	1970:	1971-1972:
Top	0.0017-0.0032 in.	0.0017-0.0032 in.
2nd	0.0017-0.0032 in.	0.0017-0.0032 in.
Oil control	0.0005-0.0065 in.	0.0005-0.0065 in.
Piston pins		
Diameter	0.9895-0.9898 in.	0.9895-0.9898 in.
Clearance	All exc. 1970 375 hp:	1970 375 hp:
In piston	0.00025-0.00035 in.	0.00030-0.00040 in.
In rod	0.0008-0.0016 in.	0.0008-0.0016 in.
Crankshaft		
End play	0.006-0.010 in.	0.006-0.010 in.
Main bearing journals		
Diameter	All	
Nos. 1-2	2.7487-2.7496 in.	
Nos. 3-4	2.7481-2.7490 in.	
No. 5	2.7478-2.7488 in.	
Taper	0.0002 maximum	
Out-of-round	0.0002 maximum	
	(continued)	

Table 2   ENGINE SPECIFICATIONS   (continued)

402 CID V8	
Crankshaft (continued)	
Main bearing clearance	
No. 1	0.0007-0.0019 in.
Nos. 2-3-4	0.0013-0.0025 in.
No. 5	0.0019-0.0035 in.
Crankpin	All
Diameter	2.199-2.200 in.
Taper, new (wear limit)	0.0003 in. (0.001 in.)
Out-of-round, new (wear limit)	0.002 in. (0.001 in.)
Connecting rods	All
Side clearance	0.015-0.021 in.
Bearing clearance	0.009-0.0025 in.
Camshaft	**All**
Journal diameter	1.9487-1.9497 in.
Runout	0.015 in. maximum
Valve system	All
Lifter type	Hydraulic
Rocker arm ratio	1.70:1
Valve lash	One turn down from zero lash
Intake valve	
Face angle	45°
Seat angle	46°
Seat width	$\frac{1}{32}$-$\frac{1}{16}$ in.
Stem-to-guide clearance	0.0010-0.0027 in.
Seat runout	0.002 in. maximum
Exhaust valves	
Face angle	45°
Seat angle	46°
Seat width	$\frac{1}{16}$-$\frac{3}{32}$ in.
Stem-to-guide clearance	0.0012-0.0027 in.
Seat runout	0.002 in. maximum
Valve springs (outer)	
Free length	2.12 in.
Load @ length (lb. @ in.)	69-81 @ 1.88 in.
	228-252 @ 1.38 in.
Installed height	$1\frac{7}{8}$ in.
Valve springs (inner)	
Free length	2.06 in.
Load @ length (lb. @ in.)	26-34 @ 1.78 in.
	81-99 @ 1.28 in.

5

Table 2   ENGINE SPECIFICATIONS

454 CID V8	
General	
Bore	4.25 in.
Stroke	4.0 in.
Firing order	1-8-4-3-6-5-7-2
Cylinder bore	
Diameter	4.2495-4.2525 in.
Out-of-round, new (wear limit)	0.001 in. (0.002 in.)
Piston	
Clearance in bore	0.0040-0.0050 in.
Piston rings	
Number per cylinder	3
Ring end gap	
Top	0.010-0.020 in.
2nd	0.010-0.020 in.
Oil control	0.015-0.055 in.
Ring side clearance	
Top	0.0017-0.0032 in.
2nd	0.0017-0.0032 in.
Oil control	0.0005-0.0065 in.
Piston pins	
Diameter	0.9895-0.9898 in.
Clearance	
In piston	0.00025-0.00035 in.
In rod	0.0008-0.0016 in.
Crankshaft	
End play	0.006-0.010 in.
Main bearing journal	
Diameter	
Nos. 1-2-3-4	2.7481-2.7490 in.
No. 5	2.7478-2.7488 in.
Taper, new (wear limit)	0.0002 in. (0.001 in.)
Out-of-round, new (wear limit)	0.0002 in. (0.001 in.)
(continued)	

Table 2   **ENGINE SPECIFICATIONS**   (continued)

454 CID V8	
Crankshaft (continued)	
Main bearing clearance	
Nos. 1-2-3-4	0.0013-0.0025 in.
No. 5	0.0029-0.0045 in.
Crankpin	
Diameter	2.1985-2.1995 in.
Taper, new (wear limit)	0.0003 in. (0.001 in.)
Out-of-round, new (wear limit)	0.002 in. (0.001 in.)
Connecting rods	
Side clearance	0.015-0.021 in.
Bearing clearance	0.0009-0.0025 in.
Camshaft	
Journal diameter	1.9487-1.9497 in.
Runout	0.015 in. maximum
Valve system	
Lifter type	Hydraulic
Rocker arm ratio	1.70:1
Valve lash	One turn down from zero lash
Intake valve	
Face angle	45°
Seat angle	46°
Seat width	$\frac{1}{32}$-$\frac{1}{16}$ in.
Stem-to-guide clearance	0.0010-0.0027 in.
Seat runout	0.002 maximum
Exhaust valve	
Face angle	45°
Seat angle	46°
Seat width	$\frac{1}{16}$-$\frac{3}{32}$ in.
Stem-to-guide clearance	0.0012-0.0027 in.
Seat runout	0.002 in. maximum
Valve springs (outer)	
Free length	2.12 in.
Load @ length (lb. @ in.)	69-81 @ 1.88
	228-252 @ 1.38
Installed height	$1\frac{7}{8} \pm \frac{1}{32}$ in.
Valve springs (inner)	
Free length	2.06 in.
Load @ length (lb. @ in.)	26-34 @ 1.78 in.
	81-99 @ 1.28 in.
Installed height	$1\frac{25}{32} \pm \frac{1}{32}$ in.

5

CHAPTER SIX

FUEL SYSTEM

The fuel system consists of a fuel tank, a mechanical fuel pump, and a carburetor with interconnecting lines.

A large number of carburetors are used on the vehicles covered. They are designed to meet the requirements of particular engine/transmission combinations as well as for emissions control. Carburetors that look alike are not necessarily interchangeable. To obtain the correct replacement carburetor, copy the part number stamped on the carburetor body or on a metal tag and take it with you to purchase a new or rebuilt unit.

It is recommended that carburetors be exchanged with a new or rebuilt equivalent model rather than rebuilding them. The exchange price of a rebuilt unit is little more than the price of a kit and hardly worth the time involved. In addition, the rebuilt unit will be correctly adjusted to ensure good operation and compliance with emission control standards. Exploded views are presented in this chapter to aid you in the unlikely event you cannot obtain a new or rebuilt carburetor.

Basic carburetor adjustments are shown in Chapter Four, *Tune-Up*.

CARTER YF

The Carter YF carburetor is used on 1967 L6 engines equipped with the Air Injection Reactor system (**Figure 1**).

The automatic choke is operated by a temperature sensing coil mounted on the exhaust manifold. The carburetor has a conventional float, low and high speed circuits, and an accelerator pump circuit. A metering rod controls the high speed circuit. The accelerator pump circuit and metering rod are mechanical and vacuum controlled.

Removal/Installation

1. Remove air cleaner.

2. Disconnect carburetor vacuum and fuel lines.

3. Disconnect choke rod and accelerator linkage.

4. If vehicle has automatic transmission, disconnect the throttle valve linkage.

5. Remove attaching nuts and remove the carburetor.

6. To install, clean all gasket sealing surfaces on carburetor and manifold and, using new gasket, reverse the procedure above.

CARTER YF CARBURETOR

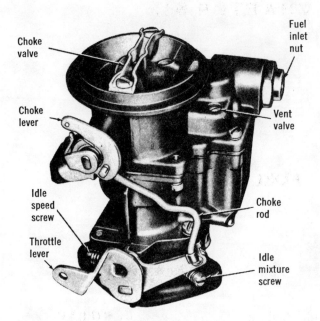

Choke valve

Fuel inlet nut

Choke lever

Vent valve

MANUAL CHOKE MODEL

Idle speed screw

Choke rod

Throttle lever

Idle mixture screw

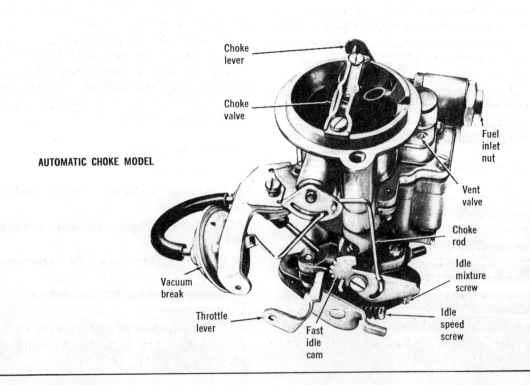

Choke lever

Choke valve

Fuel inlet nut

AUTOMATIC CHOKE MODEL

Vent valve

Choke rod

Idle mixture screw

Vacuum break

Idle speed screw

Throttle lever

Fast idle cam

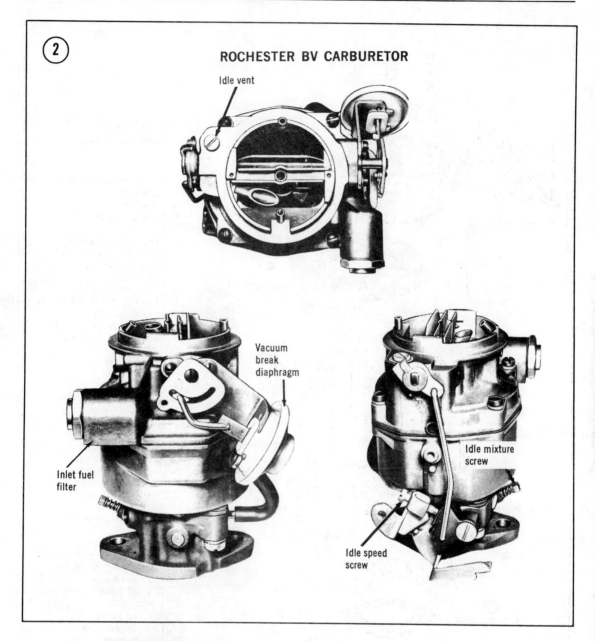

② ROCHESTER BV CARBURETOR

Idle vent

Vacuum
break
diaphragm

Inlet fuel
filter

Idle mixture
screw

Idle speed
screw

ROCHESTER BV

The Rochester BV was used on some 1967 6-cylinder engines. Refer to **Figures 2 and 3** for these procedures.

Removal/Installation

1. Remove air cleaner.

2. Disconnect carburetor vacuum and fuel lines.

3. Disconnect choke rod and accelerator linkage.

4. Disconnect throttle valve linkage on automatic transmission equipped models.

5. Remove attaching nuts and remove the carburetor.

6. To install carburetor, clean all gasket sealing surfaces on carburetor and manifold and using new gaskets, reverse Steps 1 through 5.

ROCHESTER 1MV

The Rochester 1MV was used on 1968-1976 6-cylinder engines (**Figure 4**).

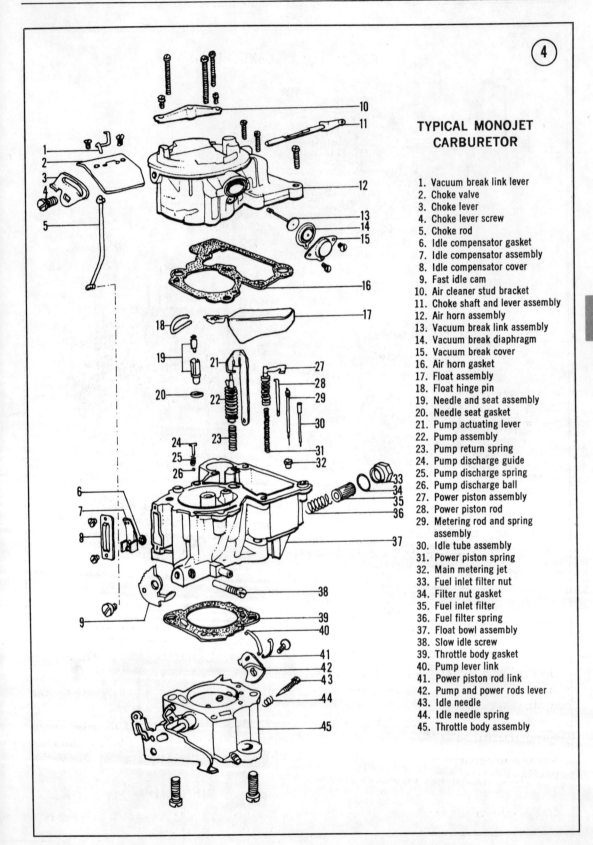

TYPICAL MONOJET CARBURETOR

1. Vacuum break link lever
2. Choke valve
3. Choke lever
4. Choke lever screw
5. Choke rod
6. Idle compensator gasket
7. Idle compensator assembly
8. Idle compensator cover
9. Fast idle cam
10. Air cleaner stud bracket
11. Choke shaft and lever assembly
12. Air horn assembly
13. Vacuum break link assembly
14. Vacuum break diaphragm
15. Vacuum break cover
16. Air horn gasket
17. Float assembly
18. Float hinge pin
19. Needle and seat assembly
20. Needle seat gasket
21. Pump actuating lever
22. Pump assembly
23. Pump return spring
24. Pump discharge guide
25. Pump discharge spring
26. Pump discharge ball
27. Power piston assembly
28. Power piston rod
29. Metering rod and spring assembly
30. Idle tube assembly
31. Power piston spring
32. Main metering jet
33. Fuel inlet filter nut
34. Filter nut gasket
35. Fuel inlet filter
36. Fuel filter spring
37. Float bowl assembly
38. Slow idle screw
39. Throttle body gasket
40. Pump lever link
41. Power piston rod link
42. Pump and power rods lever
43. Idle needle
44. Idle needle spring
45. Throttle body assembly

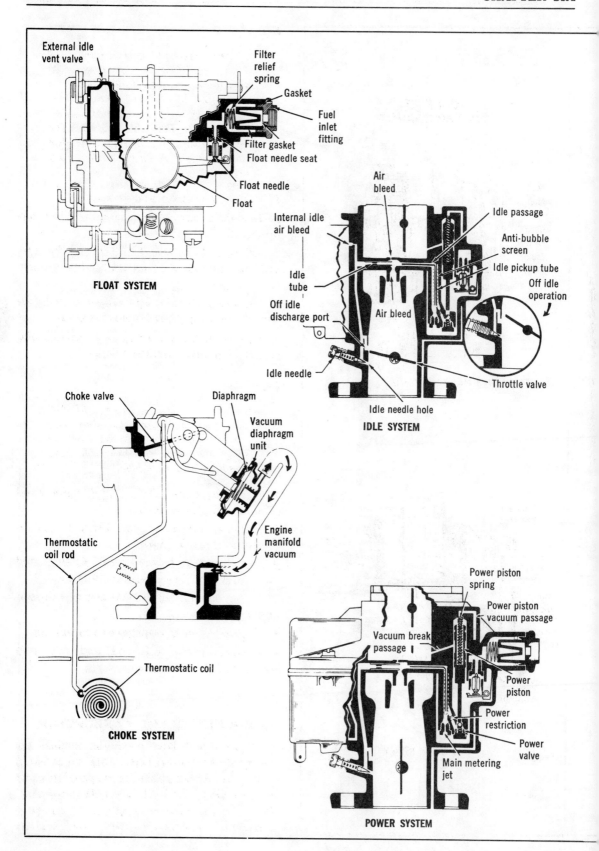

External idle
vent valve

Filter
relief
spring

Gasket

Fuel
inlet
fitting

Filter gasket

Float needle seat

Float needle

Float

FLOAT SYSTEM

Air
bleed

Internal idle
air bleed

Idle passage

Anti-bubble
screen

Idle pickup tube

Off idle
operation

Idle
tube

Air bleed

Off idle
discharge port

Idle needle

Throttle valve

Idle needle hole

IDLE SYSTEM

Choke valve

Diaphragm

Vacuum
diaphragm
unit

Engine
manifold
vacuum

Thermostatic
coil rod

Thermostatic coil

CHOKE SYSTEM

Power piston
spring

Power piston
vacuum passage

Vacuum break
passage

Power
piston

Power
restriction

Power
valve

Main metering
jet

POWER SYSTEM

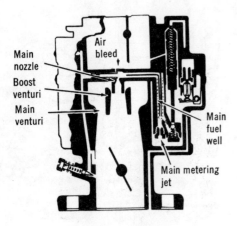

ROCHESTER
BV CARBURETOR

Main nozzle
Air bleed
Boost venturi
Main venturi
Main fuel well
Main metering jet

MAIN METERING SYSTEM

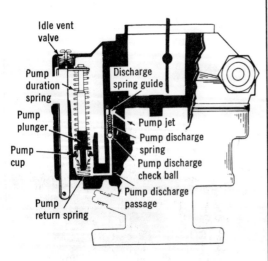

Idle vent valve
Pump duration spring
Pump plunger
Pump cup
Discharge spring guide
Pump jet
Pump discharge spring
Pump discharge check ball
Pump discharge passage
Pump return spring

PUMP SYSTEM

Removal

NOTE: *Acceleration stumbling and other performance problems are sometimes caused by foreign matter in the carburetor. When removing carburetor, take care to avoid draining fuel from bowl so that contents of bowl can be examined for contamination when the carburetor is disassembled. Also, check fuel filter.*

1. Remove air cleaner and gasket.

2. Disconnect fuel and vacuum lines from carburetor.

3. Disconnect choke coil rod, throttle linkage, and idle stop solenoid electrical lead (at connector).

4. Remove carburetor attaching nuts and then remove carburetor and solenoid assembly.

5. Remove insulator, air cleaner bracket, and gasket from intake manifold flange.

Installation

NOTE: *For ease of starting, fill carburetor bowl before installing carburetor. Operate throttle lever several times and verify fuel discharge from pump jets prior to installation.*

1. Verify that sealing flanges on carburetor and intake manifold are clean.

2. Install gasket, air cleaner bracket, and insulator over manifold studs.

3. Install carburetor over manifold studs and install and securely tighten attaching nuts.

4. Install and tighten vacuum and fuel lines at carburetor.

5. Connect accelerator linkage to carburetor.

6. Connect choke coil rod and idle stop solenoid electrical connector.

ROCHESTER 1ME CARBURETOR

All 1977 and later 6-cylinder engines are equipped with the Rochester 1ME single-barrel carburetor. Although similar in appearance and in operation to the Rochester 1MV carburetor, this carburetor is an integral part of the emission control system and has been set to meet the

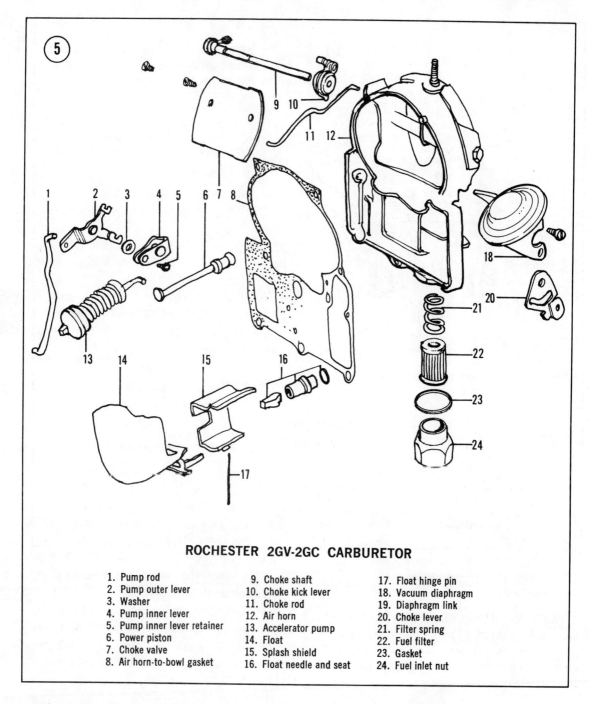

ROCHESTER 2GV-2GC CARBURETOR

1. Pump rod	9. Choke shaft	17. Float hinge pin
2. Pump outer lever	10. Choke kick lever	18. Vacuum diaphragm
3. Washer	11. Choke rod	19. Diaphragm link
4. Pump inner lever	12. Air horn	20. Choke lever
5. Pump inner lever retainer	13. Accelerator pump	21. Filter spring
6. Power piston	14. Float	22. Fuel filter
7. Choke valve	15. Splash shield	23. Gasket
8. Air horn-to-bowl gasket	16. Float needle and seat	24. Fuel inlet nut

requirements of the U.S. Department of Health, Education, and Welfare and of certain state air pollution control agencies. Except for adjusting idle speed and idle mixture (without disturbing the limiter cap) as described in Chapter Four, no attempt should be made to adjust, repair, or overhaul this carburetor. This is a job for an expert.

ROCHESTER 2GV-2GC

Refer to **Figure 5** for the following procedure.

> NOTE: *Carburetors on late models (1975 and later) are a part of the emission control system. Service by the home mechanic should be limited to adjusting idle speed and idle mixture as*

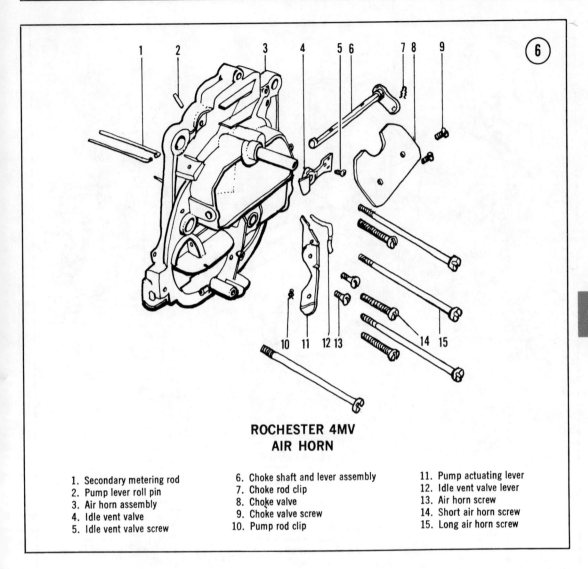

**ROCHESTER 4MV
AIR HORN**

1. Secondary metering rod
2. Pump lever roll pin
3. Air horn assembly
4. Idle vent valve
5. Idle vent valve screw
6. Choke shaft and lever assembly
7. Choke rod clip
8. Choke valve
9. Choke valve screw
10. Pump rod clip
11. Pump actuating lever
12. Idle vent valve lever
13. Air horn screw
14. Short air horn screw
15. Long air horn screw

described in Chapter Four. Other service should be referred to an expert.

The 2GV and 2GC carburetors are basically the same, except the automatic choke coil is located on the exhaust manifold in the 2GV series, and is attached to the carburetor in the 2GC series.

Removal/Installation

1. Remove air cleaner.

2. Disconnect vacuum and fuel lines.

3. On 1974 and earlier models, remove choke coil rod. On 1975 models, remove fresh air and choke hoses from choke system.

4. Disconnect accelerator linkage.

5. If equipped with automatic transmission, disconnect downshift linkage.

6. Remove all vacuum and electrical connectors, including idle stop solenoid wiring (if so equipped).

7. Remove attaching nuts or bolts and remove carburetor.

8. Remove gasket or insulator.

9. To install carburetor, clean all gasket sealing surfaces and, using new gasket or insulator, reverse Steps 1 through 8.

ROCHESTER 4MV

Refer to **Figures 6, 7,** and **8** for the following procedure.

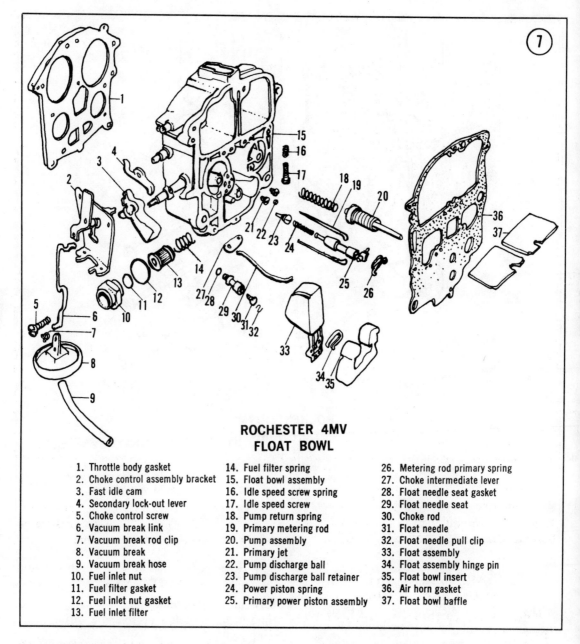

ROCHESTER 4MV
FLOAT BOWL

1. Throttle body gasket	14. Fuel filter spring	26. Metering rod primary spring
2. Choke control assembly bracket	15. Float bowl assembly	27. Choke intermediate lever
3. Fast idle cam	16. Idle speed screw spring	28. Float needle seat gasket
4. Secondary lock-out lever	17. Idle speed screw	29. Float needle seat
5. Choke control screw	18. Pump return spring	30. Choke rod
6. Vacuum break link	19. Primary metering rod	31. Float needle
7. Vacuum break rod clip	20. Pump assembly	32. Float needle pull clip
8. Vacuum break	21. Primary jet	33. Float assembly
9. Vacuum break hose	22. Pump discharge ball	34. Float assembly hinge pin
10. Fuel inlet nut	23. Pump discharge ball retainer	35. Float bowl insert
11. Fuel filter gasket	24. Power piston spring	36. Air horn gasket
12. Fuel inlet nut gasket	25. Primary power piston assembly	37. Float bowl baffle
13. Fuel inlet filter		

Removal/Installation

This is a 4-barrel, 2-stage carburetor which is easily adapted for small to large engines without design changes.

The fuel bowl is centrally located to avoid fuel slosh. The float needle valve is pressure balanced to permit use of a small single float.

The primary side has small bores and a triple venturi for fine fuel control in the idle and economy ranges. The secondary side has large bores and an air valve for high air capacity.

1. Remove air cleaner, gasket, and stud.

2. Disconnect vacuum, fuel, and choke pipes at carburetor.

3. On automatic models, disconnect transmission control rod from throttle lever.

4. On models with positive crankcase ventilation (PCV), disconnect ventilation hose at valve on carburetor base.

5. Disconnect accelerator rod and throttle return spring at carburetor.

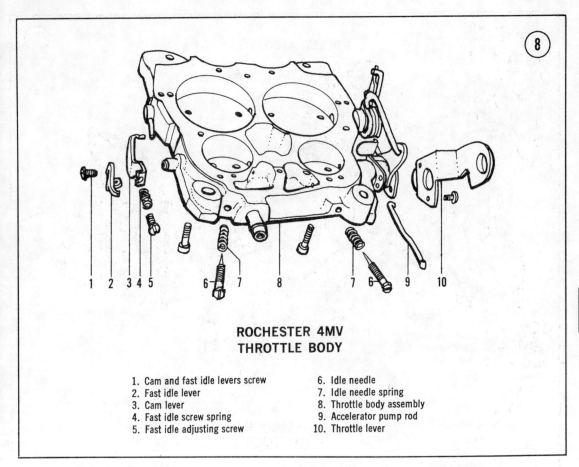

ROCHESTER 4MV
THROTTLE BODY

1. Cam and fast idle levers screw
2. Fast idle lever
3. Cam lever
4. Fast idle screw spring
5. Fast idle adjusting screw
6. Idle needle
7. Idle needle spring
8. Throttle body assembly
9. Accelerator pump rod
10. Throttle lever

6. Remove mounting nuts and lift carburetor from manifold.

7. Reverse procedures to install. Be sure carburetor base and manifold flange are clean.

HOLLEY 4150 AND 4160 CARBURETORS

Refer to **Figures 9-12** for illustrations of these carburetors.

These 4-barrel, 2-stage carburetors consist of seven subassemblies: throttle body, main body, primary and secondary fuel bowls, primary and secondary metering bodies, and the secondary throttle operating assembly.

The primary and secondary metering bodies on the Model 4150 are similar. The primary metering body on the Model 4160 is similar to the one on the 4150, but the secondary metering body is different. The secondary throttle operating assembly on both models is vacuum operated.

FUEL PUMP

Chevrolet/GMC engines use a non-serviceable fuel pump which cannot be repaired or rebuilt; the pump is replaced as a unit.

FUEL TANK

Removal/Installation

1. Remove ground cable from battery.

2. Disconnect meter wire at rear harness connector. Push out grommet and thread meter wire through trunk floor.

3. Raise vehicle and drain fuel tank.

4. Remove gauge ground wire screw from floor pan.

5. Disconnect fuel line at gauge pickup line.

6. Remove vent hoses.

7. Remove tank strap bolts and lower tank.

8. Reverse procedure to install tank.

9. Lower vehicle.

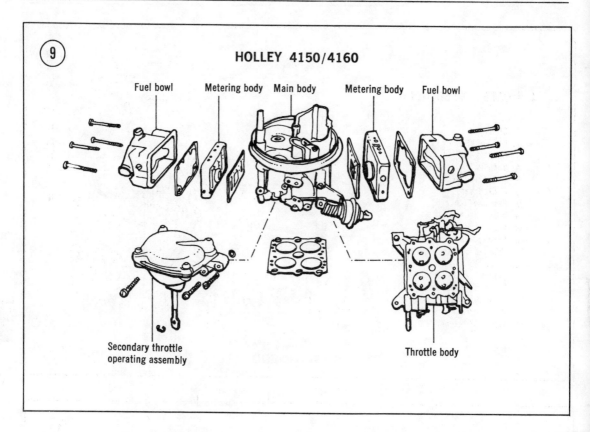

⑨ **HOLLEY 4150/4160**

Fuel bowl   Metering body   Main body   Metering body   Fuel bowl

Secondary throttle
operating assembly

Throttle body

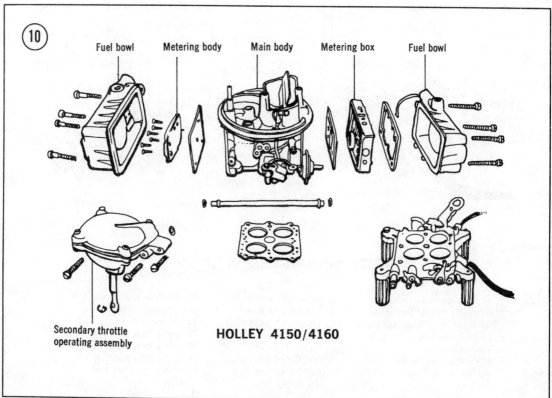

⑩

Fuel bowl   Metering body   Main body   Metering box   Fuel bowl

Secondary throttle
operating assembly

HOLLEY 4150/4160

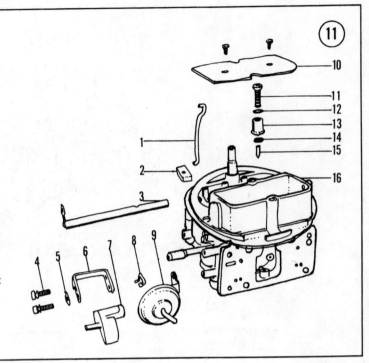

HOLLEY 4150/4160

1. Choke rod
2. Choke rod seal
3. Choke shaft and lever
4. Vacuum break screw
5. Choke lever retainer
6. Choke lever
7. Fast idle cam
8. Vacuum break link
9. Vacuum break
10. Choke valve
11. Pump discharge nozzle screw
12. Pump discharge nozzle screw gasket
13. Pump discharge nozzle
14. Pump discharge nozzle gasket
15. Pump discharge needle
16. Main body assembly

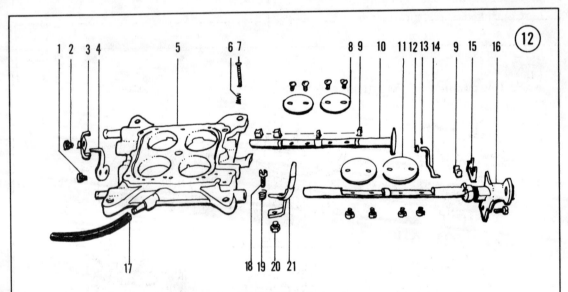

HOLLEY 4150/4160 THROTTLE BODY

1. Fast idle cam lever screw
2. Secondary throttle lever screw
3. Secondary throttle operating lever
4. Fast idle cam lever
5. Throttle body
6. Idle speed screw spring
7. Idle speed screw
8. Secondary throttle plate
9. Throttle shaft bushing
10. Secondary throttle shaft
11. Primary throttle plate
12. Throttle link washer
13. Throttle link cotter pin
14. Throttle connector link
15. Accelerator pump cam
16. Primary throttle shaft
17. Vacuum break hose
18. Pump lever adjusting screw
19. Pump lever adjusting screw spring
20. Pump lever adjusting nut
21. Pump operating lever

CHAPTER SEVEN

EMISSION CONTROL SYSTEM

Harmful emissions are minimized by a number of systems, depending on year:

a. Positive crankcase ventilation (PCV)
b. Controlled combustion system (CCS)
c. Air injection reaction (AIR)
d. Combination emission control system (CEC)
e. Fuel evaporation control system (ECS)
f. Exhaust gas recirculation system (EGR)
g. Carburetor calibration
h. Distributor calibration
i. Catalytic converter
j. Early evaporation system (ECS)

POSITIVE CRANKCASE VENTILATION

All vehicles covered have positive crankcase ventilation. Clean air is drawn from the air cleaner; the oil filler cap is not vented. The clean air scavenges emissions (e.g., piston blow-by) from the crankcase, and manifold vacuum draws the emissions into the carburetor. Eventually they can be reburned in the normal combuston process. **Figure 1** shows the closed system.

Either a PCV valve or fixed metered orifice mounted on the carburetor controls the volume of flow from crankcase to manifold.

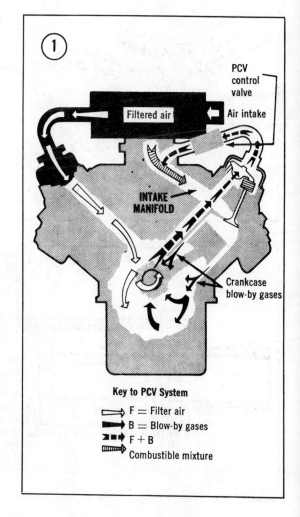

①

PCV control valve

Air intake

Filtered air

INTAKE MANIFOLD

Crankcase blow-by gases

Key to PCV System

F = Filter air
B = Blow-by gases
F + B
Combustible mixture

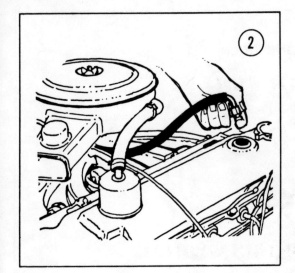

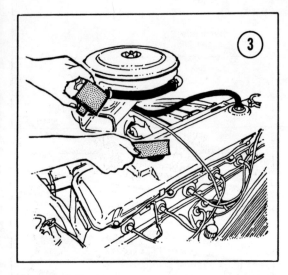

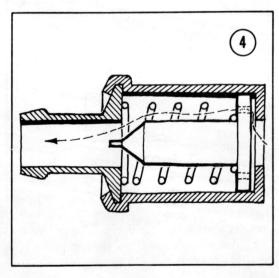

The PCV valve should be checked and replaced, if necessary, at each tune-up. Remove the valve from the rocker cover but leave it connected to the vent hose.

If the valve is clear, a hissing sound will be heard when the engine is idling, and a strong vacuum will be felt when a finger is placed over the valve (**Figure 2**).

Reinstall the valve in the rocker cover and disconnect the crankcase inlet air cleaner from the rocker cover. Hold a stiff piece of paper over the opening (**Figure 3**). After about a minute, when the crankcase pressure has subsided, the paper should be sucked down against the hole. Shut off the engine and once again disconnect the PCV valve from the rocker cover. Shake it and listen for a clicking sound that indicates the valve is free. If it is not, it should be replaced.

When a new valve is installed, check it as before, with a piece of paper held over the inlet. If the force is not considerable, it is necessary to clean the vent hose and the passages in the carburetor. Clean the hose with solvent and blow it dry with compressed air. The carburetor must be removed to clean the passages; this should be entrusted to a dealer. **Figure 4** shows a cross section of a PCV valve.

CONTROLLED COMBUSTION SYSTEM

The controlled combustion system on 1970 and later models includes a special thermostatically controlled air cleaner, special calibrated carburetor and distributor, and a higher temperature thermostat (**Figure 5**).

The thermostatically controlled air cleaner maintains air to the carburetor at a temperature of 100°F or higher. The air cleaner includes a temperature sensor, vacuum motor, and control damper assembly (**Figure 6**).

Operation of the air cleaner is shown in **Figure 7**. When the engine is off, absence of manifold vacuum permits the vacuum motor to close off the hot air pipe. When the engine is running and underhood temperatures are below 85°F, the temperature sensor bleed valve is closed and manifold vacuum operates the vacuum motor. The vacuum motor closes off the underhood air supply and the carburetor

7

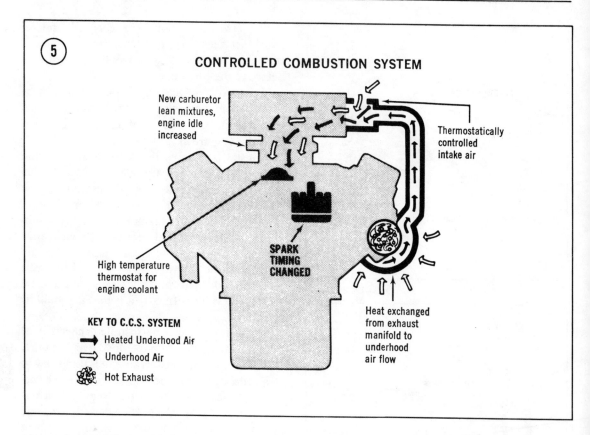

⑤

CONTROLLED COMBUSTION SYSTEM

New carburetor
lean mixtures,
engine idle
increased

Thermostatically
controlled
intake air

High temperature
thermostat for
engine coolant

**SPARK
TIMING
CHANGED**

Heat exchanged
from exhaust
manifold to
underhood
air flow

KEY TO C.C.S. SYSTEM

➡ Heated Underhood Air

⇨ Underhood Air

🔥 Hot Exhaust

draws the much hotter air from the hot air pipe. Between 85°F and 128°F, the temperature sensor air bleed is partially open. The vacuum motor opens both the underhood air inlet and the hot air tube inlet. The resulting blend is maintained around 100°F or higher. Finally, if the underhood temperature is above 128°F, the temperature sensor air bleed is fully open, the vacuum motor cannot operate and carburetor air is drawn from the underhood air inlet only.

Inspection

1. Check all heat pipe and hose connections.

2. Check for kinked or deteriorated hoses.

3. Remove the air cleaner cover and place a thermometer as close as possible to the sensor. Install the cover. Lift the cover after temperature stabilizes and read thermometer; temperature must be below 85°F before proceeding. Put cover back in place.

> NOTE: *Use a relatively fast acting thermometer such as a photographic darkroom thermometer. These are available for less than $10.*

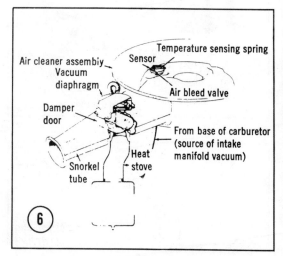

Air cleaner assembly

Temperature sensing spring

Sensor

Vacuum
diaphragm

Air bleed valve

Damper
door

From base of carburetor
(source of intake
manifold vacuum)

Snorkel
tube

Heat
stove

⑥

4. With the engine off, the snorkel passage should be completely open (**Figure 7**, View A). If not, check for binds in the linkage.

5. Start the engine. With the air temperature below 85°F, snorkel passage should close. When the damper door begins to open, remove air cleaner cover and check the temperature; it should be between 85-115°F.

⑦

A—ENGINE OFF

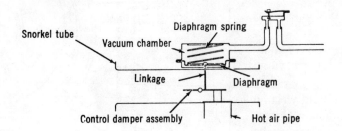

Snorkel tube
Vacuum chamber
Diaphragm spring
Linkage
Diaphragm
Control damper assembly
Hot air pipe

**B—UNDERHOOD TEMPERATURE
BELOW 85°F**

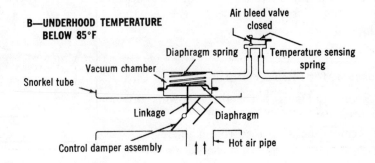

Air bleed valve closed
Diaphragm spring
Temperature sensing spring
Vacuum chamber
Snorkel tube
Linkage
Diaphragm
Control damper assembly
Hot air pipe

**C—UNDERHOOD TEMPERATURE
ABOVE 128°F**

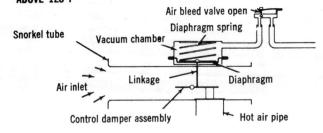

Air bleed valve open
Diaphragm spring
Snorkel tube
Vacuum chamber
Air inlet
Linkage
Diaphragm
Control damper assembly
Hot air pipe

**D—UNDERHOOD TEMPERATURE
BETWEEN 85°F AND 128°F**

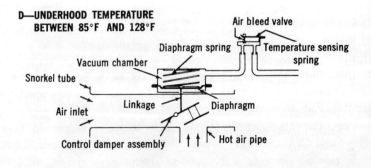

Air bleed valve
Diaphragm spring
Temperature sensing spring
Vacuum chamber
Snorkel tube
Air inlet
Linkage
Diaphragm
Control damper assembly
Hot air pipe

6. If the damper door does not close completely or open at the right temperature, check the vacuum motor as described below.

Vacuum Motor Checking

1. Turn the engine off and disconnect the vacuum hose from the sensor.

2. Suck on the hose. The damper door should completely close. If not, check for a vacuum leak at other end of hose.

3. With vacuum applied, bend or tightly clamp hose. The damper door should remain closed. If not, the vacuum motor leaks and must be replaced.

4. If the vacuum motor is good but the system does not work properly, replace the temperature sensor.

Vacuum Moter Replacement

Refer to Figure 8 for the following procedure.

1. Remove the air cleaner from engine.

2. Drill out the spot welds that fasten the motor to the snorkel.

3. Unhook the motor from the damper door.

4. Drill a 7/64 in. hole in the snorkel tube at the center of the motor retaining strap.

5. Connect the motor to the damper door.

6. Fasten the retaining strap to the air cleaner with a sheet metal screw.

7. Install the air cleaner and check the operation of vacuum motor as described above.

Temperature Sensor Replacement

1. Remove the air cleaner from engine and disconnect the vacuum hose at the sensor.

2. Pry up the sensor clip tubes. See Figure 9.

3. Remove the clip and sensor from the air cleaner.

4. Install the sensor and gasket in the air cleaner in exactly the same position as the old one.

5. Press the clip on sensor. Hold sensor by its sides only; do not touch control mechanism.

6. Install air cleaner and connect vacuum hoses.

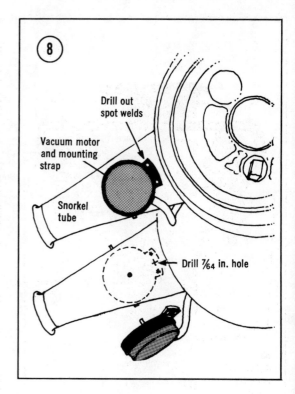

Drill out spot welds

Vacuum motor and mounting strap

Snorkel tube

Drill 7/64 in. hole

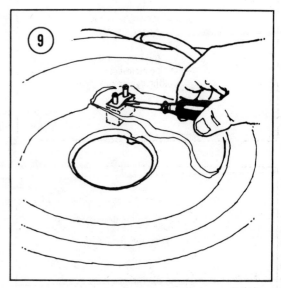

AIR INJECTION REACTOR SYSTEM

The air injection reactor system reduces air pollution by oxidizing hydrocarbons and carbon monoxide as they leave the combustion chamber. See Figure 10 and 11.

The air injection pump, driven by the engine, compresses filtered air and injects it at

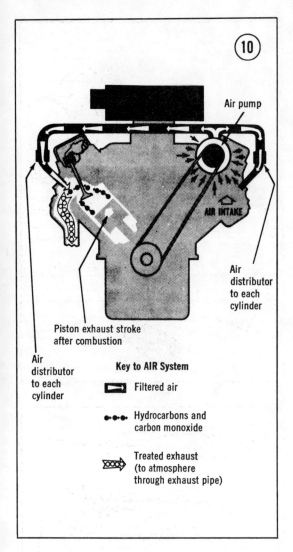

Air pump

Air distributor to each cylinder

AIR INTAKE

Piston exhaust stroke after combustion

Air distributor to each cylinder

Key to AIR System

→ Filtered air

•◦•◦• Hydrocarbons and carbon monoxide

⋙ Treated exhaust (to atmosphere through exhaust pipe)

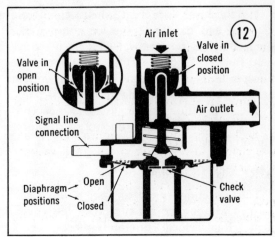

Air inlet

Valve in open position

Valve in closed position

Air outlet

Signal line connection

Diaphragm positions

Open

Closed

Check valve

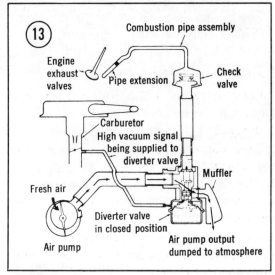

Combustion pipe assembly

Engine exhaust valves

Pipe extension

Check valve

Carburetor

High vacuum signal being supplied to diverter valve

Fresh air

Muffler

Diverter valve in closed position

Air pump

Air pump output dumped to atmosphere

7

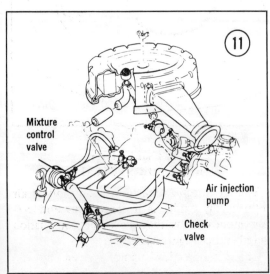

Mixture control valve

Air injection pump

Check valve

the exhaust port of each cylinder. The fresh air mixes with the unburned gases in the exhaust and promotes further burning.

On 1967 systems, the mixture control valve (**Figure 12**) senses sharp increases in manifold vacuum, such as closed throttle deceleration. The increased vacuum opens the valve admitting fresh air into the intake manifold. This leans out the air/fuel mixture and prevents exhaust system backfire.

On 1968 and later systems, a diverter valve performs a function similar to the earlier mixture control valve. However, rather than admitting air from the pump into the intake manifold, backfire is prevented by cutting the fresh air to the exhaust system and diverting the pump output to the atmosphere (**Figure 13**).

The check valves prevent exhaust gases from entering and damaging the air pump if the pump becomes inoperative, e.g., from a drive belt failure. Under normal conditions, the pump delivers sufficient air pressure to prevent exhaust gases from entering the pump.

The air injection reactor system also depends on a special calibrated carburetor, distributor, and other related components.

AIR System Inspection

The inspections to the AIR system can be performed without the aid of special test equipment. Replacement of faulty hoses, check valves, diverter valve, or drive belt are routine. However, when replacing hoses, make sure they are designed for use with the AIR system and will withstand high operating temperatures. Also, use an anti-seize compound on the threads of all connectors that attach to the exhaust manifold or cylinder head.

Drive Belt

Check the condition of the drive belt. If it is cracked, worn, excessively glazed, or if the rubber is deteriorated, replace it. Also check the tension of the belt. If the belt is in good condition, it should be adjusted to a tension of 50 lb. using a belt tension gauge.

If adjustment is required, loosen the pump pivot bolt and the bracket adjustment bolt. Move the pump as required until the tension is correct.

> WARNING
> *Do not pry on the pump housing to move it. This can severly damage the pump.*

Air Manifold, Hoses, and Tubes

Inspect the hoses for deterioration and check the hoses and tubes for cracks. Replace any that are not satisfactory. Check the connections to make sure they are tight and leak free. Test the pressure side of the system with a soapy water solution applied to each of the connections with the engine idling **(Figure 14)**. Bubbling and foaming are indications that a connection is not tight and leak free. Correct any leaks that are found.

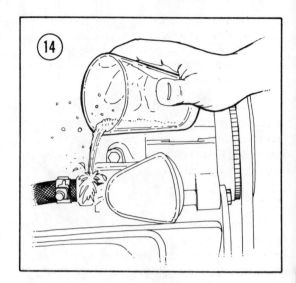

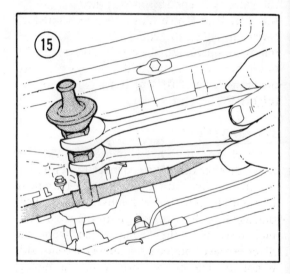

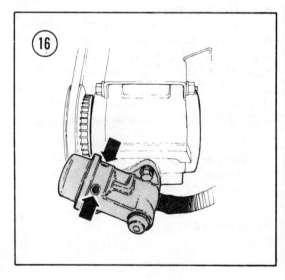

NOTE: *The connectors at the cylinder head (L6 engine) or exhaust manifold (V8 engines) are ¼-in. straight pipe threads; do not use a ¼-in. tapered tap to clean them.*

If a hose or tube is to be replaced, pay careful attention to the routing of the piece being removed and route the new piece in the same manner. Tighten all the connections securely and check for leaks as described above.

Check Valve

If a check valve is suspected of being faulty, disconnect its hose from the diverter valve and blow through it. There should be no resistance. Then, attempt to suck air through the hose. If the valve is in good condition this will not be possible. If the valve fails to perform satisfactorily in either direction, replace it. When removing and installing a check valve be careful not to bend the air manifold. Use two wrenches of comparable shaft length for equal torque (**Figure 15**).

Diverter Valve

Check the condition and tightness of the lines to the diverter valve. Pay particular attention to the vacuum line from the carburetor base plate or manifold to the valve; it must not be kinked, damaged, or deteriorated. With the engine idling, disconnect the vacuum line from the diverter valve and see if vacuum is present. If it is not, the line or the ports in the carburetor base plate may be clogged.

Check the outlets in the diverter valve muffler. At idle, no air should escape through the muffler. Quickly open and close the throttle; a blast of air at least one second in duration should be discharged through the muffler (**Figure 16**). If the valve fails to operate correctly in either mode, it should be replaced.

NOTE: *Make certain a new valve is the same as or equivalent to the one being replaced to ensure that it was designed for your engine and its operating specifications.*

Air Injection Pump

All of the inspections, checks, and corrections just described should be carried out first.

Then, with the air pressure hoses disconnected from the check valves, accelerate the engine to about 1,500 rpm and check the air flow from the hoses. It should increase as engine speed increases. If it does not, or if there is no air pressure at all, the air pump can be assumed to be faulty. Service to or replacement of the pump should be entrusted to a dealer.

NOTE: *If, after inspection and correction of any defects found in the AIR system have been carried out, the vehicle performs poorly or does not idle smoothly, the earlier tune-up procedures and inspections should be rechecked. The pump and the pressure-side lines and fittings have no effect on engine performance. Rough idling or poor performance could be caused by a leaking diverter valve vacuum line, or backfiring could be caused by a defective diverter valve or connections. The AIR system has no effect on performance other than these points.*

Air Injection Pump
Removal/Installation

1. Disconnect the hoses from the pump.
2. Hold the pump pulley with the belt and loosen the bolts.
3. Loosen the pump mounting bolt and pump adjustment bracket bolt. Swing the pump until the drive belt can be removed.
4. Remove the pump pulley.
5. Remove the pump mounting bolts and remove the pump.
6. Installation is the reverse of these steps.
7. Adjust belt tension (Chapter Three).

Mixture Control Valve Replacement

1. Refer to **Figure 17**. Disconnect the vacuum signal line.
2. Disconnect the air inlet and outlet hoses.
3. Remove the valve.
4. Install a new valve by reversing these steps.

NOTE: *The mixture control valves, though similar in appearance, are designed for a particular engine. Be sure you install the correct valve.*

7

Check Valve Replacement

Refer to **Figure 17** for following procedure.

1. Disconnect pump outlet hoses from valve.

2. Unscrew check valve from air manifold. Be careful not to bend the manifold.

3. Installation is the reverse of these steps.

Air Hose Replacement

To remove any hose or tube, first note the routing, then remove the hose or tube and install a new piece and tighten the connection.

> CAUTION
> *Air reactor system hoses are made from special materials to withstand high temperatures. Do not use substitutes.*

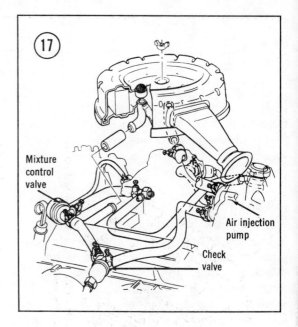

COMBINED EMISSION CONTROL SYSTEM

This system reduces exhaust emissions by permitting vacuum spark advance while in high gear only. It also prevents dieseling common to emission controlled engines.

The system consists of an electrically operated solenoid which shuts off the vacuum line between the carburetor and the distributor. See **Figure 18**. A switch on the transmission detects when the transmission is in a high gear.

Figure 19 is a more detailed diagram of the 1970-1971 system. When the solenoid is not energized, vacuum to the distributor vacuum advance unit is shut off. The distributor is vented to atmosphere through a filter at the opposite end of the solenoid. When the solenoid is energized, the vacuum ports uncover and the plunger shuts off the clean air vent.

The solenoid performs another function besides that of a vacuum switch. When idling in a low gear, e.g., during high gear deceleration with throttle closed, the solenoid is energized and the plunger is extended. This provides a higher idle rpm for reduced hydrocarbon emissions during high gear deceleration.

Two switches and two relays control the solenoid. When the transmission is in low gear, the transmission switch contacts are closed and the reversing relay contacts are open and the solenoid is de-energized. When the transmission shifts to high gear, the transmission switch

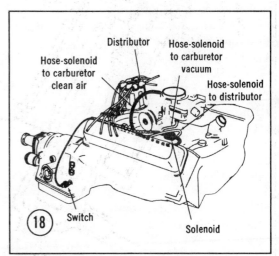

contacts open, the reversing relay de-energizes, and the reversing relay contacts close. The solenoid energizes.

Two other circuits can energize the solenoid. The time delay relay holds its contacts closed for about 15 seconds after the ignition is turned on. The voltage developed across the resistor energizes the solenoid. Full vacuum during this time improves acceleration and eliminates stalling after a start. Finally, the water temperature switch provides an override when the temperature is below 82°F. The switch closes to ground below this temperature and energizes the solenoid.

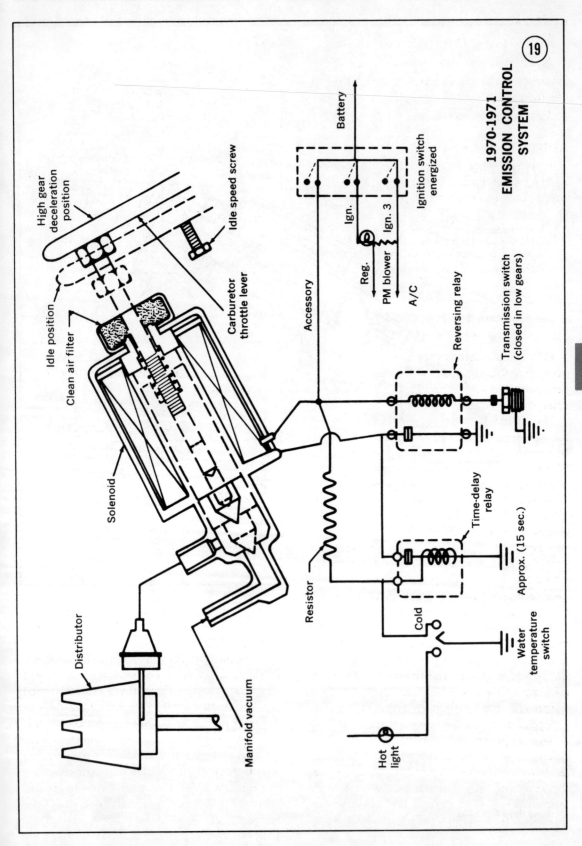

1970-1971
EMISSION CONTROL
SYSTEM

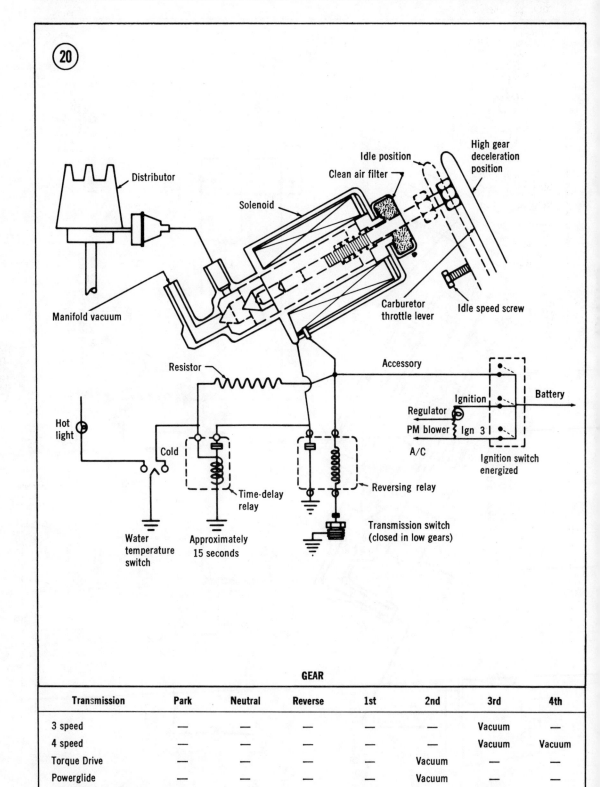

Transmission	GEAR						
	Park	Neutral	Reverse	1st	2nd	3rd	4th
3 speed	—	—	—	—	—	Vacuum	—
4 speed	—	—	—	—	—	Vacuum	Vacuum
Torque Drive	—	—	—	—	Vacuum	—	—
Powerglide	—	—	—	—	Vacuum	—	—
Turbo Hydra-Matic 350	—	—	Vacuum	—	—	Vacuum	—
Turbo Hydra-Matic 400	—	—	Vacuum	—	—	Vacuum	—

The combined emission control system also provides methods to prevent dieseling which is a problem with emission controlled engines. One method is a by-product of the much lower "curb" idle rpm which occurs when the CEC solenoid is de-engergized. The engine runs at such a low rpm it cannot diesel.

On air-conditioned vehicles with automatic transmission, the throttle is open more with the engine idling, and the engine tends to diesel if the air conditioner compressor happens to be off. To prevent this, a solid state timer engages the air conditioner clutch for 3 seconds after the ignition is turned off. The additional compressor load stops the engine quicker, reducing its tendency to diesel. **Figures 20 and 21** show the location of components in the 1970-1971 system.

The system on 1972 and later L6 250 and V8 350 cu. in. engines is similar to the earlier system with the following exceptions:

a. The transmission switch is open in low gears, eliminating the need for reversing relay.

b. A separate idle stop solenoid closes throttle completely when ignition is turned off to prevent dieseling.

c. The water temperature override operates below 82°F as before, but also operates above 232°F.

d. No time delay relay operates during startings.

e. A time delay prevents energizing vacuum advance solenoid for 23 seconds after shifting to high gear.

Figure 22 is a simplified schematic of the L6 250 and V8 350 cu. in. systems. When the ignition is turned on, the idle stop solenoid cracks the throttle open to idle. If the engine cools and temperature is below 82°F, the solenoid operates. Vacuum advance when the engine is cold improves acceleration and helps minimize stalling. If the coolant is above 82°F, the solenoid does not energize.

When engine coolant rises above 82°F, the solenoid can energize only when the transmission is in high gear and the 20-second time delay period has passed. In low gear, the transmission switch opens, de-energizing the solenoid. When the transmission is shifted to high gear, the transmission switch closes, but the time delay relay holds its contacts open for 20 seconds, preventing the solenoid from energizing. After 20 seconds, the solenoid energizes. If the

7

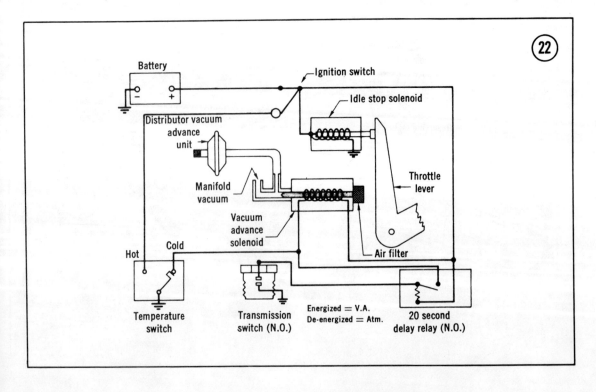

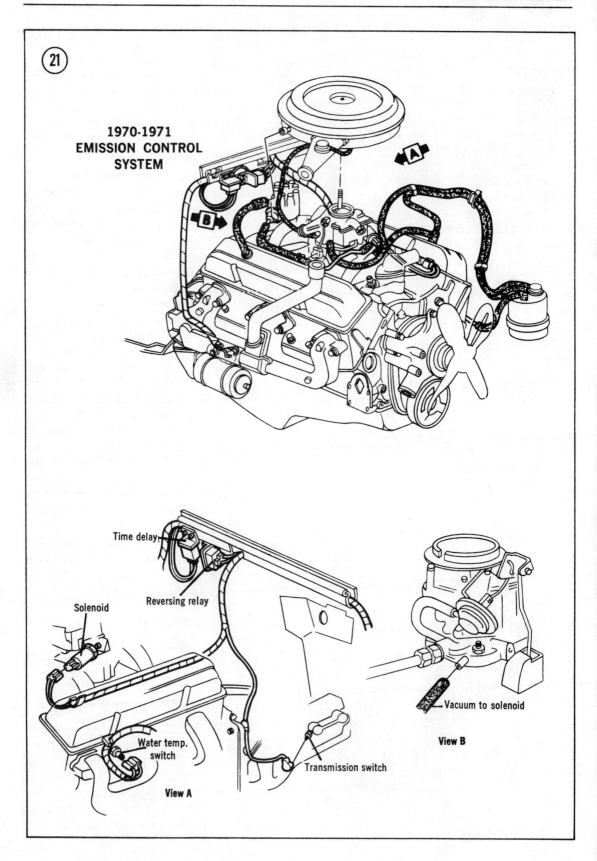

㉑

**1970-1971
EMISSION CONTROL
SYSTEM**

A

B

Time delay

Reversing relay

Solenoid

Water temp.
switch

Transmission switch

View A

Vacuum to solenoid

View B

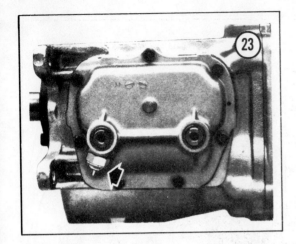

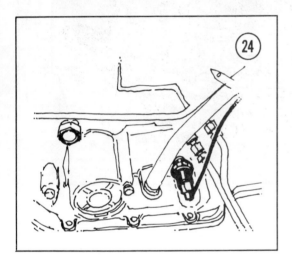

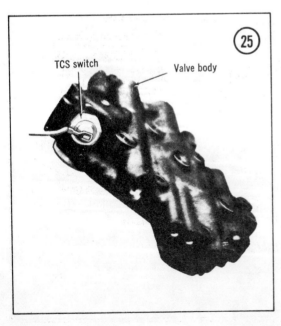

TCS switch   Valve body

transmission downshifts, even momentarily, from high gear, the time delay relay will still prevent energizing the solenoid for 20 seconds.

If coolant temperature exceeds 232°F, regardless of gear, the temperature switch overrides the system and operates the solenoid to supply vacuum advance.

Transmission Switch Replacement (1970-1971)

Refer to **Figures 20 and 21**.

Disconnect the electrical lead, unscrew the switch, and screw in new switch and connect the lead. Test the switch as described above.

Transmission Switch Replacement (1971-1974 Manual and Turbo-Hydramatic 350)

Figures 23 and 24 show location of the switch on the manual and Turbo-Hydramatic 350 transmission, respectively.

Disconnect the electrical lead. Unscrew the switch, screw in a new switch and connect the lead. Test the switch as described above.

Transmission Switch Replacement (1972-1974 Turbo-Hydramatic 400)

The switch is located internally (**Figure 25**). The transmission oil pan must be removed to reach the switch. See Chapter Ten—*Hydramatic Draining/Filling*, and remove the pan.

A wire connects the switch to the externally mounted detent solenoid TCS connector (**Figure 26**). The switch can be tested externally as described in Chapter Three.

CEC Solenoid Replacement (1970-1971)

See *Disassembly* procedure for your carburetor in Chapter Six.

Vacuum Advance Solenoid Replacement (1972-1974)

On 350 engines, the solenoid is located on the right rear portion of the intake manifold. See **Figure 27**. On the 1972 and 1973 L6 engines, the solenoid is located on the carburetor. See **Figure 28**. On 1974 L6 engines, the solenoid is bracket mounted to ignition coil (**Figure 29**).

7

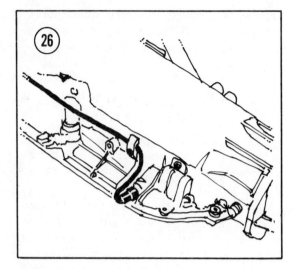

1. Disconnect the vacuum hoses and electrical wires from the solenoid.

2. Remove the solenoid from the bracket.

3. Install a new solenoid. Connect the vacuum hoses and wires.

Idle Stop Solenoid Replacement (1972-1974)

The idle stop solenoid is mounted on the carburetor. See **Figure 30**. Refer to *Disassembly* procedure in Chapter Six for your carburetor.

Relay Replacement (1970-1971)

Refer to **Figures 20 and 21**.

1. Disconnect the cable from the relay.

2. Unscrew the relay bracket.

3. Install a new relay and reconnect the cable.

Time Delay Relay (1972-1974)

The time delay relay is located on the instrument panel reinforcement immediately behind the console instrument cluster assembly (or on the cowl vertical wall on L6 engines).

1. Disconnect the cable from the relay.

2. Unscrew the relay bracket.

3. Install a new relay and reconnect the cable.

Water Temperature Switch Replacement (1970-1974)

The water temperature switch is located on the left cylinder head on 1970-1971 V8 engines

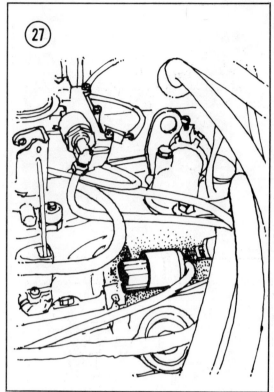

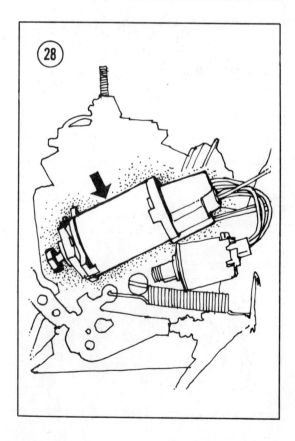

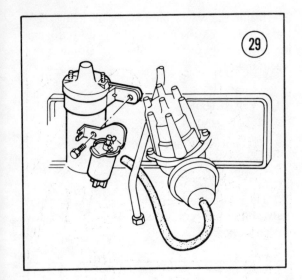

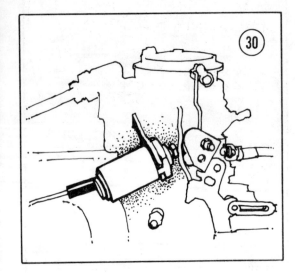

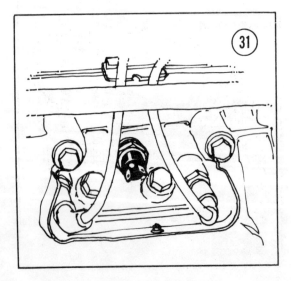

(Figure 21) and on the right cylinder head on 1972-1973 V8 engines **(Figure 31)**. On L6 engines, the switch is on the left side of the cylinder head.

FUEL EVAPORATION CONTROL SYSTEM

All 1972 and later vehicles (1970 and later in California) are equipped with a fuel evaporation control system which prevents release of fuel vapor into the atmosphere.

Fuel vapor from the fuel tank passes through the liquid/vapor separator to the carbon canister. The carbon absorbs and stores the vapor when the engine is stopped. When the engine runs, manifold vacuum draws the vapor from the canister. Instead of being released into the atmosphere, the fuel vapor takes part in the normal combustion process.

There is no preventive maintenance other than replacing the filter on the bottom of the carbon canister every 12,000 miles and checking tightness and condition of all lines connecting the parts of the system.

Canister Filter Replacement

1. From beneath the vehicle, first note the locations of the canister hoses then disconnect them from the top of the canister.

2. Loosen the canister mounting clamp and remove the canister.

3. Remove the filter from the bottom of the canister.

4. Check the hose connections in the canister and clean them of any obstructions.

5. Install a new filter in the canister and assemble the canister.

6. Set the canister in the clamp and tighten the bolts.

7. Reconnect the lines to the canister.

EXHAUST GAS RECIRCULATION (1973 and LATER)

The Exhaust Gas Recirculation (EGR) system is used to reduce the emission of nitrogen oxides (NOX). Relatively inert exhaust gases are introduced into the combustion process to

slightly reduce peak temperatures. This reduction in temperature reduces the formation of NOX.

The exhaust gases are introduced into the intake manifold by way of an EGR valve. See **Figure 32.** This shutoff and metering valve operates on vacuum from the intake manifold via a signal port in the carburetor. On 1974 and later models, a thermal vacuum switch cuts off vacuum to the EGR valve until water temperature reaches 100-130°F. At idle speed, recirculation is not required. Thus, the carburetor signal port is located above the throttle valve and vacuum to the EGR valve diaphragm is cut off at idle speeds. This causes the EGR to close, halting the inroduction of exhaust gas to the intake manifold. As the throttle valve is opened, the signal port is again exposed to manifold vacuum. This actuates the EGR valve diaphragm, which opens the valve and allows exhaust gas to be metered (through an orifice) into the intake manifold. See **Figure 33.**

On L6 engines, the EGR valve is located on the intake manifold next to the carburetor (**Figure 34**). On V8 engines, the valve is located externally on the right side of the intake manifold next to the rocker arm cover (**Figure 35**).

EGR Valve Replacement

1. Disconnect the vacuum line from the valve.
2. Remove the bolt and clamp, then remove valve from manifold.

3. Install the valve on manifold, using new gasket. Tighten the bolt to 25 ft.-lb. and bend the lock tab up over the bolt head. Connect the vacuum line.

EGR Valve Cleaning

CAUTION
Do not wash valve assembly in solvent or degreaser. Permanent damage could result.

1. Use a wire brush or wire wheel to clean the valve base and remove exhaust deposits from the mounting surface.

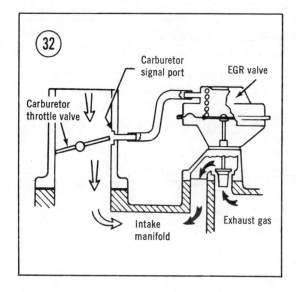

Carburetor signal port

EGR valve

Carburetor throttle valve

Intake manifold

Exhaust gas

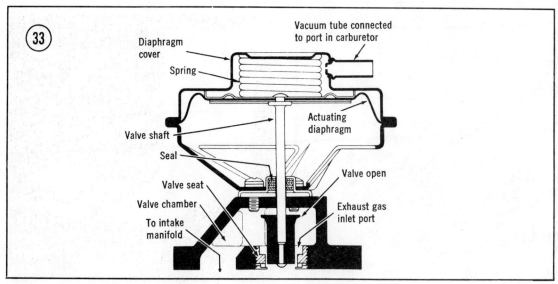

Vacuum tube connected to port in carburetor

Diaphragm cover

Spring

Valve shaft

Seal

Valve seat

Valve chamber

To intake manifold

Actuating diaphragm

Valve open

Exhaust gas inlet port

2. A spark plug cleaner (sandblaster) can be used to clean valve seat and pintle. Insert valve and pintle into machine and blast for 30 seconds.

NOTE: *Many service stations have this type of spark plug cleaner and will clean the valve for a small fee.*

3. Compress the diaphragm spring so the valve is fully unseated and repeat sandblasting for 30 seconds.

4. Make sure all exhaust deposits have been removed. Repeat cleaning if required.

5. Use compressed air to remove all abrasive material from the valve.

Thermal Vacuum Switch Replacement (1974)

1. Disconnect the vacuum lines and remove the switch from the thermostat housing.

2. Apply a sealer to threads and install the switch in the thermostat housing. Tighten the switch to 15 ft.-lb.

3. Rotate the head of the switch for correct hose routing and install the vacuum hoses.

NOTE: *The thermal vacuum switch is non-repairable. If defective, replace it.*

CARBURETOR CALIBRATION

In addition to providing the engine with a combustible mixture of air and fuel, the carburetor is also calibrated to maintain proper emission levels. The idle, off-idle, power enrichments, main metering, and accelerating pump systems are all calibrated to provide the best possible combination of performance, economy, and exhaust emission control.

Calibration is especially critical on 1975 and later models, and the tasks involved require special skills and test equipment the home mechanic is not likely to have. Except for the adjustments of idle speed and idle mixture described in Chapter Four, carburetor work on late models should be entrusted to an expert.

DISTRIBUTOR CALIBRATION

Distributor calibration consists of adjusting initial timing, centrifugal advance, and vacuum advance to obtain the best combination of engine performance, fuel economy, and exhaust emission level control. Timing specifications for each engine are given on the Vehicle Emission Control Information (VECI) decal located in the engine compartment. See *Ignition*

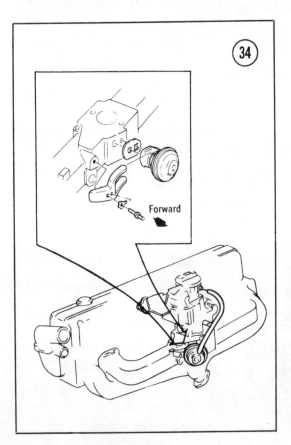

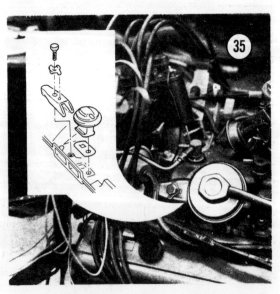

Timing Adjustment, Chapter Four, for instructions on how to set the initial timing. Adjustment or repair of the centrifugal and vacuum spark advance systems should be left to an expert.

CATALYTIC CONVERTER

Catalytic converters, used since 1975, reduce air pollutants by promoting further burning of the exhaust gases. The converter is located in the exhaust line ahead of the muffler and contains a material coated with platinum and palladium. Both of these materials are catalysts, and cause the reduction of hydrocarbons and carbon monoxide by burning as the exhaust gases pass over them. The catalytic converter should be checked for general condition at the same time the remainder of the exhaust system is checked (see *Periodic Maintenance*, Chapter Three). See *Catalytic Converter*, Chapter Nine, for replacement procedure.

EARLY FUEL EVAPORATION SYSTEM

The early fuel evaporation (EFE) system, used on 1975 and later models, provides heating to the intake manifold while the engine is cold, to promote vaporization of the fuel. This helps cut down on choke time and also promotes more thorough burning of the fuel. This, in turn, reduces the amount of pollutants released into the air. The heart of the system is the EFE valve, which controls the amount of heat (exhaust gas) directed under the intake manifold. The valve is controlled by a thermostatic switch in the cooling system that applies or removes vacuum to the EFE valve according to the temperature of the engine coolant. Use the following procedure to check operation of the EFE system.

EFE System Check

Refer to **Figure 36** (V8 engines) or **Figure 37** (L6 engines).

1. With the engine cold, place the transmission in NEUTRAL or PARK, apply the handbrake, and start the engine. Observe the movement of EFE actuator rod and heat valve. The valve should move to the closed position.

2. If the valve does not close, remove the vacuum hose from the actuator and check for the presence of vacuum. If vacuum is present, replace the actuator. If no vacuum is present, remove the vacuum input hose at thermo-vacuum switch (TVS) and check for vacuum. If vacuum is present, replace the TVS. If no

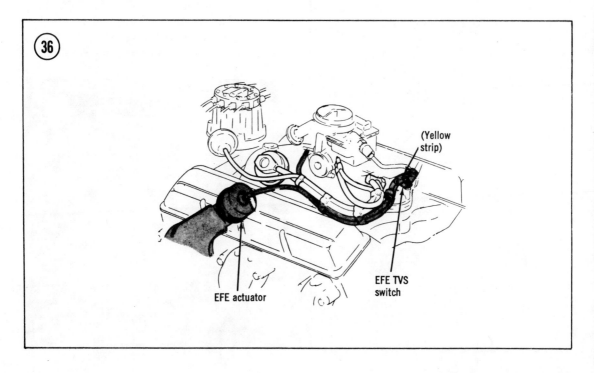

(36)

(Yellow strip)

EFE actuator

EFE TVS switch

vacuum is present, check for damaged vacuum hose and replace it as required.

3. If the valve closes, allow the engine to warm up until coolant temperature reaches 180°F (V8) or 150°F (L6). The exhaust heat valve should move to the open position. If not, remove the hose from the actuator and check for vacuum. If no vacuum is present, replace the actuator. If vacuum is present, replace the TVS.

NOTE: *When replacing the* TVS *on the V8 engines, drain the coolant below the level of the coolant outlet housing. Apply a soft setting sealant to the replacement switch threads before installation, and tighten it to 120 in.-lb.*

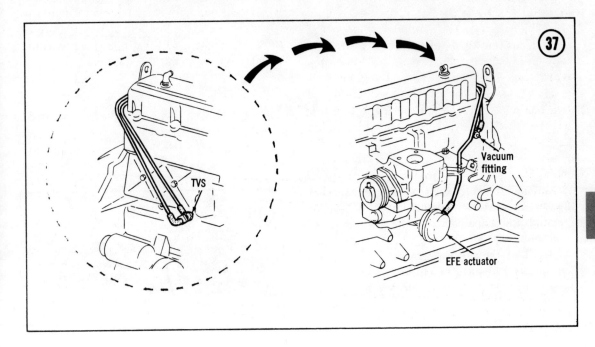

CHAPTER EIGHT

ELECTRICAL SYSTEM

Making repairs to electrical components such as the alternator or starter motor is usually beyond the capability of the inexperienced mechanic and his tool box. Such repairs are best left to the professional mechanic who is equipped with specialized tools.

By using the troubleshooting procedures given in Chapter Two it is possible, however, to isolate problems in many cases to a specific component.

In most cases, it will be faster and more economical to obtain new or rebuilt components instead of making repairs. Make certain, however, that the new or rebuilt part is an exact replacement. Also, make sure that the cause of the failure has been isolated and corrected before installing a replacement. For instance, an uncorrected short in an alternator circuit will in all probability burn out a new alternator as quickly as it damaged the old one. If in doubt, always consult an expert.

Wiring diagrams are at the back of the book.

BATTERY MAINTENANCE

The level of the electrolyte in each cell of the battery should be checked regularly, especially in hot weather. The proper level is even with the split vent located at the bottom of the vent well in each cell. See **Figure 1**. Colorless, odorless drinking water should be added as required to

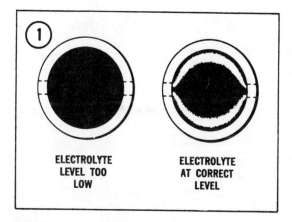

ELECTROLYTE LEVEL TOO LOW   ELECTROLYTE AT CORRECT LEVEL

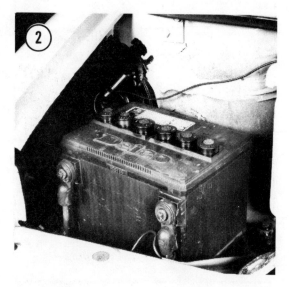

maintain this level in each cell. Never add electrolyte (acid) to a battery that is in service.

If water must be added frequently, chances are that the battery is being overcharged (normal usage is one or two ounces per month per battery — not each cell). Common causes of overcharge are high battery operating temperature, voltage regulator set too high, and a poor ground connection from the regulator.

The battery terminals, top, carrier, and hold-down should be kept free of corrosion, oil, and dirt. The carrier should be in sound mechanical condition and the hold-down bolts should be tight to keep the battery level and prevent excessive shaking of the battery. However, the bolts should not be so tight that a severe strain is placed on the battery case.

Cleaning

To clean the battery, make certain the cell vent plugs are fully seated. Cover the vent holes, if accessible, with small pieces of tape. Wash the top and sides of the battery case and carrier, and the hold-down with a mild solution of ammonia or baking soda to neutralize any acid or corrosion present, then flush with clean water. Pay special attention to terminals and the areas around them. Be sure to remove the tape from the holes in the vent caps.

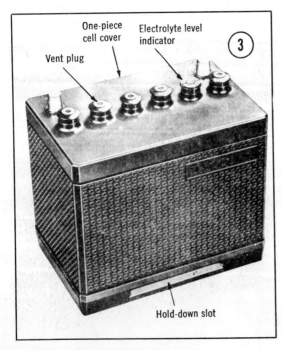

One-piece cell cover
Electrolyte level indicator
Vent plug
③
Hold-down slot

Late models (1970 on) use a battery with "sealed" terminals on the side. See **Figure 2**. This positions them out of the "wet" area on the top of the battery surrounding the vent wells. Normal spillage and other sources of moisture are far less likely to collect around the terminal. These terminals, as a rule, do not require maintenance.

Older models use the "conventional" type battery with the terminals on the top **(Figure 3)**. These terminals should be cleaned, as described above, whenever they become corroded. Following cleaning they should receive a light coat of petroleum jelly to help control future corrosion.

Common Causes of Battery Failure

All batteries eventually fail. Their life can be prolonged, however, with a good maintenance program. Some of the reasons for premature failure are listed below.

1. Vehicle accessories left on overnight or longer, causing a discharged condition.
2. Slow driving speeds on short trips, causing an undercharged condition.
3. Vehicle electrical load exceeding the generator capacity.
4. Charging system defects, such as high resistance, slipping generator belt, or faulty generator or regulator.
5. Abuse of the battery, including failure to keep the battery top and terminals clean, failure to keep cable attaching bolts clean and tight, and failure to add water when needed, or habitually adding too much water.

BATTERY TESTING

Use of the following test procedures will provide a basis for deciding whether a battery is good and usable, requires recharging, or should be replaced. A complete analysis of battery condition requires a visual inspection, an instrument test, and a full-charge hydrometer test.

Visual Inspection

This test is accomplished as follows:
1. Check the outside of the battery for breaks or cracks. If any such damage is present, replace the battery.

8

2. Check the electrolyte level. Levels too high or too low may cause poor performance.

3. Check for loose and corroded cable connections. If necessary, clean and tighten the connections before proceeding with instrument tests.

Instrument Tests

If an instrument with battery testing capabilities is available, follow the manufacturer's instructions. If such an instrument is not available, use a hydrometer to make a specific gravity cell comparison test as follows:

1. Measure the specific gravity of each cell. After taking a reading, return the electrolyte to the cell from which it was removed.

2. Compare readings of all cells. If readings between highest and lowest cell show a difference of 0.050 (50 points) or more, the battery is defective and should be replaced.

Full-Charge Hydrometer Test

This test should only be made on batteries which check out OK after the test in Step 2 above but which subsequently fail in service.

1. Remove the battery from the vehicle and add colorless, odorless drinking water to adjust electrolyte level.

2. Fully charge the battery at the slow charging rate. See *Charging*.

3. When battery is fully charged, use a hydrometer to measure the specific gravity of the electrolyte in each cell. Interpret results as follows:

    a. Full charge hydrometer reading of less than 1.230, corrected for temperature, indicates battery is defective and should be replaced.

        NOTE: *For every 10° above 80°F electrolyte temperature, add 0.004 to specific gravity reading. For every 10° below 80°F, subtract 4 points (0.004).*

    b. Hydrometer readings above 1.310, corrected for electrolyte temperature, indicate that cells have been improperly filled (activation) or improperly serviced. Poor service and short battery life will result.

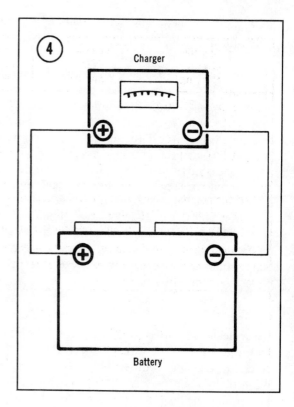

    c. Readings between 1.250 and 1.290 in all cells indicate that battery condition is good. The problem is probably in the charging system or battery cables.

Charging

There is no need to remove the battery from the vehicle to charge it. Just make certain that the area is well ventilated and that there is no chance of sparks or open flames being in the vicinity of the battery; during charging, highly explosive hydrogen is produced by the battery.

Disconnect the ground lead from the battery. Remove the caps from the battery cells and top up each cell with distilled water. Never add electrolyte to a battery that is already in service. The electrolyte level in the cells should be about ¼ in. above the plates.

Connect the charger to the battery — negative to negative, positive to positive (**Figure 4**). If the charger output is variable, select a low setting (5-10 amps), set the voltage selector to 12 volts, and plug the charger in. If the battery is severely discharged (below 1.125), allow it to charge for at least 8 hours. Less charge deterioration requires less charging time.

Table 1   CHARGING RATES

Specific Gravity Reading	Charge Rate Amperes	Battery Capacity — Ampere Hours				
		45	**55**	**70**	**80**	**85**
1.125 — 1.150 ①	35	65 min.	80 min.	100 min.	115 min.	125 min.
1.150 — 1.175	35	50 min.	65 min.	80 min.	95 min.	105 min.
1.175 — 1.200	35	40 min.	50 min.	60 min.	70 min.	75 min.
1.200 — 1.225	35	30 min.	35 min.	45 min.	50 min.	55 min.
Above 1.225	5	②	②	②	②	②

① If the specific gravity is below 1.125, use the indicated high rate of charge for the 1.125 specific gravity, then charge at 5 amperes until the specific gravity reaches 1.250 at 80°F.

② Charge at 5 ampere rate only until the specific gravity reaches 1.250 at 80°F.

Warning: At no time during the charging operation should the electrolyte temperature exceed 130°F.

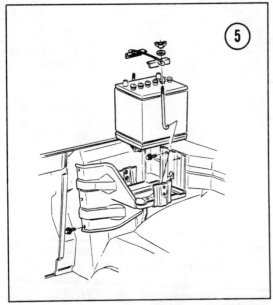

⑤

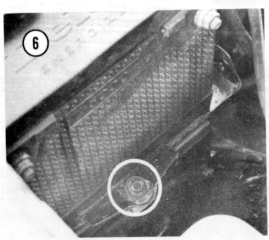

⑥

NOTE: *If time permits, it is recommended that the battery be charged at the lower rate and for a longer period of time; however, if there is not sufficient time for slow charging, the high-rate charging times and rates shown in* **Table 1** *should be followed.*

After the battery has been charged for a suitable period of time, unplug the charger and disconnect it from the battery. Be extremely careful about sparks. Test the condition of each cell with a hydrometer as described above and compare the results with **Table 1**.

If the specific gravity indicates that the battery is fully charged, and if the readings remain the same after one hour, the battery can be considered to be in good condition and fully charged. Check the electrolyte level and add distilled water if necessary, install the vent caps, and reconnect the ground lead.

Removal/Installation

1. Loosen the bolts in the terminal clamps far enough so the clamps can be spread slightly. Lift straight up on the clamps (negative first) to remove them from the posts. Twisting or prying on the clamps or posts can result in serious damage to a battery that may otherwise be in good condition.

2. Unscrew the nuts from the hold-down bolts **(Figure 5)** and remove the hold-down frame. For batteries retained with a hold-down lug **(Figure 6)**, unscrew the bolt and remove the lug. Lift the battery out of the engine compartment.

8

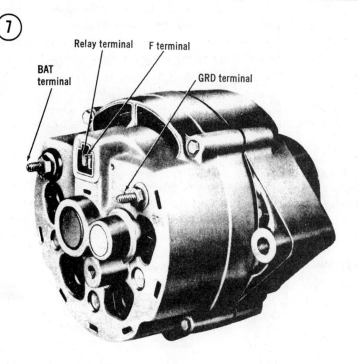

⑦

BAT terminal

Relay terminal   F terminal

GRD terminal

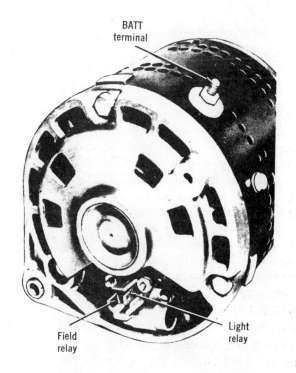

BATT terminal

**DELCOTRON
SERIES 1D AND 2D
ALTERNATORS**

Field relay

Light relay

3. Reverse these steps to install the battery. Before setting the battery in place, clean the battery holder with a solution of baking soda and water to neutralize any acids that may have formed. Allow the solution to stand for several minutes, then carefully flush it away with clean water, and dry it with an old rag. Set the battery into the holder making sure it's squarely seated. Install the hold-down frame and screw on the nuts snugly.

Connect the positive lead to the battery first, then the negative. Tighten the clamp bolts securely and check their tightness by trying to rotate them on the posts by hand. Coat the terminals liberally with Vaseline to inhibit corrosion and formation of ash-like acid deposits.

CHARGING SYSTEMS

The charging system consists of the battery (discussed above), the generator or alternator, the voltage regulator, the "tell-tale" lamp or ammeter, and the wiring necessary to connect these components. Two basic types of alternators are used. The Series 1D and 2D Delcotrons (see **Figure 7**), used on the older models, were alternating current generators (alternators) requiring an external mechanical or transistorized voltage regulator. The Series 10-SI Delcotron (see **Figure 8**), also an alternating current generator, has an internal solid state voltage regulator which employs an integrated circuit.

All models have an internal bridge which changes the stator AC voltages to DC voltages. The blocking action of the diodes in the bridge prevents battery discharge back through the alternator.

Neither type of alternator requires periodic maintenance, other than a check for loose mounting bolts and belt tension. Certain precautions should be observed, however, since the alternator and regulator are designed for use only on negative polarized systems. These precautions are as follows:

1. Do not attempt to "polarize" the alternator.

2. Do not short across or ground any of the terminals in the charging system except as specifically instructed in these procedures.

3. Never operate the alternator with the output terminal open-circuited.

4. Make sure the alternator, external voltage regulator (if so equipped), and battery are of the same ground polarity.

5. When connecting a charger or booster battery to the vehicle battery, connect the negative terminal to negative terminal and positive terminal to positive terminal.

6. Whenever a lead is disconnected from the alternator, the battery ground cable should be disconnected.

Static Checks (All Series)

Before making any electrical checks on the charging system, visually inspect all connections to make sure thay are clean and tight. Verify that battery is serviceable and charged. Inspect all the wiring for frayed, broken, or cracked insulation. Check for loose mounting bolts and proper belt tension.

10-SI DELCOTRON TROUBLESHOOTING

NOTE: *If vehicle is equipped with an ammeter instead of an indicator lamp, omit the indicator lamp circuit check.*

Indicator Lamp Circuit Check

Check the indicator lamp for normal operation as follows:

Switch	Lamp	Engine
Off	Off	Stopped
On	On	Stopped
On	Off	Running

If the indicator lamp operated normally, use procedures described under *Undercharged Battery* or *Overcharged Battery*. Otherwise, make the appropriate abnormal condition checks below:

1. *Switch off, lamp on* — Disconnect the leads from Delcotron No. 1 and No. 2 terminals. If the lamp remains on, there is a short circuit between the 2 leads. If the lamp goes out, the rectifier bridge is faulty and must be replaced, as this condition will result in an undercharged battery.

2. *Switch on, lamp off, engine stopped* — This defect can be caused by the defects listed in Step 1 above, or by reversal of the No. 1 and No. 2 leads at these 2 terminals, or by an open circuit.

8

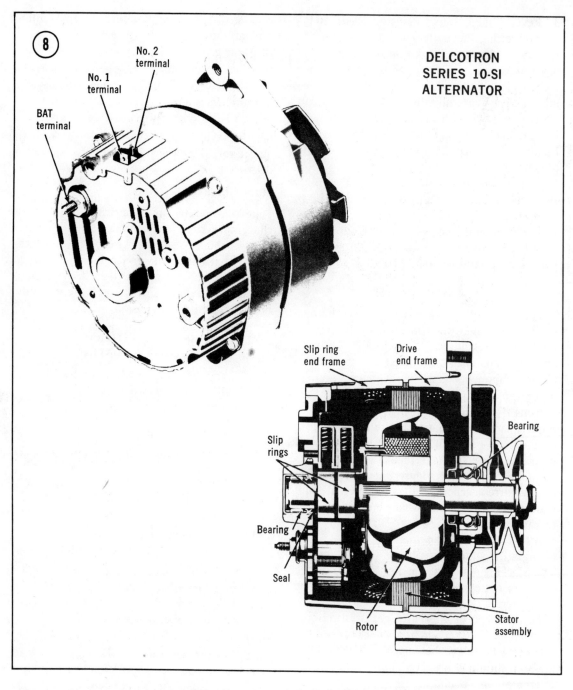

⑧

No. 2 terminal

No. 1 terminal

BAT terminal

DELCOTRON SERIES 10-SI ALTERNATOR

Slip ring end frame

Drive end frame

Slip rings

Bearing

Bearing

Seal

Rotor

Stator assembly

To determine where the open exists, proceed as follows:

    a. Connect a voltmeter between Delcotron No. 2 terminal and ground. If the reading is obtained, proceed to Step b. If the reading is zero, repair open circuit between No. 2 terminal and battery. If lamp comes on, no further check is required.

    b. Disconnect the leads from No. 1 and No. 2 terminals on the Delcotron and turn the ignition switch on. Momentarily ground No. 1 terminal lead.

CAUTION
Do not ground No. 2 lead. If the lamp does not come on, check for a blown fuse or fusible link, burned out lamp

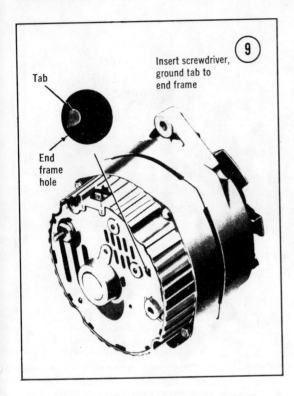

*bulb, defective bulb socket, or open in
No. 1 lead circuit between the Delcotron
and ignition switch. If the lamp lights,
remove the ground at No. 1 terminal
and reconnect No. 1 and No. 2 wires to
the Delcotron. Insert a screwdriver in
test hole (see **Figure 9**) to ground wiring.
If the lamp does not go on, check connection between wiring harness and Delcotron No. 1 terminal. If the wiring is
OK, have Delcotron brushes, slip rings,
and field winding checked. If the lamp
lights, repeat voltmeter check in Step
(a). If a reading is obtained, have the
regulator replaced.*

3. *Switch on, lamp on, engine running* — See
Undercharged Battery Condition Check, below, for possible causes.

Undercharged Battery Condition Check

Symptoms of this condition are slow crank-
ing and low specific gravity readings (battery
cells). The condition can be caused by one or
more of the following, even though the ammeter may be operating properly.

1. Accessories left on for extended periods.

2. Incorrect belt tension.

3. Defective or discharged battery (see battery
tests above).

4. Wiring defects. Check all connectors for
tightness and cleanliness, including connectors
at Delcotron and firewall, cable clamps, and
battery posts.

5. Open circuit between Delcotron and battery.
Check by connecting a voltmeter between BAT
terminal on the Delcotron and ground, No. 1
terminal and ground, and No. 2 terminal and
ground. A zero reading indicates an open between the voltmeter connection point and the
battery.

CAUTION
*An open in the Delcotron No. 2 lead cir-
cuit will cause uncontrolled voltage,
battery overcharge, and possible
damage to the battery and accessories.
The 10-SI series Delcotron has a built-in
feature to prevent overcharge and accessory damage by preventing the Delcotron from turning on if there is an
open in the No. 2 lead circuit. Such an
open could occur between terminals, at
the crimp between the harness wire or
terminal, or in the wire itself.*

Overcharged Battery Condition Check

1. Verify that the battery is in serviceable condition and fully charged.

2. Connect a voltmeter from Delcotron No. 2
terminal to ground. If the reading is zero, an
open exists in No. 2 lead circuit.

3. If the battery and No. 2 lead circuit are OK,
but an obvious overcharge condition, such as
excessive battery water usage, exists, have the
following items checked:

   a. Field winding (for shorts)

   b. Brushes and brush leads (for grounding or
     defective regulator)

1D AND 2D DELCOTRON
TROUBLESHOOTING

Charging System Condition Test

This test may be used to indicate overall
charging system condition and to isolate a malfunctioning component (if present).

1. Turn ignition off and make static tests
outlined above. If tests fail to isolate trouble,

8

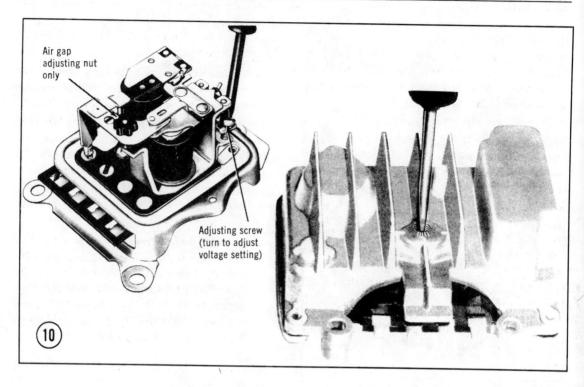

Air gap adjusting nut only

Adjusting screw (turn to adjust voltage setting)

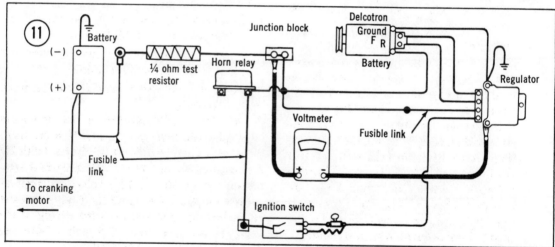

set the handbrake and place the transmission in neutral.

2. Connect a voltmeter from the junction block on the horn relay to ground at the voltage regulator base.

CAUTION
Make certain the voltmeter lead does not touch a resistor or terminal extension under the regulator; this could cause damage.

3. Connect a tachometer to the engine, using the tachometer manufacturer's instructions.

4a. *On models equipped with indicator lamp in charging circuit* — Turn the ignition switch ON. If the indicator fails to light, perform *Indicator Lamp Circuit Tests* below, and make corrections as required before proceeding.

4b. *On ammeter-equipped models* — Turn the ignition switch to ACC. If the ammeter fails to register discharge, perform *Field Circuit Resistance Check* below before proceeding.

5a. *On "indicator lamp" models* — If the lamp lights, start the engine and run it at 1,500 rpm or above. If the lamp fails to go out, perform *Indicator Lamp Circuit Tests* and make corrections before proceeding.

5b. *On "ammeter lamp" models* — If the ammeter shows discharge, start the engine and run it at 1,500 rpm or above. If the meter fails to move toward charge, perform *Field Circuit Tests* below before proceeding.

6. Start the engine and run it at 1,500 rpm a few minutes to develop a battery surface charge. Turn on the headlights and heater blower motor (high speed), run the engine at 1,500 rpm and read the voltmeter. If reading is 12.5 volts or more, turn off the headlights and heater blower and stop the engine. Have the voltage regulator adjusted (see procedure below). If reading was below 12.5 volts, check Delcotron output using the procedure given below.

   a. *Delcotron tests bad* — Have the Delcotron repaired or replaced.

   b. *Delcotron tests OK* — Disconnect the regulator connector, remove the cover, and reconnect the connector. Repeat the load test at beginning of Step 6. Turn the adjusting screw (see **Figure 10**) to raise voltmeter reading to 12.5 volts. On a transistorized regulator, remove the pipe plug, insert screwdriver into the slot and turn clockwise one or two turns to increase voltage. Turning counterclockwise decreases voltage. If 12.5 volts cannot be obtained, install new regulator and repeat Step 6. Turn off loads and stop engine.

Regulator Voltage Adjustment

1. Connect a ¼-ohm, 25-watt resistor into charging circuit at the horn relay junction block as shown in **Figure 11** (between both leads and terminals).

2. Operate the engine at 1,500 rpm for at least 15 minutes (longer in cold weather), then cycle the regulator voltage control (by disconnecting and reconnecting the regulator connector) and read the voltage. If the reading is 13.5-15.2, the regulator is OK. If it is not within these limits,

leave the engine running at 1,500 rpm and perform the following:

   a. Disconnect the regulator and remove the regulator cover. Reconnect the connector and set the voltage to 14.2-14.6 volts. See Step 6 under *Charging System Condition Test*.

   b. Disconnect the connector, reinstall the cover, and reconnect connector.

   c. Allow the engine to operate another 5-10 minutes at 1,500 rpm to reestablish regulator internal operating temperature.

   d. Cycle the regulator voltage (by disconnecting and reconnecting the connector), then read the voltage. A reading between 13.5 and 15.2 volts indicates that regulator is OK. Stop engine, remove voltmeter and resistor, and reconnect leads to the horn relay junction block.

Alternator Output Test (Voltmeter Method)

1. Disconnect the 2-terminal connector from the Delcotron "F" and "R" terminals.

2. Connect a jumper between BAT terminal to F terminal to provide field excitation.

3. Connect a voltmeter between BAT terminal and GRD terminal.

4. Start the engine and turn on the high beam headlights and high-speed heater blower. Slowly increase engine speed to 1,500 rpm (with 2D 6.2 in. Delcotron run at 600 rpm) and read voltage. A reading of 12.5 volts or higher indicates output is OK. Stop the engine, remove the voltmeter, and reconnect the wiring. If the reading was less than 12.5 volts, have the Delcotron repaired or replaced.

Indicator Lamp Initial Field Circuit Tests

The indicator lamp circuit (on models so equipped) provides initial field excitation, causing the indicator lamp to glow. The light is cancelled by closing the field relay which applies battery voltage to both sides of the bulb (bulb goes out). Thus the indicator lamp should go on when the ignition switch is turned on but should go out almost immediately when the engine is started. Ammeter-equipped models

8

use the same initial field excitation and control circuits, except that the indicator lamp is not used. Continuity tests on both circuits can be made as follows:

1. If the lamp fails to light or the ammeter fails to function, probable causes are faulty bulb or socket, faulty ammeter, an open circuit in the wiring, regulator, or field, or a shorted positive diode (which also may cause lamp to light when switch is off). Test as follows. See **Figure 12**.

   a. Disconnect the connector from the regulator and turn the ignition switch to ON. Connect a continuity test lamp from connector terminal 4 to ground as shown in Step I of **Figure 12**. If the test lamp does not light, check for faulty bulb, socket, or open circuit between switch and regulator connector. Repair as required. If the test light goes on, the failure is in regulator, Delcotron, or wire between regulator F terminal and Delcotron. In this case, proceed to Step b.

   b. Disconnect a test lamp lead from ground and connect between connector F and "4" terminals as shown in Step II of **Figure 12**. If the test lamp lights, the problem is an open circuit in the regulator or relay contacts are stuck closed. Have the regulator repaired or replaced. If the test lamp fails to light, the trouble is in the wire between connector F terminal on Delcotron and regulator or in field windings. In this case, proceed to Step c.

   c. Connect the test lamp between F terminal on Delcotron and "4" terminal in regulator connector, as shown in Step III of **Figure 12**. If the lamp lights, there is an open circuit in the wire between the Delcotron and regulator F terminals. Correct as required. If the lamp fails to light, an open exists in the Delcotron field windings. Have it repaired or replaced.

2. If the indicator lamp fails to go out, or the ammeter shows discharge while the engine is running, possible causes are loose drive belt (adjust as required), faulty field relay (see *Field Relay Checks and Adjustments* below), or a defective alternator (see *Alternator Output Test* procedure above). Other causes could be (at normal idle) parallel resistance wire open (see

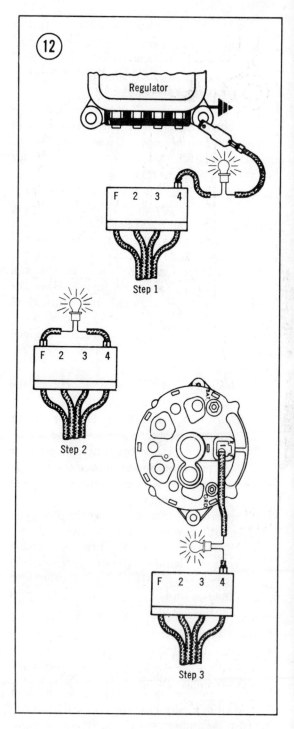

Field Circuit Resistance Wire Check below), or, on ammeter models, the initial field excitation wire to ACC terminal is open. Correct as required. If the lamp fails to go out after the switch is turned off, the positive diode is shorted (see *Diode Test* below).

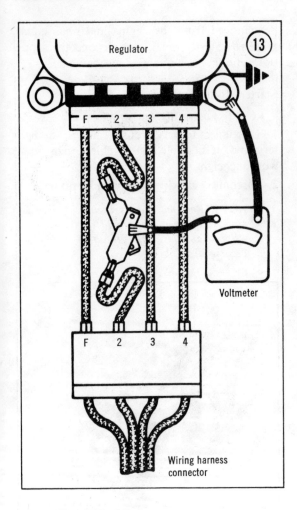

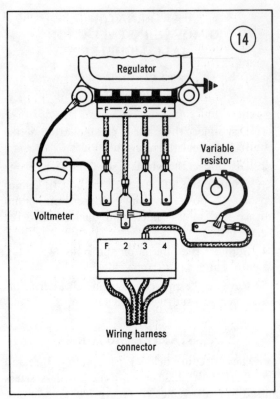

Field Circuit Resistance Wire Checks

The resistance wire is a part of the wiring harness. It cannot be soldered, however. All splices must be made with crimp-type connectors. The wire is rated at 10 ohms, 6.25 watts minimum. To check for open resistor or field excitation wire (connected to ignition switch ACC terminal), proceed as follows.

1. Connect a test lamp between regulator connector terminal "4" and ground as shown in Step I of **Figure 12**.

2. Turn the ignition switch on. If the test lamp lights, the resistance wire is OK. If the lamp fails to light, the resistor wire is open circuited and must be replaced. Note that the dash indicator lamp does not light in this test because series resistance of the 2 bulbs causes amperage to be too low.

Field Relay Checks and Adjustment

To check for a faulty relay, proceed as follows.

1. Connect a voltmeter between the regulator connector terminal "2" and ground. See **Figure 13**.

2. Operate the engine at fast idle (1,500-2,000 rpm). If the voltmeter shows zero reading, check voltage between No. 2 terminal on regulator and R terminal on Delcotron. If the voltage at regulator exceeds closing voltage (1.5-3.5 volts), regulator field relay is faulty. Check and adjust the regulator, using the procedure given below.

Closing Voltage Adjustment

1. Make the connections shown in **Figure 14**, using a 50 ohm variable resistor.

2. Turn the resistor to the OPEN position.

3. Turn the ignition switch off.

4. Slowly decrease resistance and note the closing voltage of relay. Adjust (1.5-3.5 volts) by bending heel iron as shown in **Figure 15**, as required.

ALTERNATOR REMOVAL/INSTALLATION (ALL MODELS)

NOTE: *Service of the alternator, except for removal and installation, is beyond the scope of this book.*

1. Disconnect the battery ground cable at the battery to prevent damage to diodes.

2. Disconnect the wiring leads from Delcotron.

3. Remove the alternator brace bolt (if equipped with power steering), loosen the pump brace and mount nuts, and then remove the drive belt(s).

4. Support the alternator and remove bolt(s). Remove alternator from vehicle.

5. Reverse the procedure to install alternator, and then adjust drive belt(s) tension.

STARTER MOTOR

The procedure below is general in nature and applies, with slight variations, to all starters used on all vehicles. **Figure 16** is a cross-sectional view of a typical starter motor/solenoid assembly. **Figure 17** shows typical starter installations on various engine models. **Table 2** shows starter specifications.

Periodic lubrication or other maintenance is not required for either the starter motor or the solenoid.

Diagnostic procedures for troubleshooting the starter motor are given in Chapter Two. If these procedures are used and it is determined that the starter motor and/or solenoid are defective, the starter/solenoid assembly should be removed from the engine and repaired or replaced. Starter repairs are beyond the scope of this book. See a qualified mechanic.

Starter Motor Replacement

Refer to **Figure 17**.

1. Disconnect battery ground cable at the battery and, if possible, raise vehicle to a good working height.

2. Disconnect all wires at solenoid terminals.

NOTE: *Reinstall nut as each wire is removed. Thread sizes are different and stripped threads could result if nuts become mixed.*

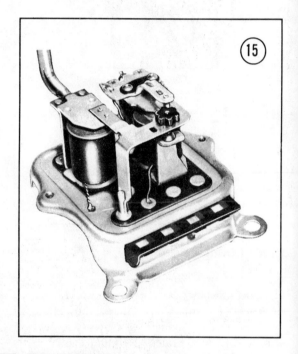

Table 2   STARTER SPECIFICATIONS

			(No Load)			
	1108799 1108365 1108774 1108512 1108367 1109056	1109059 1108418 1108775 1108430 1108776 110952	1108427 1108338	1108361	1107368 1107320 1107388	1107399
Voltage	9	9	9	9	10.6	10.6
Current	50-80	65-95	50-80	55-85	65-100	49-87
RPM	5,500- 10,500	7,500- 10,500	3,500- 6,000	3,100- 4,900	3,600- 5,100	6,200- 10,700

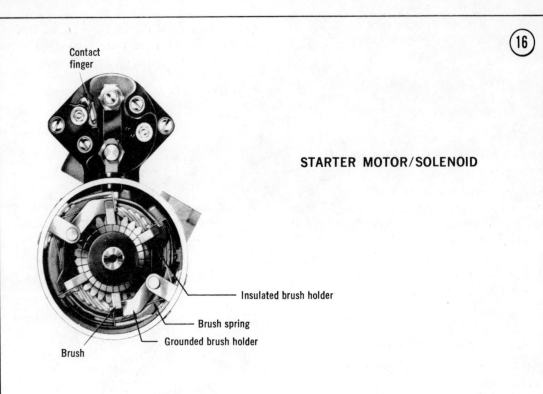

Contact finger

STARTER MOTOR/SOLENOID

Insulated brush holder

Brush spring

Grounded brush holder

Brush

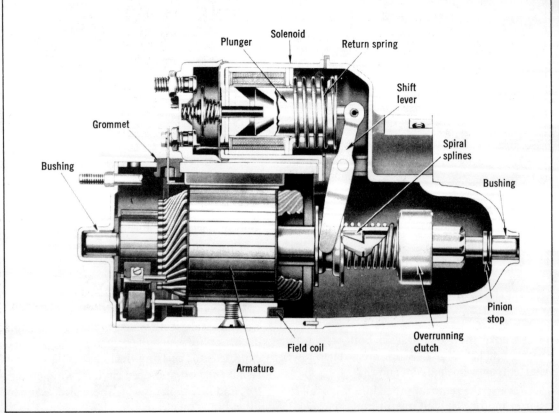

Plunger

Solenoid

Return spring

Shift lever

Grommet

Spiral splines

Bushing

Bushing

Pinion stop

Field coil

Overrunning clutch

Armature

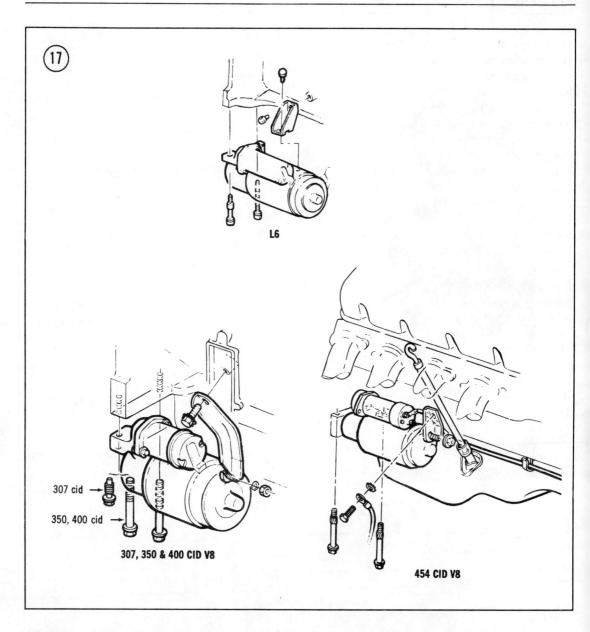

L6

307 cid →

350, 400 cid →

307, 350 & 400 CID V8

454 CID V8

3. Loosen starter front bracket (nut on V8 engines, bolt on 6-cylinder engines), and then remove 2 mount bolts.

> NOTE: *On V8 engines using a solenoid heat shield, remove the front bracket upper bolt and detach bracket from starter motor.*

4. Remove the front bracket bolt or nut and rotate bracket clear of work area. Then lower starter from vehicle, front end first.

5. Reverse the removal procedure to install the starter motor. Tighten mount bolts first (25-35

ft.-lb.), then tighten bracket nut or bolt. Make sure all electrical connections are tight.

6. Check starter operation.

BODY ELECTRICAL SYSTEM

Instructions and pointers for troubleshooting the electrical wiring system are given in Chapter Two. Service which the owner/mechanic can be expected to perform includes isolation and repair of short and open circuits, wire, connector, and fuse replacement, and sealed beam and other bulb replacement.

Maintenance of the lighting and wiring systems consists of an occasional check to see that wiring connections are tight and clean, that lighting units are tightly mounted and that headlights are properly adjusted. The latter task should be performed by a qualified mechanic having access to the specialized equipment required.

Loose or corroded connectors can result in a discharged battery, dim lights, and possible damage to the alternator or voltage regulator. Should insulation become burned, cracked, abraded, etc., the affected wire or wiring harness should be replaced.

Rosin core solder (never use acid core solder on electrical connections) must always be used when splicing wires. Splices should be covered with insulating tape.

Replacement wires must be of the same gauge as the replaced wire — never use a smaller gauge. All harnesses and wires should be held in place with clips, cable ties, or other holding devices so that chafing and abrasion can be avoided.

CHARGE INDICATOR RELAY

If the alternator and voltage regulator are operating satisfactorily and the charge indicator warning light remains on, or the ammeter registers discharge, the charge indicator relay, located inside the voltage regulator, must be tested. See *Field Relay Checks and Adjustment.*

FUSES

Whenever a failure occurs in any part of the electrical system, always check the fuse box to see if a fuse has blown. If one has, it will be evident by blackening of the fuse or by a break in the metal link in the fuse. Usually the trouble can be traced to a short circuit in the wiring connected to the blown fuse. This may be caused by worn-through insulation or by a wire which has worked loose and shorted to ground. Occasionally, the electrical overload which causes the fuse to blow may occur in a switch or a motor.

A blown fuse should be treated as more than a minor annoyance; it should serve also as a warning that something is wrong in the electrical system. Before replacing a fuse, determine what caused it to blow and then correct the trouble.

WARNING
Never replace a fuse with one of a higher amperage rating than that of the one originally used. Never use tinfoil or other metallic material to bridge fuse terminals. Failure to follow these basic rules could result in heat or fire damage to major parts, or loss of the entire vehicle.

Use the wiring diagrams and the function/color coding charts at the end of this book to determine the circuits protected by a particular fuse.

The fuse panel **(Figure 18)** is located at the left end of the firewall, beneath the dashboard.

The fuse amperage and the circuits protected are shown in **Table 3**. To replace or inspect a fuse, carefully pry it out of its holder with the end of a pencil or similar non-metallic probe and snap a new one into place.

Fusible Links

Fusible links provide protection to circuits which are not normally fused, such as the ignition system circuit. The links are usually four gauges smaller than the wiring in the circuit they are protecting, and are covered with heavy red insulation. The gauge size is plainly marked on the insulation. If a link burns out, the cause must be isolated and corrected. A new fusible link must then be spliced into the circuit. The following procedure should be used to replace fusible links.

1. Disconnect battery ground cable at battery.

2. Disconnect old fusible link from components to which it is attached.

3. Cut harness behind connector **(Figure 19)** to remove damaged fusible link.

4. Strip harness wire insulation to approximately ½ inch.

5. Position clip around ends of new fusible link **(Figure 20)** and harness wire and crimp so that both wires are securely fastened.

6. Solder the connection, using rosin core solder. Use sufficient heat to obtain a good solder joint, but do not overheat.

8

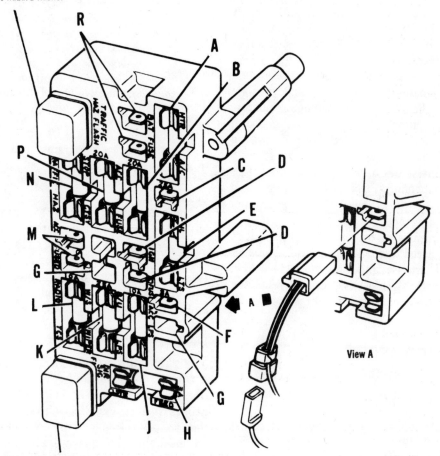

Traffic hazard flasher

Directional signal flasher

View A

FUSE PANEL

A. Fuse—heater/air conditioner
B. Fuse—accessory
C. Receptacle—C62
D. Receptacle—NL2/A33/U16
E. Fuse—panel lights
F. Receptacle—accessory lamps
G. Receptacle—(not used)
H. Fuse—cluster feed

J. Fuse—backup lamps
K. Fuse—windshield wiper
L. Fuse—radio and TCS
M. Receptacle—TP2/M40
N. Fuse—traffic hazard
P. Fuse—tail/stop/courtesy lamps
R. Receptacle—C91/UF2/U35/U37

Table 3   FUSE RATINGS

Circuit	Fuse Rating (amps)								
	1967	1968	1969	1970	1971	1972	1973	1974	1975
Wiper	20	20	25	25	25	25	25	25	25
Back-up lamp and gauges	10	20	20	25	20	20	20	20	20
Heater/AC	25	25	25	25	25	25	25	25	25
Radio	10	10	10	10	10	10	10	10	10
Instrument lamps	4	4	4	4	2	3	3	4	4
Stop and taillamp	20	20	20	20	20	20	20	20	20
Clock, lighter and courtesy	20	20	20	20	25	20	20	20	20
In-line AC	30	30	30	30	30	30	30	30	30
Gauges and telltales		10	10	10	10	10	10	10	10
Tail, license, and park						20	20	20	20

Circuit	Fuse Rating (amps)		
	1976	1977	1978
Wiper	25	25	25
Back-up lamp and gauges	20	20	20
Heater/AC	25	25	25
Radio	10	10	10
Instrument lamps	4	4	4
Stop and taillamp	20	20	20
Clock, lighter and courtesy	20	20	20
In-line AC	30	30	30
Gauges and telltales	10	10	10
Tail, license, and park	20	20	20

8

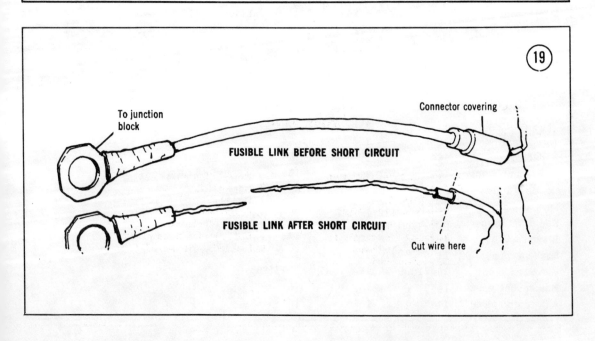

To junction block

Connector covering

FUSIBLE LINK BEFORE SHORT CIRCUIT

FUSIBLE LINK AFTER SHORT CIRCUIT

Cut wire here

⑲

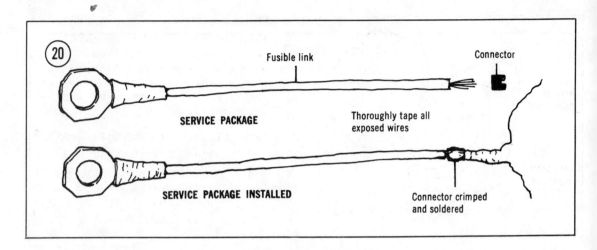

Table 4   LAMP BULB DATA

Circuit	1967	1968	1969	1970	1971	1972	1973	1974	1975
Headlamp	6012	6012	6012	6014	6014	6014	6014	6014	6014
Front park/turn	1034A	1157NA	1157NA	1157NA	1157NA	1157NA	1157NA	1157NA	1157NA
Tail stop/turn	1157	1157	1157	1157	1157	1157	1157	1157	1157
Turn signal ind.	194	194	194	194	194	194	194	168	168
High beam ind.	194	194	194	194	194	194	194	168	168
Instrument lamps	194	194	194	194	194	194	194	168	168
Courtesy lamp	211	211	211	211	211	211	212	212	212
License plate lamp	67	67	67	67	67	194	67	168	168
Radio dial lamp	1893	1893	1893	293/1893	1816	1816	1816	1816	1816
Brake alarm	194	194	194	194	194	194	194	194	194
Back-up lamp	1156	1156	1156	1156	1156	1156	1156	1156	1156
Glove box lamp	1895	1895	1895	1895	1895	1895	1895	1895	1895
Heater cont. panel	1895	1445	1445	1895	1445	1445	1445	1445	1445
A.C. control panel	1895	1445	1445	1895	1445	1445	1445	1445	1445

Circuit	1976	1977	1978
Headlamp	6014	6012	6012
Front park/turn	1157NA	1156NA	1156NA
Tail stop/turn	1157	1157	1157
Turn signal ind.	168	194	194
High beam ind.	194	194	194
Instrument lamps	194	194	194
Courtesy lamp	212	631	631
License plate lamp	67	194	194
Radio dial lamp	564	216/1893	216/1893
Brake alarm	194	194	194
Back-up lamp	1156	1156	1156
Glove box lamp	194/1895	194/1895	194/1895
Heater cont. panel	1445	161	161
A.C. control panel	1445	161	161

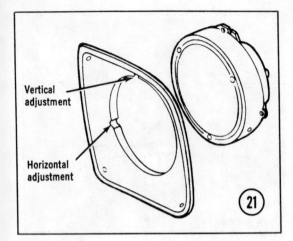

Vertical adjustment

Horizontal adjustment

㉑

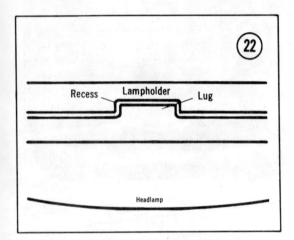

㉒

Recess Lampholder Lug

Headlamp

that there is a short in the wiring to that particular lamp. Check the fuse to make sure it is the correct amperage rating and replace it if it is not. Carefully inspect the wiring and connector too for chafing or damage and correct any breaks in the insulation.

1. Unscrew the screws which hold the headlight trim ring in place and remove the ring.

2. Loosen the 3 headlight retaining screws, turn the light unit counterclockwise to line up the large cutouts with the screws, and remove the unit. Unplug the connector from the rear of the light.

NOTE: *Do not turn headlight beam adjusting screw (Figure 21). Otherwise setting will be disturbed and headlight beam will require adjustment.*

3. Reverse the above to install a new light unit. Make sure the connector is firmly seated before installing the unit. Set the light in place, making sure the lugs on the light engage the recesses in the lamp holder (**Figure 22**). Set the retainer ring in place and turn it clockwise so the small end of each cutout engages a screw. Tighten the screws and install the outer trim ring.

8

7. Tape all exposed wires with insulating tape.

8. Connect fusible link to component from which it was removed.

9. Reconnect ground cable to battery.

LIGHTS

All of the lighting elements with the exception of instrument illumination bulbs, are easily replaced. Individual replacement procedures follow, along with a bulb chart in **Table 4**.

Headlight Replacement

The headlights are replaceable sealed-beam units. Both the high- and low-beam circuits and filaments are included in one unit. Failure of one circuit requires replacement of the entire unit.

NOTE: *If both filaments in the lamp unit fail at the same time, it is possible*

Headlight Beam Adjustment

Headlight beam adjustment should be entrusted to a specialist. Most states license some dealers and general repair shops to correctly adjust headlights so that they comply with safety standards. However, it's possible to make a temporary adjustment that will allow the vehicle to be driven until the beams can be correctly adjusted.

1. Park the vehicle on level ground, about 25 feet from a flat vertical surface such as a wall.

2. Measure the distance from the center of the headlight lens to the ground.

3. Turn the lights on high beam. Measure the distance from the center of the right beam pattern to the ground. It should be about 6 inches lower than the center of the headlight from the ground. Also, it should be about 6 inches to the right of the center of the headlight.

Measure the left beam in the same manner.

4. If adjustment is required correct it with the screws shown in **Figure 21**. To raise the beam, turn the top screw in (clockwise) and lower it by turning the screw out (counterclockwise). To move the beam to the left, turn the left screw in (clockwise) and move the beam to the right by turning the screw out (counterclockwise).

> CAUTION
> *Have the headlight beams correctly adjusted by a licensed specialist. Incorrect beam adjustment is unsafe both for you and for oncoming traffic.*

Signal Light Replacement

To change bulbs in the rear combination light (**Figure 23**), license plate light (**Figure 24**), parking/turn indicator lights (**Figure 25**), or side marker lights (**Figure 26**), remove the screws that hold the lens. Remove the lens, press in on the bulb, turn it counterclockwise, and withdraw it. Clean the socket before installing a new bulb. Don't overtighten the lens screws; they will crack the lens.

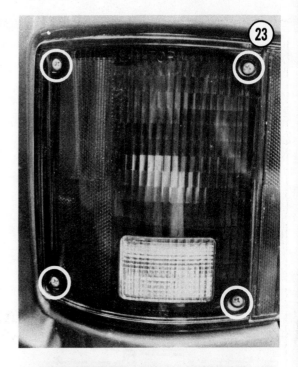

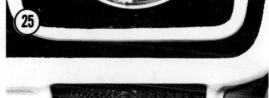

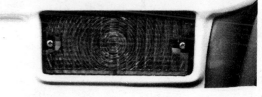

DISTRIBUTOR

Removal

1. Remove the distributor cap.

2. Disconnect the distributor primary lead at the coil.

3. Scribe an alignment mark on the distributor and the engine, in line with the rotor.

4. Disconnect the vacuum line(s) and the tachometer cable (if installed).

5. Unscrew the distributor clamp bolt and remove the clamp.

6. Note the position of the vacuum diaphragm for reference during installation and remove the distributor from the engine.

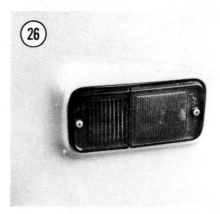

Installation

If the engine was not disturbed after the distributor was removed, reverse the above to install it. Refer to *Ignition Timing Adjustment* in Chapter Four and check and adjust timing.

If, during the course of engine work, the crankshaft is rotated with the distributor off the engine, it is necessary to time the distributor with the crankshaft and camshaft.

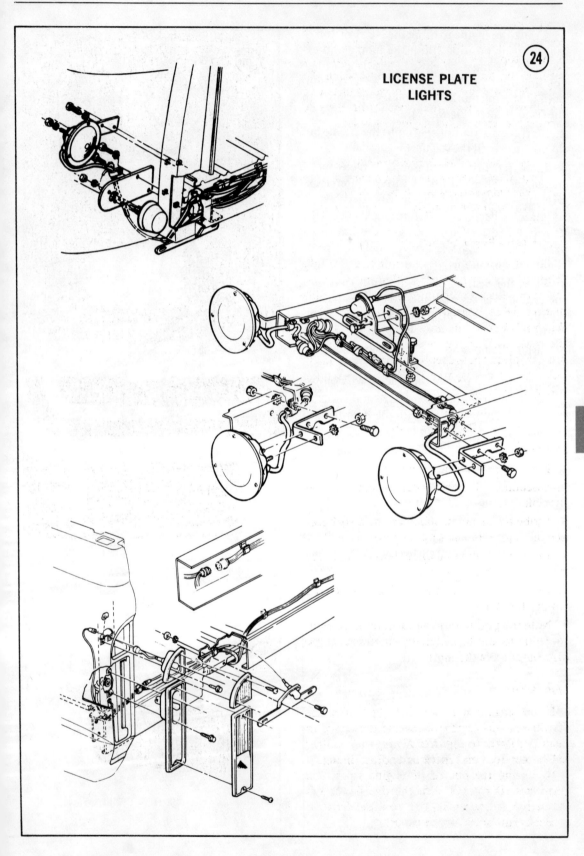

LICENSE PLATE
LIGHTS

㉔

1. Crank the engine to bring the No. 1 piston to TDC in firing position. Both the intake and exhaust valves must be closed. Slowly continue rotating the crankshaft (about ⅓ revolution) until the timing mark on the pulley lines up with the fixed pointer (**Figure 27**).

2. Start the distributor shaft into the engine but do not push it all the way in.

3. Line up the rotor so it points to the front of the engine. Then, turn it ⅛ turn counterclockwise and carefully push the distributor down into place. Check, by feel, to make sure the distributor drive gear engages the camshaft gear. It may be necessary to rock the rotor slightly to obtain engagement.

4. Press the distributor down firmly and turn the engine over several times to ensure that the distributor drive shaft engages the oil pump shaft.

5. Install the hold-down clamp and bolt. Turn the distributor body until the points just begin to open and then tighten the hold-down bolt.

6. Set the distributor cap in place and check to see that the rotor lines up with the high-tension terminal for the No. 1 cylinder (**Figure 28**).

7. Connect the high-tension leads between the distributor and the spark plugs. Route the wires as shown in **Figure 28**.

8. Connect the vacuum line and the primary electrical lead.

9. Refer to Chapter Four, *Tune-Up*, and set the point gap (1974 and earlier) and the timing.

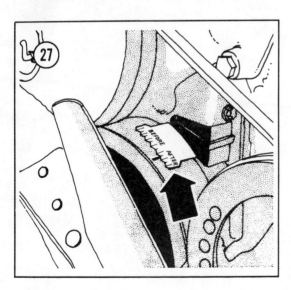

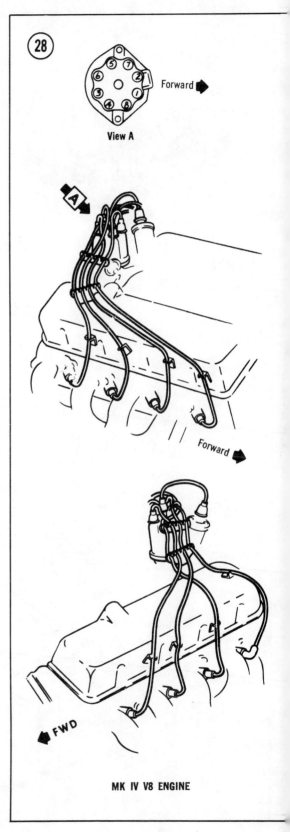

MK IV V8 ENGINE

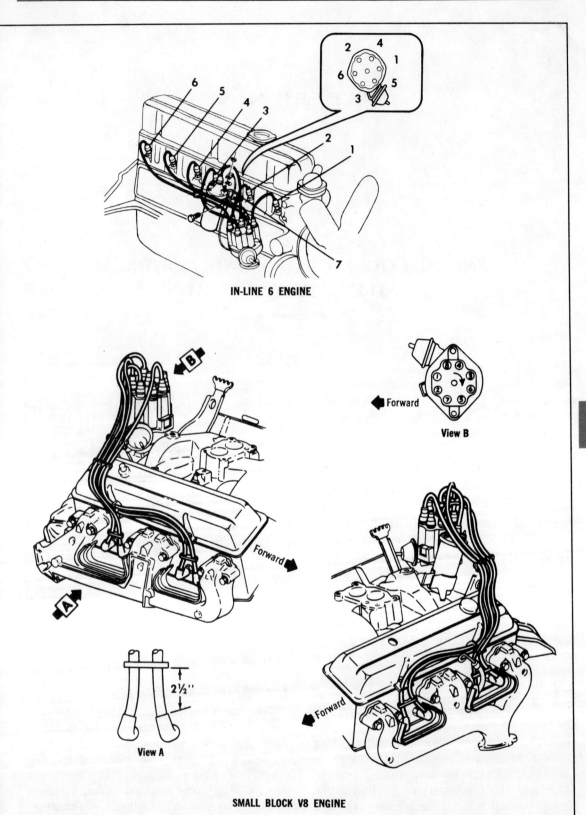

IN-LINE 6 ENGINE

View B

Forward

View A

2½"

Forward

Forward

SMALL BLOCK V8 ENGINE

8

CHAPTER NINE

ENGINE COOLING, AIR CONDITIONING, AND EXHAUST SYSTEM

All vehicles use pressurized cooling systems, sealed with a pressure type radiator cap. The higher operating pressure of the system raises the boiling point of the coolant. This increases the efficiency of the radiator.

COMPONENTS

Cooling system components are the radiator, pressure cap, water pump, thermostat, fan, thermostatic fan clutch (on 1972 and later models so equipped), coolant recovery system and associated hoses and water passages.

Radiator

The cross-flow type radiator cools the coolant fluid by allowing it to flow from side to side through the radiator and transferring heat to the air passing through the radiator.

Radiator Cap

The pressure-type radiator cap (**Figure 1**) allows the cooling system to operate at higher atmospheric pressure, thus raising the boiling point of the coolant. This permits operation of the vehicle with coolant temperatures between 245 °F and 260 °F without vaporization of the coolant through boiling. The pressure cap has a pressure relief valve which allows excessive

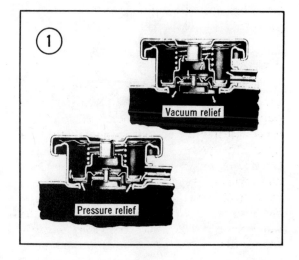

pressure to be vented. It also has a vacuum valve which opens to relieve the vacuum created when the system cools.

Fan and Fan Clutch

The cooling fan increases cooling system efficiency by drawing air through the radiator. Two types of fans are used. One is a fixed drive fan which rotates at water pump speed. The other type has a thermostatically-controlled clutch which ensures adequate cooling at reduced engine speeds and eliminates overcooling, excessive noise, and power loss at high speeds.

Thermostat

The thermostat is a heat-controlled valve in the cooling system, located in the engine water passage outlet to the radiator. When the engine and coolant are cold, the valve remains closed, preventing the circulation of coolant through the radiator. When the engine and coolant approach normal operating temperature, the thermostat opens to allow coolant to flow to the radiator for cooling.

Coolant

Only ethylene glycol-based coolant meeting the requirements of GM Specification 1899-M should be used.

The coolant should be mixed with water (preferably distilled) in accordance with the coolant manufacturer's instructions to provide freeze protection to $-20°F$. Even if your climate does not require this degree of protection, the antifreeze makes an excellent rust inhibitor.

Water Pump

The centrifugal vane impeller water pump in the cooling system has sealed bearings and requires no periodic maintenance. The pump inlet is connected to the bottom of the radiator by a hose. The pump causes water to circulate through the water passages in the engine block and cylinder heads, where engine heat is transferred to the water. The engine and head passages are connected and terminate at the water outlet of the thermostat housing, which is connected to the top of the radiator by a hose.

MAINTENANCE

Coolant Level

NOTE: *On vehicles equipped with coolant recovery systems, the coolant is checked by observing the liquid in the recovery system reservoir. The radiator cap should not be removed. If additional coolant is required, it should be added to the recovery reservoir. Level should be at* COLD FULL *mark when engine is cool or at* HOT FULL *mark when engine is hot.*

If the vehicle does not have a coolant recovery system, the coolant level should be checked only when the engine is cool.

CAUTION
Removal of the radiator cap from a hot engine, especially if an air conditioner has been in use, can result in coolant "blow out." This results in coolant loss and could cause injuries to bystanders.

Coolant level in cross-flow radiators should be maintained at 3 inches below the bottom of the filler neck when the system is cold.

Cooling System Checks

1. Check the radiator by warming up the engine. Turn the engine off and feel the radiator. A cross-flow radiator should be hot along the left side and warm along the right side with an even temperature rise from the right to left. Cold spots indicate obstructed radiator sections.

2. Check water pump operation by running the warmed up engine while squeezing upper radiator hose. If pressure surge is felt, the water pump is functioning. If not, check for a plugged vent hole in the pump.

3. Check for exhaust leaks into the cooling system by draining coolant until level is just above top of cylinder head. Disconnect upper radiator hose and remove thermostat and fan belt. Start the engine and accelerate it several times while observing the coolant. If the level rises or bubbles appear, chances are that exhaust gases are leaking into the cooling system.

Periodic Maintenance

The concentration of antifreeze in the coolant should be maintained to provide protection to $-20°F$, regardless of expected temperatures. This is required for protection from corrosion and for proper temperature indicator light operation.

Every two years the cooling system should be drained and back flushed with clear water. If required, the system should be cleaned with a good cleaning solution (follow manufacturer's instructions). Back flush the system by removing the radiator upper and lower hoses and

9

replacing radiator cap. Attach a lead-away hose to upper radiator opening and a length of garden hose to lower opening. Connect the garden hose to a pressurized water supply and back flush until water from the lead-away hose runs clear. Then the system should be refilled with ethylene glycol-based coolant/water solution sufficient to provide protection to at least −20°F. GM Cooling System Inhibitor and Sealer, or equivalent, should also be added at this time to retard the formation of rust or scale. This inhibitor should also be added every Fall thereafter.

CAUTION

Alcohol or methanol coolants or plain water are not recommended for use at any time.

Fan Belt Adjustment

Loosen the bolts at the alternator mounting and lock (**Figure 2**) and pull the alternator away from the engine until desired tension (75 ± 5 lb. new) is reached (use strand tension gauge). Tighten all alternator bolts securely and repeat the tension check.

Thermostat Check and Replacement

1. Drain the coolant until the level is slightly below the thermostat housing base.
2. Remove the upper radiator hose.
3. Remove the thermostat housing bolts and then remove the water outlet and gasket from the thermostat housing. See **Figure 3**.
4. Remove and inspect the thermostat valve (**Figure 4**). Test it as follows:

   a. Place the thermostat in a 33% solution of glycol heated to 25°F above the temperature stamped on the thermostat.

   b. Submerge the thermostat and agitate the liquid. The valve should open fully.

   c. Remove the valve and place it in another 33% glycol solution heated to 10°F less than the temperature stamped on the thermostat.

   d. The thermostat should close completely when it is completely submerged and the liquid is agitated.

5. If the thermostat fails the above test it

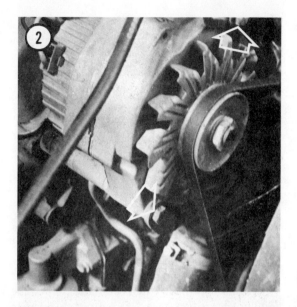

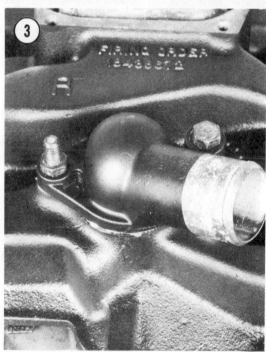

should be replaced. If it is OK, reinstall it in the housing, using a new gasket.

6. Install the radiator hose and fill the system with coolant.

Belts and Hoses

All engine belts and hoses should be inspected for wear and damage at each oil change period. Belts which show signs of wear, crack-

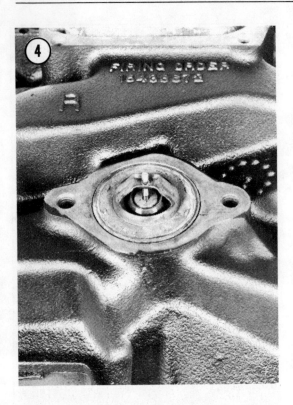

ing, etc., and hoses with bulges, soft spots, leaks, etc., should be replaced. The inspection should include heater hoses as well as radiator hoses.

Thermostatic Fan Clutch

With the engine cool, the fan blade should rotate with only a slight drag. If fan does not move, or drag is either excessive (or a rough grating is felt) or not present (fan revolved over 5 times when spun by hand), the clutch should be replaced.

WATER PUMP

Removal

1. Siphon or drain coolant from the radiator and break loose fan pulley bolts.

> ### WARNING
> *If coolant is siphoned from radiator, do not use mouth to start siphon. Coolant solution is poisonous and can cause serious illness or death if swallowed.*

2. Disconnect heater hose, lower radiator hose and bypass hose (if so equipped) from the water pump.

3. Remove the alternator upper brace (V8 engines), loosen the swivel bolt, and remove the fan belt. On Mark IV engines, disconnect power steering and air conditioner belts and swivel power steering pump unit to one side.

4. Remove the fan blade attaching bolts, fan, and pulley.

> ### CAUTION
> *Bent or damaged fans should not be reused, as any distortion will affect fan balance and operation. Damaged fans cannot be properly repaired and should be replaced.*

> NOTE: *When a thermostatic fan clutch is removed from the car it should be supported so that clutch disc remains vertical to prevent silicone fluid leakage.*

5. Remove the pump-to-cylinder block and power steering-to-pump bolts. Remove the water pump and old gasket from the engine.

> ### CAUTION
> *On 6-cylinder engines, pull the pump straight forward out of the block first to avoid impeller damage.*

Installation

1. Install the water pump assembly on engine block, using a new sealer-coated gasket. Tighten the bolts to 15 ft.-lb. for inline engines, 30 ft.-lb. for V8's.

2. Install the pump pulley and fan on the pump hub and tighten to 15 ft.-lb.

> NOTE: *For ease in aligning pulley and fan, install a ⁵⁄₁₆ in.-24 guide stud (bolt with head removed) in one hole of fan hub. Remove stud and install bolt after other 3 bolts have been started.*

3. On Mark IV engines, install the power steering and air conditioner bolts.

4. Connect the hoses and fill the cooling system with a solution of ethylene glycol antifreeze sufficient to withstand −20°F.

5. Install the Delcotron upper brace (V8 only) and power steering pump bolt. Install the fan belts and tension them to 75 ± 5 lb. (used belt) or 125 ± 5 lb. (new belt).

6. Start the engine and check for leaks.

9

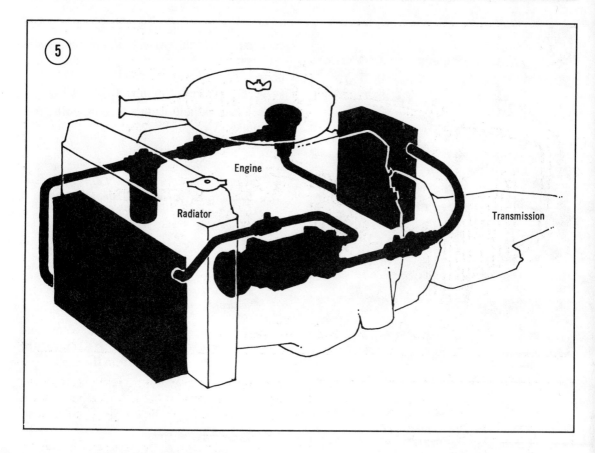

(5)

Engine

Radiator

Transmission

AIR CONDITIONING

Major service and repair to air conditioning systems requires specialized training and tools, and the difficulty of the work is compounded in the late heating/air conditioning systems. However, most air conditioning problems do not involve major repair; they are well within the ability of an experienced hobbyist mechanic, armed with an understanding of how the system works.

SYSTEM OPERATION

A typical air conditioning system is shown in **Figure 5**. (Actual component locations may differ, depending on model.)

The five basic components are common to all air conditioning systems:

   a. Compressor
   b. Condenser
   c. Receiver-drier
   d. Expansion valve
   e. Evaporator

WARNING
*The components, connected with high-pressure hoses and tubes, form a closed loop. A refrigerant, dichlorodiflouro-methane — more commonly referred to as R-12, circulates through the system under high pressure — as much as 300 psi. As a result, work on the air conditioning system is potentially hazardous if certain precautions are ignored. For safety's sake, **read this entire section** before attempting any troubleshooting, checks, or work on the system.*

A typical system is shown schematically in **Figure 6**. For practical purposes, the cycle begins at the compressor. The refrigerant, in a warm, low-pressure vapor state, enters the low-pressure side of the compressor. It is compressed to a high-pressure hot vapor and pumped out of the high-pressure side to the condenser.

Air flow through the condenser removes heat from the refrigerant and transfers the heat to the outside air. As the heat is removed, the

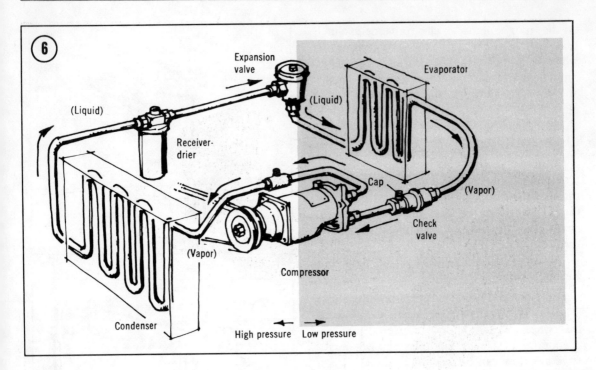

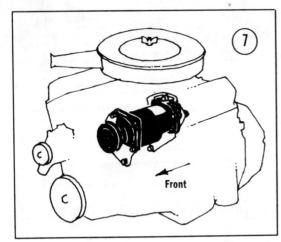

refrigerant condenses to a warm, high-pressure liquid.

The refrigerant then flows to the receiver/drier where moisture is removed and impurities are filtered out. The refrigerant is stored in the receiver/drier until it is needed. Generally, the receiver/drier incorporates a sight glass that permits visual monitoring of the condition of the refrigerant as it flows. This is discussed later.

From the receiver/drier, the refrigerant flows to the expansion valve. The expansion valve is thermostatically controlled and meters re-

frigerant to the evaporator. As the refrigerant leaves the expansion valve it changes from a warm, high-pressure liquid to a cold, low-pressure liquid.

In the evaporator, the refrigerant removes heat from the cockpit air that is blown across the evaporator's fins and tubes. In the process, the refrigerant changes from a cold, low-pressure liquid to a warm, high-pressure vapor which flows back to the compressor where the refrigeration cycle began.

GET TO KNOW YOUR VEHICLE'S SYSTEM

With **Figure 5** as a guide, begin with the compressor and locate each of the following components in turn:

a. Compressor
b. Condenser
c. Receiver/drier
d. Expansion valve
e. Evaporator

Compressor

The compressor is located on the front of the engine, like an alternator, and is driven by one or two drive belts (**Figure 7**). The large pulley

on the front contains an electromagnetic clutch that is activated and operates the compressor when the air conditioning controls are switched on. There are two compressor types — piston-and-crank (**Figure 8**) and swashplate (axial plate, **Figure 9**).

Condenser

In most cases, the condenser is mounted in front of the radiator (**Figure 10**). Air passing through the fins and tubes removes heat from the refrigerant in the same manner it removes heat from the engine coolant as it passes through the radiator.

Receiver/Drier

The receiver/drier is a small tank-like unit (**Figure 11**), usually found mounted to one of the wheel wells. Many receiver/driers incorporate a sight glass through which refrigerant flow can be seen when the system is operating (**Figure 12**). Some systems have an in-line sight glass (**Figure 13**). Some early systems do not have a sight glass but it's not essential to system operation — just handy to help diagnose air conditioning problems.

Expansion Valve

The expansion valve (**Figure 14**) is located between the receiver/drier and the evaporator. It is usually mounted on or near the firewall, in the engine compartment. In some very late systems, the valve is concealed in a housing on the firewall.

Evaporator

The evaporator is located in the passenger compartment, beneath the dashboard, and is hidden from view by the fan shrouding and ducting (**Figure 15**). Warm air from the passenger compartment is blown across the fins and tubes in the evaporator where it is cooled and dried and then ducted back into the compartment through the air outlets.

ROUTINE MAINTENANCE

First echelon preventive maintenance for your air conditioning system couldn't be simpler; at least once a month, even in cold

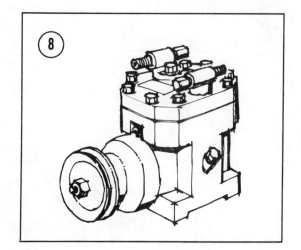

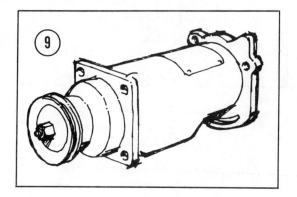

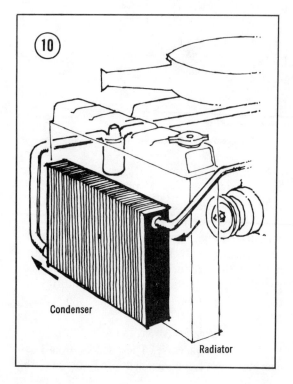

Condenser

Radiator

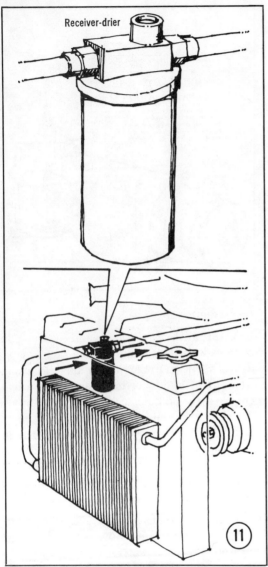

Receiver-drier

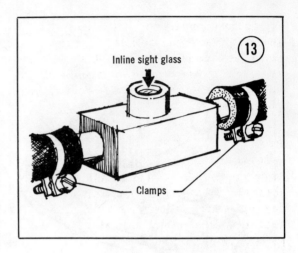

Inline sight glass

Clamps

13

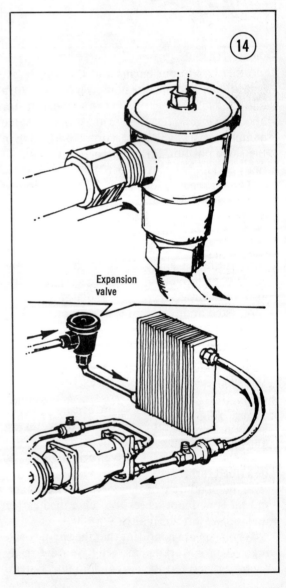

14

Expansion
valve

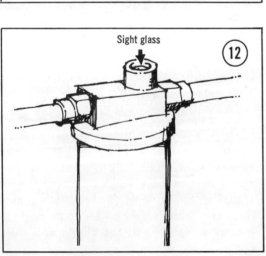

Sight glass

12

9

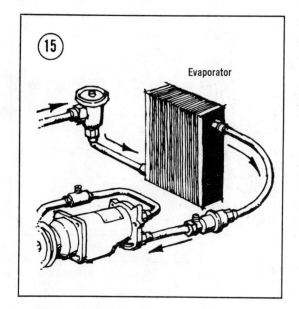

Evaporator

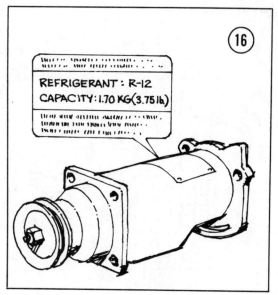

REFRIGERANT : R-12
CAPACITY: 1.70 KG (3.75 lb)

weather, start your engine and turn on the air conditioner and operate it at each of the switch and control settings. Allow it to operate for about five minutes. This will ensure that the compressor seal will not deform from sitting in the same position for a long period of time. If this occurs, the seal is likely to leak.

The efficiency of your air conditioning system depends in great part on the efficiency of your engine cooling system. Periodically check the coolant for level and cleanliness. If it is dirty, drain and flush the system and fill it with fresh coolant and water, following the coolant manufacturer's instructions for coolant/water ratio. Have your radiator cap pressure tested and replace it if it will not maintain 13 psi pressure. If the system requires repeated topping up and the radiator cap is in good condition, it is likely that there is a leak in the system. Pressure test it as described earlier in this chapter.

With an air hose and a soft brush, clean the radiator fins and tubes to remove bugs, leaves, and any other imbedded debris.

Check and correct drive belt tension as described earlier.

If the condition of the cooling system thermostat is in doubt, check it as described earlier and replace it if it is faulty.

When you are confident that the engine cooling system is working correctly, you are ready to inspect and test the air conditioning system.

Inspection

1. Clean all lines, fittings, and system components with solvent and a clean rag. Pay particular attention to the fittings; oily dirt around connections almost certainly indicates a leak. Oil from the compressor will migrate through the system to the leak. Carefully tighten the connection, taking care not to overtighten and risk stripping the threads. If the leak persists it will soon be apparent once again as oily dirt accumulates. Clean the sight glass with a clean, dry cloth.

2. Clean the condenser fins and tubes with a soft brush and an air hose, or with a high-pressure stream of water from a garden hose. Remove bugs, leaves, and other imbedded debris. Carefully straighten any bent fins with a screwdriver, taking care not to dent or puncture the tubes.

3. Check the condition and tension of the drive belts and replace or correct as necessary.

4. Start the engine and check the operation of the blower motor and the compressor clutch by turning the controls on and off. If either the blower or the clutch fails to operate, shut off the engine and check the condition of the fuses. If they are blown, replace them. If not, remove them and clean the fuse holder contacts. Then, recheck to ensure that the blower and clutch operate.

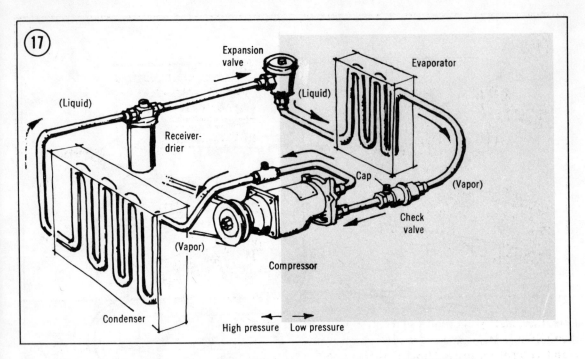

Testing

1. With the transmission in PARK (automatic) or NEUTRAL (manual) and the handbrake set, start the engine and run it at a fast idle.

2. Set the temperature control to its coldest setting and turn the blower to high. Allow the system to operate for 10 minutes with the doors and windows open. Then close them and set the blower on its lowest setting.

3. Place a thermometer in a cold-air outlet. Within a few minutes, the temperature should be 35-45°F. If it is not, it's likely that the refrigerant level in the system is low. Check the appearance of the refrigerant flow through the sight glass. If it is bubbly, refrigerant should be added.

REFRIGERANT

The majority of automotive air conditioning systems use a refrigerant designated R-12. However, a commercial grade, designated R-20, is used in heavy-duty systems. The two are not compatible. Look for an information sticker, usually mounted near the compressor, to determine which refrigerant your system uses (**Figure 16**). Also, check the system capacity indicated on the sticker. Capacity can range from two to five pounds, depending on the system.

WARNING
That harmless-looking little can of refrigerant is potentially hazardous. If it is hooked up to the high-pressure side of the compressor, or is hooked up without a gauge set, it becomes almost like a hand grenade.

Charging

WARNING
Do not attempt to add refrigerant to the system without using a gauge set; it's essential that the system pressure during charging not exceed 50 psi. Wear safety goggles.

1. Carefully read and understand the gauge manufacturer's instructions before charging the system.

2. Remove the cap from the Schrader valve on the low-pressure side of the compressor (**Figure 17**). The low-pressure is labelled SUCTION, SUCT., or SUC.

3. Connect the gauge set to the low-pressure Schrader valve. Connect the refrigerant can to the gauge set and hang the gauge set on the hood (**Figure 18**).

4. Start the engine and run it at a fast idle (about 1,000 rpm).

9

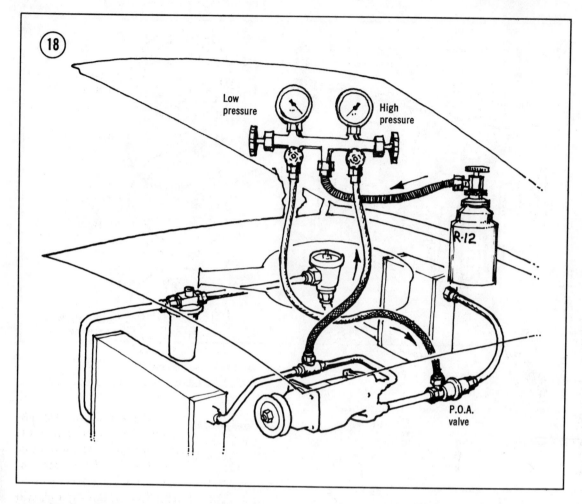

Low pressure

High pressure

R-12

P.O.A. valve

5. Set the temperature control at its coldest setting. Set the blower at its lowest setting.

6. Slowly open the refrigerant feed valve on the gauge set **(Figure 19)**. Do not allow the refrigerant pressure to exceed 50 psi.

7. Watch the refrigerant as it flows through the sight glass **(Figure 20)**. When it's free of bubbles, the system is charged. Shut off the refrigerant feed valve on the gauge set.

TROUBLESHOOTING

Preventive maintenance like that just described will help to ensure that your system is working efficiently. Still, trouble can develop and while most of it will invariably be simple and easy to correct, you must first locate it. The following sequence will help to diagnose system troubles when your air conditioning ceases to cool the passenger compartment.

1. First, stop the vehicle and look at the control settings. One of the most common sources of air conditioning trouble occurs when the temperature control is set for maximum cold and the blower is set on low. This arrangement promotes ice buildup on the fins and tubes of the evaporator, and particularly so in humid weather. Eventually, the evaporator will ice over completely, and restrict air flow. Turn the blower on high and place a hand over an air outlet. If the blower is running but there is little or no air flowing through the outlet, the evaporator is probably iced up. Leave the blower on high and turn off the temperature control or turn it down to its lowest setting — and wait; it will take 10 or 15 minutes before the ice begins to melt.

2. If the blower is not running, the motor may be burned out, there may be a loose connection, or the fuse may be blown. First check the fuse

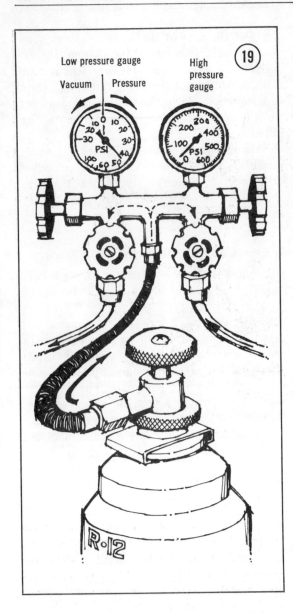

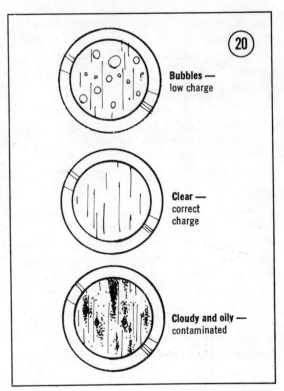

5. If all components checked so far are OK, start the engine, turn on the air conditioner and watch the refrigerant through the sight glass; remember, if it's filled with bubbles after the system has been operating for a few seconds, the refrigerant level is low. If the sight glass is oily or cloudy, the system is contaminated and should be serviced by an expert as soon as possible. Corrosion and deterioration occur rapidly, and if it's not taken care of at once it will result in a very expensive repair job.

6. If the system still appears to be operating satisfactorily but the air flow into the passenger compartment is not cold, check the condenser and cooling system radiator for debris that could block the air flow. Recheck the cooling system as described under *Inspection*.

7. If the above steps do not uncover the difficulty, have the system checked and corrected by a specialist as soon as possible.

DISCHARGING THE SYSTEM

The pressure in the system must be relieved before any fittings are disconnected. To do this, connect the gauge set in the same manner as

panel for a blown or incorrectly seated fuse. Then, check the wiring for loose connections.

3. Shut off the engine and check the condition and tension of the compressor drive belt. If it is loose or badly worn, tighten or replace it.

4. Start the engine and check the condition of the compressor clutch by turning the air conditioner on and off. If the clutch does not energize, it may be defective, its fuse may be blown, or the evaporator temperature-limiting switches may be defective. If the fuse is defective, replace it. If the clutch still does not energize, refer the problem to an air conditioning specialist.

though the system were to be charged; however, do not attach a refrigerant can to the center hose. Slowly open both the high- and low-pressure valves on the gauge set. Then, slowly open the valve for the center hose.

WARNING
Route the center hose down through the engine compartment so it will discharge on the ground. Wear safety goggles and take care not to let the refrigerant touch your skin.

When the system pressure has been relieved, disconnect the gauge set. Slowly loosen any fittings that are involved until you are sure the system is not pressurized. *Wear safety goggles.*

Immediately plug any open fittings to keep moisture out of the system; corrosion will begin almost instantly if the system is left open to the atmosphere, and it will quickly make some very expensive components unserviceable.

When all of the system components and lines have been reconnected, charge the system as described earlier.

EXHAUST SYSTEMS

The exhaust system consists of an exhaust pipe (or pipes in dual systems), mufflers, and tailpipes. Resonators, located between the muffler and the rear of the vehicle, are used on some models. In a typical installation, the exhaust pipes are constructed in one piece and are clamped to the muffler inlet. Tailpipes, except in installations having resonators, are also one piece and are, as a rule, welded to the muffler outlets.

Exhaust system components are extremely difficult or impossible to work on without a hoist, a torch, and power chisels. Muffler shops specialize in this work, and can do the work for less money than you can.

CATALYTIC CONVERTER

Exhaust systems on some 1975 and later models have a catalytic converter between the front exhaust pipe and the tailpipe. This is an emission control device which reduces hydrocarbon and carbon monoxide pollutants in the exhaust gases. The converter contains beads which are coated with a catalytic material containing platinum and palladium. The converter does not require periodic maintenance. However, it may become necessary to replace either the converter or catalytic beads. Replacement of the catalytic beads requires expensive special tools, making it more economical to have the job done by a dealer or qualified garage.

CHAPTER TEN

CLUTCH AND TRANSMISSION

This chapter provides procedures for replacement of manual and automatic transmissions and for clutch removal, replacement, and adjustment.

Repairs requiring disassembly are not recommended for home mechanics or garage mechanics without special skills and a large assortment of special tools. In fact, the cost of the necessary tools far exceeds the price of a professionally rebuilt transmission.

Considerable money can be saved by removing the old transmission and installing a new or rebuilt one yourself. See Chapter Two, *Troubleshooting*, for procedures which will help isolate the fault.

Table 1, at the end of the chapter, gives tightening torques for installation.

CLUTCH

There is one linkage adjustment (clutch fork pushrod or pedal pushrod) to compensate for all normal clutch wear. The clutch should have a specified amount of free travel before the throwout bearing engages clutch diaphragm spring levers (see individual procedures below for amounts specified). Lash is required to prevent clutch slippage which would occur if the bearing was held against the fingers or to prevent the bearing from running continually until failure.

A clutch that was slipping before adjustment may still slip after adjustment because of prior heat damage. Allow clutch to cool for at least 12 hours, then check for slippage as follows:

1. Drive in high gear at 20-25 mph.

2. Depress clutch pedal to floor and accelerate engine speed to about 3,000 rpm.

3. Snap foot off clutch pedal and at the same time press accelerator to floor board. Engine speed should drop and then accelerate. If clutch is bad, engine speed will increase immediately (before vehicle accelerates).

> NOTE: *Clutch will overheat if this test is repeated before allowing clutch to cool for at least 12 hours.*

Clutch Linkage Adjustment

1. Disconnect the clutch return spring from the clutch fork (**Figure 1**).

2. Remove the cotter key and washers from the swivel.

3. Rotate the cross shaft until the clutch pedal contacts the rubber stop on the pedal bracket.

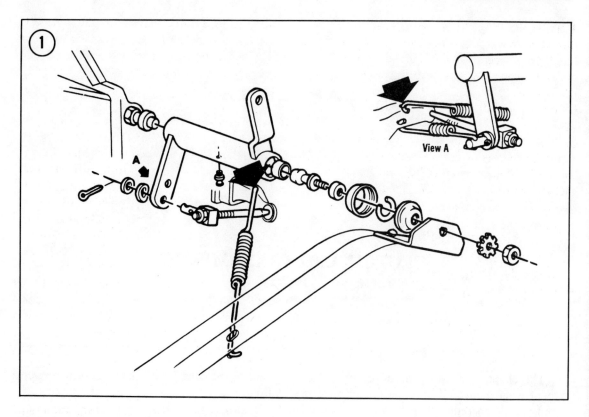

View A

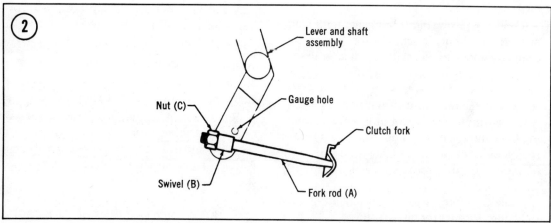

Lever and shaft assembly

Nut (C)

Gauge hole

Clutch fork

Swivel (B)

Fork rod (A)

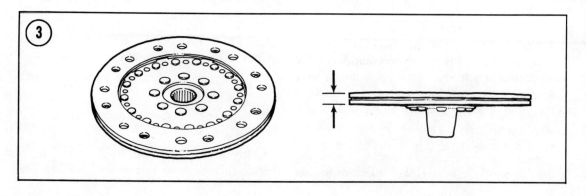

4. Push the clutch arm to the rear until the throwout (release) bearing can be felt to just touch the fingers on the clutch. Loosen the locknut on the rod and turn the adjuster until the swivel can be engaged with the gauge hole (**Figure 2**) and the end of the rod rests firmly against the clutch arm.

5. Pull the swivel out of the gauge hole and reinstall it in the lower hole in the lever. Install the washers and the cotter key and tighten the locknut without further changing the adjustment.

6. Install the return spring and check the free travel of the clutch pedal. It should be 1⅜-1⅛ in. When the free travel is correctly adjusted, road test the vehicle to ensure that the clutch releases and engages correctly.

Clutch Mechanism Removal

1. Support the engine and remove the transmission as described later.

2. Disconnect clutch fork pushrod and spring.

3. Remove the flywheel housing.

4. Slide the clutch fork from the ball stud and remove the fork from dust boot.

NOTE: *The ball stud is threaded into clutch housing and is easily replaced.*

5. Install tool J-5824 or an equivalent clutch pilot to support clutch.

6. Look for the "X" mark on the flywheel and clutch cover. If not visible, make small punch marks on these parts to aid reassembly.

7. Loosen the clutch-to-flywheel bolts evenly, one turn at a time, until spring pressure is released.

8. Remove the bolts and clutch assembly.

Inspection

Never replace clutch parts without giving thought to the reason for failure. To do so only invites repeated troubles.

1. Clean the flywheel face and pressure plate assembly in a non-petroleum base cleaner such as alcohol or lacquer thinner.

2. Check the friction surface of the flywheel for cracks and grooves. Attach a dial indicator and check runout. Compare with specifications for your engine. If necessary, have the flywheel reground; replace it in cases of severe damage.

3. Check the pressure plate for cracked or broken springs, evidence of heat, cracked or scored friction surface, and looseness. Check release lever ends for wear. On diaphragm spring clutches, check the spring fingers for wear. If there is any damage, replace with a professionally rebuilt pressure plate assembly.

4. Check the clutch disc (drive plate) lining for wear, cracks, oil, and burns. The assembled thickness of the disc should be at least 0.36 in. See **Figure 3**. Check for loose rivets and cracks in the spring leaves or carrier plate. Ensure that the disc slides freely on the transmission spline without excessive radial play. If the disc is defective, replace it with a new one.

5. Check the release bearing for wear to determine if it caused the original trouble. Never reuse a release bearing unless necessary. When other clutch parts are worn, the bearing is probably worn. If it is necessary to reinstall the old bearing, do not wash it in solvent; wipe it with a clean cloth.

Installation

1. Wash your hands *clean* before proceeding.

2. Sand the friction surface of the flywheel and pressure plate with a medium-fine emery cloth. Sand lightly across the surfaces (not around) until they are covered with fine scratches. This breaks the glaze and aids seating a new clutch disc.

3. Clean the flywheel and pressure plate with a non-petroleum base cleaner.

4. Position the clutch disc and pressure plate on engine and support with tool J-5824 or an equivalent pilot tool. Clutch disc damper springs face the pressure plate.

NOTE: *An excellent pilot tool can be made by cutting off about one foot from the forward end of an old transmission main shaft. Other tools made from wooden dowellings are available from most auto parts suppliers.*

10

5. Align "X" marks or punch marks on the clutch cover and flywheel. Install the bolts finger-tight.

6. Tighten diagonally opposite bolts a few turns at a time until all are tight. Then tighten to 11 ft.-lb.

7. Remove the pilot tool.

8. Unhook the clutch fork. Lubricate the ball socket with high melting point grease, e.g., graphite, and reinstall the fork on the ball stud.

9. Lubricate the recess on inside of throwout bearing with molybdenum grease. See **Figure 4**.

10. Install the clutch fork and dust boot into the clutch housing.

11. Install the throwout bearing on the fork.

12. Install the flywheel housing.

13. Install the transmission.

14. Connect the fork pushrod and spring.

15. Adjust the clutch pedal travel and free play.

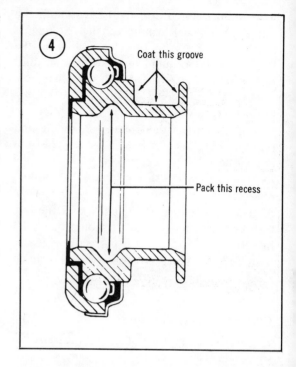

Clutch Pilot Bearing Removal/Installation

The clutch pilot bearing should be removed for inspection whenever the clutch is removed.

1. Pull bearing from crankshaft with tool J-1448 or equivalent puller. See **Figures 5 and 6**.

If this tool is not available, fill the bearing cavity with grease, insert a length of bar stock (with an OD comparable to the ID of the bearing) into the bearing and rap sharply on the end of the bar. In most cases, the hydraulic effect of the grease will drive the bearing out of the crankshaft.

2. Clean the bearing with a clean cloth dipped in solvent.

3. Check the bearing for excessive wear or other damage. Replace if necessary.

4. Drive the bearing into the crankshaft with tool J-1522 or an equivalent driver. See **Figure 7**.

TRANSMISSION REPLACEMENT

NOTE: *This procedure is general and covers all transmissions, manual or automatic.*

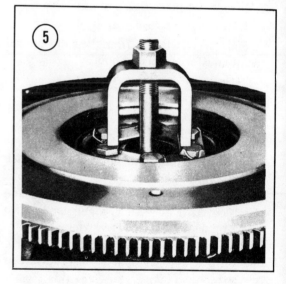

1. On manual transmissions, remove the shifter knob.

2. Raise the vehicle and support it with jackstands.

3. Disconnect the speedometer cable and all electrical leads from transmission.

4. On automatic transmissions, disconnect the shift control linkage, oil cooler pipes (if present), and vacuum line modulator (if so equipped).

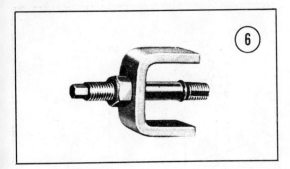

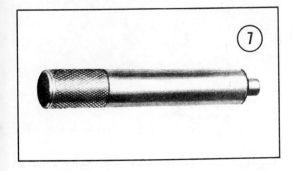

5. Disconnect and remove the drive shaft (see Chapter Twelve).

6A. Remove manual transmission:

a. Remove the transmission mount-to-crossmember bolts and crossmember-to-frame bolts. Raise and support the engine and remove crossmember.

b. Remove the shift levers from transmission and disconnect back drive rod at bell housing (floor shift models).

c. Remove shift control assembly-to-transmission support attaching bolts (floor shift models) and pull unit down until shift lever clears boot. Remove assembly.

d. Remove the upper bolts holding transmission to clutch housing and install guide pins in holes. Then remove the lower bolts.

e. Support the transmission while sliding it to the rear to remove it from the vehicle.

6B. Remove automatic transmission:

a. Support the transmission with a suitable jack.

b. Disconnect the rear mount from crossmember. Then remove the attaching bolts and remove the crossmember from frame.

c. Remove the converter under-pan.

d. Remove the converter-to-flywheel bolts.

e. Lower the transmission until the jack is barely supporting it and then remove the transmission-to-engine mounting bolts. Remove the oil filter tube at the transmission.

f. Raise the transmission to normal position, support the engine with a jack, and remove the transmission by sliding it rearward. Lower it away from the vehicle.

7. Reverse the above procedures to install transmission.

NOTE: *Tighten all nuts and bolts to specifications (see **Table 1**).*

NOTE: *On automatic transmissions, before installing flexplate-to-converter bolts, make certain weld nuts on converter are flush with the flexplate and the converter freely rotates in this position. Then hand start all bolts and tighten finger-tight before torquing to specifications. This will ensure proper alignment of converter.*

SHIFT LINKAGE ADJUSTMENT

3-Speed Column Shift

1. Install the control rods on the second/third shifter lever and the first-reverse shifter lever (**Figure 8**). Set both levers at NEUTRAL.

2. Align the levers on the steering column, in neutral, and insert a ¼ in. pin in the gauge holes to maintain the alignment.

3. Connect the control rods to the transmission shift levers and the column levers, adjusting them so that both sets of levers remain in neutral when the bolts are tightened.

4. Remove the ¼ in. pin from the column levers and move the gear selector through all of the gear positions to ensure that there is sufficient overtravel to permit the gears to engage.

Powerglide Column Shift Linkage Adjustment

Refer to **Figure 9**.

1. Verify that the shift tube and lever assembly move freely in steering column jacket.

10

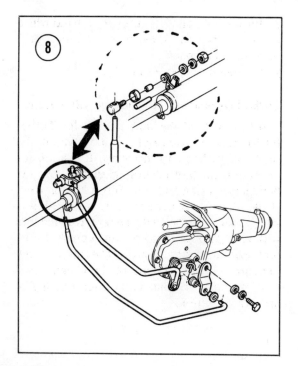

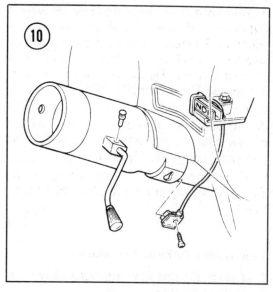

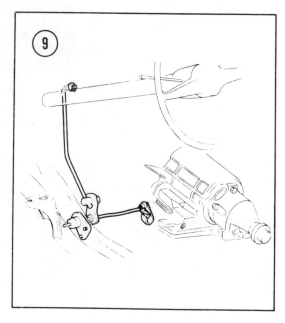

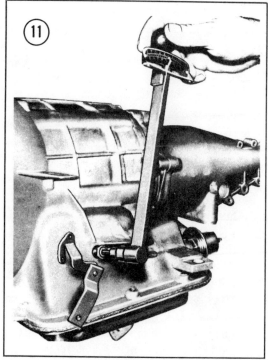

2. Lift the shift lever toward the steering wheel and place the transmission in DRIVE (D) detent.

> NOTE: *Do not use pointer to position selector, as pointer is adjusted last in this procedure.*

3. Release the lever, then try to move it to low range without lifting it. The lever should not go

into low range unless it is lifted toward the steering wheel.

4. Lift the lever and place the transmission in NEUTRAL (N) detent.

5. Release the lever, then try to move it to REVERSE (R) without lifting it. The lever should not go into reverse unless it is lifted toward steering wheel.

6. If adjustment is required, place the lever in (D) detent and loosen the adjustment swivel or clamp at the cross shaft. Rotate the transmission lever until it contacts the drive stop in the steering column. Tighten the swivel or clamp and recheck the adjustment.

7. Readjust the indicator pointer to agree with detent positions. Loosen the screw on the pointer shaft clamp, adjust as required, and tighten the screw. See **Figure 10**.

8. If required, readjust the neutral safety switch using the procedure given in Chapter Eight.

Powerglide Low Band Adjustment

1. Tighten the low servo adjusting screw to 40 in.-lb. See **Figure 11**.

2. Back off 4 complete turns for a band which has been used for 1,000 miles or more, or 3 turns for a new band.

3. Tighten the locknut to 15 ft.-lb.

Turbo-Hydramatic Shift Linkage Adjustment

Adjustment of the shift linkage for Turbo-Hydramatic transmissions is not within the scope of the hobbyist mechanic. It is a job for an automatic transmission specialist with experience working with the Turbo-Hydramatic. If the controls are not accurately adjusted, it is still possible to partially engage the clutches with enough pressure to provide apparent normal operation of the vehicle. The resulting low pressure will cause failure of the clutches and possibly other internal parts after just a *few miles* of operation.

10

Table 1   CLUTCH/TRANSMISSION TIGHTENING TORQUES

3-speed

Transmission case to clutch housing bolts	75 ft.-lb.
Crossmember to frame nuts	25 ft.-lb.
Crossmember to mount bolts	40 ft.-lb.
2-3 crossover shaft bracket retaining nut	18 ft.-lb.
1-revolution swivel attaching bolt	20 ft.-lb.
Mount to transmission bolt	50 ft.-lb.

4-speed

Universal joint front flange nut	95 ft.-lb.
Parking brake	22 ft.-lb.
Transmission to clutch housing bolts	75 ft.-lb.
Crossmember to mount	40 ft.-lb.
Mount to transmission	50 ft.-lb.

Powerglide

Transmission case to engine	35 ft.-lb.
Oil pan bolts	8 ft.-lb.
Low band adjustment locknut	15 ft.-lb.
Converter to engine bolts	35 ft.-lb.
Oil pan drain plug	20 ft.-lb.

Turbo-Hydramatic

Transmission to engine bolts	35 ft.-lb.
Rear mount to transmission bolts	40 ft.-lb.
Rear mount to crossmember bolt	40 ft.-lb.
Crossmember mounting bolts	25 ft.-lb.
Strainer retainer bolt	10 ft.-lb.
Converter to flywheel bolts	35 ft.-lb.

CHAPTER ELEVEN

BRAKES

The brake systems on all Chevrolet/GMC vehicles covered in this handbook have two independent hydraulic circuits. One circuit operates the front brakes and the other circuit operates the rear brakes. Failure of one of the brake circuits will normally be indicated by the brake warning light turning on. However, if the light is burned out or the wiring faulty, the first indication of a brake failure may occur when the brakes are applied, requiring much more pedal pressure than normal.

If the warning light comes on, carefully slow and stop the vehicle, taking into account that the braking effectiveness is greatly reduced. Remove the cap from the master cylinder reservoir (**Figure 1**) and check to see if there is fluid in both reservoirs. If the level is low in one, or it is empty, check further for leaks along the brake lines and at each wheel. If the level is correct in both reservoirs, the fault may lie in the switch, wiring, or the differential pressure valve in the master cylinder. In any case, drive the vehicle with extreme care until the system can be checked and the trouble corrected.

This chapter describes routine inspections and services, and most major work — brake and shoe replacement, and wheel cylinder and caliper service. When working on brake system components, your hands, tools, and work area

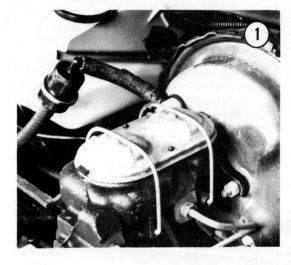

must be scrupulously clean. Work carefully and make certain a step is satisfactorily completed before proceeding to the next. If you have any doubt about your ability to correctly carry out major brake system service, trust it to a specialist: your life can depend on your brakes.

BRAKE FLUID LEVEL

The brake fluid level in the master cylinder reservoir should be checked routinely every 6,000 miles or at any time there is suspected leakage in the brake hydraulic system.

The fluid level must be within ¼ in. of the upper edge of the filler opening (**Figure 2**). If the fluid level is extremely low in one or both reservoirs, inspect the lines and fittings for leakage, and check wheel cylinders as described in Chapter Three, *Drum Brakes and Parking Brake*. Correct any leaks before adding fluid and bleed the system as described later.

Add only GM Hydraulic Brake Fluid (Supreme No. 11) or an equivalent fluid (DOT-3). This fluid grade is identified by "DOT-3" embossed on the container and is recommended for all conditions.

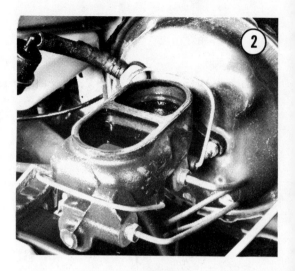

WARNING
Never add low-temperature brake fluid to the fluid that is already in the system. The fluid could vaporize, causing total brake failure.

BRAKE FLUID CHANGING

After long usage, brake fluid absorbs sufficient atmospheric moisture to significantly reduce its boiling point and make it prone to vapor lock during repeated hard brake applications (such as in mountain driving). While no hard and fast rule exists for changing the fluid in the system, it should be checked at least annually by bleeding fluid from one of the wheel cylinders and inspecting it for signs of moisture. If moisture is present, the entire system should be drained, flushed, filled, and bled as described below.

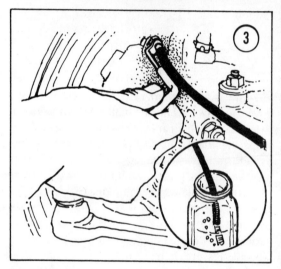

FLUSHING THE BRAKE SYSTEM

The brake system should be flushed after new parts have been installed, such as wheel cylinders, master cylinder, proportioning valve, etc., or if the fluid is contaminated with dirt or water.

Flushing is carried out in much the same manner as bleeding which is described below. However, during flushing, each bleeder valve must be opened about 1½ turns and fluid pumped through the lines until it is clear and free of contamination.

Make certain the master cylinder is kept full; otherwise air will be drawn into the system. And be sure to fill the reservoir to the correct level after the entire system has been flushed. About one quart of brake fluid is required to

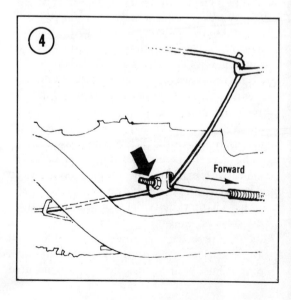

completely flush the system, and nothing other than the brake fluid recommended above should be used.

BLEEDING THE BRAKE SYSTEM

The brake system must be bled following any repairs in which a portion of the system is disconnected, after a leak has been corrected, or when water is present in the hydraulic fluid. The system can be bled using a pressure tank type bleeder or manually with the aid of an assistant. Because it is unlikely that a hobbyist mechanic will have a pressure tank bleeder, the second method is described.

It is a good idea to bleed the system beginning with the brake located closest to the master cylinder and then working away from the master cylinder. As with adding fluid to the system, use only the fluid specified earlier.

1. Check the brake fluid level in the reservoirs and top them up to within ¼ in. of the lower edge of the filler opening with fresh fluid. Leave the cap and diaphragm off the master cylinder but cover it with clean, lint-free shop rags to prevent fluid from being ejected and getting onto painted surfaces.

2. Wipe any dirt or oil from the bleeder screw (**Figure 3**) of the first brake to be bled and attach a length of hose to the screw. The hose must fit snugly over the screw. Place the other end of the hose in a container partially filled with fresh brake fluid.

3. Using an assistant, open the bleeder valve about ¾ turn and have your assistant depress the brake pedal and hold it. Just before the pedal bottoms, close the bleeder valve and instruct the assistant to release the brake pedal. When the brake pedal is all the way up, open the bleeder valve and have the brake depressed once again. Close the bleeder valve and have the brake released. Continue this sequence until the brake fluid running out of the hose and into the container is free of air bubbles. Then close the bleeder valve and tighten it and remove the bleeder hose. Top up the fluid in the master cylinder reservoirs and re-cover the reservoirs with the rags.

4. Bleed the other brakes in the same manner, topping up the reservoir with fresh fluid after each unit has been bled. When the entire system

has been bled and the fluid levels in the master cylinder reservoirs topped up to within ¼ in. of the lower edge of the filler opening, check the feel of the brake pedal. If it is not firm, some air remains in the system and it must be bled again in the manner just described.

5. When the pedal feel is correct, road test the vehicle to ensure that the brakes operate correctly. Begin checking at low speed until you are confident that the braking action is good.

SERVICE BRAKE ADJUSTMENT

Front disc brakes are self-adjusting. As the brake lining wears down, more fluid is drawn into the caliper cylinders from the master cylinder to compensate for the increased volume in the caliper cylinders.

Drum type service brakes are adjusted when the vehicle is driven in reverse and the brakes are applied. If the brake pedal can be pushed within a couple of inches of the floor, the brakes should be adjusted by backing the vehicle up several times and sharply applying the brakes. Test the adjustment by driving the vehicle at about 20 mph and then braking to a smooth stop. If the pedal travel is still long, adjust them once again as just described.

PARKING BRAKE ADJUSTMENT

The parking brake should be adjusted whenever the foot control can be depressed six or more clicks. Before adjusting the parking brake, adjust service brakes as just described.

1. Depress the parking brake pedal one click.

2. Tighten the adjuster nut (**Figure 4**) until there is a slight drag on the rear wheels when they are rotated forward.

3. Release the parking brake control and rotate the wheels. There should be no drag.

BRAKE INSPECTION AND CLEANING

The brake inspections described below should be performed every 6,000 miles for disc brakes and 12,000 miles for drum brakes, providing that the vehicle is not used extensively under adverse road and weather conditions. For extremely adverse conditions, such as deep sand or mud, the brakes should be inspected

11

and cleaned more frequently, such as at 1,000-mile intervals or each time the wheel bearings are cleaned, repacked, and adjusted.

Disc Brakes

1. Slightly loosen the front wheel lug nuts. Raise the front of the vehicle and support it on frame stands. Remove the front wheels.

2. Check the thickness of the lining at both ends of the outboard shoes. If the lining is worn to within $\frac{1}{32}$ in. of the shoe on bonded linings, or to within $\frac{1}{32}$ in. of the rivet heads on riveted linings, the shoes should be replaced as a set on both front wheels. Also check the thickness of the inboard lining through the inspection hole in the center of the caliper. The minimum lining for the inboard shoe is the same as for the outboard (**Figure 5**).

3. Check the linings for grease, oil, or brake fluid. If they are soaked, they must be replaced in spite of the amount of brake lining material remaining.

4. Inspect the brake rotors for scratches and grooves. If grooves are deep enough to snag a fingernail, the rotors should be serviced by a dealer or a brake specialist.

Drum Brakes

1. Raise the vehicle and support it on frame stands. Remove the wheels and tires from one side. To remove the front drum, first remove the outer grease cup from the hub, remove the cotter key, unscrew the axle nut and pull out on the drum to remove it. For rear brakes, remove the screws that attach the drum to the axle, pull out sharply on the drum and remove it. If the drum is difficult to remove, loosen the parking brake adjuster; the shoes may be in contact with the drum.

> NOTE: *If the brakes are simply being inspected for lining condition and remaining service life, it is not necessary to remove the drums and wheels from both sides; the condition of the linings and drums on one side is indicative of the condition of those on the opposite side. However, if the drums and linings on the first side require cleaning and dressing, this service should be carried out on the opposite side also.*

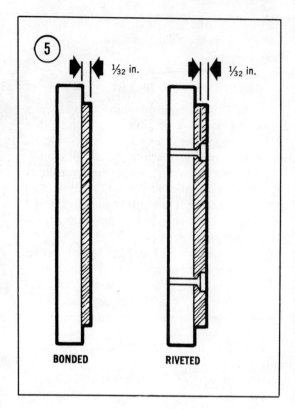

BONDED   RIVETED

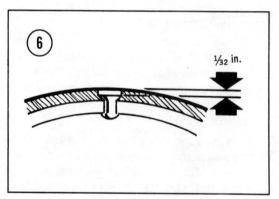

2. Wipe the brake shoes and insides of the drums with a clean dry cloth to remove sand, dirt, and any other foreign matter. *Do not use solvent.* Inspect the drums for scoring and scratches. Any score deep enough to snag a fingernail is reason for having the drums turned and the linings replaced. Minor scoring and scratches can be removed with fine emery cloth, following which the drum must be thoroughly cleaned with compressed air to remove any abrasive.

Inspect the linings for dirt, oil, grease, and brake fluid. Dirt and foreign particles that are

Applying for a
social security
number

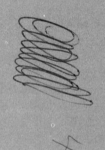

Applying for a social security number

The social security law requires that you furnish evidence of age, identity, and U.S. citizenship or lawful admission status when you apply for a social security number. If you are 18 or older, you must apply in person. If you are applying for a replacement card or changing your name or other information on your record, you must establish your identity. For a change-of-name request, the evidence must identify you with both your old name and your new name. If you need help in obtaining any documents, get in touch with any social security office.

Documents are subject to verification with the agency that issued them.

Please do not submit uncertified photocopies of your documents. We must see either the original documents or a copy certified by the agency which issued it. We will return any documents you send us.

It usually takes about 6 weeks to get your social security card after we receive your application and necessary documents.

If you were born in the United States
A variety of documents can be submitted as evidence of your age, identity, and citizenship. Examples of these documents are included in the following lists.

Evidence of age and citizenship
▶ Public or hospital record of birth established before age 5.
▶ Religious record of birth or baptism established before age 5.

HEW Publication No. (SSA) 79-10064

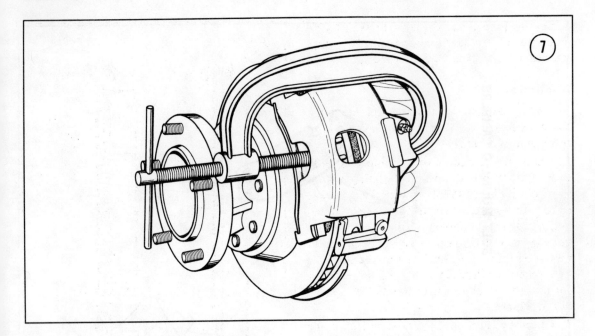

imbedded in the lining can be removed with a wire brush, but if the lining is soaked with grease, oil, or brake fluid, it must be replaced.

Measure the depth of the rivet holes with a depth gauge (**Figure 6**). If the lining is worn to within $\frac{1}{32}$ in. of the rivet heads, it must be replaced.

> NOTE: *It is important that brakes be reconditioned at least in pairs — both fronts or both rears — or all 4 at the same time. In addition, if the linings are replaced, they must be arced to the contour of the drums which in most cases require truing. This is a job for a dealer or automotive brake specialist.*

3. Refer to *Front Wheel Bearings and Hubs*, Chapter Twelve, and install the drums and service and adjust the wheel bearings.

DISC BRAKE PAD REPLACEMENT

Vacuum-Boosted Brakes

1. Remove the cap from the master cylinder reservoir and siphon all but about $\frac{1}{3}$ of the brake fluid. If this is not done, brake fluid will be ejected from the reservoir when the pistons are pushed back into the calipers. As a further precaution to fluid being ejected and damaging painted surfaces, cover the reservoir with a clean, lint-free shop cloth.

2. Carefully press the piston back into the caliper with a C-clamp (**Figure 7**).

3. On bolt-mounted calipers (**Figure 8**), unscrew the bolts and lift the caliper off the disc. Remove the shoes from the caliper.

4. Remove the shoe support spring from the front of the piston. Remove the sleeves from the inboard caliper mounting lugs. Remove the rubber bushings from the grooves in both the inboard and outboard caliper mounting lugs.

5. Thoroughly clean the mounting bolts and the caliper, taking care to remove any dirt from the holes in the mounting lugs. Clean the caliper only with a dry, clean cloth; solvent may damage the piston boot. If solvent is required to clean the mounting bolts, use only fresh brake fluid; make sure the bolts are wiped dry. Inspect the caliper for signs of leakage and check the boot for damage. If it is cracked or torn, dirt and water may have entered the caliper. In such a case, the caliper should be referred to a dealer or brake specialist to determine if the caliper should be rebuilt.

6. Lubricate new sleeves and rubber bushings, the bushing grooves in the caliper mounting lugs, and the ends of the mounting bolts (**Figure 9**) with Delco Moraine Silicone Lubricant or an equivalent.

7. Press the bushings into the grooves in the mounting lugs. Press the new sleeves into the

11

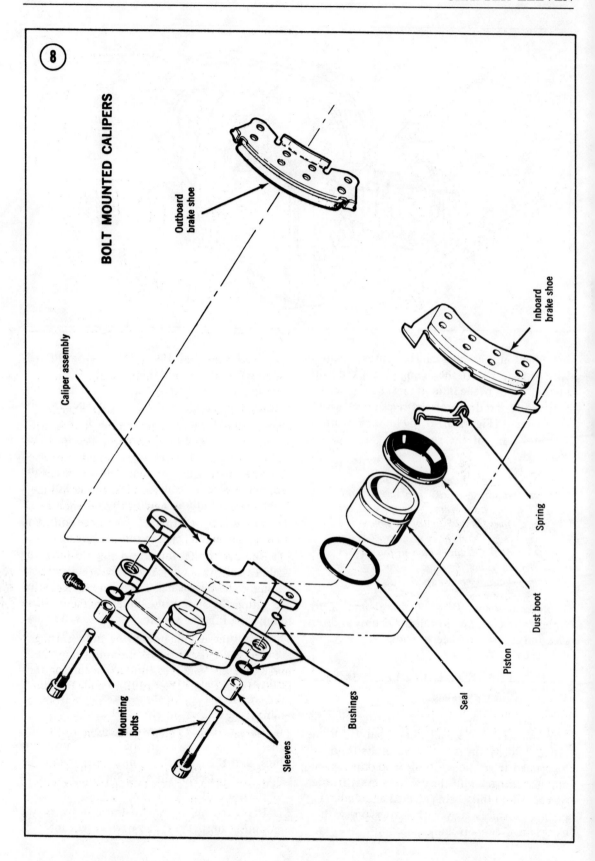

⑧

BOLT MOUNTED CALIPERS

Outboard brake shoe

Inboard brake shoe

Caliper assembly

Spring

Dust boot

Piston

Seal

Bushings

Mounting bolts

Sleeves

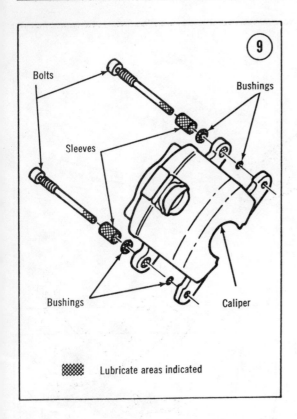

Lubricate areas indicated

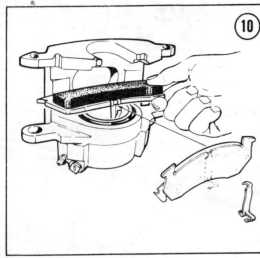

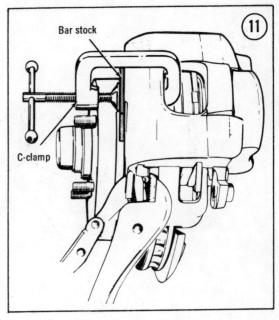

caliper and that the tab at the bottom of the shoe fits in the recess in the claiper with no clearance.

10. With a piece of barstock and a clean C-clamp to prevent contamination to the new brake lining, lightly clamp the shoes into the caliper (**Figure 11**). Use just enough force to hold the shoes firmly in place but not so much that there is risk of deforming the new shoe. Bend the ears of the new outboard shoe over the caliper lugs so there is a clearance of 0.005 in. or less between the ears and the lugs.

11. Remove the C-clamp and the old inboard shoe. Install the new inboard shoe and carefully fit the caliper over the disc. Line up the holes in the caliper lugs with the holes in the caliper mounting bracket.

12. Insert the caliper mounting bolts through the sleeves in the inboard mounting lugs and make sure the bolts pass under the ears on the inboard brake shoe (**Figure 12**). Guide the bolts through to engage the holes in the outboard shoe and in the outboard lugs on the caliper. Then, screw them in and tighten them to 35 ft.-lb.

13. Service the opposite caliper in the manner just described. After reinstalling the wheels and lowering the vehicle, fill the master cylinder reservoir to within ¼ in. of the top with fresh brake fluid and install the reservoir cap. Apply

inboard mounting lugs until the ends of the sleeves facing the disc are flush with the inside machined surface of the lugs.

8. Install the old inboard shoe and the shoe support spring in the piston (**Figure 10**) and push the shoe down until it contacts the caliper.

9. Install the new outboard shoe, making sure that the ears on the shoe are over the lugs on the

11

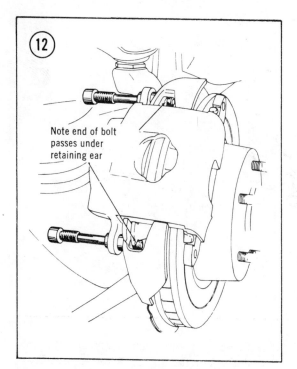

Note end of bolt passes under retaining ear

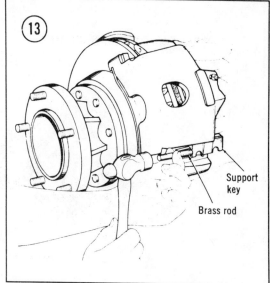

Support key

Brass rod

the brakes several times or until there is a firm pedal pressure and normal pedal travel. Then, recheck the fluid level in the master cylinder reservoir and correct it if necessary.

WARNING
Do not drive the vehicle until pedal pressure and travel are correct. If pressure cannot be obtained by pumping the brake pedal with the vehicle stationary, refer to the instructions for bleeding the system at the beginning of this chapter and correct system operation first.

NOTE: *Avoid hard brake applications as much as possible for the first 100 miles or so after installing new linings. This will permit the lining to bed into the discs and will permit them a long service life.*

Hydraulic-Boosted Brakes

1. Carry out Steps 1 and 2 described for *Vacuum Boosted Brakes*.

2. Unscrew the screw that locks the caliper support key in place and drive out the key with a soft drift **(Figure 13)**.

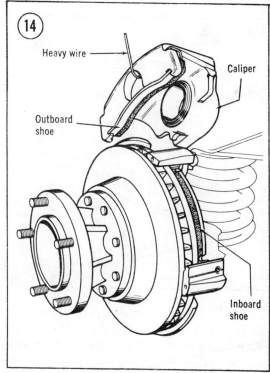

Heavy wire

Caliper

Outboard shoe

Inboard shoe

3. Slide the caliper off the disc and suspend it with a piece of wire **(Figure 14)**. *Never allow the caliper to hang by the brake hose.*

4. Remove the inboard brake shoe from the steering knuckle and the outboard shoe from the caliper. Remove the inboard shoe clip **(Figure 15)** and discard it.

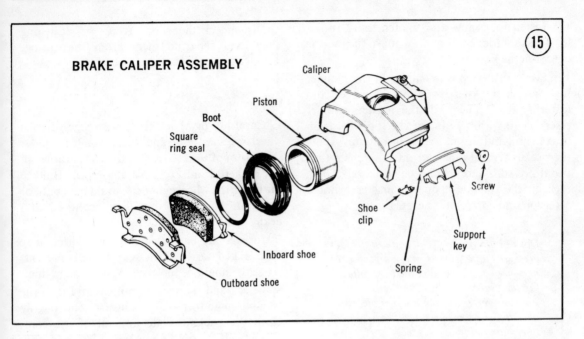

BRAKE CALIPER ASSEMBLY

knuckle using a wire brush. Lubricate the contact (sliding) surfaces with Delco Silicone Lube No. 5459912 or an equivalent.

7. Install a new inboard shoe clip in the steering knuckle with the loop spring on the clip facing away from the disc. Start the lower end of the inboard shoe into the groove in the steering knuckle then move the upper end into place. Make certain the clip remains in place.

8. Install the outer shoe in the caliper. The ears at the top of the shoe must fit over the caliper ears, and the tab on the bottom of the shoe must fit into the recess in the caliper. Make sure that there is no clearance between the tab on the shoe and the caliper recess. The shoe must fit tightly without rattling.

9. Set the caliper over the disc and engage it with the upper mount on the steering knuckle. Then swing it down into contact with the lower mount.

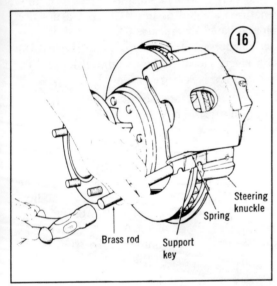

CAUTION
Make certain the brake hose is not twisted or kinked before setting the caliper in place.

10. Install the spring on the caliper support key and set them in place between the steering knuckle and the groove in the caliper. Tap the key into place with a soft drift to lock the caliper to the steering knuckle (**Figure 16**).

5. Check the inside of the caliper for leakage, and if any is present the caliper should be rebuilt. This is a job for a dealer or brake specialist. Wipe the inside of the caliper with a clean, dry cloth and inspect the rubber dust boot for cracks, tears, and damage that permit water and dirt to get into the caliper. If this type of damage is evident, it is likely that the caliper has been contaminated. It should be entrusted to a dealer or brake specialist for service.

6. Clean rust, corrosion, and dirt from the contact surfaces of the caliper and the steering

11. Install lockscrew and tighten to 12-18 ft.-lb. The shoulder on the screw must fit into the cutout in the key.

12. Service the opposite caliper in the manner just described. After installing the wheels and lowering the vehicle, fill the master cylinder reservoir to within ¼ in. of the top with fresh brake fluid and install the reservoir cap. Apply the brakes several times or until there is a firm pedal pressure and normal pedal travel. Then, recheck the fluid level in the master cylinder reservoir and correct it if necessary.

> WARNING
> *Do not drive the vehicle until pedal pressure and travel are correct. If pressure cannot be obtained by pumping the brake pedal with the vehicle stationary, refer to the instructions for bleeding the system and correct system operation first.*

NOTE: *Avoid hard brake applications as much as possible for the first 100 miles or so after installing new linings. This will permit the lining to bed into the discs and will permit them a long service life.*

DRUM BRAKE SHOE REPLACEMENT

Removal

1. Remove the brake drums as described above (See *Drum Brakes*). Unhook the pull-back springs from the anchor pin (**Figure 17**). If possible, a tool like the one shown (GM tool No. J-8049) should be used to overcome the spring stiffness.

> NOTE: *At no time, when the brake drums are removed, should the brake pedal be depressed. This would result in the pistons being ejected from the wheel cylinders.*

2. Remove the return spring from the actuator. Unhook the wire link from the anchor pin and remove it from the secondary shoe.

3. Press down on the hold-down spring cups and remove the anchor pins from the posts. Remove the springs and cups.

4. Remove the actuator and spring assembly. Unless a part of this unit is damaged, it should remain assembled.

5. Disconnect the shoes from the adjusting screw and separate them from the spring. Remove the parking brake lever.

Inspection

1. Carefully pry back the lower edge of each wheel cylinder boot and check for leakage. A slight film of brake fluid on the rods is normal, but if there is an excessive amount of fluid in the boots the wheel cylinder should be rebuilt or replaced. This work should be entrusted to a dealer or a brake specialist.

2. Inspect the backing plate for oil that may have leaked past the axle seal. If oil is present, the seals should be replaced. See Chapter Nine.

3. Check and tighten the bolts that attach the backing plate to the axle housing. Thoroughly clean the backing plate and all of the components. If a solvent must be used, use only denatured alcohol or brake fluid. Do not use mineral-based detergents. Clean the shoe contact surfaces on the backing plate (**Figure 18**) with emery cloth. Make certain all loose dirt, rust, or abrasives are removed.

4. Check the operation of the adjuster screw. If it does not turn smoothly, disassemble, clean, and lubricate it.

5. Work on the drums and shoes should be entrusted to a dealer or a brake specialist. The drums must be measured for roundness and the contact surface checked for serviceability. Often they must be trued with a brake drum lathe. In addition, the shoes and new linings must be arced to the contour of the drums.

Installation

1. Clean your hands thoroughly and check the new linings to make sure they are not nicked or burred. If they are bonded linings, check for and remove any bonding cement along the edges.

2. Use brake lubricant to lubricate the following items:

    a. Parking brake cable

    b. Fulcrum end of parking brake lever

    c. Bolt for parking brake lever

    d. Adjusting screw

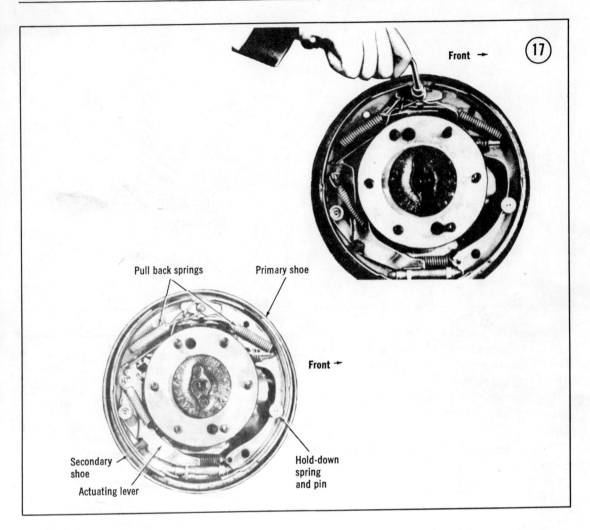

Pull back springs   Primary shoe

Front →

Secondary
shoe

Actuating lever

Hold-down
spring
and pin

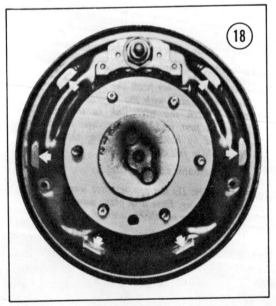

Attach the parking brake lever to the secondary shoe with the bolt, spring washer, lockwasher, and nut and then make sure it moves freely.

3. Connect the adjusting screw spring to one set of brake shoes then assemble them to the adjusting screw. Install the assembly on the backing plate.

WARNING

The right-hand thread adjusting screw must go on the left backing plate and the left-hand thread adjusting screw must go on the right backing plate. The star wheel on the adjusting screw must be toward the secondary shoe and must line up with the window in the backing plate. Make sure the adjusting screw spring does not interfere with the star wheel.

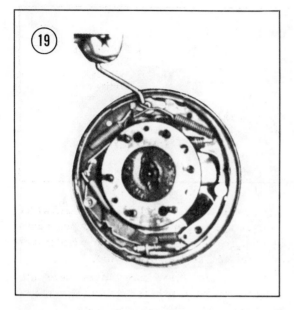

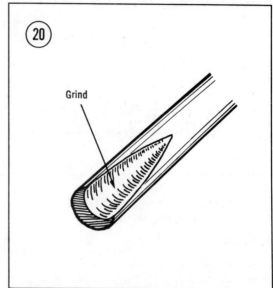

Grind

4. Connect the parking brake cable. Install the hold-down spring, cup, and pin on the primary shoe. Then connect the shoes with the wheel cylinder piston rods.

5. Install the actuator assembly and the hold-down spring, cup, and pin for the secondary shoe.

6. Install the guide plate on the anchor pin. Connect the wire link to the actuator, then hold the actuator all the way down and connect the wire link to the anchor pin. Install the return spring on the actuator, using a flat screwdriver to carefully guide it into place. *Do not bend the actuator lever out.*

7. Connect the pull-back spring to the primary brake shoe and then hook it over the anchor pin. If a tool such as the one shown (**Figure 19,** GM tool No. J-22348) is not available, a suitable tool can be made by grinding the end of a length of ¼ in. steel rod as shown in **Figure 20,** or a sturdy wire loop can be fashioned from a coat hanger. Connect the return spring to the secondary shoe and then connect it to the end of the wire link.

8. Carefully pry the shoes away from the backing plate and lightly lubricate them with brake lubricant where they contact the backing plate contact surfaces. Be careful to keep lubricant off the facing of the brake linings.

9. Check the operation of the actuator lever **(Figure 21).**

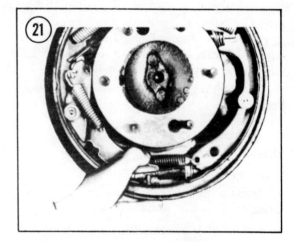

10. When both brakes have been assembled, make a preliminary adjustment. Pull the actuator away from the star wheel slightly and turn the star wheel until the brake drum can be installed with just a slight drag on the shoes. Then, back the star wheel off 1¼ turns to slightly retract the shoes. Install the drums and wheels and the metal covers on the adjusting windows in the backing plates. Make certain the locating tang in the drum engages the locating hole in the hub.

11. Make a final brake adjustment by repeatedly driving the vehicle backward and forward and stopping with firm pedal pressure until the pedal height and resistance are satisfactory.

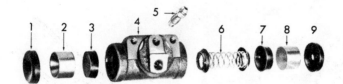

WHEEL CYLINDER

(22)

1. Pushrod boot
2. Piston
3. Piston cup
4. Housing
5. Fluid inlet
6. Spring
7. Piston cup
8. Piston
9. Pushrod boot

WHEEL CYLINDER SERVICE (DRUM BRAKES)

Removal

1. Raise vehicle and remove wheel and brake drum (see *Drum Brake*), and brake shoe pull back springs, using procedure given above.

2. Carefully clean all dirt away from line to wheel cylinder connection. Disconnect hydraulic line from cylinder and cover end of line with clean, lint-free cloth to prevent contamination from entering hydraulic system.

3. Remove screws securing cylinder to flange plate. Disengage cylinder pushrods from brake shoes and remove cylinder.

Disassembly

Refer to **Figure 22**.

1. Remove boots from cylinder ends and discard.

2. Remove and discard pistons and caps.

Cleaning and Inspection

NOTE: *Most brake fluids are colored to assist in detecting hydraulic leaks. Staining from this coloring should not be confused with corrosion, which can be identified by pits or roughness in the cylinder bore.*

1. Check cylinder bore for staining and corrosion. Discard if corroded (see NOTE above) and obtain new cylinder.

2. Remove stains by polishing the cylinder bore with crocus cloth. This can be done by revolving the cylinder while supporting the cloth in the bore with a finger. Do not polish by sliding the cloth lengthwise in the bore under pressure.

3. Clean hands thoroughly with soap and water (do not use gasoline or any other petroleum based solvent) and then clean the cylinder and all metal parts in clean brake fluid.

4. Shake excess fluid from cylinder. Never use a rag to dry cylinder bore as even the smallest fragment of lint could cause problems.

Assembly

1. Lubricate cylinder bore and counterbore with clean brake fluid and insert spring expander assembly.

2. Install new cups with flat surfaces toward center of cylinder. Do not lubricate cups prior to assembly.

3. Install new pistons with flat surfaces toward center of cylinder. Do not lubricate pistons before assembly.

4. Press new boots into cylinder counterbore by hand. Do not lubricate boots prior to installation.

Installation

1. Position wheel cylinder to flange plate and install and securely tighten screws.

2. Replace all pushrods and pull back screws.

3. Reconnect hydraulic line to wheel cylinder.

4. Use the star wheel adjuster to adjust the brake shoes so that the drum will just fit over them with a slight drag. Then, turn the adjuster back 1¼ turns to retract the shoes and provide sufficient shoe-to-drum clearance.

5. Install the brake drums and wheels. For front brakes, refer to *Front Wheel Bearings and Hubs* in Chapter Twelve and service and adjust the wheel bearings.

11

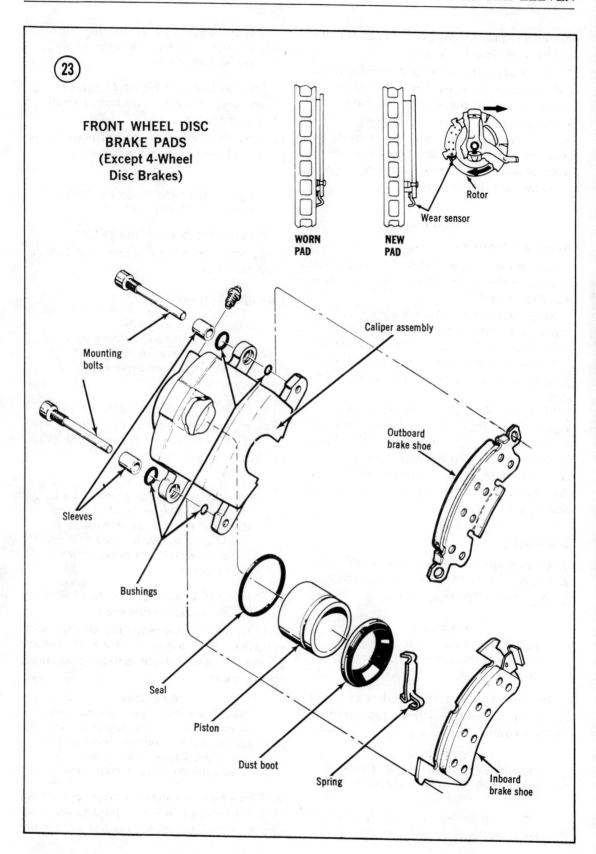

(23)

**FRONT WHEEL DISC
BRAKE PADS
(Except 4-Wheel
Disc Brakes)**

WORN
PAD

NEW
PAD

Rotor

Wear sensor

Caliper assembly

Mounting
bolts

Outboard
brake shoe

Sleeves

Bushings

Seal

Piston

Dust boot

Spring

Inboard
brake shoe

6. See *Bleeding the Brake System* earlier in this chapter and bleed the system.

7. See *Brake Adjustment* and *Parking Brake Adjustment* in Chapter Three and adjust the service brakes and then the parking brake.

8. Road test the vehicle. Drive slowly at first and check to make sure the brakes are operating correctly. If the shoes and drums were reconditioned, use the brakes sparingly at first and allow them to seat.

CALIPER

Removal/Installation

Caliper removal and installation is described in detail earlier in this chapter (see *Disc Brake Pad Replacement*).

After disconnecting the brake hose from the caliper, tape the end of the hose to prevent the entry of dirt and moisture. When reconnecting the hoses, use new copper gaskets. Position the hose between the locating beads on the caliper gate.

When installation is complete, refer to *Bleeding the Brake System* and bleed the system. Then road test the vehicle. Drive slowly at first to ensure that the brakes are operating correctly. If the pads and rotors were reconditioned, use the brakes sparingly at first to allow them to seat.

Disassembly

1. Clean caliper exterior with clean brake fluid and place caliper on a clean working surface.

2. Drain brake fluid from caliper.

WARNING
Follow Step 3 and do not attempt to catch or protect piston with fingers, as injury could result.

3. Pad interior of caliper with clean shop towels and remove piston by application of compressed air.

CAUTION
Do not blow piston out of bore. Use only enough air to ease the piston out.

NOTE: *If compressed air is not available, remove piston by applying*

brake pedal after caliper has been removed from disc, but before disconnecting hydraulic line.

4. Pry dust boot (see **Figure 23**) out of caliper piston bore, exercising care not to scratch or damage piston bore.

5. Use a small piece of wood or plastic to pry piston seal from its groove in piston bore.

CAUTION
Do not use a metal tool of any kind, as damage to bore may result.

6. Remove bleeder valve from caliper.

7. Remove and discard sleeves and bushings from caliper ears.

Cleaning and Inspection

CAUTION
Dust boot, piston seal, rubber bushings, and sleeves must be discarded when the caliper is overhauled. Replace them with new parts.

1. Clean all parts (except those discarded) in clean brake fluid. Use only dry, filtered, compressed air to blow out all passages in caliper and bleeder valve.

CAUTION
Use of unfiltered shop air may leave a film of mineral oil on internal passages. Mineral oil may damage rubber parts. If filtered air is not available, allow parts to drain completely dry before attempting reassembly.

2. Examine all mounting bolts and replace any that appear corroded or damaged.

3. Carefully examine piston for scoring, nicks, corrosion, and worn or damaged chrome plating. If any surface defects are noted, replace piston.

CAUTION
Piston surfaces and plating are manufactured to close tolerances. Do not attempt to resurface the piston by any means. The use of any abrasive, including crocus cloth, is not acceptable.

4. Check bore of caliper for same defects listed in Step 3. Piston bore is not plated and stains or minor corrosion can be polished out with a

11

crocus cloth. A thorough clean-up is required after the use of crocus cloth.

CAUTION
Do not use emery cloth or any other type of abrasive. If crocus cloth does not remove the stain or corrosion, the caliper must be replaced.

Assembly

1. Lubricate caliper piston bore and new piston seal with clean brake fluid and place seal in caliper bore groove.

2. Lubricate piston with clean brake fluid and assemble new dust boot into groove in piston. Fold must face open end of piston as shown in **Figure 24**.

3. Insert piston into caliper bore, using care not to disturb the seal seating. Force piston to bottom of bore (50-100 lb. of force required).

4. Position dust boot in caliper counterbore and seat, using a boot installer tool (GM No. J-22904) as shown in **Figure 25**.

CAUTION
Check boot installation carefully to ensure that retaining ring molded into boot is not bent and that boot is installed below caliper face and evenly all around.

NOTE: *If boot installer tool is not available, the inventive mechanic can improvise a substitute. Care should be taken, however, not to damage the boot, piston, or caliper. A better alternative is to take the assembly to a brake shop and have the boot installed there.*

5. Install bleeder valve and torque to 65 in.-lb. (If valve will not seal at 65 in.-lb., torque to 100 in.-lb. maximum to obtain seal. If valve will not seal at 100 in.-lb., replace valve).

POWER BRAKE UNIT

Inspection

1. Check vacuum line and connections, including check valve, for vacuum loss.

2. Inspect hydraulic lines and connections for leaks.

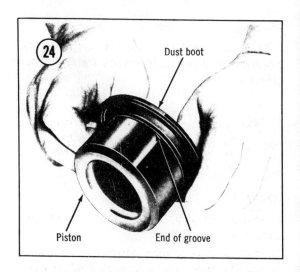

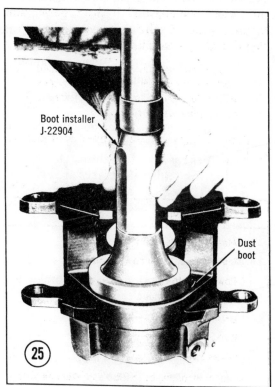

3. Check for scored brake drums and for worn or contaminated linings.

4. Check and fill fluid reservoirs, as required.

5. Inspect for loose master cylinder and power unit mounting bolts.

6. Check power piston air filter and replace if indicated.

7. Check for misalignment and/or binding of brake pedal linkage.

Bleeding

Bleeding of brake hydraulic system should be done in accordance with procedure given earlier in this chapter.

CAUTION
Do not use power assist when bleeding brake lines. Engine must be off. Pump brake pedal several times to expend vacuum reserve before starting.

Removal

1. Disconnect vacuum line from power unit check valve.

2. Remove nuts holding power unit to master cylinder (in models so attached). Pull forward on master cylinder until it clears power unit mounting studs. Carefully move cylinder to one side with all hydraulic lines attached.

NOTE: *On older models, the power unit and master cylinder must be removed as a unit. In this case, disconnect hydraulic lines from master cylinder.*

3. Remove nuts holding power cylinder to dash.

4. Remove retainer holding pushrod to brake pedal. Remove power unit from engine compartment.

NOTE: *Repair of the power unit requires special tools and knowledge. Instead of attempting to make repairs, the home mechanic should take the unit to a dealer or competent power brake mechanic for repairs or replacement. Always replace vacuum check valve and grommet when power unit is overhauled.*

Installation

1. Install all components in reverse order of the removal procedure. See **Table 1** for torque specifications.

2. Check brake operation. If hydraulic lines were removed, the system must be bled to remove all air from lines and components. Check stoplight switch adjustment.

CAUTION
Start engine and allow time for vacuum to build up in power unit before operating brake pedal.

Table 1   TORQUE SPECIFICATIONS

Component	Torque
Master cylinder to dash	24 ft.-lb.
Master cylinder to power unit	24 ft.-lb.
Power unit to dash	24 ft.-lb.
Brake line nuts (all)	150 in.-lb.
Brake bleeder valves	65-100 in.-lb.
Brake shoe to anchor pin	120 ft.-lb.
Wheel cylinder to flange plate	50 in.-lb.
Caliper mounting bolt (1968-and later one piston)	35 ft.-lb.
Caliper mounting bolt (1969 four piston)	70 ft.-lb.
Caliper mounting bolt (1967-1968)	130 ft.-lb.
Flex hose-to-caliper bolt	22 ft.-lb.
Pedal mounting pivot bolt (nut)	28 ft.-lb.
Combination valve mounting	150 in.-lb.

11

CHAPTER TWELVE

CHASSIS

Major work on Chevrolet/GMC chassis frequently requires the use of special tools that are available only to dealers. In addition, a great deal of specialized experience is required that places such work beyond the abilities of a hobbyist mechanic.

Chassis work should be confined to the procedures described below. All other work should be entrusted to a dealer or a qualified specialist.

SHOCK ABSORBERS

The shock absorbers can be routinely checked while installed on the vehicle. However, this is only a general indication of their condition; if there is any doubt about their serviceability, they should be removed as described later and checked more accurately.

To check their general condition, bounce first the front and the rear of the vehicle up and down several times, then release it. The vehicle should not continue to bounce more than twice. Excessive bouncing is an indication of worn shock absorbers. Keep in mind, however, that this test is not conclusive. If there is doubt about the condition of the units, remove them and have them tested.

NOTE: *Conventional shock absorbers usually last 20-30,000 miles.*

Removal/Installation (Front)

1. Jack up the front of the vehicle and support it on frame stands. Remove the front wheels.

2. Unscrew the nut and bolt from the lower mount (**Figure 1**).

3. Unscrew the nut and bolt from the upper mount, remove the washer and bushings, and pull the shock absorber out of the mount.

4. Install the new shock absorbers with new rubber bushings. Install the upper end of the shock absorber first, but do not tighten the nut until the bottom has been installed. Then, retighten both nuts and bolts to 65-75 ft.-lb.

Removal/Installation (Rear)

1. Jack up the rear of the vehicle and support it on frame stands. Remove the rear wheels.

2. Unscrew the upper mounting nut (**Figure 2**) and remove the washer and bushing. Unscrew the nut from the bottom bolt and tap the bolt out with a soft mallet. It may be necessary to drive the bolt out with a soft drift such as a hardwood dowel.

3. Install the new shock absorbers with new bushings. Install the upper end of the shock absorber first, but do not tighten the nut until the lower end has been lined up with the bracket

REAR SHOCK ABSORBERS

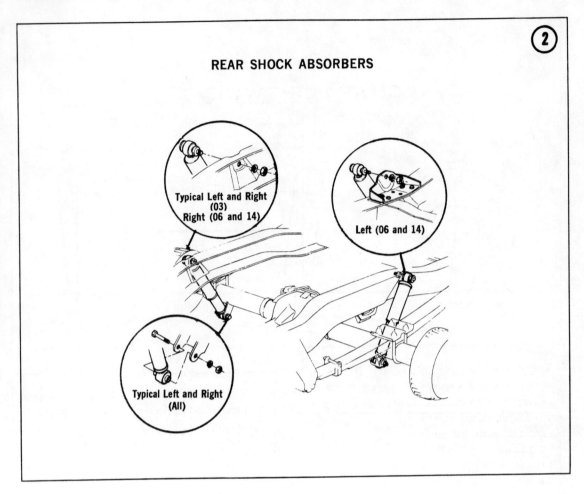

Typical Left and Right
(03)
Right (06 and 14)

Left (06 and 14)

Typical Left and Right
(All)

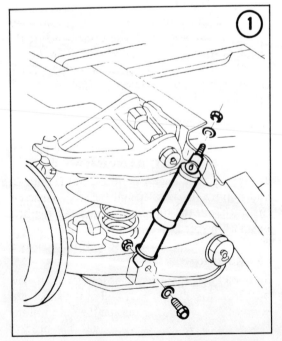

and the bolt installed. Then, tighten the nuts to the values shown in **Table 1**.

Inspection

1. Check the piston rod for bending, galling, and abrasion. Any one of these conditions is reason for replacement.

2. Check for fluid leakage. A light film on the rod is normal, but severe leakage is reason for replacement.

3. With the shock absorber in the installed position, completely extend the rod, then invert the shock absorber and completely compress the rod. Do this several times to expel trapped air. Clamp the lower end of the shock absorber in a vise fitted with jaw protectors. Compress and extend the piston rod as fast as possible and check damping action. The resistance should be smooth and uniform throughout each stroke, and the resistance during extension should be

12

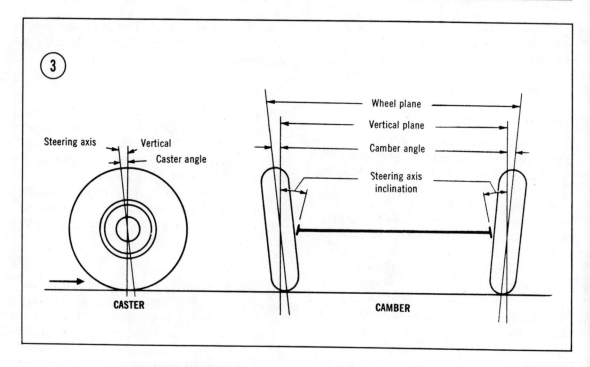

CASTER

CAMBER

Steering axis
Vertical
Caster angle

Wheel plane
Vertical plane
Camber angle
Steering axis
inclination

Table 1
REAR SHOCK ABSORBER
TIGHTENING TORQUES

Year	Torque
1967-1972	
Upper and lower	65 ft.-lb.
1973 and Later	
Upper	140 ft.-lb.
Lower	115 ft.-lb.

greater than during compression. Also, the action of both shock absorbers in a pair should feel the same. If the damping action is erratic, or resistance to quick extension and compression is very low, or if resistance is the same in both directions, the shock absorbers should be replaced, preferably as a set. The exception here would be for a shock absorber that has failed because of physical damage while the opposite unit performs satisfactorily.

> NOTE: *Comparison of a used shock absorber, that is believed to be good, to a new shock absorber is not a valid comparison; the new shock absorber will seem to offer more resistance because of the greater friction of the new rod seal.*

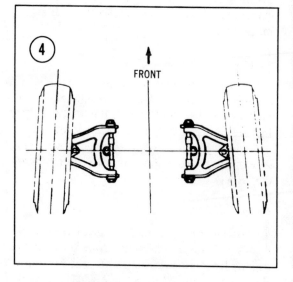

FRONT

WHEEL ALIGNMENT

Wheel alignment should be checked periodically by a dealer or an alignment specialist. Misalignment is usually indicated first by incorrect tire wear (see *Tire Wear Analysis*, Chapter Two), or steering or handling difficulties.

> NOTE: *Precision frame and wheel alignment equipment is required to accurately measure caster, camber, and toe-in. If steering, handling, and tire*

wear difficulties cannot be corrected by the checks and corrections presented below, the vehicle should be entrusted to a Chevrolet dealer or an automotive alignment specialist.

Inspection

A proper inspection of front tire wear can point to several alignment problems. Tires worn primarily on one side show problems with toe-in. If toe-in is incorrect on one wheel, the vehicle probably pulls to one side or the other. If toe-in is incorrect on both wheels, the vehicle is probably hard to steer in either direction.

Incorrect camber may also cause tire wear on one side. Tire cupping (scalloped wear pattern) can result from worn shock absorbers, one wheel out of alignment, a bent spindle, or a combination of all. Tires worn in the middle, but not the edges, or worn nearly even on both edges, but not in the middle, are probably overinflated or underinflated, respectively. These conditions are not caused by suspension misalignment.

Camber

Camber is the inclination of the wheel from vertical as shown in **Figure 3**. Note that camber angle is positive camber, i.e., the top of the tire inclines outward more than the bottom.

Camber is adjusted by adding or removing shims at both front and rear bolts of upper control arm shaft.

Caster

Caster is the fore and aft inclination of the steering knuckle centerline from vertical. See **Figure 3**. Caster is positive, i.e., the bottom of the wheel is shifted forward. Caster causes the wheel to return to a position straight ahead after a turn. It also prevents the car from wandering due to wind, potholes, or uneven road surfaces.

Caster is adjusted by adding or subtracting shims to the front bolt or the rear bolt of the upper control arm shaft.

Steering Axis Inclination

Steering axis inclination, shown in **Figure 3**, is the inward inclination of the steering knuckle centerline from vertical. This angle is not adjustable, but can be checked with proper front end racks to find bent suspension parts.

Toe-in

Camber and rolling resistance tend to force the front wheels outward at their forward edge. To compensate for this tendency, the front edges are turned slightly inward when the car is at rest. This is toe-in. See **Figure 4**.

Toe-in is adjusted by lengthening or shortening the tie rods. Each tie rod is threaded so that the center section can be rotated to make the adjustment.

Inspection

Steering and handling problems which may appear to be caused by misalignment may very well be caused by other factors which are readily correctable without expensive equipment. The checks and inspections which follow should be carried out if steering, handling, or tire wear problems exist, and also before toe-in is adjusted.

1. Check all tire pressures and correct them if necessary, referring to Table 1, Chapter Three. It is essential that the pressures be checked when the tires are cold.

2. Raise the front of the vehicle and support it with frame stands as described in Chapter One. Check the end play of the wheel bearings by grasping the tire front and rear and attempting to move it in and out. If bearing end play can be felt, refer to the section on wheel bearing service in this chapter and inspect and adjust the bearings.

3. Refer to the section on steering service in this chapter and check the steering components for wear and all of the fasteners for looseness. Pay particular attention to the steering gear mounting bolts.

4. Check radial and lateral runout of both front tires with a dial indicator (**Figure 5**). Place the indicator against the tread first and slowly rotate the wheel. Then place the indicator against the outer sidewall of the tire and again slowly rotate the wheel. If either the radial or lateral runout is greater than 0.080 in., the tire should be deflated and rotated 90 degrees on the wheel.

12

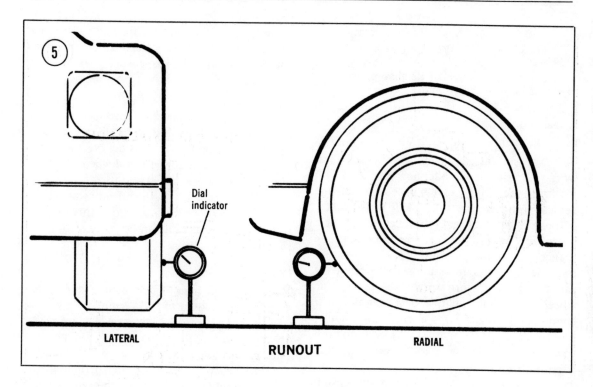

NOTE: *It will probably be necessary to soap the wheel rim before the tire can be turned.*

Reinflate the tire to the correct pressure shown in Table 1, Chapter Three, and recheck the runout. If necessary, the tire should be rotated again if the runout is still excessive.

If steering, handling, and tire wear problems cannot be corrected by carrying out the above inspections and adjustments, the vehicle should be referred to a dealer or alignment specialist for a precision inspection and corrective work.

STEERING

Service to the steering gear is limited to checking and correcting the lubricant level (Chapter Three), checking and correcting play in the steering wheel and column, and checking and tightening the steering gear mounting bolts. The tightening torque for the steering gear mounting bolts (**Figure 6**) is 65 ft.-lb.

FRONT WHEEL BEARINGS AND HUBS

The factory-recommended service interval for the front wheel bearings is 12,000 miles or

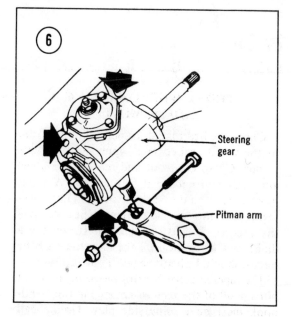

12 months. This interval assumes operation in generally dry weather and on good roads. If the vehicle is operated under adverse conditions (mostly off-road, continually wet weather, in mud or snow) the bearings should be serviced more frequently. For vehicles operated in deep water or mud, where the axles are likely to be submerged, bearings should be serviced daily.

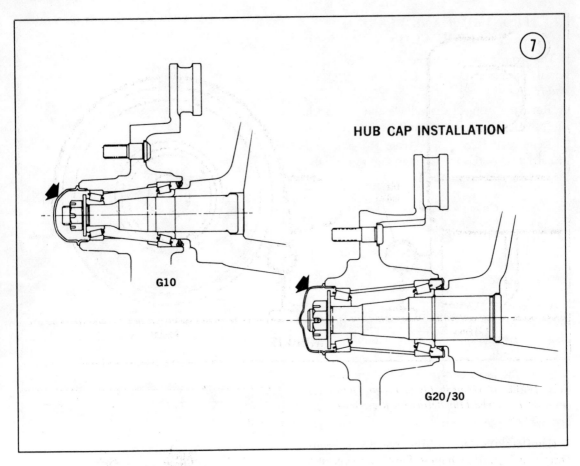

⑦

HUB CAP INSTALLATION

G10

G20/30

FRONT WHEEL BEARING ADJUSTMENT

Check the bearing adjustment with the front of the vehicle raised and supported by frame stands. Grasp the front and rear of the wheel and attempt to move it in and out. A slight movement should be felt. If there is no movement, or if the movement seems to be excessive, the bearings should be adjusted. If you use a dial indicator to measure the movement of the hub, it should be between 0.001 and 0.005 in.

The tapered roller bearings used in the front hubs of all of the vehicles covered in this handbook must have some side play. Unlike ball bearings which can be preloaded, roller bearings can be damaged by a constant preload on the ends of the rollers.

1. Remove the hub cap or wheel cover. Carefully pry the dust cap from the hub, taking care not to damage or deform it (**Figure 7**).

2. Remove the cotter pin from the axle and discard it.

3. Tighten the axle nut to 12 ft.-lb. and at the same time rotate the wheel back and forth to seat the bearings. This is necessary to remove any burrs and displace grease so that the movement present is the true movement of the bearing.

4. Unscrew the nut until it is just loose. Then tighten it by hand, without a wrench.

5. Install a new cotter pin. It may be necessary to back off the nut slightly to line up one of the notches in the nut with one of the holes in the axle. Not more than ½ flat of movement should be required.

6. Bend the ends of the cotter pin over and clip them so the dust cap can be installed. If possible, measure the end play of the hub with a dial indicator. It should be between 0.001-0.005 in. If necessary, readjust the bearings as described above.

7. Install the dust cap, wheel cover, or hub cap. Check and correct the adjustment of the opposite wheel in the manner just described.

12

FRONT HUB AND BEARING LUBRICATION

The front hubs should be serviced at the intervals discussed under *Front Wheel Bearings and Hubs*.

1. Raise the front of the vehicle and support it on frame stands as described in Chapter One.

2. Remove the cotter pin from the axle and discard it. Unscrew the axle nut and remove the large flat washer from the hub.

> NOTE: *On models equipped with front disc brakes, refer to Chapter Eight and remove the brake calipers. Be sure the calipers are suspended by heavy wire and are not allowed to hang by the brake lines.*

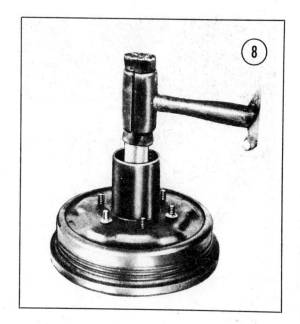

3. Pull out on the wheel to remove the wheel, brake drum, and hub as an assembly. This will also remove the outer bearing assembly from the axle spindle.

4. Drive the inner bearing cup and the bearing out of the hub using either a bearing driver **(Figure 8)** or soft drift, tapping progressively around the inner edge of the bearing assembly.

5. Thoroughly clean the bearings and the inside of the hub with solvent and blow them dry with compressed air.

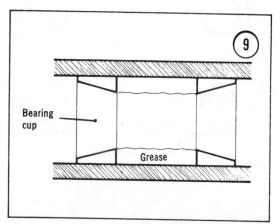

WARNING
Do not spin the bearings with the air jet; it is capable of rotating the bearings at speeds far in excess of those for which they were designed. The likelihood of a bearing disintegrating under this condition and causing damage and injury is very real.

Check the bearing rollers and the cups for signs of wear and damage and replace them as a set if they are less than satisfactory. If the bearings are to be replaced, carefully drive the outer cups out of the hub using a soft drift and tapping evenly around the edges of the cups. Seat the new cups squarely in the hub and carefully tap them into place with the drift, evenly around the circumference of each cup.

6. Clean the brake assembly as much as possible, using a stiff, *dry* brush; do not use any solvents to clean any of the brake components and in particular make sure no solvents come in

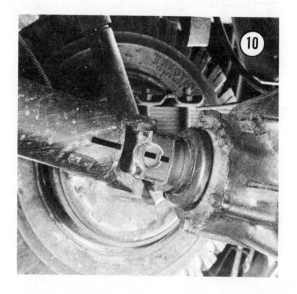

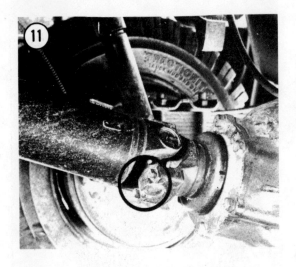

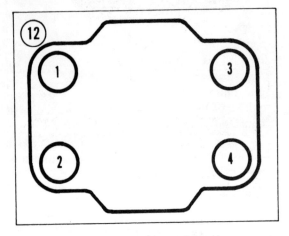

8. Pack the inside of the hub with a multi-purpose grease until it is level with the inside diameter of the outer bearing cups (**Figure 9**). Thoroughly pack the bearing assemblies with grease, working it in carefully by hand, and apply a film of grease to the inner cone. Install inner bearing assembly into the outer cup. Set a new seal squarely into the hub and carefully tap it into place evenly around the circumference.

9. Install the wheel, keeping the hub centered around the spindle to prevent damage to the spindle threads and the seal. Install the outer bearing assembly and screw on the bearing adjusting nut. Refer to the procedure for bearing adjustment and adjust the end play of the hub and complete the reassembly. Repeat the above procedures for the opposite wheel.

DRIVE SHAFT

When the vehicle is to be towed for long distances, it is essential that the drive shaft be disconnected.

1. Mark both halves of the yoke at the axle with light-colored chalk or crayon so the phasing of the drive shaft and differential will be the same when the drive shaft is reconnected (**Figure 10**).

2. Unscrew the 4 nuts at the axle end of the drive shaft (**Figure 11**), remove the straps, and disconnect the end of the shaft. Tape the bearing cups in place so they will not fall off.

3. Securely tie the end of the drive shaft up and out of the way of the differential.

4. Before reconnecting the drive shaft, thoroughly clean the yoke, bearing caps, and straps. Line up the end of the shaft with the differential yoke making sure the marks are on the same side.

5. Install the straps and screw on the nuts and tighten them in a crisscross pattern (**Figure 12**) to 8-15 ft.-lb.

contact with the brake lining material. Solvent will render the lining unserviceable, requiring that it be replaced.

> NOTE: *This is a good opportunity to check the serviceability of the brake linings. Refer to Chapter Eight and inspect and measure the lining as described.*

7. When the brake has been cleaned and all of the dirt and foreign matter removed, carefully clean the spindle with solvent, taking care not to get any on the brake.

CHAPTER THIRTEEN

CUSTOMIZING

So far in this book, we have assumed that the pickup you're driving is exactly like the tens of thousands of similar vehicles that the manufacturer turns out each year. Sure, there are differences in load capacity, wheelbase, engine and the like, but basically it's pretty much like any other pick-up you might see coming down the road or sitting on your friendly dealer's lot.

What we're going to talk about in this chapter is how to change all that. Customizing basically consists of apply all those little tricks that go together to make your truck uniquely yours, different from any other one on the road.

We will explain the four major areas of customizing: exterior, interior, handling, and performance. We'll see how they work together, describe what you ought to look for in, and expect from, a given accessory or procedure, and help you avoid some common mistakes. There is a tremendous variety of equipment available and, in the space available to us, we can only touch on some of the most basic items.

Most of the accessories we will talk about in this chapter are of the "bolt-on" variety. "Bolt-on," as we use it here, means accessories that you can add to your truck with ordinary hand tools and a reasonable degree of mechanical expertise. Generally speaking, if you can carry out the service procedures out-lined in this manual, you can install the bolt-on accessories described in this chapter.

It is impossible for us to show you how to install all of the items discussed in this chapter (it would take an entire book), but we will show you some of the things that are available, give you an idea of how they are installed, and supply you with manufacturer's addresses and other vital information.

EXTERIOR CUSTOMIZING

Most people start with customizing the exterior, because even the slightest change is instantly visible to all who see the truck. The problem with exterior customizing is that many of the modifications are tightly linked to other areas, such as suspension. Wheels and tires are both a good example and starting place. They have as much, if not more, effect on the ride and handling of the vehicle as they have on its appearance. Still, a set of chrome, polished aluminum, or white enameled wheels fitted with wide, low-profile tires does more to change the appearance than almost any other accessory.

Wheels are available from a host of manufacturers, in literally hundreds of designs. **Table 1**, at the end of this chapter, gives names and addresses of sources for good wheels.

Most ½ ton or ¾ ton trucks can use five stud

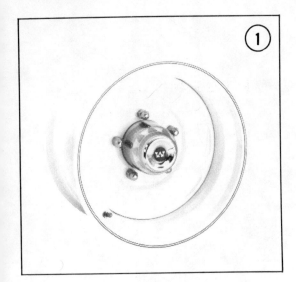

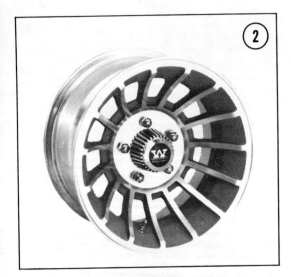

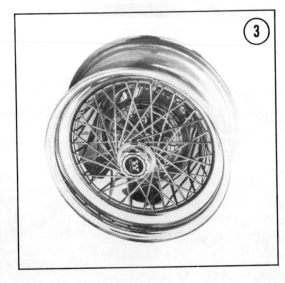

wheels, providing the widest choice of styles. Some ¾ ton vehicles and all one ton models are equipped with eight stud wheels, which are currently available in fewer varieties. That is changing, however, as manufacturers offer new designs on an almost monthly basis to meet the needs of this expanding market.

Later in this chapter, when we talk about the improvements that can be made in handling, we'll look at terms like "offset" and "rim width," since they affect handling more than appearance. Here, the most important thing to know is that there are basically three types of custom wheels available. The first type is the stamped steel wheel. You will probably find wheels of this type listed in the manufacturer's option book as "styled steel" or "rallye" wheels. This is the least expensive type of custom wheel, and it is available in chrome, polished metal, or white epoxy enamel finish. **Figure 1** shows a steel wheel. Next is the cast wheel. This is usually refered to as a "mag" wheel, but most of the ones that you'll see are cast from an aluminum alloy. **Figure 2** shows a typical cast wheel. Real magnesium "mag" wheels are available for those who want to spend the extra money for them, but their great advantage of lighter weight is lost on most trucks anyway. The original advantage of cast wheels was in racing, where they cut down the "unsprung weight" when fitted with lightweight racing tires. On a truck, shod with an oversize steel belted radial, the advantage may be in appearance only. The third type of custom wheel is the wire wheel. This is also the most expensive type, as well as being the most exotic in appearance. There are also what are called "wire spoke" wheels which are essentially stamped steel wheels with a wire spoke "basket" over them for decoration. See **Figure 3**.

Stamped steel wheels are the easiest to take care of, requiring little or no more care than any of the rest of the painted or chrome-plated parts of your vehicle. Cast wheels are usually covered with a clear epoxy coating that is designed to prevent corrosion. Cheaper or older wheels that do not have this coating will have to be polished often to retain their shine. Special compounds for this purpose are available at most auto supply stores.

13

Wire wheels are the most difficult to care for, since all the nooks and crannies between the spokes tend to fill up with road grime every time the vehicle is driven. Their other shortcoming is that they are the weakest of all the types of wheels. They will not stand up to severe cornering stresses the way a cast wheel will, particularly on a heavy vehicle. The sparkle and flash from a rotating wire wheel is certainly desirable, but be sure that you are willing to pay the cost in terms of additional upkeep. This upkeep consists of occasionally tightening the spokes and re-trueing the wheels. Spokes loosen, bend, or even break from hitting curbs or other road hazards, therefore, the wheels must be re-trued on a regular basis to keep the runout within specifications. An out-of-true wheel can cause excessive wear on tires and suspension, will give a rough ride, and could even collapse, throwing the vehicle out of control.

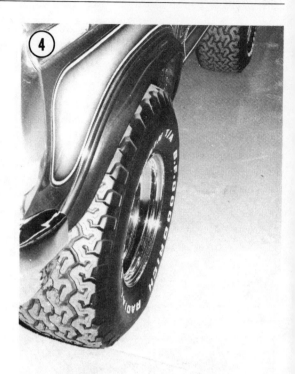

Flares and Spoilers

Most states have laws that say that those fancy wide wheels you've just installed cannot extend out beyond the width of the fenders, so manufacturers of accessories have developed fender flares that extend the fenders out to cover the wheels. These flares may be made of rubber, plastic or metal. **Figure 4** shows a typical flexible flare. Most of the ones in use today are made from fiberglass or ABS plastic materials. They are relatively easy to install with simple tools, and can be painted to contrast or blend in with the body color.

Metal flares are custom built by hand in good body shops. They are much stronger than the plastic ones, and can be shaped to any special contour desired. They are expensive, however, and time consuming to construct and install, so they are most often used on show trucks.

Front fender flares are very often joined by what is called a spoiler or air dam. This is a streamlined flap under the front bumper that keeps as much air as possible from moving under the vehicle. In racing, this is important since it creates a partial vacuum under the car, forcing it down tighter to the road surface and causing more air to travel through any scoops or grilles than would otherwise happen. A small side benefit is a slight increase in economy,

since the underside of any vehicle is notoriously non-aerodynamic, and the less air that moves underneath, the less the drag. Considering the speeds at which your truck will be operated, and its weight and general shape, spoilers and air dams are mostly cosmetic.

As with the flares, there are kits for plastic spoilers, while metal ones usually have to be made and installed by a custom body shop. **Figure 5** shows a typical plastic spoiler. A spoiler may have holes for ducts to lead air to the front brakes, or for mounting fog lights close to the ground.

Plastic flares can be installed with "pop" rivets or sheet metal screws and left as is, or molded to the body in a smooth contour. Metal ones are welded on, and become a part of the fenders.

Hood Scoop and Grille

Another pair of items that can considerably change the appearance of your truck are a hood scoop and a new grille. The hood scoop gives the same effect in appearance as the "power bulge" added to the hood of a sports car. Originally, this was installed to accommodate

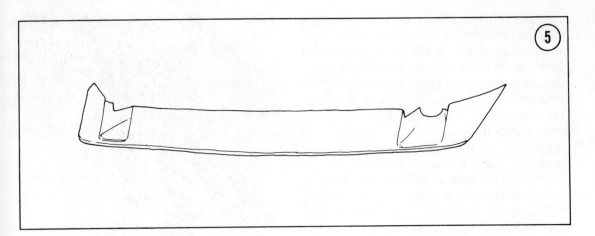

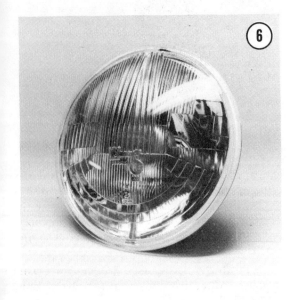

larger carburetors on a high performance intake manifold. It indicates subtly that there is a high performance engine living under the hood. For maximum effect, a "shaker" scoop can be installed. With this type, the scoop is attached directly to the carburetor, and extends up through a hole in the top of the hood. This allows it to move as the engine vibrates on its mounts.

Hood scoops are available molded from plastic or fiberglass, or a scoop can be custom-made from metal by a good bodyshop. Often, hood scoops and bulges are for appearance only, and are not even functional.

Changing the grille offers a complete "personality" change for the truck, since the grille is the major item of recognition for any vehicle. Custom grilles are available from several sup-

pliers. Most of them are made of various types of steel rod, welded together and chrome plated, but one increasingly popular model is made from chrome plated plastic, much as stock grilles are. Installing a custom grille is a matter of unbolting the stock grille and bolting the new one into its place.

Lights

Rectangular headlights have become a new style. Actually, they are slightly more efficient than their round predecessors, and in any case they are standard equipment on all new trucks starting with the 1979 model year. Many of the custom grilles on the market incorporate openings for fitting these lights on earlier models. The main thrust for the installation of the rectangular lights is not for the tiny extra amount of light they put onto the road. It came from the stylists, who find it easier to work with rectangular shapes on the front of a vehicle than trying to integrate round ones into a basically rectangular form.

If your reasons for changing the lighting setup on your truck include improving your night vision, however, there are several things which you can do, all of which, incidentally, add to the custom look of your truck. The first of these is to replace the headlights with quartz-halogen units. These are an exact plug-in replacement for most styles of sealed-beam lamp, and provide a brighter, whiter, longer-lasting light that lets you see farther down the road. **Figure 6** shows a quartz-halogen replacement headlight unit. Up until July of 1978,

13

lighting of this type was of questionable legality, but at that time legislation was passed making quartz-halogen sealed-beam lights legal for highway use in the United States. Unfortunately, the non-sealed-beam types, which are still more efficient, are still not legal in many states. Check with your local highway authority for the legality of these lamps.

Because of their intense beam, these lights require more accurate aiming than the standard tungsten types of lights. The results are worthwhile, however, in terms of increased safety and decreased fatigue if you plan to do much long distance driving at night.

Driving lights project a long, narrow beam that will show distant objects clearly for high speed driving. Fog lights project a wide, fan shaped beam with a sharp cutoff on top, so that the sides of the road will be clearly lit during fog. Unfortunately, many states require that the low beam headlights remain lit when the fog lights are on, negating much of the value of the fog lights.

Fog lights should be mounted as close to the road as possible, so that as little light as possible will be reflected back into the driver's eyes. **Figure 7** shows some good fog lights. Driving lights are best mounted at approximately the same height as the headlights, for minimum glare with maximum range. **Figure 8** shows some driving lights. Some enthusiasts mount auxiliary lights on a light bar that is clamped to the rain gutters at the top of the cab, or on a roll bar mounted in the bed behind the cab, but these locations are best for show or serious off-road driving, rather than normal highway functions. See **Figure 9**. Installation of lights is easy, and complete instructions are supplied with most makes of lamps. Most lamps mount with a $\frac{7}{16}$ in. bolt, and can be mounted to the bumper by simply drilling holes in the desired locations. **Figure 10** shows a typical bumper installation, including a "brush cutter" type bumper guard.

Wiring of auxiliary lights follows standard procedures. A relay must be used with each 100 watts of lighting. This means that if you use lamps with 55 watt bulbs, one relay is sufficient for a pair. If you use lamps with 100 watt bulbs, one relay is needed for each lamp. In normal use, 100 watt bulbs are not recommended, as

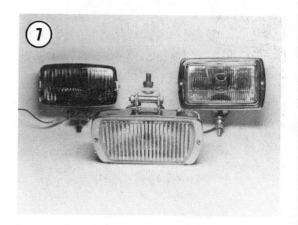

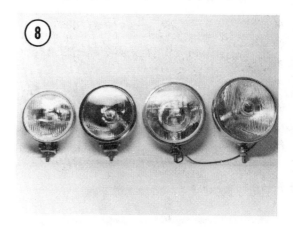

they put a considerable load on the electrical system. Auxiliary lamps should also be wired so that a pilot lamp somewhere on the dashboard indicates that they are on. This eliminates the chance of leaving the lights on and running the battery down.

Auxiliary lighting can put a heavy load on your electrical system, so you must be sure that there is sufficient output from the alternator and capacity in the battery to handle what you wish to install. If necessary, replace the alternator or add an auxiliary battery in parallel with the existing one to increase the electrical capacity of the system.

INTERIOR CUSTOMIZING

Customizing the interior of a pickup truck cab is not terribly difficult, but it is harder than the small space would seem. Carpeting and insulation can quiet the interior to a car-like level. Comfortable seats and a thick-rim steering wheel make long distance trips easier. A

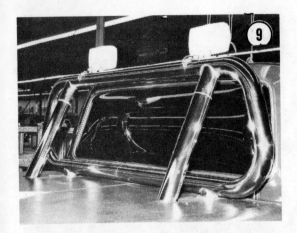

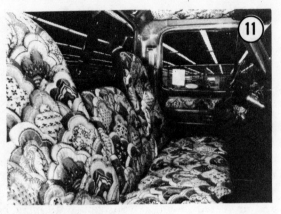

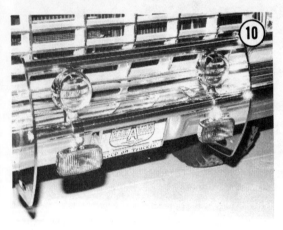

that can be set to give proper support to every inch of your body — supremely comfortable, and, unfortunately, supremely expensive.

Installation of aftermarket seats is not difficult. The old seats, cushions and backrests should be removed, and all the mounting hardware unbolted. New holes must be drilled into the floor pan to hold the pedestals of the new seats. Bolt these into place, and then attach the seats to them.

CAUTION
Be sure to fully plug any extra holes left in the floor pan. If they are left unplugged, there is the possibility that poisonous gases may be admitted to the interior of the vehicle.

A common method of upgrading the interior of a rig's cab is to install a pair of improved bucket seats with a handy console between them. The console can be purchased ready-made from plastic or fiberglass, or made from wood and finished or covered with vinyl, leather, or cloth to match the seats. If the console is fitted with a locking lid, valuables such as cameras or binoculars can be safely stored in it on trips, while depressions formed or cut into the lid allow drinks to stand upright when in a drive-in or when eating by the roadside.

A unique solution to the problem of carrying more than one passenger while at the same time maintaining the convenience of a console is shown in **Figures 11 and 12**. This seat is a bench type, contoured for three passengers. The center backrest folds down, however, and is fitted with a storage compartment and drink receptacles.

sunroof and sliding rear window aid ventilation and make the cab seem roomier. And finally, a good set of instruments makes keeping track of what is going on under the hood that much easier.

Seats

Seating is the first consideration in making over the cab of your rig. The stock seat, which usually has as its only virtues the fact that it is long wearing and can carry four friendly adults abreast, should be replaced by more anatomically designed bucket seats. The cabs of modern pickups are wide enough so that three seats can be installed, if desired.

The least expensive type of seat is the thickly padded seat sold as a van replacement seat. From this level it is possible to upgrade all the way to the fabulous Recaro and Scheel seats from Europe, that are used in the finest sports cars. These seats have a myriad of adjustments

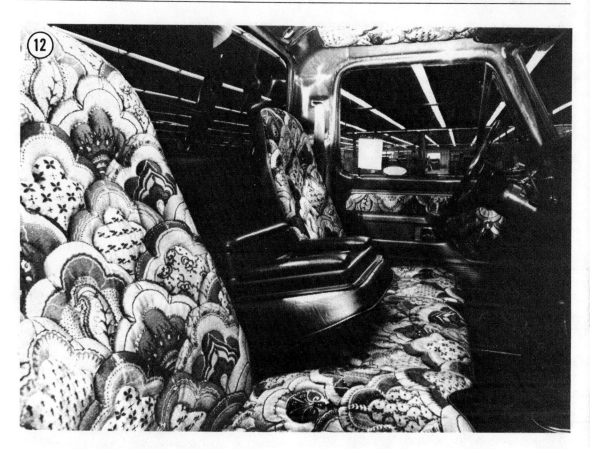

The newest models of pickups are available with consoles installed at the factory, as they are also available with high-grade nylon carpeting over the floor, the lower parts of the doors, and the back of the cab.

Those fancy car-like interiors cost a lot of money, however, and chances are that your truck came with a more plebian bench seat and rubber floor matting. This is particularly true if your rig was bought used, and its original owner used it as a real working vehicle.

A good grade of nylon carpeting, installed throughout the interior, can not only add a good deal to the appearance, but also dampen a considerable amount of road and engine noise that would otherwise penetrate the interior. Up until recently, customizers seemed to prefer long filament shag-type carpeting for this purpose. This material proved extremely difficult to keep clean, and the trend now is toward a tighter weave, denser carpet that sheds dirt as well as it keeps out sound. Carpeting is installed with glue and staples into wooden strips, much the way it is installed in homes. If you want to

run carpet over a deeply compound curved surface, such as a high transmission hump, it is best to have the piece fitted and stitched by a good interior shop.

Ventilation and Visibility

It would seem that the small dimensions of a pickup cab, with the relatively large windows in the doors, would make for really decent ventilation. This is almost the case. Those big windows also create a good deal of wind buffeting when they are opened at speed, making for a choice of being roasted or deafened during summer driving. Happily, the aftermarket provides several solutions for the home customizer. The first, and easiest of these, is to install a sliding rear window. These were originally developed for use with slide-in camping units, so that there could be comuunication between cab and camper. They proved to be so useful, however, that now all the major manufacturers offer them as optional equipment from the factory. These windows are available from most accessory suppliers for installation in vehicles

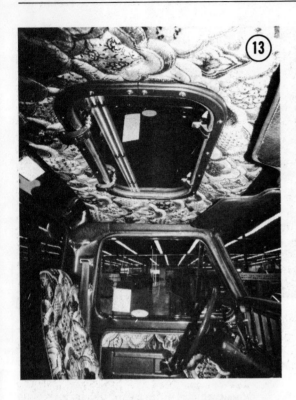

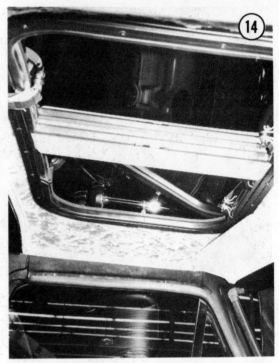

that were not originally equipped with them. Installation is an easy job, with not much more than a screwdriver required in the way of tools.

Some truck owners have opted instead to install a "bubble" window at the rear. See **Figure 9**. This is molded from plastic, and curves outward from the cab. Psychologically, this seems to provide more room in the cab, although the actual difference is no more than two or three inches. These windows are usually made from dark material, so that they add privacy and keep out heat.

Sunroofs are an increasingly popular accessory. These usually consist of one or two panels of clear or smoked glass or plastic that can be opened to provide additional ventilation. The most difficult part of the installation of one of these units is cutting the opening in the cab roof. The manufacturers provide templates for location, and the cutting can be done with an electric saber saw equipped with a metal cutting blade. If the instructions are followed carefully, the installation is not difficult, and the result is a substantial gain in the comfort and usefulness of the vehicle. **Figure 13** shows a single panel sunroof, while **Figure 14** shows a double panel type with a fluorescent lamp.

Instruments

Instruments can tell you a lot about the condition of your engine, and do it faster than so called "idiot lights." Unfortunately, full instrumentation is still optional equipment, so unless your rig is new and you've checked all the right boxes on the option list, there's a very good chance that some added instrumentation will make you feel happier and more secure on the road.

Extra instruments not only give you that added security of knowing exactly what is going on under the hood, they also add a note of interest to the interior of the cab. These new instruments may consist merely of gauges to supplement the original equipment warning lights, or new gauges to monitor extra functions not thought of by the manufacturer. An example of the first type may be a water temperature gauge to replace a "hot" warning light. An example of the second type might be a transmission fluid temperature gauge.

To fill their functions best, gauges should be as easy to read as possible. White numerals on a black background are preferable, and the numerals should be as large as possible. The needle should swing through 270 degrees rather

13

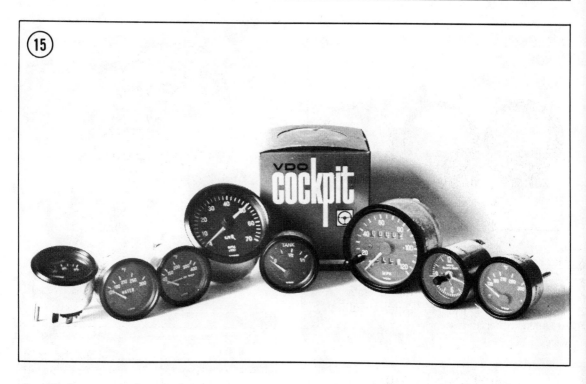

than 90 degrees, so that the largest space is between the indication marks. **Figure 15** shows a selection of gauges from one manufacturer. This may change in the near future, however, as all gauges will eventually become the direct reading digital type. There are already digital clocks available for installation on light truck dashboards.

Mounting the gauges is also important, as they must be seen easily without interfering with the driver's vision. Single gauges can be mounted on top of the dashboard, where they are easily in view. Many truck owners like to install extra instruments in an overhead "console" that runs the full width of the vehicle over the top of the windshield.

A full compliment of gauges in the dashboard or in a console lets you keep better track of what the engine, transmission, and electrical system are doing. The manufacturer offers an oil pressure gauge, ammeter, and water temperature gauge as options, but many rigs purchased second or third hand never had them installed. We would recommend these as the first extra instruments to be installed. The next most popular, and even the next most important, might be a tachometer. This indicates how fast the engine is running, and is used in high per-

formance vehicles to indicate the proper gearshift points. On a vehicle equipped with an automatic transmission, this is less important, but the tachometer is still a valuable aid in driving for economy or performance, or for keeping the engine in top tune.

A vacuum gauge can indicate optimum operating conditions in your vehicle's engine and, by the various quivers of its needle, indicate any ills that the engine might be subject to. Driving with a vacuum gauge can actually save you several miles per gallon under certain conditions.

Heat is the great killer of mechanical components, which is why the really complete gauge package will have an oil temperature gauge and a transmission temperature gauge in it. If the engine or transmission oil gets too hot, it will cease to lubricate and you will soon be without an engine or transmission. These gauges indicate the presence of such conditions before they have time to cause any damage. **Figure 16** shows a set of temperature gauges for all fluids.

The overhead console that is useful for extra gauges is also handy for other accessories. If the components of an automotive stereo system are mounted in the overhead console, the original radio location in the dash is a handy

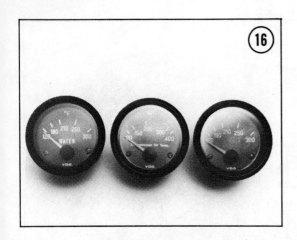

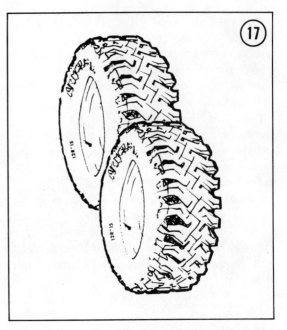

place to mount instruments while keeping wiring runs short. Remember that any and all wiring runs to an overhead console have to be made before the installation and headlining is installed, otherwise there is no place to put the wires.

SUSPENSION, RIDE, AND HANDLING

A truck is not a car. The stock ride and handling, therefore, are thoroughly trucklike, meaning a tendency to slide off the road under severe cornering stresses or a harsh, lumpy ride. Happily, there are a number of modifications that can be made to the suspension that will modify this behavior and make a truck a much more pleasant vehicle to drive and ride in.

Tires and Wheels

This area was discussed earlier in this chapter, but from the appearance aspect only. Now we must consider what effect those fat tires and fancy wheels will have on ride and road holding. We'll start with tires. The biggest improvement in ride and roadholding, for the least investment, can be made by changing the tires on the vehicle. Tires also affect rolling resistance, and with it fuel economy, and interior noise level. Poorly selected tires can actually have a negative effect, not only cancelling out any improvements made elsewhere in the suspension, but producing a ride and handling that is worse than what it was with the stock tires the vehicle came with from the factory.

Many custom rigs are rolling along the streets on tires that the owners chose for cosmetic reasons only. The owners of these vehicles may be happy, but they may not realize how much happier they could be if they had paid more attention to the letters and numbers and less to the macho lettering on the sidewalls.

When you shop for your new tires, you'll need to know what the letters and numbers mean. An example of the type of thing you might find is a tire lettered "12 R-15 B", seen in **Figure 17**. This is a wide tread light truck type radial tire. The "15" indicates that it fits on a 15 inch wheel. The "12" is the approximate overall width of the tire in inches. The "R" indicates that it is of radial ply construction. A tire as wide as this must be mounted on a custom wide wheel. The wheel rims on most stock van wheels are 6 in. or 6.5 in. wide. The tire we are considering requires an 8 in. or even 8.5 in. wide rim in order to run with the tread and sidewalls in the proper configuration and relationship. The "B" at the end of the designation indicates the load carrying capability of the tire. The load range changes with the size of the tire and the heaviness of the construction. In the case of our subject tire, an 11-15 B tire can carry a maximum load of 1900 lb. at 30 psi. inflation, and more air should not be added. For heavier vehicles, tires are rated in

13

load ranges up to "E", but these tires, while they can carry enormous loads, are far too stiff and heavy for the purposes to which a pickup is usually put. **Figure 18** shows a tire more appropriate for serious off-road travel than highway use.

Tires contribute such a vital part of the overall safety and comfort of a vehicle that perhaps we should get into a little technical discussion of what they can, and actually do, do for you.

Two of the most important characteristics of a tire are its coefficient of friction and its slip angles. The coefficient of friction describes the ability of a tire to resist sliding when subjected to a force, such as braking. The maximum force that a tire can sustain without sliding may be described as the "limit of adhesion" for that tire.

In order for a tire to be steered (i.e., maintain a desired course), it must be rolling, not sliding. A sliding tire has absolutely no directional discretion. It will slide sideways just as willingly as it will slide forward.

Friction is only important at the "limit of adhesion." Obviously, at that point it assumes overwhelming importance as the tire "breaks loose." But tire friction does not explain any of the handling characteristics of a vehicle below the limit of adhesion of the tires.

A rolling tire normally follows a path in line with the direction of the tread. But, if the tire is subjected to a side force as it is during cornering, it can deflect. Its path then diverges from the path in line with the tread. The tire actually travels in a direction at an angle to the direction that the tire points. This angle is called a "slip angle."

Slip angle is one of those unfortunate, misleading terms that we are stuck with. It does not mean that the tire is sliding. The tire does not have to be anywhere near its limit of adhesion to operate at a slip angle. Slip angle causes the familiar effects of understeer, oversteer, and neutral steering.

Oversteer occurs when the slip angle at the rear tires changes more than at the front tires. This steers the car into a smaller circle than intended and increases centifugal force. Increased centrifugal force, in turn, causes the tires to

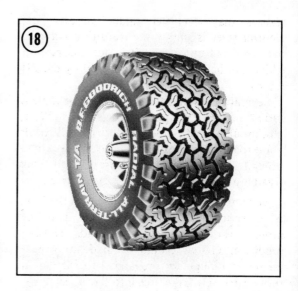

operate at even higher slip angles, making the car steer into an even smaller circle, and so on. It is truly a "vicious circle," which if allowed to continue will result in a spin-out, even in the hands of a skilled driver.

Understeer occurs when the slip angle at the front tires changes more than at the rear. The car steers into a larger circle than intended, reducing centrifugal force. This decreases the tire slip angle and further increases the circle, thereby decreasing centrifugal force, and so on. The car automatically seeks a turning circle which balances tire forces with no correction from the driver.

Understeer may seem more desirable than oversteer, but if the equilibrium turning circle is larger than the curvature of the road, the driver may helplessly watch his car head for the bushes.

Neutral steer means that slip angles change at the front and rear at the same rate. The vehicle path tends to follow the curvature of the road without a tendency to increase or decrease the turning circle.

Slip angle is not fixed for any tire. Factors that change it are centrifugal force, wind gusts, road plane (level, banked), wheel plane (camber, toe, deflection), and vertical forces (acceleration, braking, lateral weight transfers).

Since the slip angle at which a tire operates is constantly changing, there is no such thing as a "state of understeer." For example, a car which understeers under one set of circum-

stances may oversteer under another set. Neutral steer is simply the transition between oversteer and understeer; it is not a condition which can be set up and maintained by chassis tuning.

Several manufacturers produce excellent radial tires: Semperit, Veith, Michelin, Goodyear, Pirelli, and Goodrich. All offer good road holding (some better in the wet than others), reasonable ride comfort, and long tread life (a characteristic of all radial tires).

Many owners like to give their units the look of a serious off-road vehicle by installing monstrous tires with aggressive treads. This is a modification that should be made only with plenty of thought beforehand. In order to fit those extremely large tires into the wheel wells, some cutting and bodywork may have to be done on the wheel arches. In addition, the vehicle may have to be raised up on its suspension, raising the center of gravity and making cornering a more hazardous and less comfortable procedure.

In addition, there are two other problems with this type of tire. The aggressive treads are noisy on the road at normal cruising speeds. With some tread patterns, the noise level is so high as to preclude normal conversation or listening to the radio while on a trip. Finally, the sidewalls of these tires must be reinforced in order to prevent damage when traveling over rough or rocky terrain well off the pavement. These stiff sidewalls make for a hard, harsh ride when this type of tire is installed. For maximum comfort and pleasure while traveling, the best rule is to stick to highway type tires if you're going to stick to the highways.

Of course this is not to prevent your mounting wider, stickier tires on your vehicle. Generally, the more tread width, the better the handling, to a point. The point usually comes in wet weather, when water builds up under the wide tread of some of these tires, and a phenomenon known as "aquaplaning" occurs. At that instant, the tire is riding on the film of water instead of the pavement, and is totally incapable of being steered or braked. As a rule, tire manufacturers have tried to design grooves into their tread patterns that will minimize this problem. Check with a tire dealer who handles several makes of tires to see if the ones you have choosen are more than usually subject to aquaplaning.

With wider tires, you'll need wider wheels. Widened steel wheels are available, or you can have your own steel wheels widened by a specialty shop. The most popular accessory wheels are cast aluminum or magnesium "mags." Those shown in **Figure 2** are typical.

Three things need to be considered when buying wheels: whether they can be used with tubeless tires; wheel width; and wheel offset.

Some "mag" wheels require tube-type tires. If you're going to use tube-type tires anyway, this doesn't matter. Check before buying, though, to make sure your tires and wheels are compatible.

Wheel width should be proportional to the tire. As a rule of thumb, the wheel should be approximately 2 inches narrower than the tire's cross-section width. Once you've selected a specific brand of tires, the tire dealer can give you exact size recommendations.

Wheel offset (**Figure 19**) is the relationship of the wheel center to the wheel rim. Positive offset moves the wheel rim outward (the track is wider). Negative offset moves the wheel rim inward (the track is narrower). Too much negative offset can cause clearance problems between the tires and wheel wells. In front, the wheels may rub on the brake calipers or tie rod ends. Too much positive offset may cause the tires to rub on the fenders. Also, positive offset increases the strain on wheel bearings and hubs. If you use wheels with much positive offset, the wheel bearings should be checked frequently for wear.

The number of wheel manufacturers makes it impossible for us to list them all here, so you will have to do some of the detective work yourself and check through automotive magazines such as *Road & Track, Car & Driver, Autoweek,* etc., and send for some of the catalogs from these wheel manufacturers.

13

NOTE: *In addition to obtaining the catalogs offered by the various wheel manufacturers, you will find a wealth of information concerning tires and wheels in Auto World's Motorsports Catalog or in the Dick Cepek catalog. The Auto*

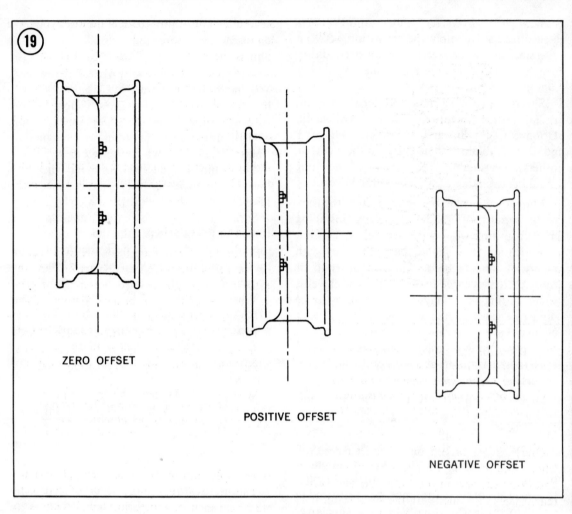

ZERO OFFSET

POSITIVE OFFSET

NEGATIVE OFFSET

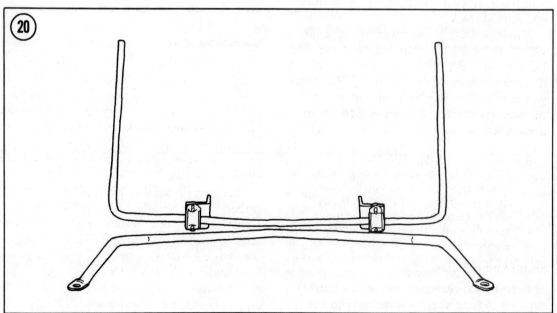

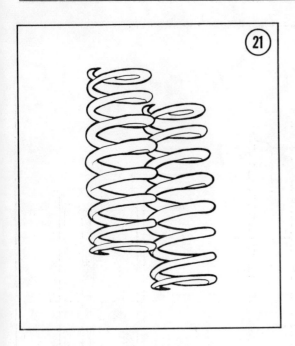

*World catalog concentrates more on the sports car and highway type of tire, while Cepek caters mainly to the truck and off-road enthusiast. Their addresses will be found in **Table 1** at the end of the chapter.*

Once you've picked out a combination of wheels and tires, have a pair of them mounted and installed, one on the front and one on the rear. Check clearance with the suspension bottomed out, and with the front wheels at full left and full right lock.

If the tire dealer doesn't want to let you try a set before buying (and you don't feel like looking for another tire dealer), offer to pay the mounting charge if the tires don't fit. When you're spending hundreds of dollars to last thousands of miles, it's worth $10 or so to avoid a bad purchase.

CAUTION
Alloy wheels can easily be chipped or gouged during tire mounting, and some are more difficult to balance than steel wheels. Have mounting and balancing done by a shop experienced with alloy wheels.

Sway (Anti-roll) Bars

These bars reduce body roll during hard cornering, resulting in a flatter cornering attitude and better control and tire adhesion. Refer to **Figure 20**.

It is necessary to "balance" the car by carefully coordinating the diameter of the rear sway bar with that of the front one. A rear sway bar should definitely not be installed without using a front sway bar which has a larger than stock diameter.

Installation of sway bars is a simple nuts-and-bolts operation requiring a couple of hours of work. Kits generally come with installation instructions.

Front and Rear Springs

Heavy duty springs are available for street or off-road conditions (refer to **Figure 21**), and installation is straightforward. Refer to the procedures outlined in the proper chapter of the main body of this manual.

The addition of stiffer springs reduces "body wallow" in corners and generally keeps the car more stable on winding or undulating roads.

> NOTE: *Heavy-duty shocks must be used in conjunction with stiffer springs, as conventional shock absorbers cannot control the movements set up by stiffer springs.*

The installation of some high-performance coil springs will reduce the height of your vehicle by an inch or more, so take this into consideration when buying wheels and tires.

Shock Absorbers

The installation of high-performance shock absorbers is an absolute necessity if you choose to install heavy-duty springs. Even if you keep the stock springs, it is a good idea to install high-performance shock absorbers, which control the road wheels much better than stock shock absorbers, due to their special valving and construction.

There are a number of popular shock absorbers available for high-performance cars: Koni, Mulholland, Bilstein, KYB, and Boge seem to be the front-runners. All are excellent; the choice is simply a personal one which you must make. Refer to **Figure 22**.

If you have never driven a car equipped with high-performance shock absorbers of this

13

quality, you will immediately appreciate the difference in handling.

Wheel Spacers

Wheel track can easily be widened by adding wheel spacers. Installation is easy: simply remove the wheels, slip the spacers over the wheel studs, and install the wheels again.

Increasing the track makes the truck more stable in corners, as it widens its stance.

Another use for wheel spacers is to gain additional brake caliper clearance when installing special alloy wheels.

> CAUTION
> *Spacers may keep the wheel nuts from threading all the way onto the studs. In this case, longer studs must be installed.*

Brake Linings

Several manufacturers offer excellent high-performance brake pads which can be installed in place of the stock brake pads. Repco pads seem to be the most popular, and they are widely available in auto parts stores. These pads offer more consistent control and less fading during heavy braking, less brake dust, and they do not squeal.

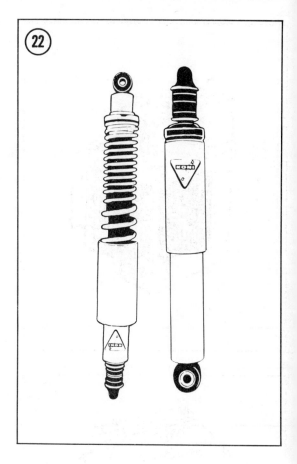

ENGINE MODIFICATION

We have left this area for the last, since it is normally regarded as the lowest priority by most customizers. There are certain items, however, that should be a must on any rig that is used for daily transportation or highway cruising.

Trucks are large vehicles, with large amounts of what is known as "frontal area." What this means is that they have to push more air out of the way than smaller vehicles. This, coupled with a truck's heavy weight as compared to passenger cars, means that fuel economy is lower.

Engine modifications can combat this to some extent, and provide you with a more responsive, crisper performing vehicle as well. There is no real point in putting a full-out, high performance engine in a pickup, since the handling, suspension, and brakes can never be brought up to that level in so large a vehicle.

While car engines are sometimes tuned to almost race track or drag strip levels and then used on the street, there is no advantage to doing this with the engine in a pickup unless shows or drag racing are your goals.

Engine modifications should be carried out in logical sequence in order to extract the most benefit from each component. The recommended modifications are given in stages, starting with components which will increase efficiency and performance, as well as laying the groundwork for more extensive modifications. In this chapter, we will be concerned only with Stages I and II, since we are dealing with vehicles for street use.

STAGE I

Many stock engines suffer from a mediocre ignition system, restricted exhaust system, and a fuel system which "breathes" through a less-than-ideal air filtering system. The simple addition of an efficient header/exhaust system, a

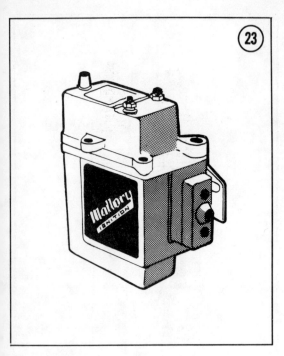

(23)

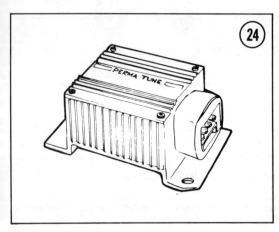

(24)

high-performance ignition coil, an electronic ignition system, and a more efficient air filter will bring a surprising increase in horsepower and make the engine start more easily, deliver better gas mileage, and (in the case of the ignition) need less maintenance than its stock counterpart.

Ignition Coil

Many manufacturers offer "hotter" ignition coils which are supposed to provide more voltage to your distributor (and therefore to your spark plugs). Some do, and some don't. Most of the reputable manufacturers (Accel,

Mallory, Bosch, etc.) offer high quality ignition coils that meet their claims. They are a simple nuts-and-bolts replacement item for your stock coil.

Electronic Ignition

There are also many manufacturers who offer electronic ignition systems such as Mallory, Permatune, Allison, Jacobs, Tiger, Piranha, etc. These units are easy to install and reasonably priced. High-performance coils are mandatory or recommended with some; others replace the coil altogether. A typical high-performance coil is shown in **Figure 23**.

There are two basic types of electronic ignition. One type retains the points, but uses them only to carry a low-voltage trigger signal. This prolongs point life. The other type replaces the points with a photo-optical or magnetic trigger. These highly accurate triggering systems provide stable ignition timing, and eliminate point bounce at high rpm.

All of the systems provide a longer lasting, higher voltage spark. This allows easier starting and may increase horsepower and gas mileage. It also ensures that the spark plugs will fire at high rpm. Within the past two years, all light trucks have been equipped from the factory with electronic ignition. Older models can use an aftermarket type as shown in **Figure 24**.

Spark Plugs and Spark Plug Wires

A modified engine usually requires plugs just slightly colder than stock.

Spark plugs are designed to work within a specific heat range. Below 1,000°F (550°C), carbon deposits do not burn off the tip and may form a conducting track which short circuits the plug. Above 1,550°F (850°C), the plug tip gets so hot it can pre-ignite the mixture like a glow plug. The spark plug operates best when center electrode is 1,300-1,400°F (700-750°C).

Modified engines usually run hotter and require a "cold" plug that can dissipate heat rapidly. This prevents the center electrode from running hotter than desired. The center electrode and insulating core are made short so that there is a short heat conduction path to the metal body and the comparatively cool cylinder head. **Figure 25** shows a cold plug.

13

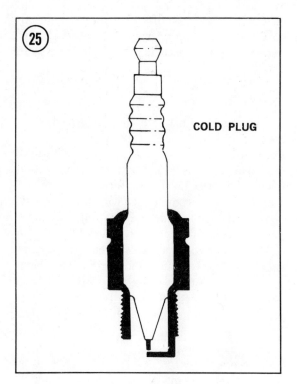

COLD PLUG

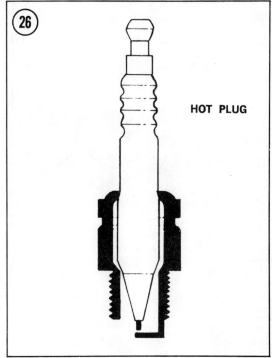

HOT PLUG

A cold-running engine requires a hot plug that does not quickly dissipate the heat. Thus, the central electrode stays hotter. Otherwise, the central electrode temperature would drop below the desired range. The central electrode is made long so that the heat conduction path is long. **Figure 26** shows a hot plug.

Most plug manufacturers use a number to indicate heat range. Champion uses higher numbers to indicate a higher heat range. For example, an N9 plug is hotter than an N5. Bosch and NGK use lower numbers for higher heat ranges. For example, a Bosch W95T2 plug is hotter than a W125T2. An NGK BP6ES is hotter than a BP7ES.

It is a good idea to replace your stock spark plug wires with high-energy capacity, high-performance spark plug wires such as the "Kool Wire" offered by Auto World (see **Table 1**). This metallic wire is made up of 19 strands of silver-plated copper (finished size is 16 ga., 7mm in diameter), and covered with special silicone rubber that is immune to ozone, corona, moisture, corrosion, cracking, and hardening. The rubber is self-extinguishing and resists extreme heat and cold (+600°F to −100°F) with a temperature rating of 550°F.

NOTE: *Metallic plug wires create radio interference, so you may have to use noise suppressors with them.*

Exhaust System

Replacing the stock exhaust system with an efficient header and complete free-flow exhaust system can improve the performance of a stock engine, and is necessary for a modified engine.

"Back pressure" (the accumulation of exhaust gas in the exhaust system which has not found its way out of the engine from the previous exhaust stroke at the time that the intake stroke takes place) can rob an engine of 15-20% of its horsepower. By simply providing a smooth, uninterrupted path for this exhaust gas to be expelled from the engine, the maximum fresh charge of air and fuel can be drawn into the cylinders, providing all of the horsepower that your engine was designed for.

NOTE: *The addition of a more efficient exhaust system is occasionally against the law, due to Federal smog regulations. Check the laws in your state to see if they apply.*

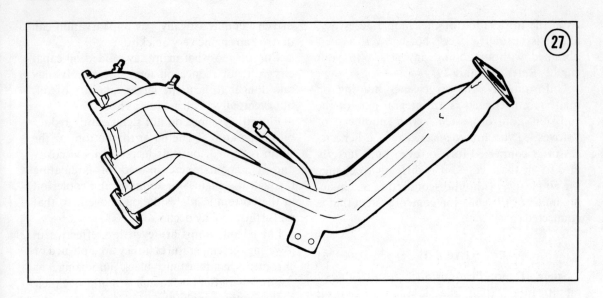

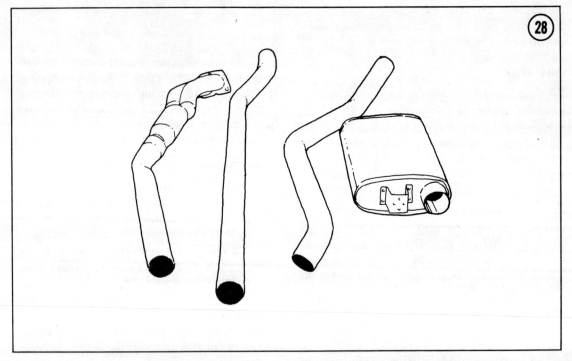

An example of a truly efficient header is shown in **Figure 27**, and a free-flow exhaust system is shown in **Figure 28**. Installation can be done by anyone with average mechanical ability and a moderate tool collection.

Header quality can vary widely from one maufacturer to another. Before buying, note whether the mounting surface is flat and smooth. If not, it must be surface ground to prevent exhaust leaks. Make sure welds are strong, even, and gas-tight. Poor fit is a common problem, so some drilling and filing may be necessary.

Air Cleaners

Replacing the standard air cleaner with a more efficient unit is a simple operation. It improves the appearance of the engine compartment, and permits the engine to breathe better. Approximately 2-3 horsepower can be gained

13

from the installation of this simple accessory, and it is virtually "free" horsepower, as it is obtained without adding any strain to your engine. Refer to **Figure 29**.

Unfortunately, the air cleaner housing on many recent engines is an integral part of the emission control system, with numbers of "stoves", vacuum devices, and other accessories connected to it or even built directly into it. In these cases, it is difficult to change the air cleaner without disconnecting or replacing much of the emission control system that is connected to it.

STAGE II

Stage II modifications include all Stage I modifications, plus the addition of an oil cooler; baffled, high-capacity oil sump; and heavy-duty clutch or modified automatic transmission valve body.

Oil Cooler

In the interests of making your engine live as long as possible while putting out all of the horsepower your require, it is a good idea to install an engine oil cooler.

Accessory oil coolers built especially for your truck are available from some of the manufacturers listed in **Table 1**, or you can install one of the universal accessory oil coolers.

These bolt-on, multi-finned alloy coolers keep the oil from reaching extreme temperatures which can eventually destroy an engine. There are many sizes and configurations to choose from. **Figure 30** shows a typical oil cooler.

Oil Sump

The installation of a baffled, high-capacity oil sump only takes a few minutes (it is installed the same way as a stock one), and it is a worthwhile addition to your engine because of the extra margin of safety it provides. The baffles and extra oil capacity prevent oil starvation during hard cornering or acceleration. (Oil starvation can occur even when negotiating a freeway on-ramp; it is a result of oil sloshing to one side of the oil sump, away from the oil pump pickup.) This extra safety is vital for any vehicle

driven "enthusiastically" as oil starvation can destroy an engine very quickly.

Contrary to what many say, added oil capacity will not reduce oil temperatures. It may take longer to heat the larger quantity of oil, but eventually it will get just as hot.

Finned oil sumps do not significantly reduce oil temperatures. The oil at the bottom of the sump is cooled, but this increases its viscosity and it remains there instead of circulating through the engine. In addition, the cooler oil in the bottom insulates the oil above it so that no further cooling occurs.

Finned oil sumps are even less effective in lowering oil temperatures if they are polished or chromed. Sandblasting, black anodizing, or painting with flat black paint will improve their heat radiating capability.

Clutch

Most stock clutches are not capable of handling increased horsepower without slipping. Before you really dig into the engine's internal parts, it is wise to replace the stock clutch with a heavy-duty, balanced one.

Transmission

Shifting in an automatic transmission is controlled by a complex valve that responds to changes in vacuum and oil pressure to initiate the shifts. In the interests of a smooth and comfortable ride, the manufacturers have set the control valves to produce a slow, smooth shift. These slow shifts cause slippage, which wastes fuel, slows acceleration and can cause the shifting clutches or bands to wear faster.

Kits are now available from several manufacturers that modify this shifting pattern, in order to produce quicker, more positive shifts. If you do much traffic driving, one of these kits installed in your transmission could concievably save you several gallons of gas from each tankful.

The kits are easy to install, and complete instructions are included with them. When you select one, be sure you get one designed for street or RV use. Models designed for competition use produce shifts that are far too harsh for comfort in normal driving.

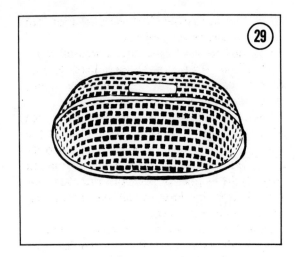

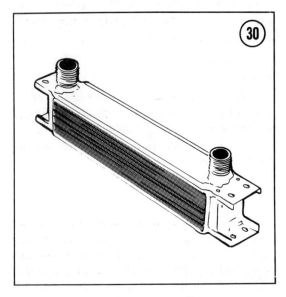

The quicker shifts produced by one of these kits will lengthen the life of the shifting clutches and bands in your transmission. You must be sure, however, that the transmission is in perfect condition before you install the kit, or its effectiveness will be lost.

TURBOCHARGING

The easiest way to obtain a significant increase in horsepower is by turbocharging your engine.

> NOTE: *It is advisable to discuss any engine modifications which you have already made (or would like to make) with the turbocharger manufacturer*

prior to purchasing and installing the turbocharger kit.

Turbocharging Theory

Special high-lift cams, multiple carburetors such as the big Webers, high-compression heads, and tuned exhaust systems can't compare to simply forcing more air/fuel mixture into the cylinders with a properly designed turbocharger system. Furthermore, if properly maintained, a turbocharged engine seems to live approximately as long as a normally aspirated one.

Anyone reading this chapter is probably familiar with the basic operation of a naturally-aspirated, 4-cycle, spark-ignition engine. On the intake stroke, the descending piston draws an air/fuel charge through the intake valve. Theoretically, the volume of the incoming air/fuel charge should equal the volume of the cylinder at full throttle. In fact, this is impossible to achieve. The incoming charge volume is less than the cylinder volume. The reasons are:

a. Small, but unavoidable pressure drop through the fuel induction system

b. Restrictions in intake manifold ports and valves

c. Incomplete exhaust of burned gases from previous cycle

d. Exhaust valve and exhaust manifold port restrictions

The ratio between induced air/fuel volume (at 60°F and 14.7 psi) and calculated cylinder volume (piston area x stroke) is usually expressed as a percentage and is called "volumetric efficiency." If the induced charge equals the cylinder volume, the volumetric efficiency is 100%; most engines have a volumetric efficiency of about 80%.

In order to increase power from an engine, all we have to do is get more air/fuel charge into the cylinder. One method is to design very low restriction intake and exhaust systems. This explains how some exotic racing engines with tuned intake and exhaust systems achieve nearly 100% volumetric efficiency over a very narrow speed range. However, they are not nearly flexible enough for everyday street driving.

Another method is to force the air/fuel

13

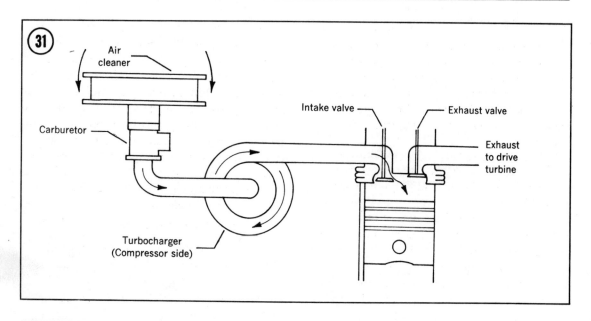

③ Air cleaner — Carburetor — Turbocharger (Compressor side) — Intake valve — Exhaust valve — Exhaust to drive turbine

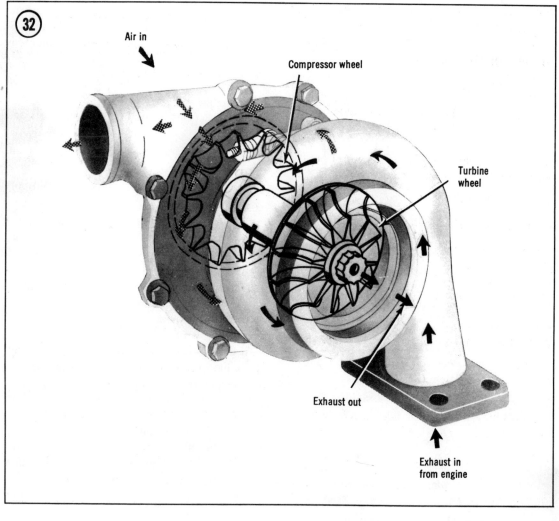

③ Air in — Compressor wheel — Turbine wheel — Exhaust out — Exhaust in from engine

charge into the combustion chamber under pressure, using a compressor. This will force more charge into an engine than is possible with low restriction and tuned intake/exhaust systems, and it will do it over a much broader speed range. This is how a turbocharger works. **Figure 31** is a diagram of the principle of turbocharging.

A turbocharger consists of a tubine wheel and a compressor wheel. Exhaust gases from the engine drive the turbine wheel at speeds of up to 120,000 rpm. The compressor wheel, in turn, pumps a tremendous volume of air to the engine, under pressure. The turbocharger sucks through the standard fuel intake system, although some turbocharger kit manufacturers offer a Weber carburetor as an option, which increases the efficiency still more. The compressor is sealed to ensure that the oil is not drawn into the intake system from the turbocharger lubrication system.

Turbocharger Installation

Most turbocharger kits come with complete instructions. Installation time depends upon your own mechanical skill, but an average time is approximately 12 hours, depending on your working conditions and tool collection (although no special tools are required other than normal mechanic's tools). **Figure 32** shows the parts of a typical turbocharger.

Turbocharger Maintenance

The primary maintenance requirement is simply changing the oil every 3,000 miles, in order to provide the turbocharger with a clean supply of lubricant.

Fuels Recommended For Turbocharger Operation

Catalytic converter-equipped vehicles must use unleaded gasoline; non-catalytic converter-equipped cars must use premium fuel.

> NOTE: *Always use the highest octane fuel that you can buy.*

Turbocharger Performance

At low rpm, the turbocharger is hardly a factor in engine performance — this is one of the main advantages of this efficient, power- producing unit; when you don't need it, it literally "loafs"; when you do need it, stand on the throttle and watch what happens. The turbo boost comes on at medium rpm and steadily increases to its maximum boost. The power is delivered smoothly, as the turbo just starts pumping air in increased volume as the exhaust gases flow faster. The "turbo-lag" that you hear so much about has been reduced to a minimum and presents very little problem.

IN CONCLUSION

The modifications we have discussed in this chapter, if carefully done and selected with taste, will give you a vehicle that will stand out from the others of its kind. In addition, it will be more practical, useful, and fun to drive.

Table 1	SOURCES	
AMERICAN RACING EQUIPMENT 2600 Monterey St. Torrance, CA 90501		Wheels
AUTO WORLD 701 N. Keyser Ave. Scranton, PA 18508		Accessories
BAE 3032 Kashiwa St. Torrance. CA 90505		Turbochargers
DICK CEPEK 9201 California Ave. South Gate, CA 90280		Accessories
HEHR INTERNATIONAL, INC. 333 Casitas Ave. Los Angeles. CA 90039		Windows
MG MITTEN, INC. 44 S. Chester Ave. Pasadena. CA 91106		Accessories
MOTOR RIM AND WHEEL SERVICE 666 Union St. Montebello, CA 90640		Wheels
QUICKOR ENGINEERING 6710 S.W. 111th Beaverton. OR 97005		Suspension
SUPERIOR INDUSTRIES 14721 Keswick St. Van Nuys. CA 91409		Wheels
WESTERN WHEEL COMPANY 6861 Walker St. La Palma. CA 90623		Wheels

13

INDEX

14

MAINTENANCE LOG

DATE	TYPE OF SERVICE	COST	REMARKS

MAINTENANCE LOG

DATE	TYPE OF SERVICE	COST	REMARKS

MAINTENANCE LOG

DATE	TYPE OF SERVICE	COST	REMARKS

NOTES

NOTES

NOTES

1967 ENGINE COMPARTMENT WIRING (L6)

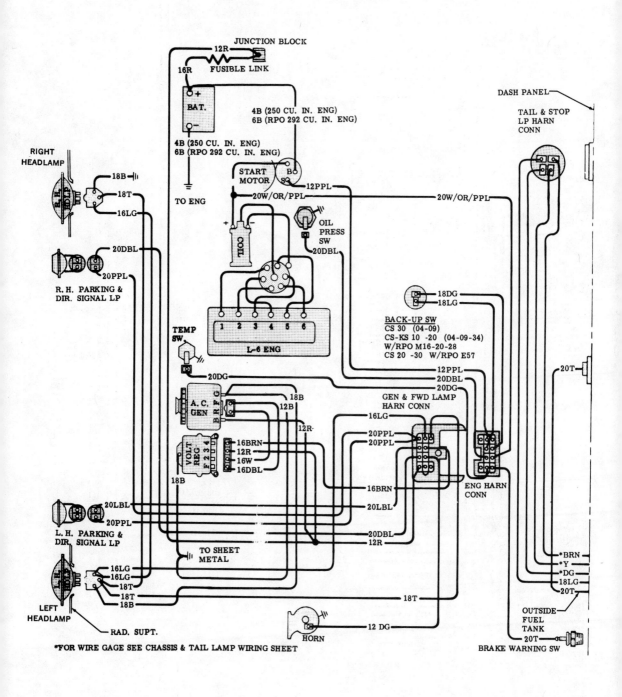

JUNCTION BLOCK

12R

16R FUSIBLE LINK

BAT.

4B (250 CU. IN. ENG)
6B (RPO 292 CU. IN. ENG)

4B (250 CU. IN. ENG)
6B (RPO 292 CU. IN. ENG)

TO ENG

START MOTOR

DASH PANEL

TAIL & STOP
LP HARN
CONN

RIGHT HEADLAMP

18B
18T
16LG

20DBL
20PPL

R. H. PARKING &
DIR. SIGNAL LP

20W/OR/PPL
12PPL
20W/OR/PPL

COIL

OIL PRESS SW

20DBL

18DG
18LG

BACK-UP SW
CS 30 (04-09)
CS-KS 10 -20 (04-09-34)
W/RPO M16-20-28
CS 20 -30 W/RPO E57

TEMP SW

20DG

L-6 ENG

1 2 3 4 5 6

20T

12PPL
20DBL
20DG

A.C. GEN

18B
12B
12R

GEN & FWD LAMP
HARN CONN

16LG

20PPL
20PPL

VOLT REG

16BRN
12R
16W
16DBL

18B

16BRN

ENG HARN CONN

L. H. PARKING &
DIR. SIGNAL LP

20LBL
20PPL

20LBL

20DBL
12R

16LG
16LG
18T
18T
18B

TO SHEET METAL

*BRN
*Y
*DG
18LG
20T

18T

LEFT HEADLAMP

RAD. SUPT.

HORN

12 DG

OUTSIDE FUEL TANK

20T

BRAKE WARNING SW

*FOR WIRE GAGE SEE CHASSIS & TAIL LAMP WIRING SHEET

1967 ENGINE COMPARTMENT WIRING (V8)

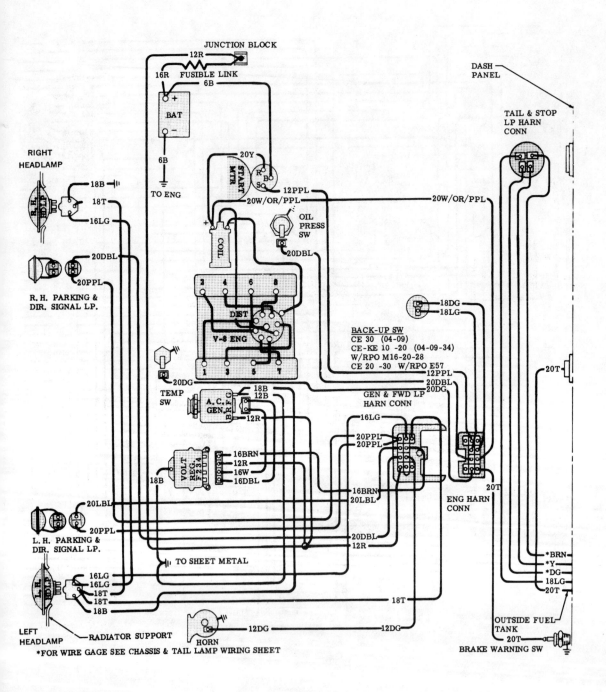

JUNCTION BLOCK

12R
16R   FUSIBLE LINK
6B

BAT
+
−

6B

TO ENG

RIGHT
HEADLAMP

18B
18T
16LG

20DBL
20PPL

R. H. PARKING &
DIR. SIGNAL LP.

START
MTR

20Y
R
B
S

12PPL
20W/OR/PPL

COIL
+

OIL
PRESS
SW

20DBL

DIST

V-8 ENG

2 4 6 8
1 3 5 7

TEMP
SW

20DG

A. C.
GEN.

18B
12B
12R

VOLT
REG.
F 2 3 4

16BRN
12R
16W
16DBL

18B

20LBL

20PPL

L. H. PARKING &
DIR. SIGNAL LP.

TO SHEET METAL

16LG
16LG
18T
18B

LEFT
HEADLAMP   RADIATOR SUPPORT

HORN

12DG

*FOR WIRE GAGE SEE CHASSIS & TAIL LAMP WIRING SHEET

DASH
PANEL

TAIL & STOP
LP HARN
CONN

20W/OR/PPL

18DG
18LG

BACK-UP SW
CE 30 (04-09)
CE-KE 10 -20 (04-09-34)
W/RPO M16-20-28
CE 20 -30 W/RPO E57

12PPL
20DBL
20DG

GEN & FWD LP
HARN CONN

16LG

20PPL
20PPL

16BRN
20LBL

20DBL
12R

18T

12DG

ENG HARN
CONN

20T

20T

20T

*BRN
*Y
*DG
18LG
20T

OUTSIDE FUEL
TANK

20T

BRAKE WARNING SW

15

1967 INSTRUMENT PANEL WIRING (PART I)

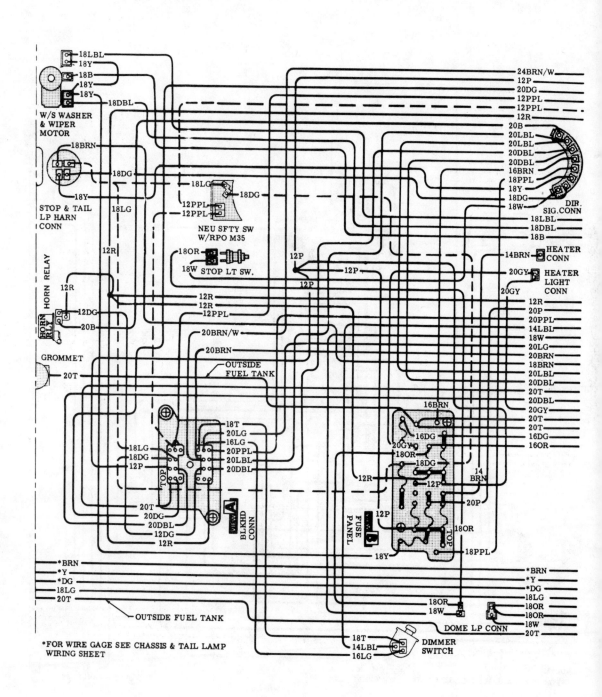

1967 INSTRUMENT PANEL WIRING (PART II)

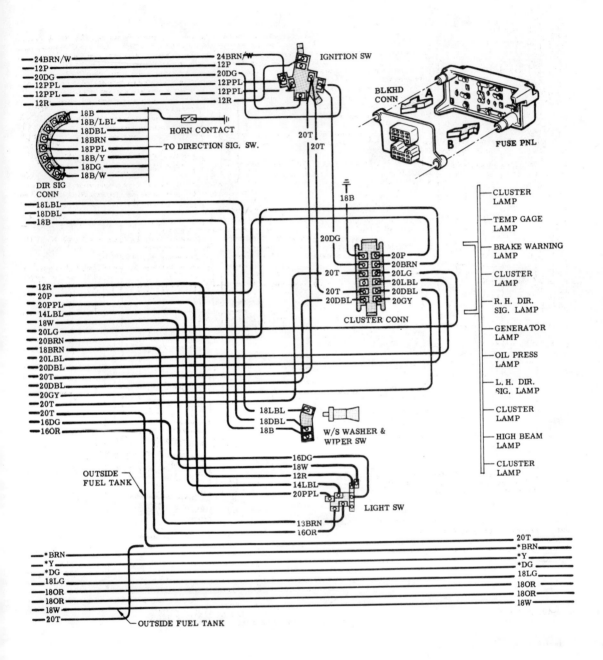

15

1967 TAIL AND STOPLIGHT WIRING

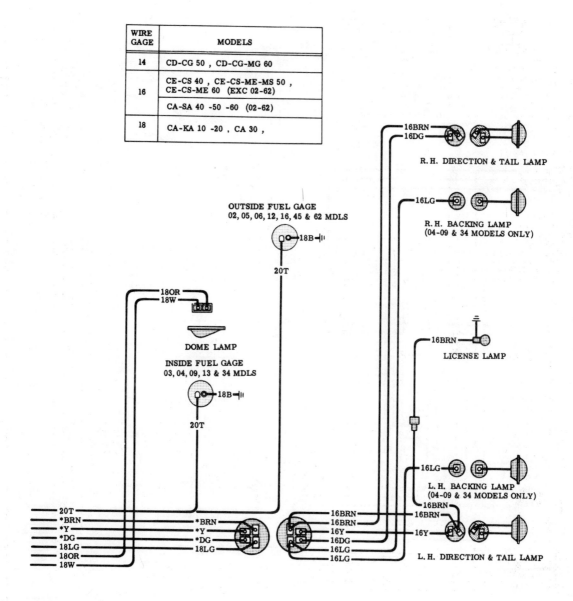

WIRE GAGE	MODELS
14	CD-CG 50 , CD-CG-MG 60
16	CE-CS 40 , CE-CS-ME-MS 50 , CE-CS-ME 60 (EXC 02-62)
	CA-SA 40 -50 -60 (02-62)
18	CA-KA 10 -20 , CA 30 ,

R.H. DIRECTION & TAIL LAMP

16BRN
16DG

16LG

R.H. BACKING LAMP
(04-09 & 34 MODELS ONLY)

OUTSIDE FUEL GAGE
02, 05, 06, 12, 16, 45 & 62 MDLS

18B

20T

18OR
18W

DOME LAMP

16BRN

LICENSE LAMP

INSIDE FUEL GAGE
03, 04, 09, 13 & 34 MDLS

18B

20T

16LG

L. H. BACKING LAMP
(04-09 & 34 MODELS ONLY)

20T
*BRN
*Y
*DG
18LG
18OR
18W

*BRN
*Y
*DG
18LG

16BRN
16BRN
16Y
16DG
16LG
16LG

16BRN
16BRN
16Y

L. H. DIRECTION & TAIL LAMP

*FOR WIRE GAGE SEE CHART ABOVE.

1968 ENGINE COMPARTMENT WIRING (L6)

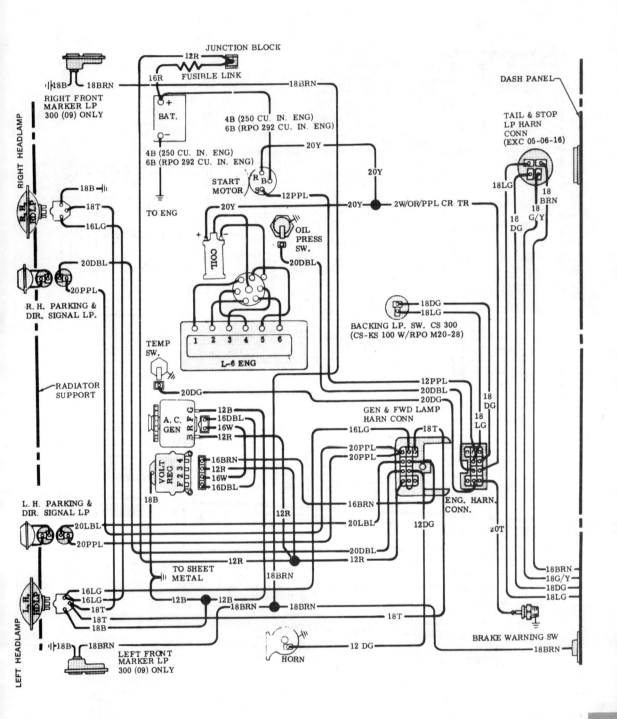

JUNCTION BLOCK

12R

16R   FUSIBLE LINK

18B   18BRN

RIGHT FRONT
MARKER LP
300 (09) ONLY

BAT.

4B (250 CU. IN. ENG)
6B (RPO 292 CU. IN. ENG)

4B (250 CU. IN. ENG)
6B (RPO 292 CU. IN. ENG)

TO ENG

START
MOTOR

20Y

12PPL

20Y

20Y

2W/OR/PPL CR TR

18BRN

DASH PANEL

TAIL & STOP
LP HARN
CONN
(EXC 05-06-16)

18LG   18
BRN

18
DG   18
G/Y

RIGHT HEADLAMP

18B

18T

16LG

20DBL

20PPL

R. H. PARKING &
DIR. SIGNAL LP.

TEMP
SW.

RADIATOR
SUPPORT

COIL

OIL
PRESS
SW.

20DBL

1 2 3 4 5 6

L-6 ENG

18DG
18LG

BACKING LP. SW. CS 300
(CS-KS 100 W/RPO M20-28)

12PPL
20DBL
20DG

18
DG

18
LG

20DG

A.C.
GEN

12B
16DBL
16W
12R

GEN & FWD LAMP
HARN CONN

16LG   18T

20PPL
20PPL

VOLT
REG

16BRN
12R
16W
16DBL

16BRN

ENG. HARN.
CONN.

18B

12R

20LBL

12DG

20T

L. H. PARKING &
DIR. SIGNAL LP

20LBL

20PPL

20DBL
12R

18BRN
18G/Y
18DG
18LG

TO SHEET
METAL

12R

18BRN

16LG
16LG
18T
18T
18B

12B   12B

18BRN   18BRN

18T

BRAKE WARNING SW

18B   18BRN   LEFT FRONT
MARKER LP
300 (09) ONLY

HORN

12 DG

18BRN

LEFT HEADLAMP

15

1968 ENGINE COMPARTMENT WIRING (V8)

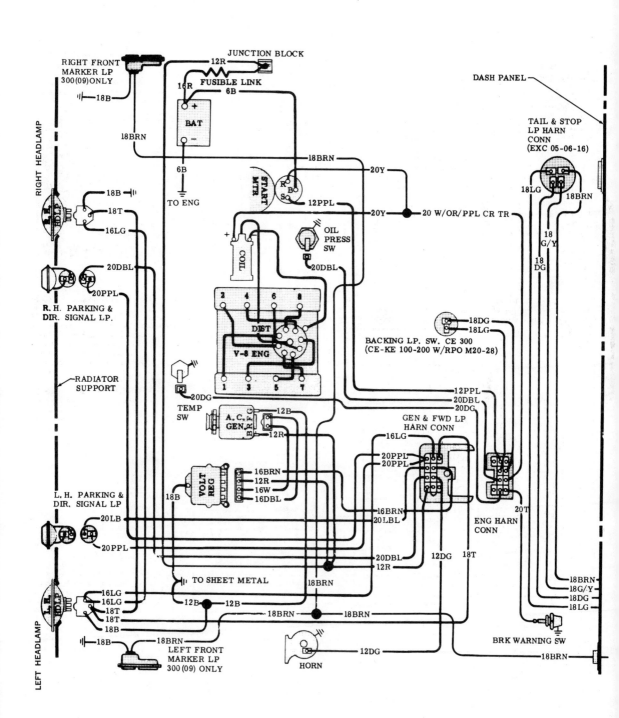

1968 INSTRUMENT PANEL WIRING (PART I)

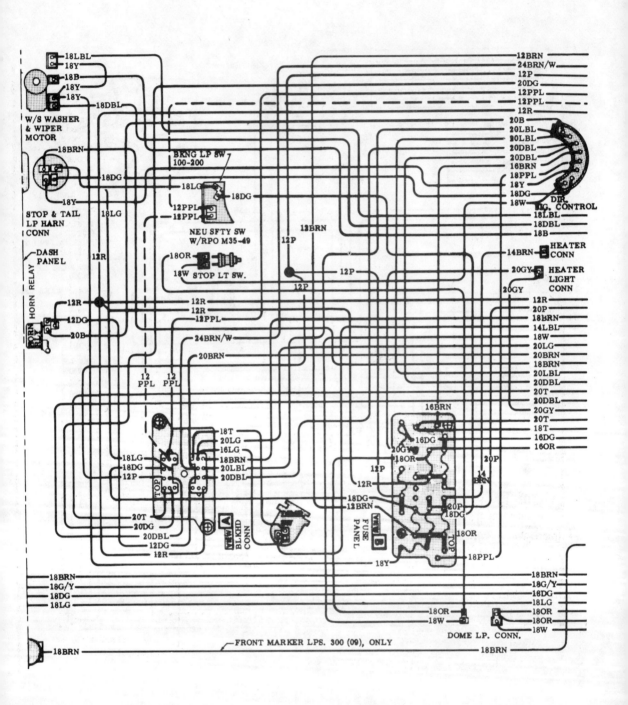

1968 INSTRUMENT PANEL WIRING (PART II)

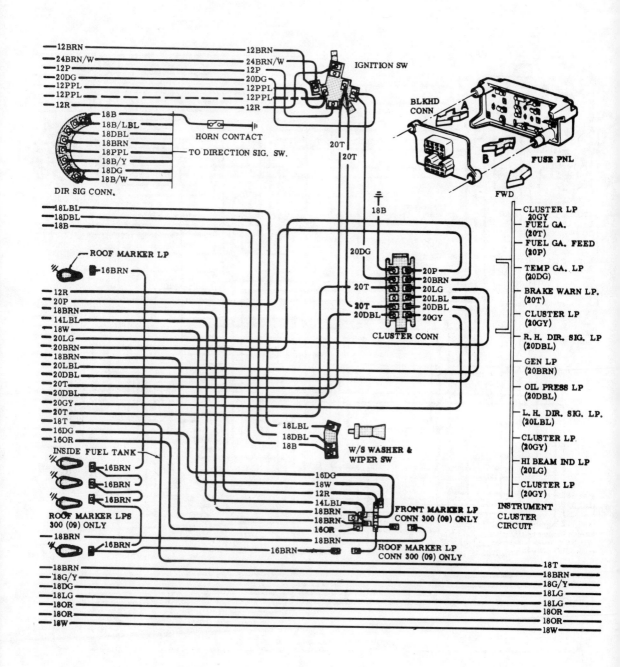

1968 TAIL AND STOPLIGHT WIRING

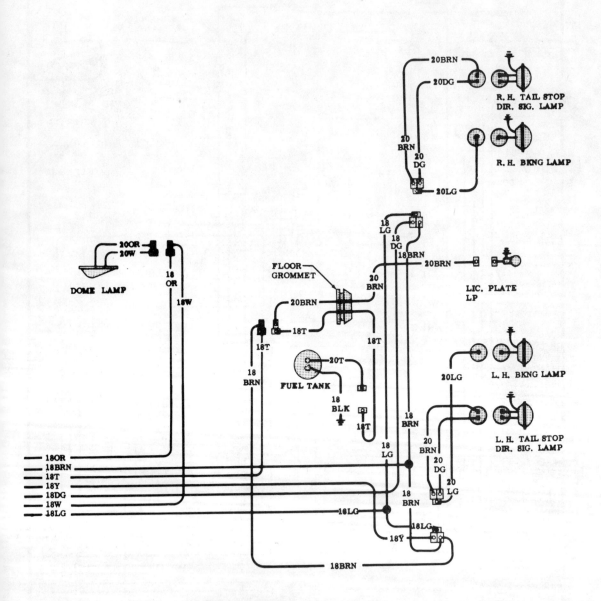

R. H. TAIL STOP DIR. SIG. LAMP

R. H. BKNG LAMP

20BRN

20DG

20 BRN

20 DG

20LG

DOME LAMP

20OR

20W

18 OR

18W

FLOOR GROMMET

20BRN

18T

18T

18T

18 BRN

18 BRN

18T

FUEL TANK

20T

18 BLK

18T

18 DG

18BRN

18 LG

20BRN

LIC. PLATE LP

20LG

L. H. BKNG LAMP

20 BRN

20 DG

20 LG

L. H. TAIL STOP DIR. SIG. LAMP

18 LG

18 BRN

18OR
18BRN
18T
18Y
18DG
18W
18LG

18LG

18Y

18LG

18BRN

1969-1970 ENGINE COMPARTMENT WIRING (L6)

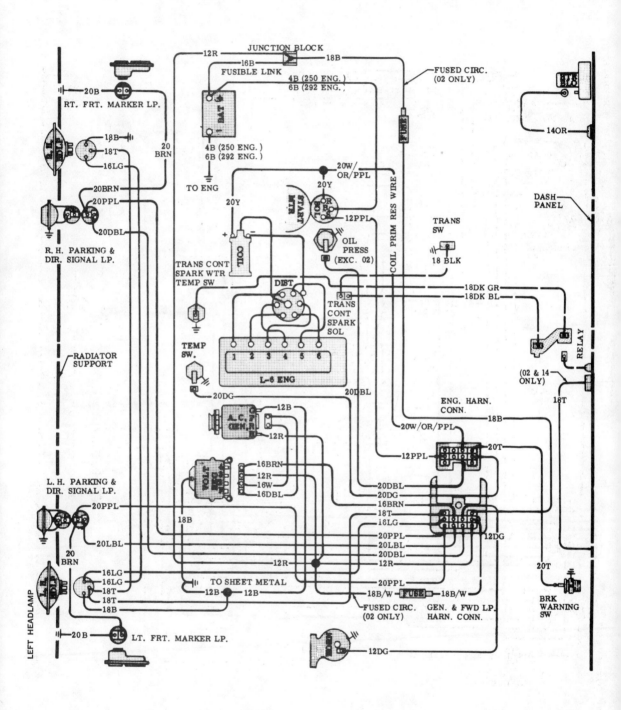

1969-1970 ENGINE COMPARTMENT WIRING (V8)

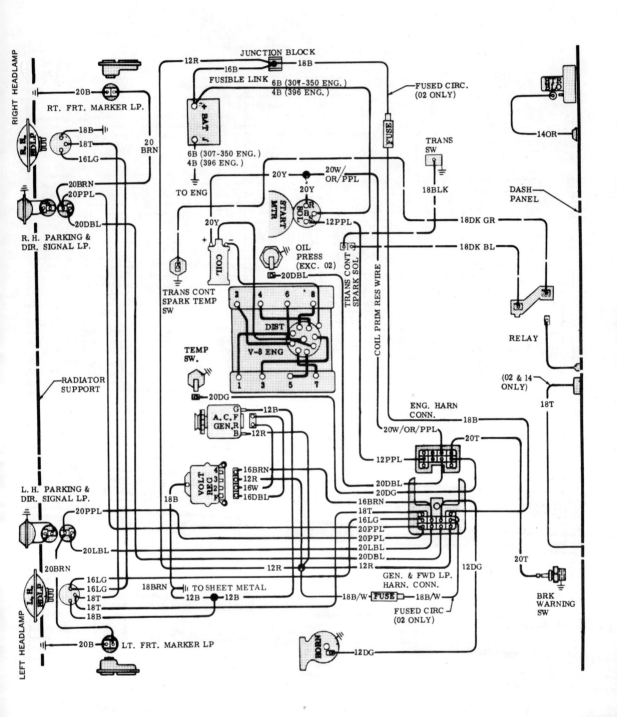

1969-1970 INSTRUMENT PANEL WIRING (PART I)

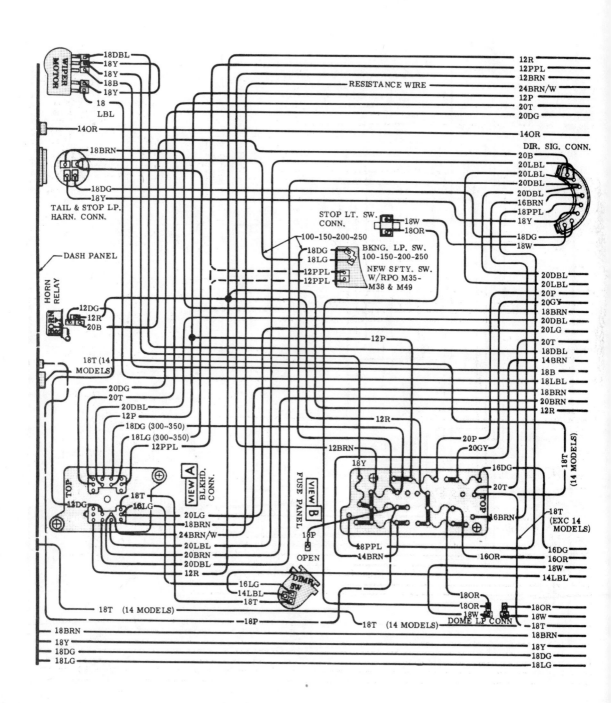

1969-1970 INSTRUMENT PANEL WIRING (PART II)

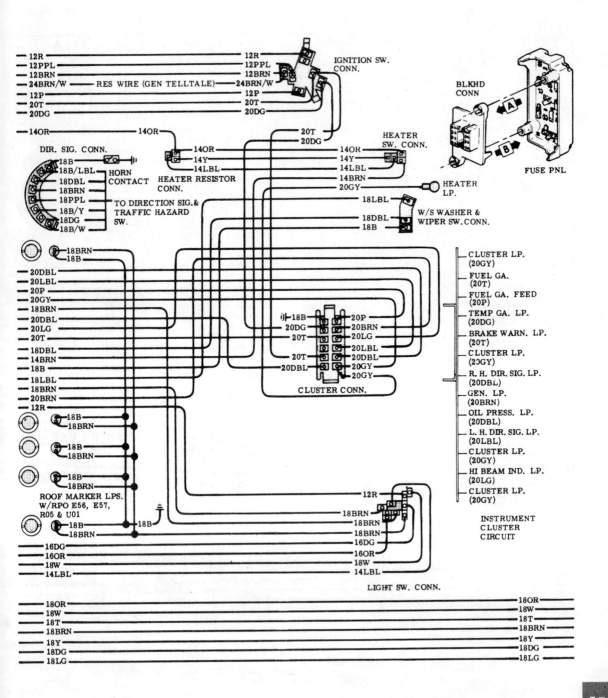

1969-1970 TAIL AND STOPLIGHT WIRING

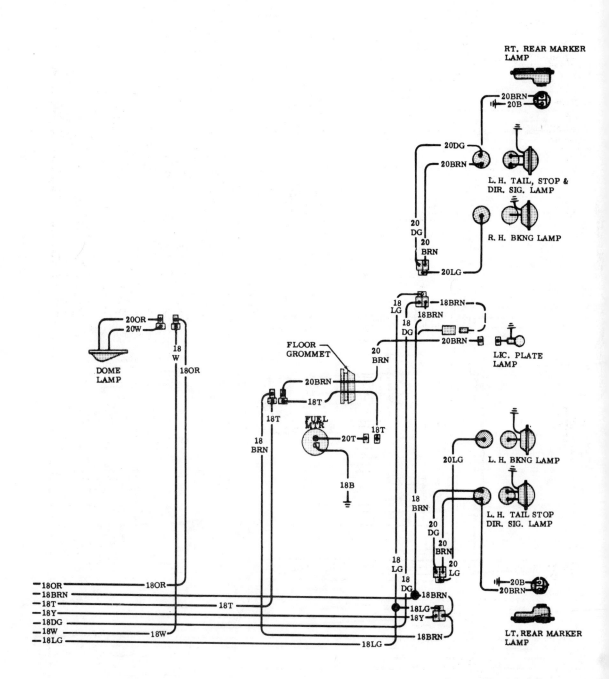

RT. REAR MARKER LAMP

20BRN
20B

20DG
20BRN

L. H. TAIL, STOP & DIR. SIG. LAMP

20
DG
20
BRN

R. H. BKNG LAMP

20LG

18
LG
18BRN
18BRN
18
DG
20BRN

LIC. PLATE LAMP

FLOOR GROMMET

20
BRN

20OR
20W

18
W

18OR

DOME LAMP

20BRN

18T

18T

FUEL MTR

20T

18T

18B

18
BRN

20LG

L. H. BKNG LAMP

L. H. TAIL STOP DIR. SIG. LAMP

20
DG
20
BRN
20
LG

18
BRN

18
LG
18
DG

18BRN

18OR
18BRN
18T
18Y
18DG
18W
18LG

18OR

18T

18W

18LG

18BRN

18LG
18Y

18BRN

20DG
20BRN
20B

20B
20BRN

LT. REAR MARKER LAMP

1971 ENGINE COMPARTMENT WIRING

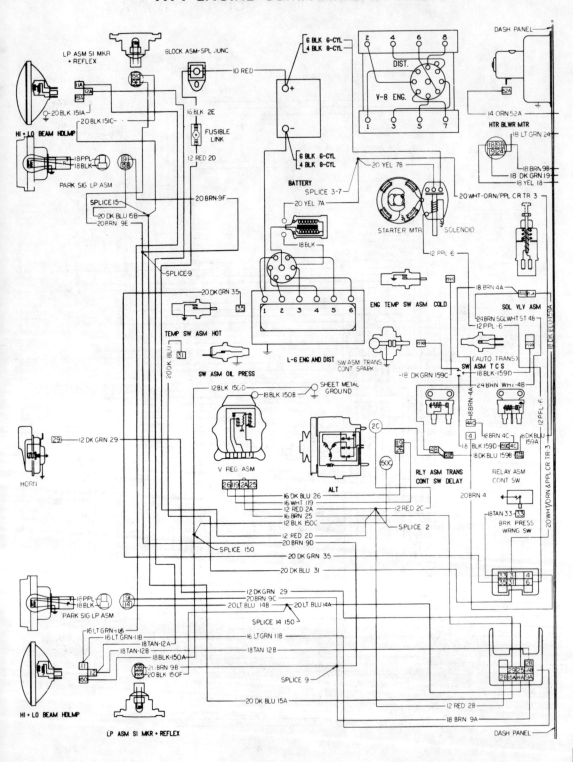

1971 INSTRUMENT PANEL WIRING (PART I)

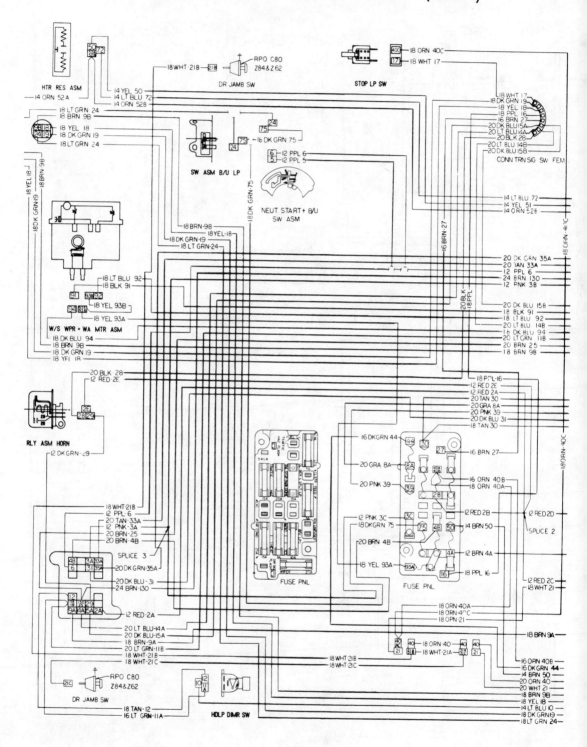

1971 INSTRUMENT PANEL WIRING (PART II)

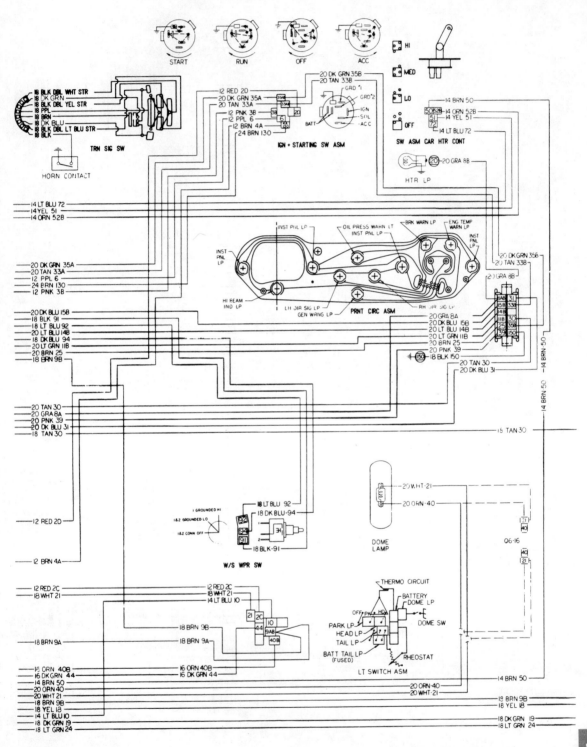

1971 TAIL AND STOPLIGHT WIRING

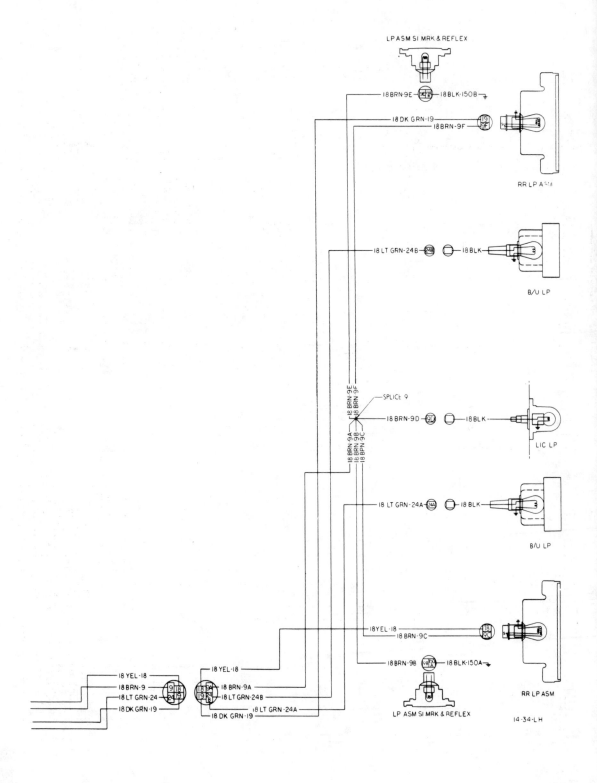

1972 ENGINE COMPARTMENT WIRING

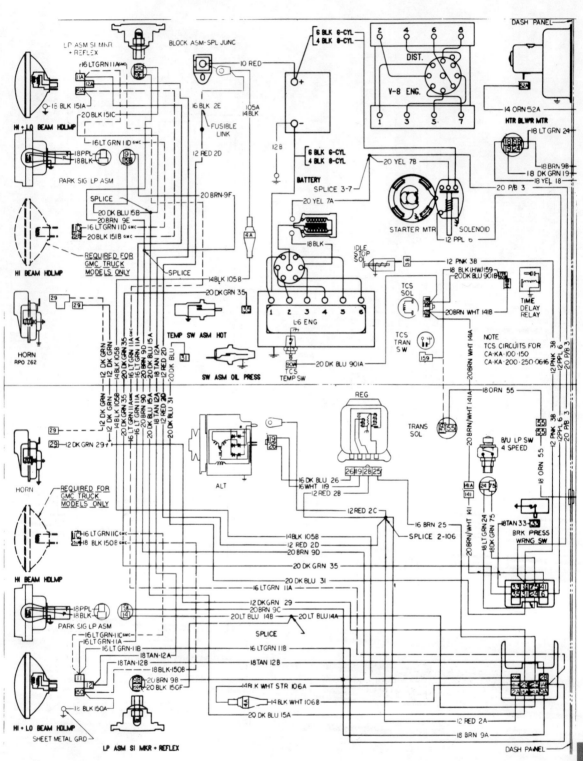

1972 INSTRUMENT PANEL WIRING (PART I)

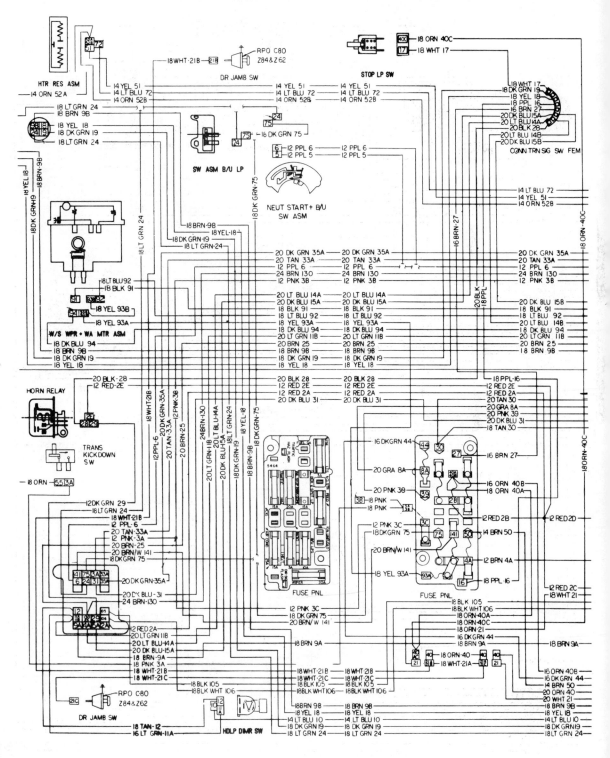

1972 INSTRUMENT PANEL WIRING (PART II)

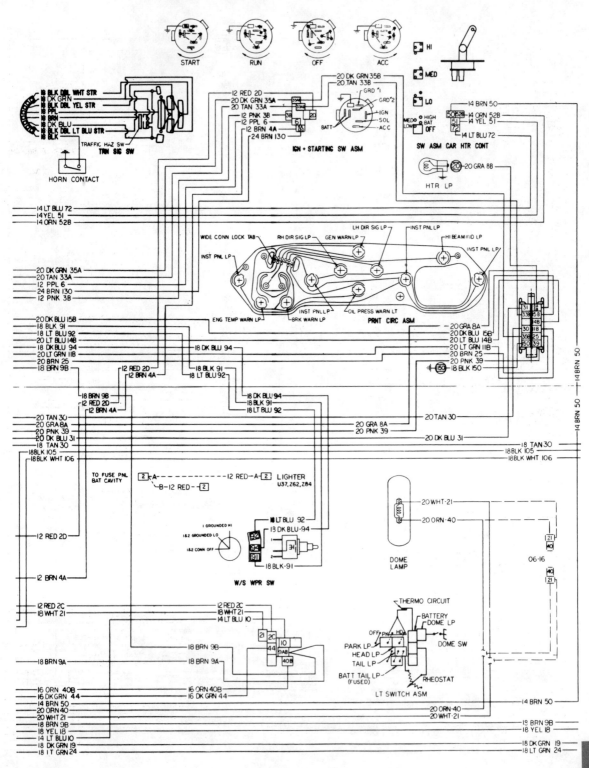

1972 TAIL AND STOPLIGHT WIRING

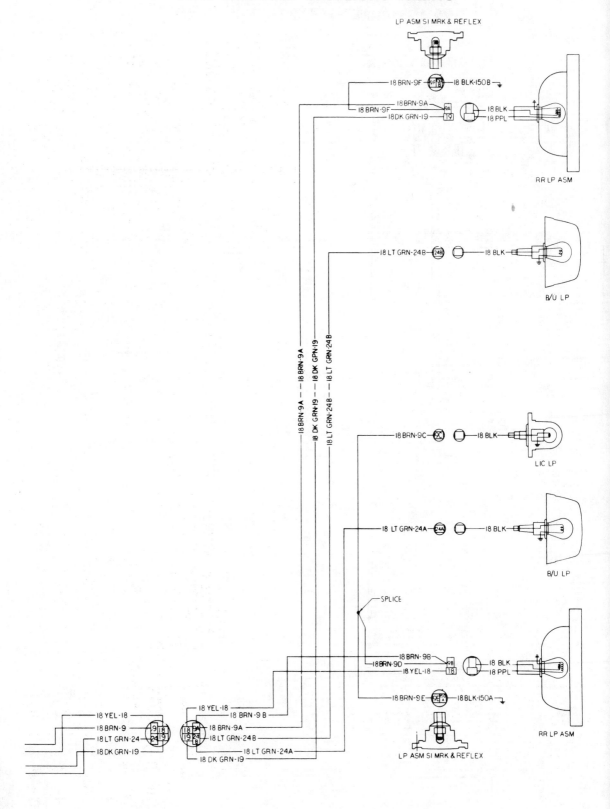

1973 WIRING (PART I)

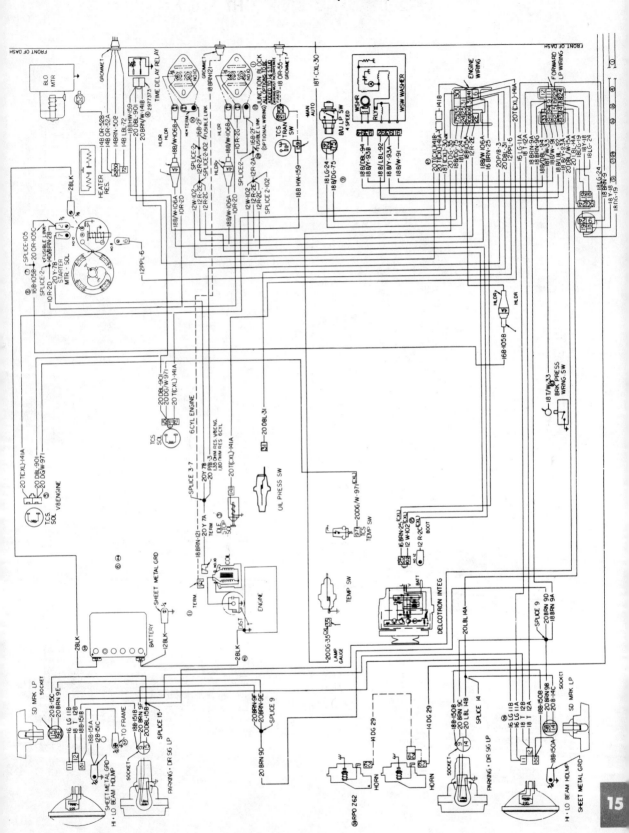

15

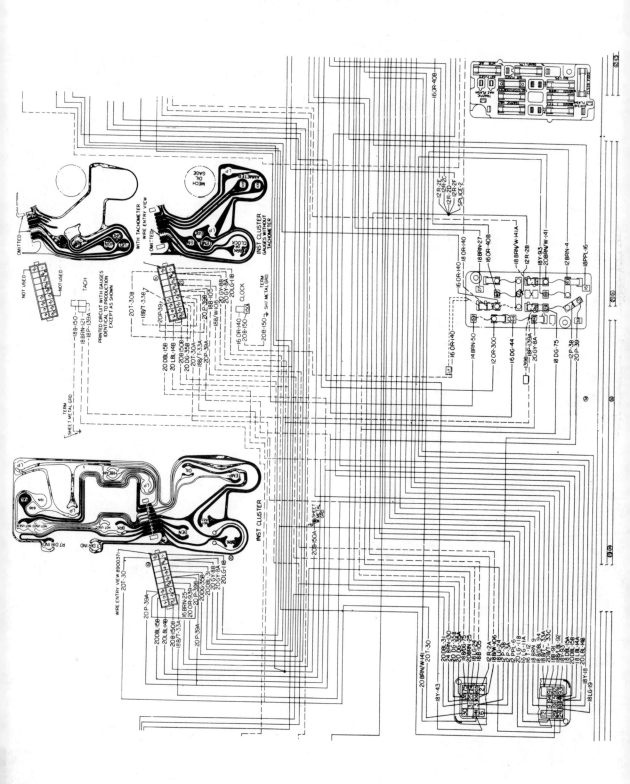

1973 WIRING (PART III)

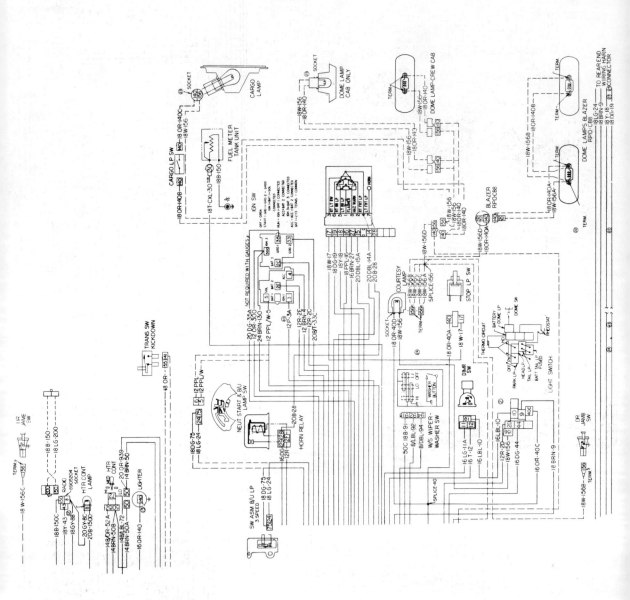

1974 Wiring (Part I)

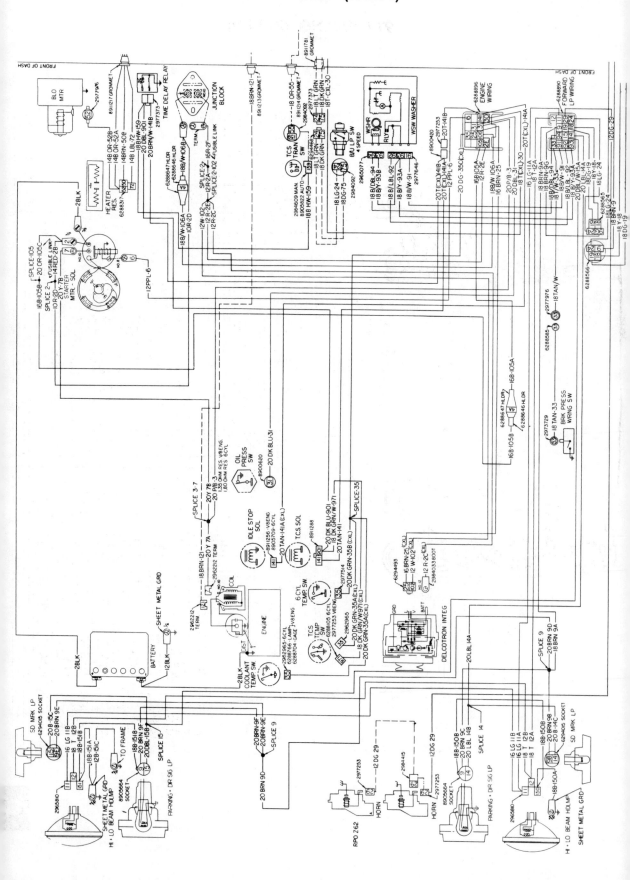

1974 WIRING (PART II)

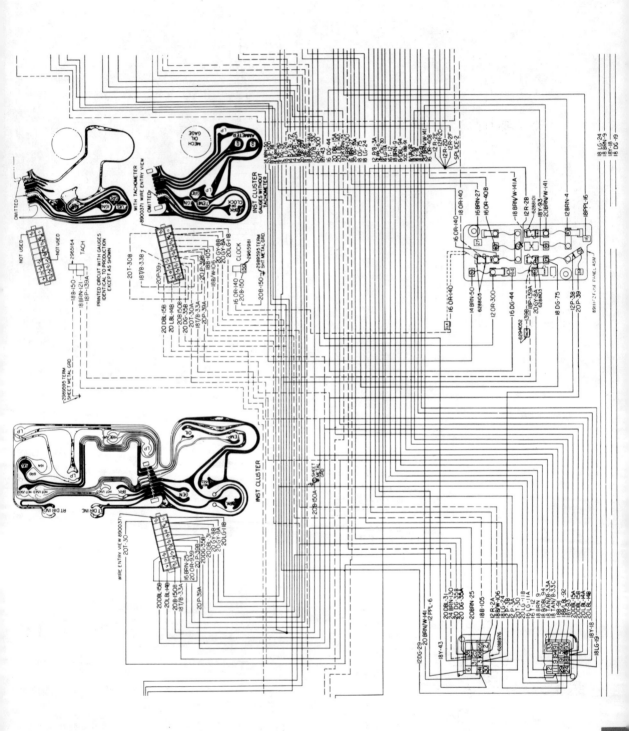

15

1974 WIRING (PART III)

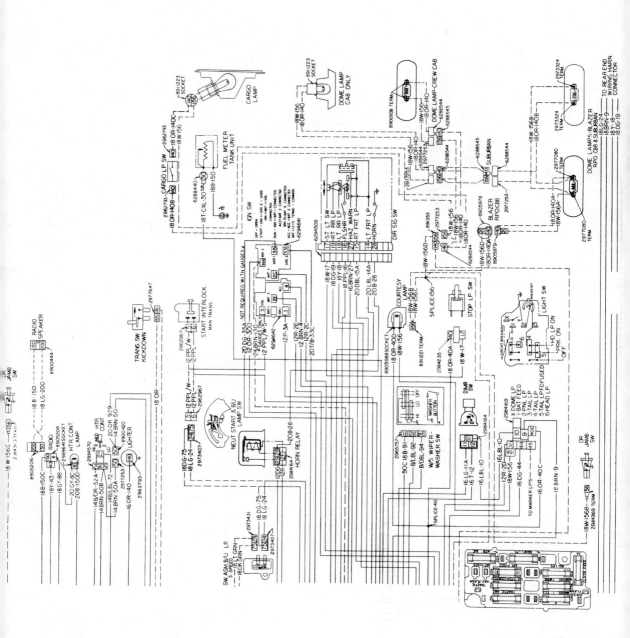

1975 WIRING (PART I)

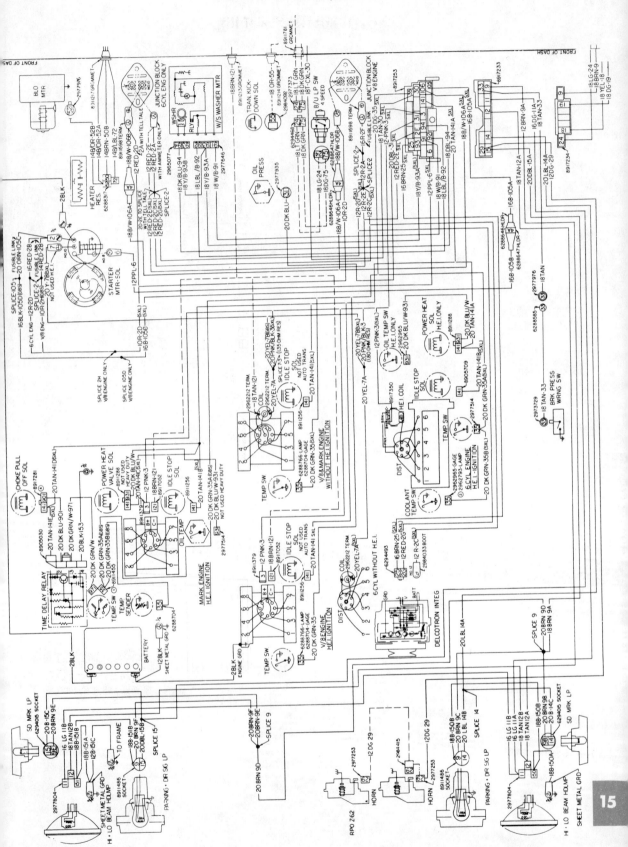

1975 WIRING (PART II)

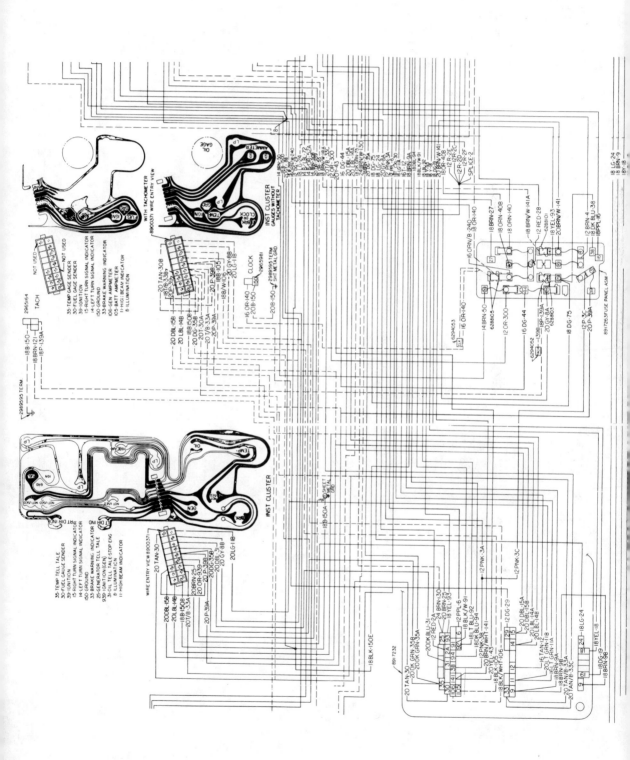

1975 WIRING (PART III)

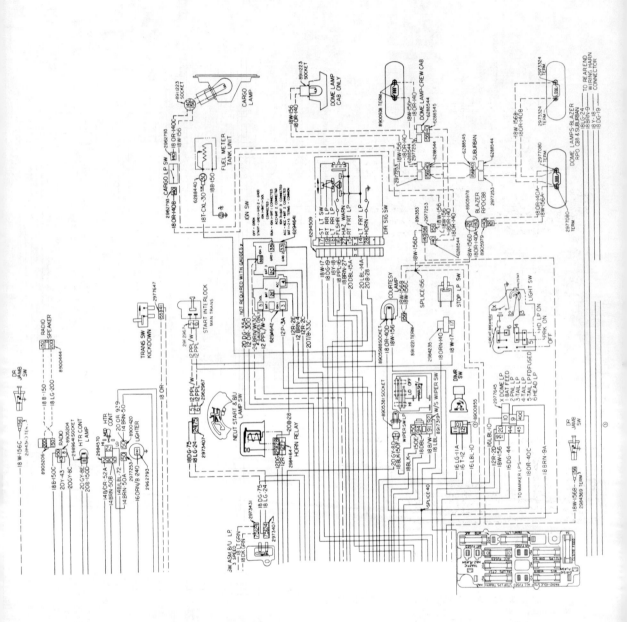

1976 Wiring (PART I)

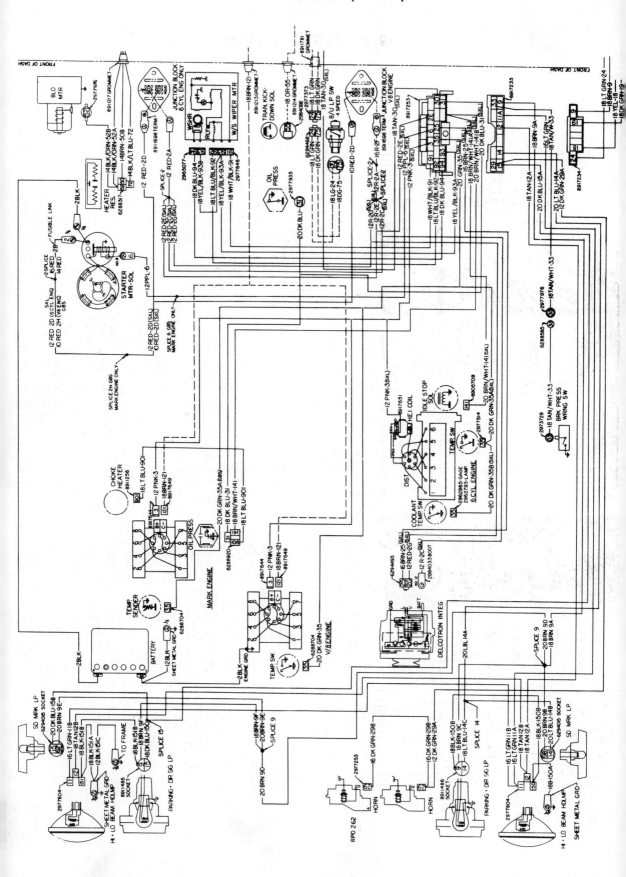

1976 WIRING (PART II)

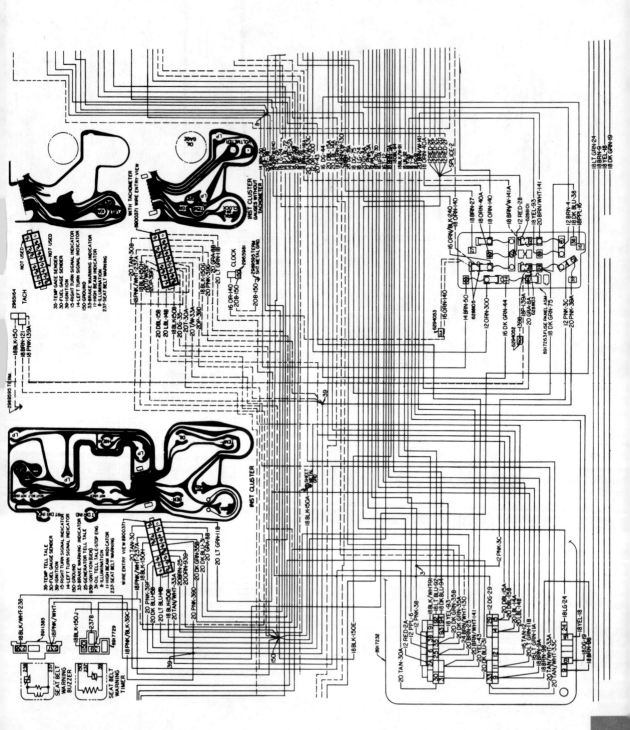

1976 WIRING (PART III)

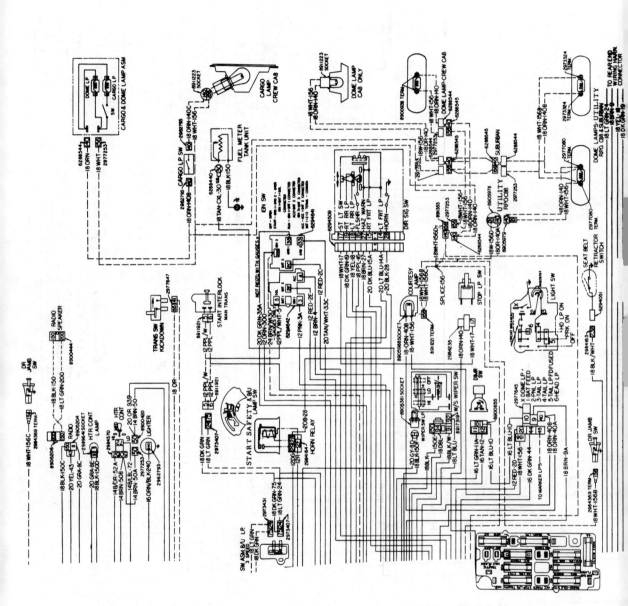

1977 WIRING (PART I)

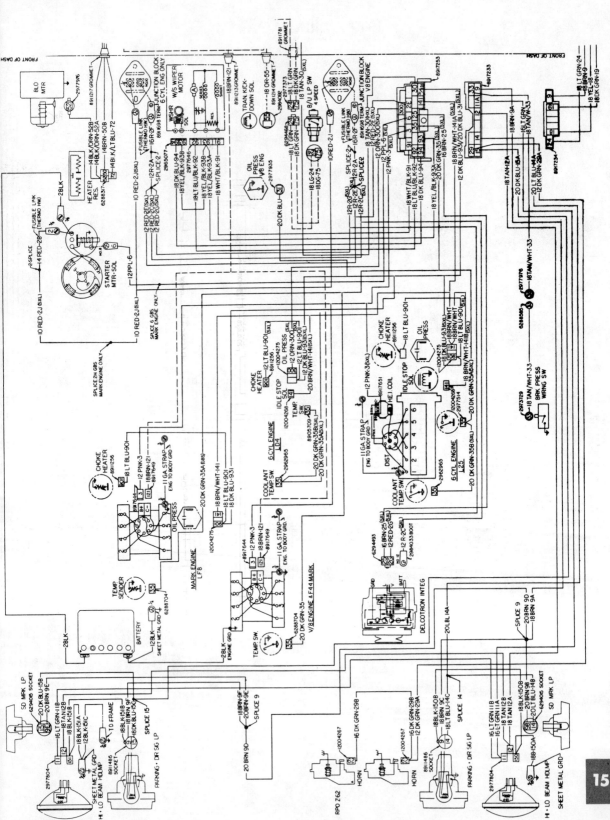

1977 WIRING (PART II)

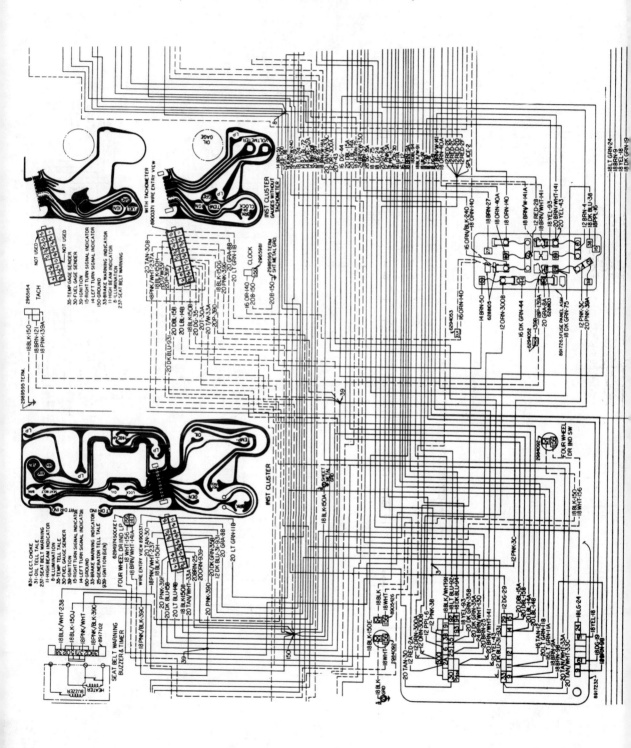

1977 WIRING (PART III)

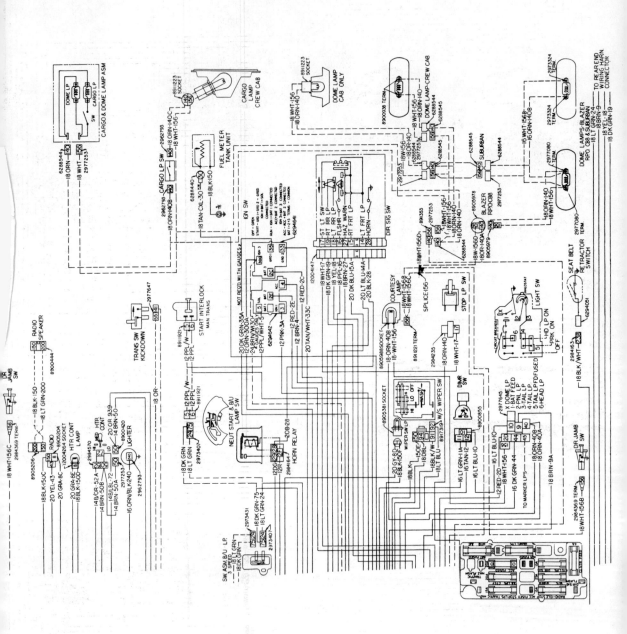

1978 WIRING (PART I)

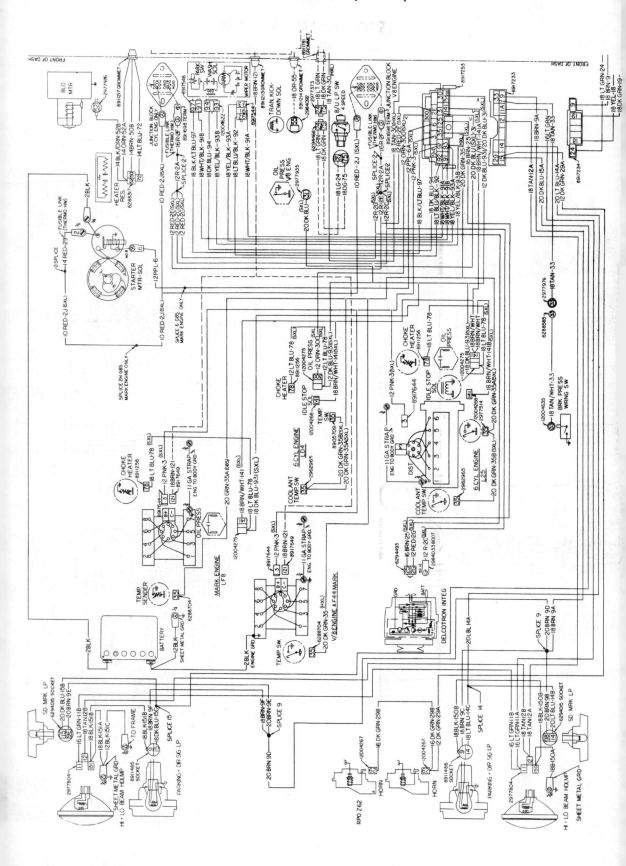

1978 WIRING (PART II)

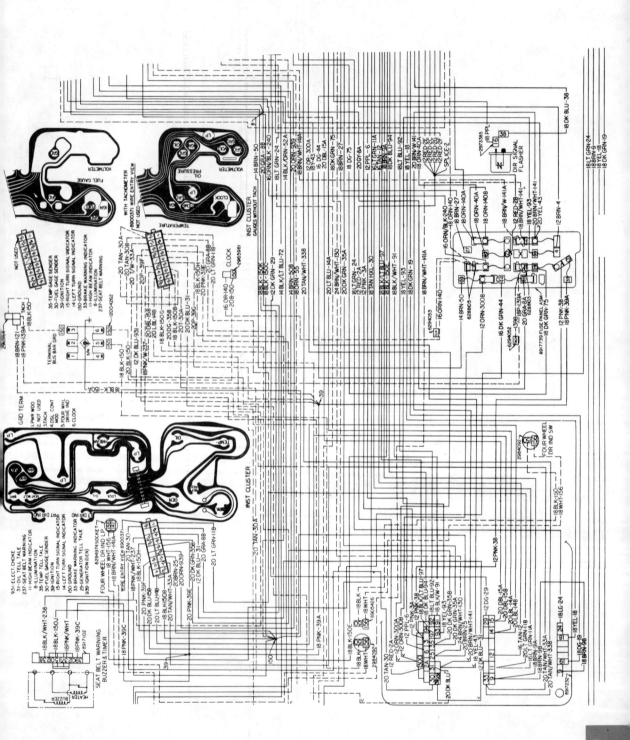

1978 WIRING (PART III)

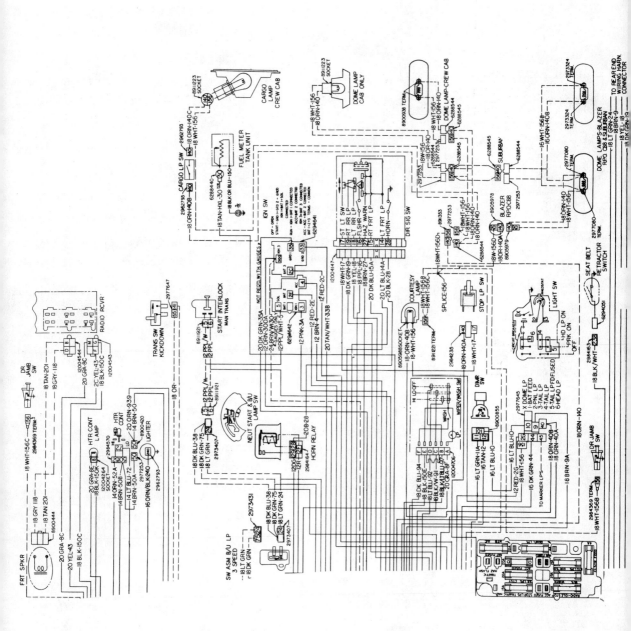